Over the last two centuries, Germans and Americans have been rivals, friends, opponents, and, most recently, allies. This cross-disciplinary collection of essays analyzes how German and American views of each other developed and periodically shifted, providing a fresh analysis of the often complex German-American relationship. The images that resulted from encounters between the two countries frequently reflected significant cross-currents of the contemporary relations, and often foreshadowed important trends. The nine German and eight American contributors to this volume analyzed travelogs, private letters, diaries, diplomatic reports, and newspaper articles from the wake of U.S. independence through the reunification of Germany, and also post-1945 movies, which reflect these cross-cultural encounters and illustrate how political agendas, prejudices, stereotypes, and pragmatic forces influenced individual, group, and mass perceptions of the other society.

PUBLICATIONS OF THE GERMAN HISTORICAL INSTITUTE
WASHINGTON, D.C.

Edited by Detlef Junker
with the assistance of Daniel S. Mattern

Transatlantic Images and Perceptions

THE GERMAN HISTORICAL INSTITUTE, WASHINGTON, D.C.

The German Historical Institute is a center for advanced study and research whose purpose is to provide a permanent basis for scholarlycooperation between historians from the Federal Republic of Germany and the United States. The Institute conducts, promotes, and supports research into both American and German political, social, economic, and cultural history, into transatlantic migration, especially in the nineteenth and twentieth centuries, and into the history of international relations, with special emphasis on the roles played by the United States and Germany.

Other books in the series

Hartmut Lehmann and James J. Sheehan, editors, *An Interrupted Past: German-Speaking Refugee Historians in the United States after 1933*

Carol Fink, Axel Frohn, and Jürgen Heideking, editors, *Genoa, Rapallo, and European Reconstruction in 1922*

David Clay Large, editor, *Contending with Hitler: Varieties of German Resistance in the Third Reich*

Larry Eugene Jones and James Retallack, editors, *Elections, Mass Politics, and Social Change in Modern Germany*

Hartmut Lehmann and Guenther Roth, editors, *Weber's Protestant Ethic: Origins, Evidence, Contexts*

Catherine Epstein, *A Past Renewed: A Catalog of German-Speaking Refugee Historians in the United States after 1933*

Hartmut Lehmann and James Van Horn Melton, editors, *Paths of Continuity: Central European Historiography from the 1930s to the 1950s*

Jeffry M. Diefendorf, Axel Frohn, and Hermann-Josef Rupieper, editors, *American Policy and the Reconstruction of West Germany, 1945–1955*

Henry Geitz, Jürgen Heideking, and Jurgen Herbst, editors, *German Influences on Education in the United States to 1917*

Peter Graf Kielmansegg, Horst Mewes, and Elisabeth Glaser-Schmidt, editors, *Hannah Arendt and Leo Strauss: German Emigrés and American Political Thought after World War II*

Dirk Hoerder and Jörg Nagler, editors, *People in Transit: German Migrations in Comparative Perspective, 1820–1930*

R. Po-chia Hsia and Hartmut Lehmann, editors, *In and Out of the Ghetto: Jewish–Gentile Relations in Late Medieval and Early Modern Germany*

Sibylle Quack, editor, *Between Sorrow and Strength: Women Refugees of the Nazi Period*

Mitchell G. Ash and Alfons Söllner, editors, *Forced Migration and Scientific Change: Emigré German-Speaking Scientists and Scholars after 1933*

Stig Förster and Jörg Nagler, editors, *On the Road to Total War: The American Civil War and the German Wars of Unification, 1861–1871*

Norbert Finzsch and Robert Jütte, editors, *Institutions of Confinement: Hospitals, Asylums, and Prisons in Western Europe and North America, 1500–1950*

Manfred Berg and Geoffrey Cocks, editors, *Medicine and Modernity: Public Health and Medical Care in Nineteenth- and Twentieth-Century Germany*

Transatlantic Images and Perceptions
GERMANY AND AMERICA SINCE 1776

Edited by

DAVID E. BARCLAY

and

ELISABETH GLASER-SCHMIDT

GERMAN HISTORICAL INSTITUTE
Washington, D.C.
and

PUBLISHED BY THE PRESS SYNDICATE OF THE UNIVERSITY OF CAMBRIDGE
The Pitt Building, Trumpington Street, Cambridge, United Kingdom

CAMBRIDGE UNIVERSITY PRESS
The Edinburgh Building, Cambridge CB2 2RU, UK
40 West 20th Street, New York NY 10011–4211, USA
477 Williamstown Road, Port Melbourne, VIC 3207, Australia
Ruiz de Alarcón 13, 28014 Madrid, Spain
Dock House, The Waterfront, Cape Town 8001, South Africa

http://www.cambridge.org

© The German Historical Institute 1997

This book is in copyright. Subject to statutory exception
and to the provisions of relevant collective licensing agreements,
no reproduction of any part may take place without
the written permission of Cambridge University Press.

Typeset in Bembo

First paperback edition 2003

A catalogue record for this book is available from the British Library

Library of Congress Cataloguing-in-Publication Data
Transatlantic images and perceptions : Germany and America since 1776 / edited by
David E. Barclay, Elisabeth Glaser–Schmidt.
p. cm. – (Publications of the German Historical Institute)
Includes index.
ISBN 0 521 58091 9 (hardcover)
1. United States – Relations – Germany. 2. Germany – Relations – United States.
3. United States – Foreign public opinion, German.
4. Germany – Foreign public opinion, American.
5. Public opinion – United States – History. 6. Public opinion – Germany – History.
I. Barclay, David E., 1948– . II. Glaser–Schmidt, Elisabeth. III. Series.
E183.8.G3T68 1997
303.48′273043 – dc20   96-31667
CIP

ISBN 0 521 58091 9 hardback
ISBN 0 521 53442 9 paperback

Contents

List of Contributors   *page* vii

Introduction   *David E. Barclay* and *Elisabeth Glaser-Schmidt*   1

1 "Through a Glass, Darkly": Changing German Ideas of American Freedom, 1776–1806   *A. Gregg Roeber*   19

2 "Germans Make Cows and Women Work": American Perceptions of Germans as Reported in American Travel Books, 1800–1840   *Hermann Wellenreuther*   41

3 Weary of Germany – Weary of America: Perceptions of the United States in Nineteenth-Century Germany *Hans-Jürgen Grabbe*   65

4 "Auch unser Deutschland muss einmal frei werden": The Immigrant Civil War Experience as a Mirror on Political Conditions in Germany   *Walter D. Kamphoefner*   87

5 Different, But Not Out of This World: German Images of the United States Between Two Wars, 1871–1914 *Wolfgang Helbich*   109

6 From Culture to *Kultur*: Changing American Perceptions of Imperial Germany, 1870–1914   *Jörg Nagler*   131

7 The Reciprocal Vision of German and American Intellectuals: Beneath the Shifting Perceptions *James T. Kloppenberg*   155

8 Germany and the United States, 1914–1933: The Mutual Perception of Their Political Systems   *Peter Krüger*   171

Contents

9 Between Hope and Skepticism: American Views of Germany, 1918–1933   *Elisabeth Glaser-Schmidt*   191

10 "Without Concessions to Marxist or Communist Thought": Fordism in Germany, 1923–1939   *Philipp Gassert*   217

11 The Continuity of Ambivalence: German Views of America, 1933–1945   *Detlef Junker*   243

12 Cultural Migration: Artists and Visual Representation Between Americans and Germans During the 1930s and 1940s   *Marion F. Deshmukh*   265

13 Representations of Germans and What Germans Represent: American Film Images and Public Perceptions in the Postwar Era   *Beverly Crawford* and *James Martel*   285

14 Chancellor of the Allies? The Significance of the United States in Adenauer's Foreign Policy   *Hans-Jürgen Schröder*   309

15 American Policy Toward German Unification: Images and Interests   *Konrad H. Jarausch*   333

16 Unification Policies and the German Image: Comments on the American Reaction   *Frank Trommler*   353

Index   363

Contributors

David E. Barclay is a professor of history at Kalamazoo College, Kalamazoo, Michigan.

Beverly Crawford is a professor of political economy and the research director of the Center for German and European Studies at the University of California at Berkeley.

Marion F. Deshmukh is a professor of history at George Mason University in Fairfax, Virginia.

Philipp Gassert is a research fellow at the German Historical Institute, Washington, D.C.

Elisabeth Glaser-Schmidt is a research fellow at the German Historical Institute, Washington, D.C.

Hans-Jürgen Grabbe is a professor of history at the Martin Luther University, Halle-Wittenberg.

Wolfgang Helbich is a professor of history at Ruhr University, Bochum.

Konrad H. Jarausch is a professor of history at the University of North Carolina at Chapel Hill.

Detlef Junker is director of the German Historical Institute, Washington, D.C.

Walter D. Kamphoefner is a professor of history at Texas A & M University.

James T. Kloppenberg is a professor of history at Brandeis University.

Peter Krüger is a professor of history at Philipps University, Marburg.

James Martel is an instructor of political economy at the University of California at Berkeley.

Jörg Nagler is director of the John F. Kennedy House, Kiel, and guest lecturer at the University of Kiel.

A. Gregg Roeber is a professor of history at The Pennsylvania State University.

Hans-Jürgen Schröder is a professor of history at the Justus-Liebig University, Giessen.

Frank Trommler is a professor of German literature at the University of Pennsylvania.

Hermann Wellenreuther is a professor of history at the University of Göttingen.

Introduction

DAVID E. BARCLAY AND ELISABETH GLASER-SCHMIDT

> Ere Babylon was dust,
> The Magus Zoroaster, my dead child,
> Met his own image walking in the garden.
> – Percy Bysshe Shelley, *Prometheus Unbound*

Like Shelley's Magus Zoroaster, European travelers to the United States may have met their own image, if not that of the Other. The same was true for Americans who visited the old continent or expressed their private thoughts about it. Do images and perceptions of another country consist of accurate observations that mirror the reality of the perceived object? Or do those perceptions reflect the subject's own psyche, prejudices, intentions, and actions? These are the major questions that inform this book. The last century of German and American relations has witnessed a close relationship emerging from the great antagonism between the two powers during the era of the world wars. The deep mutual fascination that has developed from this changing relationship finds its antecedents in the German immigration that started in the late seventeenth century and became a mass movement in the middle of the nineteenth. Interest in the other country's constitutional development and its federal system figures as another point of engagement. The history of German-American relations offers rich material for the study of German and American mutual images and group perceptions. Exploring them will in turn allow us to map patterns of communication that have powerfully shaped the evolution of German-American relations in general. The analysis of German and American mutual images thus constitutes an important chapter in the burgeoning history of transnational perceptions. In surveying the formation of individual and group perceptions on both sides of the Atlantic, the authors of this book use the tools of historical analysis to understand the processes by which perceptions of the other are generated and expressed. These processes have parallels in private relations or within the views that social, religious, gender, or ethnic groups form of each other within each society. Consequently, when we examine the images that Germans and Americans have conceived of each other, we do so within a general perceptional framework that has drawn the attention of psychologists and social scientists as well as students of literature and ethnology. The term "perceptions" originally comprises mental observations and mental images or, used in a neurobiological and psychological context, the process of converting a sensory experience into a symbolic representation.[1] As employed in this book, it also refers to the formation of group opinions and stereotypes that result from image formation of the other, the distant country, the enemy, the rival. It is thus used synonymously with the term "images," which likewise refers both to a visual representation of a mental observation and verbally expressed conceptions about an object. Historians have chiefly concentrated their efforts on presenting the expressions of perceptions and on analyzing intentions, social circumstances, and other motivations that influence such perceptions. Individuals communicate their perceptions through verbal or visual images as well as reenactments. This book concentrates on the historical analysis of written representations and some visual depictions, which are the main expressions of perceptions accessible to historical scrutiny. Moreover, it focuses primarily on perceptions of the present rather than the past of the other country, though it also includes references to traditional and persistent ethnic and cultural images.[2] The chapters in the book present historically rooted case studies that may contribute to a better understanding of how image formation takes place. They should serve as material witnesses to the ongoing development of a new theory of mutual perceptions and image formation in history and its neighboring disciplines.

Research about image formation and perceptions faces similar challenges to those that confronted European and Arabian mapmakers in the age of discovery. Before the Islamic scholar al-Idrisi sent a world map to Roger of Sicily in 1154, European and Arabian mapmakers explored the

---

1 George Goldenberg, Ivo Podreka, and Margarete Steiner, "The Cerebral Localization of Visual Imagery: Evidence from Emission Computerized Tomography of Cerebral Blood Flow," in Peter J. Hampson, David F. Marks, and John T. E. Richardson, eds., *Imagery: Current Developments* (New York, 1990), 307–33.
2 See Hermann Wellenreuther's chapter in this book.

same problem without communicating with each other. As a result, information about Asia's geography was poor and failed to advance until Jesuit missionaries used Chinese maps in the sixteenth century to prepare a more accurate atlas. Similarly, until quite recently, research on perceptions has been segregated into separate avenues of psychological, literary, social science, and historical inquiry, with little communication among the different fields. Still, some common problems have emerged. Thus, a great deal of social science research on perceptions has tended to focus on the differences between perception and object reality. Psychologists have enhanced that approach. Psychoanalysis and social psychology have added substantially to our knowledge by adumbrating the emotional foundations of individual and group images. In his study of dream interpretation, as well as through his analytical work with patients, Sigmund Freud sketched out a comprehensive theory concerning the operation of the unconscious. Through those pioneering achievements, Freud pointed to the limitations that the individual faces in correctly perceiving his or her own fears and desires. In his later work, Freud applied his empirical knowledge of individual psychology to a theoretical exploration of the emotional foundations of society. In *Totem and Taboo*, as well as in *The Future of an Illusion*, he showed the irrational roots of human thought as they were embodied in society's religious illusions. *Civilization and Its Discontents* broadened the theme to include the flight from *Unbehagen* (uneasiness) in modern culture. That work interpreted the flight into human pleasures – such as work, religion, and love – as an escape mechanism to shelter society from the inevitable dreads of aging, death, and aggression.[3] Freud underscored the emotional background behind society's perception of cultural values and implicitly provided major insights into the affective roots of image formation.

Subsequent psychoanalysts who ventured to explain links between individual image formation and mass opinion have presented a significant body of empirical evidence about perceptional processes in group behavior. Otto F. Kernberg, an American psychologist who has sought to provide a link between Freud's approach and that of the object relations school, described early individual defense operations in group processes.[4]

---

3 Sigmund Freud, *The Interpretation of Dreams*, in *The Standard Edition of the Complete Psychological Work of Sigmund Freud* (London, 1953–), 4 and 5:58–648; Peter Gay, *Freud: A Life for Our Time* (New York, 1988), 127–9, 525–53, and passim; Philip Pomper, *The Structure of the Mind in History: Five Major Figures in Psychohistory* (New York, 1985), 49–80.
4 Otto F. Kernberg, *Internal World and External Reality: Object Relations Theory Applied* (New York, 1980), 217; see also Diane Mackie and David L. Hamilton, *Affect, Cognition, and Stereotyping: Interactive Processes in Group Perception* (San Diego, 1993).

Heinz Kohut, founder of the school of self-psychology, widened the focus of research on group perceptions by calling attention to the role of individual leaders or national elites in mobilizing transferences – in other words, articulating unconscious feelings in ways that parallel the process of projection in analysis.[5] The chapters in this book on German immigrants' perceptions of the United States and of American painters' representations of Nazi Germany present clues about the crystallization of group perceptions of cultural identity as well as leadership ideals.[6] Those contributions offer historical evidence that allow us to apply psychoanalytical and other theories of image formation to larger groups.

Misperceptions form a prominent theme in political science investigations into the enemy stereotypes held by high-level American decision makers.[7] Here again, research conducted during the last thirty years emphasizes the difference between reality and perception. Gestalt psychology provides the most frequently used theoretical framework for the interpretation of the perceptional process; it hypothesizes that individual perceptions are inextricably related to the social reality and the actions of individuals that flow from that reality. This theory thus offers insights for the psychological and sociological explorations of the roots of misperceptions. Herrmann has formulated an agenda for further political science research that includes perceptions of threat and perceptions of cultural differences, two aspects addressed in several contributions in this book.[8] Despite an already large literature, both themes constitute a fruitful field for additional inquiry.[9] Social science research relating to perceptions has largely focused on stereotypes, that is to say, simplified findings and generalized statements of characteristics attributed to others and not shared by the social group of the perceiving individual. A series of essays

---

5 Heinz Kohut, *Self-Psychology and the Humanities: Reflections on a New Psychoanalytical Approach*, ed. Charles Strozier (New York, 1985), 82–4.
6 See the chapters in this book by Marion F. Deshmukh and Wolfgang Helbich; on visual images, see also Nicholas Natanson, *The Black Image in the New Deal: The Politics of FSA Photography* (Knoxville, Tenn., 1992).
7 See, e.g., Ole Holsti, "Cognitive Dynamics and Images of the Enemy: Dulles and Russia," in David J. Finlay et al., eds., *Enemies in Politics* (Chicago, 1967), 25–96.
8 Richard K. Herrmann, "Perceptions and Foreign Policy Analysis," in Donald A. Sylvan and Steve Chan, eds., *Foreign Policy Decision Making: Perception, Cognition, and Artificial Intelligence* (New York, 1984), 25–52.
9 Daniel Katz and Richard Braly, "Racial Stereotyping of One Hundred College Students," *Journal of Abnormal and Social Psychology* 28 (1933): 280–90; Joshua A. Fishman, "An Examination of the Process and Function of Social Stereotyping," *Journal of Social Psychology* 43 (1956): 27–64; William Buchanan and Hadley Cantril, *How Nations See Each Other: A Study in Public Opinion* (Urbana, Ill., 1953); Ole R. Holsti, "The Belief System and National Images: A Case Study," *Journal of Conflict Resolution* 6 (1962): 244–52.

edited by Willi Paul Adams and Knud Krakau has applied some of the resulting findings to related issues in American history and American foreign policy, and has clearly demonstrated the potency of the interdisciplinary approach.[10]

Historical research on ethnic or national stereotypes invariably confronts the question of how closely these stereotypes conform to reality. Social psychology offers some pertinent clues. Otto Klineberg has pointed out that the amount of veracity in a stereotype can often exceed the amount of error.[11] Klineberg's empirical studies suggest that stereotypes can have a positive function in that they provide a proximate reflection of some characteristics of the other. Nevertheless, Klineberg's thesis, while tantalizing, seems difficult to test. It serves mainly to remind us that relationships between objective reality and subjective perception are exceedingly complicated and cannot be sorted into simple boxes of truth and fiction.

Historical research concerning images of other nations that are separated by a large geographic distance from the perceiving individual or group has mainly tended to focus on the social and political processes of group and national image formation and on the resistance of those images to reality testing.[12] Indeed, historians are particularly inclined to emphasize the pernicious and sometimes fateful consequences of misperceptions. On the one hand, the methodological constraints of their discipline limit their ability to evaluate the reality content of stereotypes. On the other hand, historians – like social psychologists and sociologists – often find it easier to document the comic and tragic effects of stereotyping than to

---

10 Knud Krakau and Willi Paul Adams, eds., *Deutschland und Amerika: Perzeption und historische Realität* (Berlin, 1985); Hubertus-Carl Duijker and Nico H. Frijda, *National Character and National Stereotypes: A Trend Report* (Amsterdam, 1960); Sander Gilman, *Difference and Pathology: Stereotypes of Sexuality, Race, and Madness* (Ithaca, N.Y., 1985); Jean Pirotte et al., *Stéréotypes et préjugés raciaux aux XIX et XX siècles: Sources et méthodes pour une approche historique* (Louvain-la-Neuve, 1982).

11 Otto Klineberg, *Tensions Affecting International Understanding* (New York, 1950); see also Knud Krakau, "Einführende Überlegungen zur Entstehung und Wirkung von Bildern, die sich Nationen von sich und anderen machen," in Adams and Krakau, eds., *Deutschland und Amerika*, 9–18.

12 See, e.g., Peter Berg, *Deutschland und Amerika, 1918–1929: Über das deutsche Amerikabild der zwanziger Jahre* (Lübeck, 1963), 8 and passim; Charles W. Brooks, *America in France's Hopes and Fears, 1890–1920* (New York, 1987), 4–7, and passim; David Strauss, *Menace in the West: The Rise of French Anti-Americanism in Modern Times* (Westport, Conn., 1978); Christine Totten, *Deutschland – Soll und Haben: Amerikas Deutschlandbild* (Munich, 1964); Konrad H. Jarausch, "Huns, Krauts or Good Germans? The German Image in America, 1800–1980," in James F. Harris, ed., *German-American Interrelations: Heritage and Challenge* (Tübingen, 1983), 149–59; Detlef Junker, "Hitler's Perception of Franklin D. Roosevelt and the United States of America, 1933–1945," in Cornelius A. van Minnen and John F. Sears, eds., *FDR and His Contemporaries: Foreign Perceptions of an American President* (New York, 1992), 145–56.

disentangle the complicated and layered strands of accurate perceptions and misperceptions that fuse into images over time.[13]

Recent research in social psychology has emphasized the experiential factor in the genesis of stereotypes and images of the other. For example, Vamik Volkan, a psychiatrist interested in political psychology, has dealt in his work with group images of enemies and allies. Volkan's findings about affective needs for enemies, based on observations of the externalization process in groups, seem especially apposite for historical research in the fields of ethnicity and nationalism. As Volkan has stated, targets of externalization develop in each social group with a certain amount of causality; the targets are chosen as a consequence of long historical processes.[14] The reality content of stereotypes thus becomes a point of departure for further inquiry. Although Volkan comes from a different tradition and does not refer to Klineberg, his argument echoes the latter's findings about the historical foundations of stereotypes. That theme is discussed in the chapters here that deal with American diplomatic and popular perceptions of Germany during the two postwar periods.

Those of us who seek to investigate the history of perception, as well as the social function and externalization of images, must consider a variety of contingencies. Peter Gay wisely reminds us that the historian is never forced into a narrow choice between an emphasis on "objective," external realities as shapers of human experience or an emphasis on the ego's distorted apprehension of the external world.[15] The historical evidence presented in this book underlines the wide array of possible motives for the expression of human experience. These observations parallel recent findings in neurobiology that dispute previously accepted assumptions about the dominance of the right hemisphere of the brain for image formation. Thus, we are bound to reject global generalizations about the emotional or cognitive composition of mental images. Imagery, in the infelicitous diction that currently prevails, thus concerns a wide array of brain functions, and the underlying neurological process seems to be shaped by individual differences.[16] Because brain-scanning techniques that

---

13 See the chapters by Peter Krüger, Elisabeth Glaser-Schmidt, Beverly Crawford and James Martel, and Hans-Jürgen Schröder in this book.
14 Vamik Volkan, *The Need to Have Enemies and Allies: From Clinical Practice to International Relationships* (Northvale, N.J., 1988), 90–5; for a historical statement about America's need for enemies, see Detlef Junker, *The Manichean Trap: American Perceptions of the German Empire, 1871–1945*, German Historical Institute, Occasional Paper, no. 12 (Washington, D.C., 1995).
15 Peter Gay, *The Bourgeois Experience: Victoria to Freud: Education of the Senses* (New York, 1984), 226–7.
16 Goldenberg, Podreka, and Steiner, "Cerebral Localization"; see also Stephen Kosslyn, Michael H. Van Kleeck, and Kris Kirby, "A Neurologically Plausible Model of Individual Differences in

help us to localize verbal and nonverbal neurological functions remain in an early stage of research, definite conclusions about the cognitive process of image formation and its relevance for historical study appear premature. Likewise, historical research about the emotional, cognitive, and social processes underlying image formation, while abstaining from reductionist fervor, must take into account all possible contingencies concerning how human minds interact with the external world to shape individual perceptions and group attitudes.

The materials presented in this book, though different in their analytical presuppositions and thematic focus, underscore the notion that historical research about perceptions should avoid deterministic concepts about the effects of psychological and cultural factors upon perceptions. To be sure, psychological inquiry into the makeup of idle thoughts, which lie at the juncture between individual image formation and verbal representation, suggests that cultural value systems determine the contours of seemingly free associations.[17] Those findings lend empirical support to the hypothesis that underlies the contributions in this book: that individual and group perceptions are culturally constructed. Correspondingly, psychoanalytical research has led to cognate findings about the influence of emotional factors on image formation that now are widely accepted in the historical discipline.

Historians of perception, whether they study across cultures or look intraculturally at social, sexual, or ethnic groups, face three distinct challenges. The nature of our discipline imposes an obvious constraint on the researcher. Even a description of the past that is based on years of painstaking research, as well as prudent perusal of the available scholarly literature, will generate a reconstruction that remains partially rooted in the researcher's own perceptions.[18] Mindful of the methodological pitfalls in our own discipline and of the difficulties in attaining objectivity, we seek not to stray too far from our evidentiary base. In short, we explore past individual and group perceptions by describing

Visual Mental Imagery," in Hampson, Marks, and Richardson, eds., *Imagery*, 39–77; see also the contributions in Richard Davis and Kenneth Hugdahl, eds., *Brain Asymmetry* (Cambridge and London, 1995).

17 Susan Aylwin, "Imagery and Affect: Big Questions, Little Answers," in Hampson, Marks, and Richardson, eds., *Imagery*, 247–67.

18 See, e.g., Reinhard Koselleck, "Representation, Event, and Structure," in Koselleck, *Futures Past: On the Semantics of Historical Time* (Cambridge, Mass., 1985), 105–15; see also the recent discussions of "objectivity" in history, esp. Peter Novick, *That Noble Dream: The "Objectivity Question" and the American Historical Profession* (Cambridge, 1988); for a recent assessment of Ranke's concept of objectivity, see Lothar Gall, "Ranke und das Objektivitätsproblem," in Norbert Finzsch and Hermann Wellenreuther, eds., *Liberalitas: Festschrift für Erich Angermann zum 65. Geburtstag* (Stuttgart, 1992), 37–44.

and analyzing image representations where concrete documentation is available to us.

The historical task of image research therefore depends on the availability of that documentation, such as diaries and letters that may reflect the personal experience underlying the formation of perceptions. Up to a generation or so ago, historical research tended to focus on well-known individuals and their writings. The progenitor of transatlantic perceptions research, even before the field had a name, was Alexis de Tocqueville, and his writings remain a continued object of study and analysis. Although American researchers have largely focused on Tocqueville's social and political ideas, their French and German counterparts have shown more interest in his image of America. Thus, Otto Vossler, a German historian of ideas, has proposed to reconstruct the life experience that influenced Tocqueville's assessment of American and French societies.[19] Historical research during the last twenty years, following this model, has expanded the field of inquiry by examining and contextualizing the written documentation left by less prominent individuals. The results have provided substantial and often original insights into modes of thought, cultural values, and mentalities.[20] The contributions in this book reflect those findings by enlarging our field of scrutiny to embrace immigrant letters, popular travel books, and movies.

The ultimate challenge to historians studying the reality content of national images is to distinguish among many shades of gray. Although, as Klineberg and Peter Gay remind us, cultural assumptions, projections, and a host of other neurotic phenomena distort the accuracy of perceptions, we should not overlook the extent to which a core reality underlies them.[21] No doubt we must bear in mind the extent to which individual images and experiences are culturally and effectively constructed. Yet

---

19 Otto Vossler, *Alexis de Tocqueville: Freiheit und Gleichheit* (Frankfurt/Main, 1973), 9–12; see also Bernhard Fabian, *Alexis de Tocquevilles Amerikabild* (Heidelberg, 1957); Françoise Mélonio, *Tocqueville et les Français* (Paris, 1993); Jon Elster, *Psychologie politique* (Paris, 1990); André Jardin, *Tocqueville: A Biography*, trans. Lydia Davis with Robert Hemenway (New York, 1988); Larry Siedentop, *Tocqueville* (New York, 1994); Alan S. Kahan, *Aristocratic Liberalism: The Social and Political Thought of Jacob Burckhardt, John Stuart Mill, and Alexis de Tocqueville* (New York, 1992); Bruce J. Smith, *Politics and Remembrance: Republican Themes in Machiavelli, Burke, and Tocqueville* (Princeton, N.J., 1985); James T. Schleifer, *The Making of Tocqueville's Democracy in America* (Chapel Hill, N.C., 1980).

20 See, e.g., C. Vann Woodward and Elisabeth Muhlenfeld, eds., *The Private Mary Chesnut: The Unpublished Civil War Diaries* (New York, 1984); Robert C. Bray and Paul E. Bushnell, eds., *Diary of a Common Soldier in the American Revolution, 1775–1783: An Annotated Edition of the Military Journal of Jeremiah Greenman* (De Kalb, Ill., 1978); Laurel T. Ulrich, *Good Wives: Image and Reality in the Lives of Women in Northern New England, 1650–1750* (New York, 1990); Laurel T. Ulrich, ed., *A Midwife's Tale* (New York, 1990).

21 Klineberg, *Tensions*; Gay, *Education of the Senses*, 11–13.

cultural historians and social psychologists who lean toward broader notions of a constructed society and psyche go further and claim that emotions themselves are socially constructed.[22] "All theory is gray, my friend," Goethe once remarked, "but green is the everlasting tree of life." However, there exists no convincing evidence to support that claim. The historical research presented in this book, though mindful of social, cultural, and emotional experiences that shape individual and group images, assumes that perceptions remain rooted in a subsoil of reality. They may indeed be partly constructed, but those constructs constitute an additional ingredient of the complex historical and experiential reality that we seek to reconstruct. The analyses of historical images elaborated in this book take account of the well-known constraints in perceiving external reality by grounding their findings in the evidence.[23] The task of historical analysis is to distinguish carefully between misunderstandings that result from partial vision, ignorance, or lack of mobility, and misperceptions that emanate from a desire to construct a larger fiction or myth for ulterior purposes.[24] Thus, we try to reconstruct individual and group perceptions by collecting and conflating multiple sources of singular experiences and by practicing historical craftsmanship, once elegantly defined by Erich Angermann as a "work of art conveying insight not otherwise obtainable."[25]

Perceptions across the Atlantic constitute a special field for historical analysis of image formation as well as a recurrent leitmotif in the history of European-American contacts.[26] Individual travels starting in the seventeenth century, mass immigration across the Atlantic beginning in the 1830s, and detailed diplomatic reports commencing in the early twentieth century created transatlantic perceptions on a multiplicity of levels and for a variety of purposes. The United States from its earliest colonial begin-

22 The constructionist claim is spelled out in Rom Harré, ed., *The Social Construction of Emotions* (New York, 1986); a critique is offered by Ralf Nüse, Norbert Groeben, Burkhard Freitag, and Margrit Schreiber, *Über die Erfindungen des Radikalen Konstruktivismus* (Weinheim, 1991).
23 Johann Wolfgang Goethe, *Studierzimmer*; see also the chapters by Krüger and Glaser-Schmidt in this book; see also the recent contribution by Ido Oren, "The Subjectivity of the 'Democratic' Peace: Changing U.S. Perceptions of Imperial Germany," *International Security* 20, no. 2 (Fall 1995): 147–84; for an example of useful projection of social criticism on distant cultures, see Charles de Secondat, Baron de Montesquieu, *The Persian Letters* (New York, 1961).
24 For an example, see Peter Gay, "A Special View: Freud's America," in Frank Trommler and Joseph McVeigh, eds., *America and the Germans: An Assessment of a Three-Hundred-Year History*, 2 vols. (Philadelphia, 1985), 2:303–13.
25 Erich Angermann, *Challenges of Ambiguity: Doing Comparative History* (New York, 1991), 18–19.
26 Antony Pagden, *European Encounters with the New World from Renaissance to Romanticism* (New Haven, Conn., 1993); Jerry M. Williams and Robert E. Lewis, *Early Images of the Americas: Transfer and Invention* (Tucson, Ariz., 1993); Tzvetan Todorov, *The Conquest of America: The Question of the Other*, trans. Richard Howard (New York, 1984).

nings had constituted a prominent destination for European emigrants and, as a result, defined itself as what Europe was not.[27] The ensuing mass emigration, combined with an enduring interest in America's democratic institutions, resulted in a lasting German fascination with the other continent. First-time travelers and traders, ever conscious of the rigors and the expense of the journey to the New World, took special pains to report their impressions because they knew that they might never see America again. Likewise, they thought that they should report frequently to their European brethren who might not otherwise have access to anything more substantial than superficial newspaper reports about the new land.[28] The Civil War in the United States and German unification in 1871 sparkled mutual curiosity in the two countries' parallel constitutional development.[29] America's steadily increasing involvement in European conflicts, beginning with the dynastic struggles of the seventeenth century and culminating in its interventions in the great wars of 1914 and 1939 and in the subsequent Cold War, increased interest in mutual explorations of the other. From the late 1960s onward, mutual relations became more ambivalent as anti-Americanism in Germany and elsewhere brought back old misperceptions mixed with new concerns about the war in Vietnam and America's role as a nuclear hegemon.[30]

This book concentrates on political, social, and cultural perceptions at the level of the group. Individual views constitute the component parts of group images, yet they aggregate to something more; accordingly, these chapters rightly emphasize the larger social context. So, for example,

---

27 Daniel Boorstin, *America and the Image of Europe* (New York, 1960).
28 For a magisterial documentation of German immigrants' images, see Walter D. Kamphoefner, Wolfgang Helbich, and Ulrike Sommer, eds., *News from the Land of Freedom: German Immigrants Write Home* (Ithaca, N.Y., 1991); see also Helbich's and Kamphoefner's chapters in this book.
29 Angermann, *Challenges of Ambiguity*; Peter Krüger, "Die Beurteilung der Reichsgründung von 1871 in den USA," in Finzsch and Wellenreuther, eds., *Liberalitas*, 263–84. See also Detlef Junker's chapter in this book; and, by the same author, "Roosevelt and the National Socialist Threat to the United States," in Trommler and McVeigh, eds., *America and the Germans*, 2:30–44.
30 Frank Trommler, "The Rise and Fall of Americanism in Germany," in Trommler and McVeigh, eds., *America and the Germans*, 2:332–43. See also H. Stuart Hughes, *The Sea Change, 1930–1965* (New York, 1975), 148–53; for a description of Max Horkheimer's steadfastly critical image of the United States, see *The Authoritarian Personality*. For historical antecedents of German anti-Americanism in the 1960s, see Klaus Schwabe, "Anti-Americanism Within the German Right, 1917–1933," *Amerikastudien/American Studies* 21 (1976): 89–107; for more recent developments, see Paul Hollander, *Anti-Americanism: Critiques at Home and Abroad* (New York, 1992); Thomas P. Thornton, *Anti-Americanism: Origins and Context* (Newbury Park, Calif., 1988); Rob Kroos, Maarten van Rossem, and Marcus Cunliffe, *Anti-Americanism in Europe* (Amsterdam, 1986); Peter Lösche, "Amerikanische Deutschlandbilder und die deutsche Vereinigung," in Günter Trautmann, ed., *Die hässlichen Deutschen: Die Deutschen aus der Sicht ihrer Nachbarn* (Darmstadt, 1991); Hans-Georg Betz, *Post-Modern Politics in Germany: The Politics of Resentment* (New York, 1991); and the chapters by Konrad H. Jarausch and Frank Trommler in this book.

literary historians have developed comparative modes of analysis to examine fictional conceptions of other countries. Thus, the convergent research of literary critics and their historical homologues has addressed literary images of America in contemporary and historical German fiction. These scholars have generated rich material, although, as is so often the case, the works in question often tell more about the home country than the foreign one.[31] Travel reports constitute another quarry for interdisciplinary literary and historical research; some pertinent themes have been described in this book.[32] Or, to cite still another important example of the range of research methods available to scholars, Mary Nolan has recently used German business-travel reports to the United States in the 1920s to draw the larger implications for the rationalization and modernization processes during the Weimar Republic.[33] She has drawn distinctions between modernization and Americanization through close analysis of the German experience in America as reflected in travel and journalistic reports.[34] Nolan has largely focused her work on German sources, whereas this book assembles scholarship based on both German and American documentation that should facilitate comparative research about the formation of group perceptions. Among other things, the chapters show that the ease and frequency of communication form the chief variables in the evolution of mutual German-American perceptions. As, over three centuries, facilities for travel improved, encounters became more frequent. Large-scale German immigration in the nineteenth century was followed by growing tourism in the twentieth. Both developments prompted peaceful mass contacts. The two world wars and the American occupations that followed them produced a different sort of encounter. Yet the long-term results of the contacts between the

---

31 The theoretical debate in literary history has been advanced by Hugo Dyserinck, "Zum Problem der 'images' und 'mirages' und ihrer Untersuchung im Rahmen der vergleichenden Literaturwissenschaft," *Arcadia* 1 (1966): 107–20. For French and German image research see also, e.g., René Cheval, "Cent ans d'affectivité franco-allemande ou l'ère des stereótypes," *Revue d'Allemagne* 4 (1972); Alexander Ritter, ed., *Deutschlands literarisches Amerikabild: Neuere Forschungen zur Amerikarezeption der deutschen Literatur* (Hildesheim, 1977). Among the contributions in that book, see esp. Hans Galinsky, "Das Amerika-Bild in der deutschen Gegenwartsliteratur: Historische Voraussetzungen und aktuelle Beispiele," 59–81.
32 See Wellenreuther's chapter in this book; for a broad description of twentieth-century German travel reports, see Ulrich Ott, *Amerika ist anders: Studien zum Amerika-Bild in deutschen Reiseberichten des 20. Jahrhunderts* (Frankfurt/Main, 1991); for nineteenth-century antecedents, see Peter J. Brenner, *Reisen in die Neue Welt: Die Erfahrung Nordamerikas in deutschen Reise- und Auswandererberichten des 19. Jahrhunderts* (Tübingen, 1991).
33 Mary Nolan, *Visions of Modernity: American Business and the Modernization of Germany* (New York, 1994).
34 Nolan, *Visions of Modernity*, 25; see also Jeffrey Herf, *Reactionary Modernism: Technology, Culture, and Politics in Weimar and the Third Reich* (Cambridge, 1984).

cultures of occupied and occupiers were not foreordained. Perceptions and misperceptions, public and private, determined those relationships and in turn were shaped by them. The raw material for a study of perceptions continues to evolve, as does the German-American relationship itself.[35]

The chapters contained in this book grew out of a conference at Kalamazoo College in Kalamazoo, Michigan, in April 1993. Co-sponsored by the German Historical Institute in Washington, D.C., the Goethe-Institut in Ann Arbor, Michigan, and the Center for Western European Studies at Kalamazoo College, Kalamazoo, Michigan, the conference brought together German historians of America and American historians of Germany. The debates between two groups of academics who endeavored at once to transcend the boundaries of their own national histories and to maintain a critical and comparative point of view were exceptionally fruitful, and refined the contours of the assemblage's transnational perspectives.[36]

This book includes sixteen chapters, all but one of which were presented in earlier versions at the Kalamazoo conference; eight of the seventeen authors are American, and nine are German. The first group – by A. Gregg Roeber, Hermann Wellenreuther, Hans-Jürgen Grabbe, and Walter D. Kamphoefner – focuses on the evolution of mutual German and American perceptions and images during the period between the Declaration of Independence in 1776 and German unification ninety-five years later. These chapters clearly demonstrate that, during this period, the evolution of such perceptions and images was largely a grassroots phenomenon, a natural consequence of growing immigration from Germany to the young United States. Of course, that movement of population sparked the interest of intellectuals, writers, theologians, and travelers from both countries and to both sides of the Atlantic. But, as Roeber shows in his chapter on changing German ideas of American freedom, decreasing distance did not always lead to increased understanding or knowledge; by 1806, he argues, the image of America projected by

---

35 Stuart B. Schwartz, "Introduction," in Schwartz, ed., *Implicit Understandings: Observing, Reporting, and Reflecting on the Encounters Between Europeans and Other Peoples in the Early Modern Era* (New York, 1994), 1–22, discusses the concept of implicit meanings regarding encounters between groups without a common language. For public images, see, e.g., Hermann Wellenreuther, "Image and Counterimage, Tradition and Expectation: The German Immigrants in English Colonial Society in Pennsylvania, 1700–1765," in Trommler and McVeigh, eds., *America and the Germans*, 1:85–105.
36 See also Denis Lacorne, Jacques Rupnik, and Marie-France Toinet, eds., *The Rise and Fall of Anti-Americanism: A Century of French Perception* (New York, 1985); Strauss, *Menace*; Schwartz, ed., *Implicit Understandings*.

German writers had grown dimmer rather than brighter. Similarly, Wellenreuther contends that early American perceptions of Germany, largely mediated by the accounts of travelers to central Europe, "were intertwined with a larger and more fundamental search for an American identity." Again like Shelley's Magus Zoroaster, in traveling to the Old World the Americans were to a large extent confronting their images of themselves. In many ways, then, our first group of chapters suggests that the images and perceptions developed by immigrants at the grass roots were both more useful and "reliable" than those that were produced by more distant "elite" groups. As Grabbe points out in his contribution to this book, "Germans whose friends and relatives lived in the United States had access to a data base contained in the immigrants' letters. It was generally superior to the information available in print." Moreover, that data base was constantly changing; and, just as circumstances were evolving, so too were images and perceptions. As our chapters reveal, the mutual images and perceptions of Germans and Americans were rarely fixed or static, even as they often remained incomplete, contradictory, anachronistic, or self-referential. They were constantly evolving, constantly in a state of dynamic flux, as Kamphoefner shows in his chapter on German immigrants' experiences of the American Civil War. Using immigrant letters, he contends that the experience of the New World at that tragic and bloody time intensified a sense of republican (and often Republican) idealism among German-Americans of divergent backgrounds and views.

The reports of German residents in the United States, as contained in their letters back home, continued to contribute to the formation of popular images and perceptions after 1871, when German emigration to America reached its peak. After examining German images of America as reflected in literature, travel guides, press reports, and school textbooks, Wolfgang Helbich concludes, like Grabbe, that Germans who were in regular letter contact with emigrants "had a more vital connection" to images of America and represented by far the largest single group of Germans "with any meaningful 'image' of America." And within the United States, the images and perceptions developed by the majority population continued to be strongly influenced by daily encounters with ordinary German immigrants and German-Americans. Thus, Jörg Nagler suggests in his contribution to this book that before 1914 the "popular" image of Germans remained ambivalent, but it "certainly was not overwhelmingly unfavorable."

Nagler points out, though, that American elite images of Germany changed significantly (and increasingly steadily) for the worse after 1871, and by 1914 had laid the groundwork for the "vehement home-front attack against all things German" during World War I. His analysis leads us to one of this book's major themes. The reconstitution of the American republic after the Civil War, the unification of a new and powerful German Empire, and the emergence of mass industrial societies on both sides of the Atlantic radically altered the context within which mutual images and perceptions were evolving. As the relationship between the two burgeoning countries increasingly came to be characterized by feelings of competition, rivalry, and suspicion, processes of image formation themselves grew increasingly complex. Older sources of mutual images and cross-cultural contact, such as the people-to-people experiences of immigrants and travelers, remained important; but, in an age of mass communication, mass education, and mass socialization, the influence of important elite groups in both countries increased. Those elites now found themselves in a better position to affect popular images, perceptions, sentiments, and stereotypes about the other; at the same time, their own images and perceptions shaped and influenced the formation of official policy toward the other country. Accordingly, many of the chapters in the second part of this book focus on those elite groups and their own ambivalent and shifting attitudes.

James T. Kloppenberg, for example, explores the "reciprocal visions" of German and American intellectuals during the years of the *Kaiserreich*; and, like most of his fellow contributors to this book, he raises the issue of the relationship between image and perception, on the one hand, and observable social "reality," on the other. Again, like virtually all of the other writers in this book, he reminds us that "shifting perceptions on both sides of the Atlantic" reflected very real cultural transformations, which themselves were quite dramatic during this period.

Peter Krüger carries the story into the troubled years of World War I, the "return to normalcy" in the United States, and the failed experiment with republican democracy in Weimar Germany. His analysis focuses on shifting elite images of the other country's political systems during that turbulent time; and, like so many of his fellow authors, he shows how elite images of the other often reflected the concerns, feelings, and passions of those elite groups about their own society. At the same time – and here again this book points to the complexities of research into images, perceptions, and stereotypes – Elisabeth Glaser-Schmidt reminds us in her chapter of the ways in which an influential individual's own direct experience with the other country could decisively influence his or her feelings about it, as the examples of the American diplomats Jacob Gould Schurman, S. Parker Gilbert, and William R. Castle suggest.

The next group of chapters deals with the changing context of mutual German and American images and perceptions during the most painful and traumatic chapter of modern history. Detlef Junker argues in his contribution to this book that the years between 1933 and 1945 "saw no change in the traditional ambivalence that characterized the German view of America." On some occasions the United States mattered a great deal to Nazi leaders, while at other times it was quite literally "an ocean apart" in their calculations. Similarly, Philipp Gassert shows that "reactionary modernizers" in Germany also remained ambivalent about America, embracing "Fordism" in the 1920s while at the same time decrying the putatively "soulless" mass culture of the United States, in which, among other things, they saw the image of a kind of modernity that they decried and feared. If German images of America continued to be shaped by a "continuity of ambivalence," Marion Deshmukh notes that America's relationship with Germany "turned problematic" during the period that Junker and Gassert describe. Her chapter sheds fascinating new light on, among other things, the important German cultural emigration to the United States after 1933. But she too concludes that the cross-cultural interaction between American artists and their exiled German counterparts – and the American response to European modernism as mediated by the exiles – was complex and ambiguous.

Both "elite" and "popular" images have continued to shape the German-American relationship since 1945. At the same time, those images have continued to be ambivalent, even as the images themselves have been transformed as (West) Germany itself was transformed from a defeated, morally bankrupt, and occupied enemy into a trusted, prosperous democratic ally of the United States. In his chapter, Hans-Jürgen Schröder demonstrates that Konrad Adenauer – a man who played a pivotal role in the development of more positive American images about Germany – was certainly no "puppet" of the Western allies in general or of the United States in particular. Beverly Crawford and James Martel focus their analysis on the medium of film, one of the most powerful shapers of popular images and perceptions in the twentieth century. In looking at American film representations of Germans, we see yet again how images of the self are projected upon the other. They conclude on an optimistic note, however, by suggesting that the appearance of a film like *Schindler's List* suggests that the American popular media may find it possible to transcend narrow and simplistic stereotyping.

The book closes with two essays on American responses to German unification in 1989–90 and thereafter. Konrad H. Jarausch investigates the hitherto little-appreciated role of American diplomacy in the unification process. Again, he draws attention to possible discrepancies between popular images and the behavior of elite policymakers. Public opinion in the United States was, he notes, volatile and contradictory, though on the whole favorably disposed toward the idea of a unified Germany. Jarausch also evaluates the impact of television – probably the most potent shaper of images and perceptions in our time – upon American opinion. Nevertheless, the conduct of actual American policy toward German unification was largely unaffected by popular images, attitudes, and perceptions. Indeed, the Bush administration essentially pursued very traditional national-interest diplomacy in 1989–90 – and with considerable success, in Jarausch's view. In his commentary on Jarausch's chapter, Frank Trommler returns to the larger methodological issues addressed by all the contributors to this book: the "function of stereotypes," the relationship between image and memory, and the extent to which images, perceptions, and stereotypes are altered by changing conditions and circumstances. Europe, and especially Germany, he argues, "always remained an integrating part of American self-definition." But, he concludes, with the end of the Cold War and the decline of America's global position, a greater emotional distance is likely to emerge between the Americans and the Germans. That new distance, he implies, will almost certainly affect the future evolution of their mutual images and perceptions.

In sum, despite the richness and variety of the topics treated in this book, certain themes constantly recur in it: the problematic relationship between self-perception and images of the other; the relationship between "popular" and "elite" images of the other; the "continuity of ambivalence"; the relationship between image and perception, on the one hand, and "reality" (however construed), on the other; and, lastly, the complex and dynamic relationship between images and changing historical circumstances. Finally, these chapters reflect the methodological richness, the conceptual complexity, and the continuing scholarly debates connected with recent historical research on images, perceptions, and stereotypes. We hope that this collection of chapters will contribute positively to those debates.

Like all such volumes, this book is a cooperative endeavor, and we would like to express our deep thanks to our collaborators. Throughout the beginning phase of our undertaking, Hartmut Lehmann gave our project indispensable intellectual and material support. The funding for the conference derived from the Center for Western European Studies at Kalamazoo College, the German Historical Institute in Washington, D.C., and the Goethe-Institut in Ann Arbor, Michigan. At the planning stage of the conference in Kalamazoo, Janet Riley and Dieter Schneider provided invaluable administrative groundwork. During and after the conference Frank Trommler, Willi Paul Adams, Bruce Levine, James Kloppenberg, Jeffrey Herf, Geoffrey Cocks, and Hermann-Josef Rupieper provided challenging and inspiring comments on the contributions and manuscripts. Daniel S. Mattern read the whole manuscript and expertly, as well as patiently, redrafted many portions of it.

I

"Through a Glass, Darkly"

Changing German Ideas of American Freedom, 1776–1806

A. GREGG ROEBER

On May 7, 1805, Pastor Johann Georg Schäfer, Lutheran pastor of Bieber, Hanau, wrote to Johann Georg Knapp of the Francke Foundations in Halle/Saale. Schäfer, whose nephew Johann Edward Schäfer similarly labored as pastor in Germantown, Pennsylvania, inquired about a book order the Hanauer had placed with Halle's book dealer in Frankfurt. At the end of the letter, however, Schäfer could not let the opportunity pass to express his hope and that of fellow pastors that Knapp and the Halle fathers would reject "the spirit of the present times" that would "transform the Religion of Jesus into a mere natural faith. We beg you to remain faithful to the Truth and further to defend the same, which is in fact the duty of theologians."

This letter, replete with multiple ironies, provides a useful text on which to suggest a reconsideration of the image of America shared by Germans from the outbreak of the American Revolution in 1776 to the abolition of the Holy Roman Empire in 1806. Because of the collapse of the religious networks that had long supplied some of the most important impressions Germans received of the New World, a more ambiguous view of religious freedom in America and its possible implications developed, especially after 1789. This theme is explored in the first part of the chapter. The second part argues that a rather muddled view of the American constitutional system after 1789 – both at the state and the federal levels – contributed to the confused picture of American freedom available to Germans in the Holy Roman Empire. The continuing tension between European Pietism and the late Enlightenment, and especially German-Americans' own difficult relationship to these two movements, was also responsible for a shift in German perceptions of

America by 1806. Since the earliest days of migration to North America, ordinary German speakers had clearly valued the chance to attain the greater individual and family security that the New World offered to them; and many had actually found that security in their new home. Similarly, they came to appreciate the tolerance for various expressions of European Christianity that they encountered in North America, especially in Pennsylvania. These values, which looked to Europeans like hallmarks of "enlightened" and "progressive" political thinking, could not easily be reconciled with the more radical aspects of French revolutionary thought and activity. By the 1790s, then, depending on the source, the picture of American freedom available to interested readers in the Reich had become dark, confusing, and to many, increasingly irrelevant to European conditions.

I

Many German-Americans, as well as Pastor Schäfer in Hanau, seem not to have understood that Halle Pietism itself had long been thoroughly imbued with the more radical principles of later Enlightenment rationalism; indeed, Halle Pietism had itself contributed to the triumph of those principles. Certainly since the 1760s, rationalist principles had transformed the emphasis on Biblical faith toward one on rational allegory and the dismissal of supernatural interventions in history. This transformation was reflected in new philosophical emphases on empiricism and probable certainty, which pointed in turn to the utility of religion in personal and public ethics. Siegmund Jacob Baumgarten, although deceased by 1757, had influenced a younger generation of Halle Pietists who, largely unbeknownst to their American counterparts, had become sympathetic to a demythologized view of miracles, divine providence, and the individual conscience that older Halle Pietists could not have comprehended. By 1788, Christian Wilhelm Schneider, *Oberkonsistorialrat* and editor of the famous Weimar *Acta historia-ecclesiastica nostri temporis*, had already informed Pastor J. H. C. Helmuth in Philadelphia that "in our protestant churches in Germany the agitation has increased among the Socinians and deist-oriented, old-atheists and the theologians who teach through such writings." A new Prussian censorship edict in July might, Schneider thought, restrict such undertakings. But Helmuth continued to receive pleas from young pastors in Alsace and in Braunschweig as well as reports from Prussia concerning the decline of religion and requesting help in coming to America where true religion still flourished.[1]

Whether Germans other than worried pastors still thought of America as a place of flourishing religion and religious freedom after 1776, however, is a more complicated question than it first appears. Before 1776, German impressions of America were formed by descriptions of landscape and statistical compilations; from famous visitors like Franklin and Lafayette; from translations of French, English, and Dutch reports on America; from newspaper reports; from informal contacts in letters, visits from former villagers, or agents collecting inheritances in Germany for German-Americans; and from the religious network of letters and information that included the London-Halle Lutheran pietist connections as well as those of the Moravians, the Mennonites, and the German Reformed via the Classis at Amsterdam. Universally, the picture of America had gradually been transformed from one that emphasized the "wildness" of American freedom to a more positive impression of "freedom from" religious oppression as well as from taxation and feudal obligations. This impression, shared both by common villagers who caught glimpses of America from their informal contacts and by the intellectual class and middling sorts who had access to more formal sources, had to be reevaluated between 1776 and 1806. The disruption caused by the war had led to a near-collapse of older religious networks. Moreover, the disintegrating relationship between both orthodox and pietist Christians in Germany, on the one hand, and "Enlightened" observers, on the other, was not the only reason for a reassessment of what American liberty meant. The lack of an opportunity to examine the workings of the new constitutional system of the states and, after 1789, of the Federal Constitution also contributed to a blurring of the image America presented to the minds of Germans in the years after 1783.[2]

---

1 No adequate study exists of the history of the Franckesche Stiftungen in the late eighteenth century and its relationship to the university and to struggles over the Enlightenment. Both Siegmund Jakob Baumgarten and his brother Alexander Gottlieb had been students of Christian Wolff. Archiv der Franckeschen Stiftungen (hereafter cited as AFrSt) 4 D6 Philadelphische Schriftwechsel ab 1805, no. 47; Lutheran Theological Archives Center, Philadelphia, Justus Heinrich Christian Helmuth correspondence, PH 48 E7, letters from Schneider, from Johann Daniel Diehendt, Oct. 1795; August Johann Milius, Mar. 16, 1790, and from a theological candidate Horstmann in Alsace, Herbisheim, not dated.

2 On the pre-1776 notions of liberty, see A. Gregg Roeber, *Palatines, Liberty, and Property: German Lutherans in Colonial British America* (Baltimore, 1993); Jörn Garber, "Von der Natur- zur Aufklärungstopographie: Die deutsche Intelligenz und die Amerikanische Revolution (1777–1800)," in Peter Mesenhöller, ed., *Mundus Novus, Amerika oder Die Entdeckung des Bekannten: Das Bild der Neuen Welt im Spiegel der Druckmedien vom 16. bis zum frühen 20. Jahrhundert* (Dortmund, 1992), 54–75; of some significance, Garber neglects to mention the religious networks of informa-

Pastor Schäfer's letter is also ironic in that the picture it conveyed to Germany about America's own religious conditions was not unambiguously positive. If some believed that orthodox Protestantism survived in America, where in Europe it had been driven out by deism, pastors in America between 1776 and 1806 were not uniformly sanguine about their own battles with "infidelity," on the one hand, and, on the other, unrestrained evangelical "enthusiasm," by which they generally meant Baptist and Methodist revivalism. German-speakers in America also found that they were still not universally trusted. European Mennonites reacted with sharp dismay and annoyance on learning that their American counterparts after 1783 were in a poor position to advance a plan to settle persecuted Mennonites in the Ohio Country. So pro-British had the supposedly neutral Mennonites been, according to an irritated Heinrich Dulheuer in a report to an unnamed correspondent in Leer, Friesland, that even after the Treaty of Paris some Mennonites refused to believe that the war was over and hoped for further British military intervention. The belief that German-American Mennonites posed a threat to the stability of the Confederation was reflected in a European journal article to which Moravian Bishop Johann Friedrich Reichel felt obliged to respond on behalf of the peace churches.[3]

Between 1783 and 1792, reports to Halle from Philadelphia and the impressions sent to Braunschweig from missionaries in North Carolina deepened the sense among German clerics that the Revolution in America indeed portended the fulfillment of Protestant freedom. The outbreak of the Revolution in France also seemed to confirm their worst suspicions about atheism and Enlightenment emanating from this version of revolution; at the same time, events on the other side of the Rhine had created an impression among secular enthusiasts in Germany

---

tion that also contributed to German impressions of the New World. The classic work on the middling classes and their reactions to the Revolution is Horst Dippel, *Germany and the American Revolution, 1770–1800: A Sociohistorical Investigation of Late Eighteenth-Century Political Thinking* (Chapel Hill, N.C., 1978). On the economic and religious motivations of immigrants and resulting definitions of freedom, see Hermann Wellenreuther, "Image and Counterimage, Tradition and Expectation: The German Immigrants in English Colonial Society in Pennsylvania, 1700–1765," in Frank H. Trommler and Joseph McVeigh, eds., *America and the Germans: An Assessment of a Three-Hundred-Year History*, 2 vols. (Philadelphia, 1985), 1:85–105; Mark Häberlein, "German Migrants in Colonial Pennsylvania: Resources, Opportunities, and Experience," *William and Mary Quarterly*, 3d ser., 50 (1993): 555–74; Georg Fertig, "Transatlantic Migration from the German-Speaking Parts of Central Europe, 1600–1800: Proportions, Structures, and Explanations," in Nicholas Canny, ed., *Europeans on the Move: Studies on European Migration, 1500–1800* (Oxford, 1994), 192–235.

3 Donald F. Durnbaugh, "Religion and Revolution: Options in 1776," *Pennsylvania Mennonite Heritage* 1 (1978): 2–9.

that France was fulfilling the revolutionary promise of recent history. Only the resistance of a revanchist Catholicism, a regressive monarchy, and outdated, privileged estates stood in the way of freedom's historic destiny.[4]

Yet those same reports, coupled with the sharp decline after 1783 in the exposure of ordinary Germans to agents or former villagers with experiences of America, resulted in a more ambiguous picture about the possible meaning of "American freedom." To be sure, Halle continued to publish its reports, and during the 1780s and early 1790s Philadelphia's plans for an extended educational system modeled on Halle's seemed to be full of promise. On the surface, the founding of Franklin College suggested a grand future for German-speaking religion in America in the late 1780s. The *Helmstedt Reports* and the *Neu-Hannoverisches Magazin* also reprinted fulsome descriptions of the North Carolina missions where pastors enthused over the piety, gratitude, and friendliness of congregations and their great respect for preachers – virtues sadly lacking in Germany, as the missionaries liked to remind their readers.

Yet a more careful reading of the published reports, as well as veiled references in personal letters, reveals a more doubtful picture of American freedom, particularly after it began to become clear that legal freedom might impinge on other, deeply cherished values. The North Carolina reports warned against mixing German with English or Irish blood, since no German man would be able to exercise appropriate authority in a house with a wife from those more licentious nations. Apart from worrying about the "degenerating influence of race-mixture," cited by J. C. Velthusen, careful lay readers might also have wondered at the extraordinary picture of freedom described by pastor Roschen to a childhood friend in Oldenburg in 1790. Regaling his correspondent with descriptions of the generosity of his congregation, Roschen reveled in his "very independent life on my plantation; free as birds of the air. I can rise in the morning and retire in the evening when I wish, excepting when my official duties interfere.... only the wine is expensive." Surely the image of a pastor rejoicing over being *vogelfrei* and expecting freewill offerings from congregants cannot have awakened uniformly positive responses from lay readers of such reports, whatever clerical observers might have made of them.[5]

---

4 On this perception in general, see Volker Mehnert, *Protestantismus und radikale Spätaufklärung: Die Beurteilung Luthers und der Reformation durch aufgeklärte deutsche Schriftsteller zur Zeit der französischen Revolution* (Munich, 1982); Garber, "Aufklärungstopographie," 69–70.

5 On the educational experiments and Helmuth's reports to Halle/Saale, see A. Gregg Roeber, "The von Mosheim Society and the Preservation of German Education and Culture in the New

Ordinary German villagers from the southwestern territories of the Reich probably discovered none of the reports published at Weimar, Halle, or Helmstedt. Traditionally, their information had mostly come from letters, visits from former neighbors, or the agents who before 1776 had appeared in increasing numbers to pursue legacies and inheritances for claimants now living in America. Although exact numbers are impossible to reconstruct, surveys of the local and regional archives as well as the published visits of emigrants and their petitions for inheritances show that, by the late 1780s and early 1790s, America did not have quite the "presence" among villagers that it had once enjoyed. Nor was its image universally seen in a positive light. Among the rare instances of post-Revolutionary inheritance recovery efforts, one that originated in South Carolina is especially illuminating. In attempting to recover the inheritance of two orphaned children now living in Charleston, Heinrich Geiger discovered from his father, Jacob, a village *Schultheiss* and speculator in American property, that "Americans don't have the best reputation in this country, even if they may be the most honest people in the world." Even the testimony of the pastor and elders of St. John's Lutheran congregation in Charleston did not allay the suspicions of villagers in Ittlingen, in the Kraichgau, about Americans and their designs on village resources.[6]

German villagers were interested in learning more about the American religious situation as well as political and economic conditions in the New World. That curiosity is suggested by the exchanges between the Eulenberg and Betz families in Flammersfeld, Grafschaft Haagenburg, and Baltimore in the 1780s. Inquiring after the Betz family, the German villagers asked first "what exactly is the situation of Religion with you and how is it with church and school? also what is the situation with political authority, and whether the king of England is the ruler of the

---

Republic, 1789–1813," in Henry Geitz, Jürgen Heideking, and Jurgen Herbst, eds., *German Influences on Education in the United States to 1917* (New York, 1995), 157–76; Elizabeth Lewis, "Poor Children and Enlightened Citizens: German Lutheran Education in Pennsylvania, 1740–1820," senior thesis, Northwestern University, 1992; the North Carolina citations summarize the documents in William K. Boyd and Charles A. Krummel, eds., "German Tracts Concerning the Lutheran Church in North Carolina during the Eighteenth Century," *North Carolina Historical Review* 7 (1930): 79–149, 225–82, quotations on 249, 260.

6 On the Geiger case, see Roeber, *Palatines, Liberty, and Property*, 129–30; for the period before 1776, I estimate at least eighty agents were involved in collecting inheritances in the villages, and the incidences peaked in the period right before the Revolution (fifty for the period 1770–6; twenty-nine for 1783–9; twenty-eight for 1790–1800; fewer than twenty for 1800–6); for further details, see ibid., 118–20.

American provinces, and then how do your countrymen sustain themselves in your country on their farms and in raising livestock?"

The brave response from Baltimore emphasized that one could live "as well as a count or prince can in all of Germany," largely since the Betzes were innkeepers at the White Lamb in Baltimore, the sign for which Herr Betz's wife had painted herself. This exchange had been prompted by the prospect of the fourth part of an inheritance, worth no more than 100 gulden, which the sister in Flammersfeld hoped to receive from her father's estate in America. What emerged indirectly in the letters from Baltimore was the enormous geographic distance that separated family members living in New Jersey, Pennsylvania, and Baltimore; while everyone was doing well enough, family members saw little of one another because of the vastness of the country. The Baltimore letters shed little light on church and school conditions for the inquiring relatives in Flammersfeld.[7]

The vastness of America, as well as the fact that religious freedom could lead to stunning novelties among German-speakers, must have struck the family of the deceased Jacob Harginet of Bäischweiler in Alsace when news of his death reached them in 1790. Harginet had originally left for the West Indies, had prospered on a sugar plantation, but eventually made his way to Pittsburgh in Pennsylvania, where he married an African-American woman. Dying at Fort Ligonier, he left half his estate to her and the balance of some £60 to his German relatives. The authenticity of the marriage was attested to by the Reformed pastor Stephan Barrer, originally of Ansbach, at the request of Harginet's friend and fellow Alsatian Mathias Blume, who assured the relatives that the Reformed pastor was trustworthy and a good friend of the Marquis de Lafayette.[8]

The authoritative attestations by church authorities in America of the authenticity of claims advanced by former villagers now residing in the new states did not always convince skeptical Germans in the Holy

---

[7] Landeshauptarchiv Koblenz, Best. 30/ Nr. 4678, letters of Friedrich Betz and Johann Heinrich Eulenberg. For another instance of a frustrated German seeking in vain both information about relatives and money from an inheritance from the authorities in Charleston, South Carolina, see the case of Henriette Gruntzel of Grätz, Niedersächsisches Hauptstaatsarchiv Hannover, 92 LXXXV G 8, Feb. 18, 1794.

[8] Landesarchiv Speyer, Best. C 20/ Nr. 143; the authorities in Alsace noted the difficulties of confirming the authenticity of the participants in this drama, even though the death certificate and other pertinent documents were countersigned by "Louis Philippe Douret, Commissaire dans les Sudiste Colonies," indicating perhaps that the documents traveled down the Mississippi and via New Orleans back to Germany.

Roman Empire. The hope that American church members would behave well was reinforced by people like Johann Joseph Schmidt of Chambersburg in Franklin County, Pennsylvania, who in 1791 left a bequest to the Reformed school in his home town of Winweiler. But, just to be sure, correspondents often invoked the names of the rich and famous, as witnessed by the reference to Lafayette in the Pittsburgh/ Bäischweiler case. In another case, authorities in Württemberg attempted to adjudicate four competing property claims there by asking American-based pastors to authenticate one claim and seeking Benjamin Franklin's help in Paris with the others – in vain, as far as the records show. On another occasion, a family in the Palatinate sought to use the famous American's name in the hopes of securing legal and economic obligations owed to them by American relatives. Similarly, in a case from Prussia, a family from Neuruppin hoped to convince John Adams, in Ghent and Berlin, to intervene in a private dispute concerning property in Virginia.[9]

These efforts reveal the fairly sophisticated and informed nature of villagers' perceptions of how American religious and legal-economic freedoms could work either to their advantage or disadvantage. Nor should we assume that the Revolution completely disrupted contact with or interest in America. The best available statistics on immigration to the new nation after 1783 suggest that 8,700 German-speakers had arrived from the Reich by 1800, an average of about 510 per year. Germans with relatives in the United States continued to receive reasonably good information about religious and legal-economic conditions, but the numbers of people now involved in this transatlantic communication were decidedly lower than before the Revolution. Moreover, both pastoral reports and communications from other educated observers now contributed to a more ambiguous set of impressions about American freedom.[10]

By the 1790s, even the earlier, positive reports of America's religious liberty that had made their way back to Germany no longer retained quite the optimistic tone that they had expressed in the first years after the

---

9 Landesarchiv Speyer, Best. C 14/389 1791; Best. A 2/924 1784; Hauptstaatsarchiv Stuttgart A 213 Bu 94 15h 1775–84; Preussisches Geheimes Staatsarchiv, Berlin-Dahlem, Rep. 11, 21 a, Bu 2, 1780–1817; also consult copies of German archival material in the Library of Congress.

10 Hans-Jürgen Grabbe, "Besonderheiten der europäischen Einwanderung in die USA während der frühen nationalen Periode, 1783–1820," *Amerikastudien/American Studies* 29 (1984): 271–2; these represent the revised figures Grabbe has worked out for the post-1783 migration to the United States; for the distinction between information enjoyed by those with relatives as opposed to more elite impressions, see also his chapter in this book.

Revolution. The most obvious reason lay in the fact that the seventeen issues of the "brief reports" from Halle and the sixteen "continuations" of news from America were published in a complete edition in 1787. Even the overly positive reports that German friends of Halle had received since 1744 now came to an end with Heinrich Melchior Mühlenberg's death in October 1787.[11] Pastor Helmuth was still hopeful that positive relationships connected Halle to the Graf von Arnim in Berlin, since the latter had contacted Helmuth through a merchant in Bremen seeking a sample of American seeds for botanical study. But Helmuth noted privately in a diary entry in September of that same year the "insidious attacks against Jesus (I consequently read the heretic's work)" carried out by the infamous heterodox theologian Carl Friedrich Bahrdt (1741–92). Helmuth must have been especially galled by Bahrdt's catalogue of special advice for middle-class citizens on how to attain "happiness" (*Glückseligkeit*) in religious life. To Bahrdt, religion was a form of civic ethics, and he encouraged critical, rational, and enlightened discussion of sermons in meetings designed to make such ethics more practical. Little remained of traditional Christianity in Bahrdt's work.[12] In reporting on religious conditions in Pennsylvania, Helmuth could hardly overlook the connections between what Bahrdt represented in Germany and what the Philadelphia pastor believed to be an increase in deist and liberal activity in America itself. At the same time he complained that "Methodism now works powerfully on the emotions – God protect these souls." In October 1792 he was lamenting to European correspondents the attacks by Quakers against the preaching office; almost simultaneously he received a letter from Johann Jacob Carl, the bookseller in Frankfurt, informing him that Bahrdt had died. In 1793, Helmuth's reaction to religious developments in America were broken off by a yellow fever epidemic in which he played a significant role simply by staying in the city. His essay on the epidemic, published in both German and English, certainly reached German readers with access to Halle's continuing reports; to his Halle correspondents, Helmuth noted that the only remedies that had seemed to help during the fever were the medicines that he continued to receive from the Halle pharmacy.[13]

---

11 *Nachrichten von den Vereinigten deutschen evangelisch-lutherischen Gemeinen in Nord-America, absonderlich in Pensylvanien: Mit einer Vorrede von D. Johann Ludewig Schulze* (Halle/Saale, 1787).
12 Helmuth does not specify which of Bahrdt's essays he read, but almost certainly he knew Bahrdt's *Handbuch der Moral für den Bürgerstand* (Tübingen, 1789), esp. 163–86 (on religious duties and happiness).
13 J. H. C. Helmuth, *Kurze Nachricht von dem sogenannten Gelben Fieber in Philadelphia* (Philadelphia, 1793); see also Theodore G. Tappert, "Pastoral Heroism in a Time of Panic: Helmuth and the

Helmuth's reaction to Bahrdt revealed perhaps more to European correspondents than it does to casual observers of this exchange today. Bahrdt was renowned not only for his heterodox theology but also for being one of the first Europeans to praise the idea of building a republic on the basis of freedom of public opinion. For theologians such as Helmuth, such notions seemed impossible to square with a commitment to objective truth, and like many conservative thinkers then and since, Helmuth could only identify Bahrdt's enthusiastic support for freedom of press and opinion with licentious attacks on both religion and the God-given nature of public authority. Bahrdt himself had identified traditional links between state churches and censorship as the heart of the problem, while liberals like the Mainz Republican Club leader Georg Forster lamented in 1793 that "there is no German public opinion"; accordingly, both Helmuth's response as well as Bahrdt's perspective could hardly have been other than they were. Yet precisely this sort of transatlantic action and reaction suggests how German perceptions of American freedom were increasingly being refracted through a darkening glass – a glass that was becoming more obscure partly as a result of the transfer to American shores of the European debate between Enlightenment and pietism.[14]

The passing of the yellow fever epidemic, about which Germans could read in Helmuth's pamphlet, was followed by the news that Philadelphia's Zion Church had burned to the ground in December 1794. The largest church building in North America at the time had been partially funded by loans from Halle, and its building (1766–8) had been described in detail in the *Hallesche Nachrichten*. To this disaster, German pastors in Pennsylvania now had to add their horror, shared with their Anglo-

---

Yellow Fever Epidemic in Philadelphia," *Lutheran Church Quarterly* 12 (1940): 162–75; diaries of J. H. C. Helmuth, Lutheran Theological Archives Center, PH 48 K 1.6, Feb. 18, 1790, Sept. 2, 1790; AFrSt 4 D3, letter of Oct. 29, 1792, on Quakers; Helmuth correspondence, Lutheran Theological Archives Center, PH 48 E7, Oct. 9, 1792 on the death of Bahrdt; Helmuth's yellow fever essay and his labors during the plague were noted by Johann Friedrich Schmidt's letter to the Halle fathers, AFrSt 4 D3 Philadelphische Schriftwechsel 1791–6, no. 45, Sept. 3, 1793.

14 Carl Friedrich Bahrdt, *Über Pressfreyheit und deren Gränzen* (Riga, 1787); Carl Friedrich Bahrdt, *Rechte und Obligenheiten der Regenten und Untertanen in Beziehung auf Staat und Religion* (Riga, 1792); Georg Forster, "Über die öffentliche Meinung," in Georg Forster, *Werke: sämtliche Schriften, Tagebücher, Briefe*, 18 vols. (Berlin, 1974), 8:365; see also Lucian Hölscher, "Die Wahrheit der öffentlichen Meinung," and Dieter Grimm, "Soziale Voraussetzungen und verfassungsrechtliche Gewährleistungen der Meinungsfreiheit," in Johannes Schwartländer and Dietmar Willoweit, eds., *Meinungsfreiheit: Grundgedanken und Geschichte in Europa und USA* (Strasbourg, 1986), 51–64, 145–71; for the growth of the American doctrine of *Meinungsfreiheit* in one American state, see Ulrike Jordan, *Anspruch und Verwirklichung des Grundrechts auf Meinungsfreiheit in Virginia im späten 18. Jahrhundert* (Frankfurt/Main, 1990).

American counterparts, at the appearance of Tom Paine's *The Age of Reason*. Helmuth could congratulate the Yorktown, Pennsylvania, pastor Jacob Goering for his refutation of Paine's attacks on Christianity and concluded that most Germans in America had not yet read Paine and had not yet been exposed to his insidious influences. But to his European correspondents, Helmuth was much less sanguine. In his letters to Halle, he reported on the apparent early success of church schools, but noted with horror that on one Sunday occasion Joseph Priestly had preached in the Philadelphia Academy against the divinity of Christ. By 1797 Helmuth expressed his cautious hope that neither Paine nor Priestly had actually enjoyed much real success in Philadelphia, but he was clearly uncertain that this was so. Since the Halle fathers did not publish Helmuth's letters, only a select number of the clergy would ever have understood that the ideological struggles between the late Enlightenment and Christianity that raged in Europe were being faintly echoed in the national capital of the United States. For Helmuth, the triumph of deism and the destruction of the American political system were both accomplished by the death of George Washington, for whose passing the grieving pastor published an ode. The election of the deist Thomas Jefferson, for whom the enraged pastor forbade public prayers, portended disaster. To one European correspondent, Helmuth grimly remarked, "the present so-called Enlightenment has in my experience destroyed much happiness and blessedness and in their place installed a careless abandon with its sorry results – the common man has, at least, won nothing therefrom."[15]

II

If Germans received an increasingly mixed picture of the meaning of American religious liberty between 1776 and 1806, they were left even more confused by the new nation's legal-constitutional system and its relationship to "freedom." Almost none of the essays and reports on political and legal institutions in America reached the common villagers or townspeople in Germany. The dissemination of this sort of information

---

15 AFrSt 4 D3 Helmuth to Halle, no. 21 on burning of Zion; Feb. 8, 1797, on Priestly; Apr. 24, 1797, on Paine and Priestly; Lutheran Theological Archives Center, PH 48 E7 D1 Jacob Goering to Helmuth, Mar. 18, 1789; J. H. C. Helmuth, *Klagen über den Tod des General Washingtons* (Philadelphia, 1800); AFrSt 4 D5, Helmuth to Johann Georg Knapp, July 18, 1800. Goering, born in America, was educated by Helmuth and as a pastor became a fierce anti-Jeffersonian, sharing most of his mentor's views on the dangers the Virginian posed to constitutional government.

took place through published travel diaries, newspaper essays, or the learned magazines published at Göttingen, Berlin, and Halle by well-known publicists such as Albrecht Wittenberg, Johann Wilhelm von Archenholtz, Friedrich Wilhelm Hermann, and August Ludwig Schlözer. As Horst Dippel has convincingly shown, the interest among literate, urban, middle-class Germans for American subjects increased dramatically between 1776 and 1780; at the same time, the assessments offered by most university professors and other officials naturally took the pro-British side in evaluating the Revolution in North America. But actual treatises that carefully laid out the confederation system, the constitutions and legal systems of the new states, and, after 1789, the new Federal Constitution were actually quite rare. Johann Jacob Moser's treatise on North America after 1783 devoted relatively little space to an analysis of the issue of American freedom and constitutionalism. Most of his interest was dictated by his deeper preoccupation with the law of nations, and he somewhat misleadingly described the Confederation as an entity that was "one free and great state." Without interpreting for his readers, Moser summarized or transcribed the state constitutions of Massachusetts and Pennsylvania, but no one could have grasped the nature of the loose Confederation government from these sketchy summaries and translations; nor could German readers have guessed at the actual difficulties involved in applying constitutional principles to the realities of vexing economic and political issues.[16]

In theory, German-speakers could already have had access in 1781 to the Dutch compilation *Verzameling van de Constitutien der vereenigde onafhanglijke Staaten van America*, or, more likely, to French translations of key American documents. In his *Staatsanzeigen* Schlözer offered certain key texts, but in general the German reader had no access to a complete set of documents that included the Articles of Confederation, the state constitutions, and, after 1791, the Federal Constitution and Bill of Rights. Moreover, the texts, when they did appear, almost always are part of a description of landscape and geography. Indeed, only brief summaries of selected numbers of the *Federalist Papers* were available in German before the American Civil War.[17]

---

16 Johann Jakob Moser, *Nord-Amerika nach den Friedensschlüssen vom Jahr 1783*, 3 vols. (Leipzig, 1784–85), 1:697–8, 728–9; 3:496–532, 567–70.

17 The Dutch collection is Dordrecht, 1781, and includes the Declaration of Independence, the Articles of Confederation, the constitutions of the various states, the Treaty of Amity and Commerce with France, and the formal articles of alliance with France; see also Gerhard Dumbar, *De oude en nieuwe Constitutie der vereeniggde Staten van America mit de beste schriften in haare gronden ontvouwd* (Amsterdam, 1793–6), which relies on the Federalist Papers and cites the specific articles

Had the mere absence of critical and complete versions of these fundamental texts been the only obstacle facing Germans interested in assessing American freedom in the last two decades of the century, their confusion might in fact have been limited solely by lack of information. More serious, however, was a flood of positively misleading interpretations in German-language magazines that projected German writers' own hopes and fears onto supposed American legal and political institutions. Those hopes and fears were shaped in turn by the confrontation between the supposed opposites of Enlightenment and pietism, which were commonly identified with the forces of progressive liberalism and regressive monarchy.

In all fairness, it should be noted that Americans' ignorance about the actual constitutional workings of the Holy Roman Empire – expressed in contemptuous dismissal by several of the founders – was equal to any European misperception of the American legal and constitutional system. Europeans themselves, of course, had given Americans grounds for thinking of the Reich's constitution as hopelessly irrelevant to the dawning new age. As Helmut Neuhaus has reminded us forcefully, there were ulterior motives behind Johann August von Reuss's oft-cited dismissal in 1799 of the Old Reich as a "federation with no connections, a union without unity, a community without a common interest and a society where every partner thinks only of himself." In fact, the constitutional structure of the Holy Roman Empire was not as weak as Reuss or the Founding Fathers of the United States imagined. But neither was it possible – to return to the central issue of definitions of freedom – to disconnect the theory of the authority of the state from the inherited obligation to protect true religion. Although Prussia and, even later, Austria made some concessions toward religious liberty and freedom of religious opinion, what still bound much of the Old Reich together was a conviction, at least at its highest levels, that open toleration of religious liberty was tantamount to the notion that religious truth was a matter of

---

of the Federal Constitution to which they apply. The earliest publication of the Federal Constitution is, I believe, in Albrecht Wittenberg's *Historisch-Politisches Magazin nebst literarischen Nachrichten* (1789–95), where the text appears with "George Washington, 'Entwurf zur Grundlage einer neuen Conföderations-Acte des Vereinigten America, welcher in der grossen Bundes-Convention gemacht, und den vereinigten Staaten vorgeschlagen worden,'" 2 vols. (1787), 2:911–21, 989–94. One should not overlook the translation from the French of Filippo Mazzei, *Geschichte der Staatsverfassung der vereinigten Staaten von Nordamerika: Von einem virginischen Bürger*, 2 vols. (Leipzig, 1789). The first summary in German of the Federalist Papers is Wilhelm Kieselbach, *Der amerikanische Federalist*, 2 vols. (Bremen, 1864); a complete translation of the Federalist Papers did not appear in German until after World War II. On the general pattern sketched here, see also Garber, "Aufklärungstopographie," 58–9, 72nn. 33–9.

subjective opinion: an unthinkable idea, on the whole, for many inhabitants of the Reich. In short, both liberals and conservatives projected onto America certain ideas about religious freedom which were at odds with many of the constitutional assumptions in the Old Reich concerning the role of the state. Those projections in turn led liberals and conservatives to idealize or demonize the remote American experiment, but they rarely led to a closer examination of the real intricacies and compromises that shaped religious liberty within the American system.[18]

If one looks ahead into the history of the nineteenth century, it becomes increasingly clear that most historians today deny that later German thinking reflected a genuine understanding of the American legal and constitutional system at all. In other words, despite the demonstrable existence of commentaries and later documentary compilations, Germans could not draw at all on the constitutional and legal system of the United States for inspiration or guidance after the Napoleonic period, during the *Vormärz*, or in 1848. What one misses during this period is an awareness among German observers of the fundamental importance of the difference between the formal and the informal constitutions of the United States. That is, in sharp contrast to the stunningly meticulous collections of statutes, actual cases, and legal procedures that one finds in the catalogue of the *Reichsgericht* after 1871, there is not much to suggest that the major German publicists of the early nineteenth century understood the actual workings of either state or federal constitutions at the level of legal case disputes, at least if the books and treatises that have survived are any indication. It would have been odd, of course, if they had. But first-hand, close observation of the practical resolution of constitutional questions in legal disputes and of the ways in which the still uncertain balance between state and federal powers was being worked out in the arena of public opinion would have brought much of the rather abstract and idealistic

---

18 Helmut Neuhaus, "Das föderalistische Prinzip und das heilige Römische Reich Deutscher Nation," in Hermann Wellenreuther and Claudia Schnurmann, eds., *Die Amerikanische Verfassung und Deutsch-Amerikanisches Verfassungsdenken* (New York, 1991), 31–53, quotation on 53; Dietmar Willoweit, "Meinungsfreiheit im Prozess der alteuropäischen Staatswerdung," in Schwartländer and Willoweit, eds., *Meinungsfreiheit*, 105–19; Karl Otmar Freiherr von Aretin, *Heiliges Römisches Reich, 1776–1806: Reichsverfassung und Staatssouveränität, 1776–1806* (Frankfurt/Main, 1967), vols. 1–2; for a summary of the literature to 1990 treating the period 1740–1806 and the constitutional issues, see Dietmar Willoweit, *Deutsche Verfassungsgeschichte: Vom Frankenreich bis zur Teilung Deutschlands* (Munich, 1990), 179–96. Among the many dismissals of the Reich constitution, see, e.g., the letter of James Madison to Thomas Jefferson, Oct. 24, 1787, reprinted in Michael Kammen, ed., *The Origins of the American Constitution: A Documentary History* (New York, 1986), 68.

journalism published in Germany between 1789 and 1806 down to more solid, procedural ground.[19]

For example, few Germans understood that local juries in Virginia had in practice made it impossible for British creditors to recover lawful debts despite the U.S. Supreme Court's 1796 decision in their favor in *Ware* vs. *Hilton*. Despite the gradual assertion of a doctrine of judicial review over both congressional legislation and state court decisions, advanced in *Marbury* vs. *Madison* (1803) and *Martin* vs. *Hunter's Lessee* (1816), not everyone concurred or even acknowledged such curbs on local and state freedom to interpret the law. Virginia's highest court flatly refused to acknowledge the force of the latter decision in the Old Dominion. And, certainly local jurors believed they were defending American freedom when they pointed to a jury's ability to decide matters of fact in a legal case. Their refusal to award British creditors interest owed by indebted Virginia neighbors would have been difficult to convey to a German readership. But around just such complex issues, evolved the definitions of American freedom in the early nineteenth century.[20]

Moreover, since German perceptions of American freedom had for so long thought of religious freedom as a defining characteristic, they might well have approved of the confiscation of Episcopal Church properties by the state of Virginia in favor of selling these former farmlands by the overseers of the poor. The disputes surrounding the statute, however, led to a contested case, *Turpin* vs. *Locket*, in which opponents claimed the state was acting out of animosity toward the Christian religion. At the same time, legal and constitutional scholars elsewhere in the new republic

---

19 See, e.g., Michael Dreyer, *Föderalismus als ordnungspolitisches Prinzip: Das föderative Denken der Deutschen im 19. Jahrhundert* (Frankfurt/Main, 1987); for the post-1815 essays, I cite here only a few representative examples: Robert Mohl, *Das Bundes-Staatsrecht der vereinigten Staaten von Nord Amerika* (Stuttgart, 1824), an especially careful exposition of federalism and the principle of separation of powers, and a criticism of the Federalist Papers as lacking "eine umfassende systematische Darstellung des politischen Bundesstaatsrechts der vereinigten Staaten" (xi); Alexander Lixs, *Statistiken von Amerika, oder Versuch einer Darstellung des politischen und bürgerlichen Zustands der neuen Staaten-Körper von Amerika* (Frankfurt/Main, 1828); Achilles Mürat, *Darstellung der Grundsätze der republikanischen Regierung . . . in Amerika* (Braunschweig, 1833). All of these works rely on relatively careful expositions of the Federalist Papers, the state and Federal constitutions, official government reports and statistics; for a sharp, anti-American diatribe, see Johann Georg Hülsemann, *Geschichte der Demokratie in den Vereinigten Staaten von Nord-Amerika* (Göttingen, 1823). For the post-Civil War collections in Germany, see K. Schulz, *Katalog der Bibliothek des Reichsgerichts*, 4 vols. (Leipzig, 1889–96).
20 On these cases, see A. Gregg Roeber, *Faithful Magistrates and Republican Lawyers: Creators of Virginia Legal Culture, 1680–1810* (Chapel Hill, N.C., 1981), 229–30; F. Thornton Miller, *Juries and Judges Versus the Law: Virginia's Provincial Legal Perspective, 1783–1828* (Charlottesville, Va., 1994), 34–46, 74–86.

like James Kent of New York, and his young German-American admirer David Hoffman of Maryland who studied briefly at the University of Göttingen, rhapsodized that "the christian religion is a part of the law of the land." Trying to convey the complex doctrines that forbade established religion on a national scale, but just as clearly permitted it in the several states, presented a Herculean task for German observers, but the result would have been a more accurate picture of "American freedom."[21]

The explanation for the gradual eclipse of German admiration for Americans can thus be located in the period between the outbreak of the French Revolution and the dissolution of the Holy Roman Empire in 1806. More specifically, it can be located in the clash during those years between the interests of religion and reason in Germany, and the projection of that clash on an America from which reliable information regarding both religion and the legal-constitutional system had become increasingly difficult to obtain.

The extent of German misunderstanding of America can be gauged from the lack of serious information on either issue that came back to Germany in the *Reisebeschreibungen* and in the German journalism of these years. Johann David Schoepf's famous travels in rural Pennsylvania largely focused on the geographic dispersion of the population, just like the private letters that villagers received from relatives. Schoepf shed little light on legal-constitutional or religious issues in the Confederation. Nor did any later travelers provide much help to those Germans who might be interested in more precisely defining "American freedom" in its religious legal-constitutional terms.[22]

The most important descriptions and interpretations of America during this critical period have been examined with considerable precision in the recent work of Volker Depkat. Building on the work of Dippel, Depkat has analyzed some one hundred and eighty essays on America that appeared between 1750 and 1815 in the German periodical literature. Depkat suggests that the most influential commentators include the sev-

---

21 For the Virginia case, see Charles Cullen, "St. George Tucker and Law in Virginia, 1772–1804," Ph.D. diss., University of Virginia, 1971, 243–63; on Kent, see Carl F. Stychin, "The Commentaries of Chancellor James Kent and the Development of an American Common Law," *American Journal of Legal History* 37 (1993): 440–95; David Hoffman, *A Course of Legal Study*, 2 vols. (Baltimore, 1863), 1:65.

22 Johann David Schoepf, *Travels in the Confederation*, 2 vols. (New York, 1968), 1:68–70; and, in general, Peter J. Brenner, *Reisen in die neue Welt: Die Erfahrung Amerikas in deutschen Reise- und Auswandererberichten des 19. Jahrhunderts* (Tübingen, 1991), which, however, concentrates largely on the post-1830 period.

enty essays in von Archenholtz's *Minerva*; the thirty essays in Wittenberg's *Historisch-politisches Magazin nebst literarischen Nachrichten*; twenty-one essays that appeared in the *Hannoverisches Magazin*; and sixteen essays that Schlözer offered in his *Staatsanzeigen*.[23] The most striking commonality of these essays is their near-obsession with "freedom" or "liberty" understood to mean religious tolerance. On the surface, therefore, this would seem to indicate a grand continuity with pre-Revolutionary German impressions of "American freedom." On closer examination, however, the newer *Amerikabild* begins to look suspiciously like a projection of Germans' own hopes and disappointments. Perhaps most strikingly, none of the essays actually devotes any serious discussion to the actual nature of religious organizations in the new nation; none offers a commentary or an explanation of the meaning of the First Amendment to the Federal Constitution; and none comments on the inapplicability of the Bill of Rights to the states, and of how religious liberty worked under state, as opposed to federal, constitutional conditions. There seems to be no awareness, for example, that state establishments of religion were perfectly constitutional, that they continued to exist in Massachusetts and Connecticut, and that, in theory, they could have been constructed in any state, anywhere in the United States, until well into the twentieth century.

In the absence of any careful study of religious liberty under federal and state constitutional conditions, pro-French German revolutionaries as well as conservative Pietists and religious figures tended by the mid-1790s to read the American situation only as a projection of their own hopes and fears. Adam Dietrich Freiherr von Bülow's peculiar mix of mysticism and Enlightenment ideas is among the most typical of these projected images of American freedom. In an essay on America published in Berlin in 1797–8, Bülow emphasized the notion of "positive" freedom, suggesting that only the servant of the general welfare could be truly free. Using selective tales about American cupidity and American injustices to slaves and Native Americans, Bülow's rather bizarre treatise contrasts an imaginary neoplatonic vision of the state with the abuses of freedom that had emerged in America under its "new condition." A more complete misapprehension of the increasingly privatized freedom of choice in matters religious, economic, and political that would soon sweep Jefferson and his Democratic Republicans into office can hardly be imagined.

---

23 Volker Depkat, "Amerikabilder in der deutschen Publizistik von 1789 bis 1815," *Staatsexamensarbeit*, History, University of Göttingen, 1992, based on the Göttingen *Index deutschsprachiger Zeitschriften, 1750–1815*; and Horst Dippel, *America Germanica 1770–1800: Bibliographie deutscher Amerikaliteratur* (Stuttgart, 1976).

Unfortunately, the response to Bülow's essay was just as one-sided, and just as representative of the ways in which America was being used for German political purposes. Christoph Daniel Ebeling, a quondam former correspondent with Mühlenberg, sought to overturn Bülow's negative stories about the nature of American freedom by accusing him of ignorance concerning the real character of American constitutionalism. Ebeling did little to clarify for his readers what the American constitution actually did say about liberty.[24] Although he based his claim to know more than Bülow about the real conditions of America on his own correspondence with pastors like the deceased Mühlenberg, Ebeling's massive fifteen volumes on the *Genius der Zeit* and his work in the *Americanisches Magazin*, co-edited with Dietrich Hermann Hegewisch at Hamburg in the mid-1790s, show that he was not in systematic contact with churchmen in North America. Although Ezra Stiles in New England was a useful source of information on that region's point of view, it is notable that Ebeling's name is conspicuously absent from Helmuth's voluminous correspondence with interested Europeans. The absence of a correspondence between Ebeling and Helmuth, Mühlenberg's successor in Philadelphia, is perhaps indicative of the projection of tensions emanating from the Pietist-Enlightenment struggle within Germany itself.[25]

The same oddities surround the supposedly first-hand experiences of Justus Erich Bollmann, who visited the United States in 1796. Born in 1769, and a medical student at Göttingen, Bollmann's enthusiasm for the French Revolution landed him in jail as he tried to extricate Lafayette from Olmütz prison. Arriving in America, he affiliated himself with the German Republican Club of Philadelphia and immediately began publishing his assertions in the *Berlinerische Monatsschrift* that the American and French Revolutions were one and the same. Only if one compares the diametrically opposite picture of Philadelphia life being sent back to Germany by Helmuth at the very same time can one begin to appreciate why the picture of America in Germany was so unclear. That picture could do nothing more than reflect the intensely bitter struggle between

---

24 Adam Dietrich Freiherr von Bülow, *Der Freystaat von Nordamerika in seinem neusten Zustande* (Berlin, 1797–8); Christoph Daniel Ebeling, *Der Genius der Zeit: Ein Journal*, ed. A. Hennings, 15 vols. (Altona, 1794–1800); Christoph Daniel Ebeling and Dietrich Hermann Hegewisch, *Amerikanisches Magazin; oder Authentische Beiträge zur Erdbeschreibung, Staatskunde und Geschichte von Amerika, besonders aber der Vereinten Staaten*, vol. 1 (1797): "Ein paar Rezensionen, Amerika betreffend"; see also Depkat, "Amerikabilder," 105–14, 129–35.

25 I base this conclusion on my survey of all surviving letters of the Helmuth correspondence in the American archives, including the Lutheran Theological Archives Center (Philadelphia), Muhlenberg College Archives, Gettysburg College Archives, as well as all correspondence through 1815 in the Halle archives of the Francke Foundations.

the late Enlightenment and religious conservatives within the Holy Roman Empire. It was a struggle that was also played on the smaller stage of the new nation in the New World.[26]

Indeed, just before Bollmann's arrival, Helmuth and one of his students, the schoolmaster Christian Endress, had arranged for the publication of a constitutional history of the United States that was explicitly tied to Christian history. Endress presented his reflections to the von Mosheim Society, an adult educational and literary club that Helmuth had founded to combat both theological liberalism and the loss of German language and culture. He argued that the American constitutional experiment had been blessed by God, and that it was clearly part of an historical process that had begun in apostolic times, had survived Roman corruption, had been reinforced by the blessings of the English Tudor Reformation, and at last had flowered with the emergence of a Christian republic in North America. This picture corresponded, of course, to conservative German fantasies about America that in turn paralleled liberal Enlightenment projections of absolute social and personal equality and freedom on America; and it was just as fanciful as Bollmann's bizarre letters from Philadelphia.[27]

The single exception to the relatively bleak picture that has been painted here was the appearance in Friedrich von Gentz's *Historisches Journal* of a serious attempt to compare the causes and basic assumptions of the French and American Revolutions. The Berlin publicist was nearly alone, however, in sensibly pointing out the uniqueness of the American situation and in asserting that, whatever the merits of the American

---

26 See Depkat, "Amerikabilder," 73–7; oddly enough, the actual records of the German Republic Club have never surfaced in America. After the burning of Zion Church, Helmuth was accused by his political enemies of having allowed this radical club to hold meetings in the church, whereupon they showed their gratitude by burning it to the ground. Helmuth denied having given any such permission, pointing out that he had reluctantly granted permission in 1790 for the American Philosophical Society to eulogize Franklin, but a year later he had refused to let the Society of the Cincinnati use the church. The New York *Minerva* spread the German Republic Club rumor that Helmuth denounced; the German Society of Pennsylvania did meet in St. Michael and Zion's schoolhouse. For further details, see Carl F. Hussmann, "History of St. Michael's and Zion Corporation," 2 vols., M.S., Lutheran Theological Archives Center, H 10 P5M6 L2, 100–12. None of this internal exchange and dispute reached Europeans, of course.

27 I have already explicated this text elsewhere: See A. Gregg Roeber, "Citizens or Subjects? German Lutherans and the Federal Constitution in Pennsylvania, 1789–1800," *Amerikastudien/American Studies* 34 (1989): 49–68. For the German literature in the nineteenth century that saw America as the logical extension of the Protestant Reformation and responsible constitutionalism, see Volker Mehnert, *Protestantismus und radikale Spätaufklärung: Die Beurteilung Luthers und der Reformation durch aufgeklärte deutsche Schriftsteller zur Zeit der französischen Revolution* (Munich, 1982); Michael von Neumüller, *Liberalismus und Revolution: Das Problem der Revolution in der deutschen liberalen Geschichtsschreibung des 19. Jahrhunderts* (Düsseldorf, 1973), 58–76.

constitutional system, it was not transferable to Europe. Ironically, by actually paying attention to the Constitution of the United States, and especially to its historic evolution from the British common-law system he admired so much, Gentz managed to make America completely irrelevant for Germans in search of a usable revolutionary past or model. Alone among the essayists of the period, Gentz insisted that the American constitutional system drew its strength from its actual lived experience in the British constitutional past. In discussing the American experience, Gentz believed, it was historically correct to speak of the "rights of Englishmen" and the application of those specific liberties in a new American constitutional context. That basic reality fundamentally distinguished the American experiment from the French Revolution's romantic invocation of the "Rights of Man," which to Gentz were simply "chimerical."[28]

Unlike his contemporaries Herder and Goethe, Gentz had been influenced by his reading of Edmund Burke's *Reflections on the Revolution in France* not only to repudiate the French Revolution but also to idolize British common sense philosophy and empiricism. In this respect, of course, Gentz had a lot more in common with many Americans than with his fellow Germans. His own dismissal of the American experiment stemmed ultimately from his unabashedly pro-British sentiments and from his increasingly strident role as an antirevolutionary publicist thoroughly disillusioned with the Revolution in France and anything remotely associated with it. If America were truly like Britain, Gentz contended, Americans would not have revolted. Since they had done so, and thus seemed at least dimly to resemble the French, they were, in his view, even less a model of genuine freedom and order than they had been during the colonial period.[29]

---

28 Friedrich von Gentz, "Der Ursprung und die Grundsätze der Amerikanischen Revolution, verglichen mit dem Ursprunge und den Grundsätzen der Französischen," *Historisches Journal* 2, no. 2 (1800): 3140. I am not the first to note Gentz's unique contribution. See Depkat, "Amerikabilder," 81–6, and Hermann Wellenreuther, "Die USA: Ein politisches Vorbild der bürgerlich-liberalen Kräfte des Vormärz?" lecture delivered in honor of Hans R. Guggisberg, Nov. 1992, and forthcoming in the *Festschrift*. The same approach, emphasizing the experiential nature of American constitutionalism, has been pursued by the two foremost German scholars of the American constitutions; see Willi Paul Adams, *The First American Constitutions: Republican Ideology and the Making of the State Constitutions in the Revolutionary Era*, trans. Robert Kimber and Rita Kimber (Chapel Hill, N.C., 1980); Willi Paul Adams, "The State Constitutions as Analogy and Precedent: The American Experience with Constituent Power before 1787," *Amerikastudien/American Studies* 34 (1989): 7–20; Jürgen Heideking, *Die Verfassung vor dem Richterstuhl: Vorgeschichte und Ratifizierung der amerikanischen Verfassung, 1787–1791* (Berlin, 1988); Gentz's essay, "Ursprung," is excerpted in Ernst Fraenkel, ed., *Amerika im Spiegel des deutschen politischen Denkens* (Cologne, 1959), 79–81.

29 See Günter Arnold, "Herder und Friedrich Gentz," in Karl Manges, Wulf Krepke, and Wilfried Matsch, eds., *Herder Yearbook* (Columbia, S.C., 1992), 1:80–97.

By 1806, the image of America among Germans was dimmer and ever-darkening. As we have seen, this condition was attributable to several factors: the collapse after 1783 of older village- and church-related networks; the decline of migration, which only began to recover after 1783 but was stifled again by 1795 with the outbreak of war in Europe; the failure of publicists in Germany adequately to study American constitutional and legal provision within the context of experience (which of course was precisely what they lacked).[30] Although Pastor Helmuth gloomily concluded that French deism had triumphed in North America by 1800, destroying forever the possibility of true Christianity in a North American republic, the country was in fact about to experience the Second Great Awakening. Dominated by Protestant evangelicals, that Awakening represented the most comprehensive and numerically significant Christianization that North Americans had experienced at an unofficial, quasi-establishment level. A closer study both of the history of religious toleration in Britain and the varied reactions to the problem of separating politics from religion in North America between 1776 and 1791 might have provided a more concrete lesson to interested Germans about the difficulties of American religious and constitutional history. Indeed, one can only speculate on what liberal, enlightened Germans would have said had they known that, even under Jefferson, German Moravians received federal subsidies to carry out missionary work among the Native American population of North America, a fact that might have posed an interesting puzzle for radical Europeans who envisaged a complete break between the interests of religion and those of the state. But, in fact, no such careful and close study appeared in the vast array of travel reports, essays, letters, and observations about America.[31] And while Gentz was concluding at the same time that nothing very much could be

---

30 On the newest immigration statistics for the period, see Grabbe, "Besonderheiten." Some eighty-one redemptioner transports arrived in Philadelphia between 1783 and 1819, but most immigration was sandwiched between 1783 and 1794 and the period after 1816. Grabbe also notes that the illegality of labor contracts made in Europe – they were inconsistent with "American freedom" by the 1790s – was also unknown and uncommented on by European observers until after 1816.

31 On the evolution of religious liberty and constitutionalism, see J. G. A. Pocock, "Religious Freedom and the Desacralization of Politics: From the English Civil Wars to the Virginia Statute," in Merrill D. Peterson and Robert C. Vaughn, eds., *The Virginia Statute for Religious Freedom: Its Evolution and Consequences in American History* (Cambridge, 1988), 43–73; for evidence that Germans paid relatively little attention to this key issue in their fascination with England, see Michael Maurer, *Aufklärung und Anglophilie in Deutschland* (Göttingen, 1987); on the Moravian subsidies, see Gerard V. Bradley, *Church–State Relationships in America* (New York, 1987), 99–101. The reports of German travelers on the German-Americans themselves, largely stemming from the post-Napoleonic period, reveal continued admiration for upward economic ability. They contain descriptions of Sunday recreation and church services, and suggest that the retention of the German language was apparently not a "freedom" much coveted by immigrants, nor perhaps

learned from America that was transferable to the German search for constitutional freedom, his more sensible observations, grounded in the experiential, historical evolution of America's legal and constitutional past, were swept aside by the more fantastic claims projected onto America by liberal and conservative protagonists within the dying Holy Roman Empire.

Even had pre-Revolutionary networks and renewed migration not been disrupted, though, German perceptions of American freedom surely would not have remained static. The glorification of American religious freedom by ordinary German villagers before 1776 had largely reflected legal and economic concerns, and their delight at the prospect of living in a land where neither feudal dues nor taxes supported prince and pulpit. This had hardly made them irreligious. Certainly, the somewhat tenuous sources of information that had been provided to ordinary Germans via letters from former villagers, agents bearing powers of attorney, and connections through various church networks reflected genuine experience somewhat more accurately than the learned essays, travel reports, and speculative treatises on American institutions published by European literati. The latter were interested in how those institutions either fit or completely broke with Central European traditions of religious thought or with the highly elaborate constitutional structure of the Holy Roman Empire. Once the French Revolution and the intensified struggle between pietism and Enlightenment intruded into earlier patterns of information, however, it is hard to imagine how conversations about American freedom among conservative religious leaders and liberal German revolutionaries could have avoided distortion. The "spirit of the present times" that had worried the Schäfers, uncle and nephew, on both sides of the Atlantic testified to a long process in the eighteenth century of cultural transfer that had sustained an interest in American versions of freedom at various levels of German society. Ironically, as the time it took to cover geographic distance decreased, so too did interest in American freedom. A renewal of German interest in American religious and legal-political freedoms had to wait until the emergence of Congress Europe and a post-Federalist United States.

tolerated by the larger society. For an examination of these latter perceptions, see Petra Mühr, "Die Darstellung der Deutsch-Amerikaner in deutschen Berichten über Amerika (1800–1840)," *Staatsexamensarbeit*, History, University of Göttingen, 1994. I would like to thank Ms. Mühr and Prof. Wellenreuther for providing me with a copy of this work.

2

"Germans Make Cows and Women Work"
American Perceptions of Germans as Reported in American Travel Books, 1800–1840

HERMANN WELLENREUTHER

I

"In the manners and conversation of these persons, upon the whole, we found a frankness, a cordiality, and good nature truly republican, or which at least I love to consider as such," wrote John Quincy Adams upon encountering the inhabitants of Saxony during a tour of Germany in 1800.[1] Eighteen years later George Bancroft thought that the people and professors of Göttingen were friendly, too. The first professor he met, "Mr. Benecke," struck him as "a friendly man," and he also reported that "Professor Blumenbach and his family . . . are kind to me indeed."[2] Well over a decade later, the poet and frustrated Bowdoin College professor Henry Wadsworth Longfellow confided to his diary that "Counsellor Böttiger," the first person he visited upon the recommendation of his friend Washington Irving, had "received me very cordially."[3]

How does one interpret these three American reactions to Germans? Do they tell us that Germans in the early part of the nineteenth century were invariably friendly to American travelers, to Americans in general, or even to all foreigners? Longfellow's friend Washington Irving thought that such a conclusion would be rash. Upon arriving in Aachen, admittedly out of humor and feeling ill, he wrote to his sister, Sarah Van Wart: "The Germans are full of old customs and usages, which are obsolete in other parts of the world. . . . The people have an antiquated look, particu-

---

1 John Quincy Adams, *Letters on Silesia, Written During a Tour Through That Country in the Years 1800 and 1801* (London, 1804), 22.
2 M. A. DeWolfe Howe, *The Life and Letters of George Bancroft*, 2 vols. (London, 1908), 1:37–8.
3 Samuel Longfellow, ed., *Life of Henry Wadsworth Longfellow, with Extracts from his Journals and Correspondence*, 3 vols. (Boston, 1891), 1:163.

larly the lower orders. The women dress in peculiar costumes."[4] A few days later, however, with the weather improving along with his health, Irving was much less lugubrious. From Wiesbaden he wrote to his sister: "I am very much pleased with the Germans; they are a frank, kind, well-meaning people, and I make no doubt were I in a place where I could become intimate, I should enjoy myself very much among them."[5]

Almost every American who traveled through Germany offers in his journals, accounts, and letters similar contradictions. The explanation is simple. Personal reflections on other peoples and cultures are partly shaped by the mood of the moment, the particular circumstances of the writer, and by the concepts and images the traveler has brought to the new country.[6] For example, John Quincy Adams suggests another reason for the Germans' friendliness. After reporting the kind manner with which he had been greeted by a Mr. Förster in Crossen, Saxony, he explained: "This country in general is seldom visited by strangers, and in such countries strangers are always treated with the utmost attention and hospitality. Many years ago I had experience of this in Sweden; and the farther we now remove from Berlin the more we become sensible of it upon this road."[7]

There exists a large and growing literature on traveling, on travel reports, on seeing and experiencing the "other," and on efforts to interpret and incorporate it into one's own view of the world.[8] In the Enlightenment, travelers mainly focused on exploring and describing the multifaceted variations of a world that they regarded as a homogeneous entity. In the latter part of the eighteenth century this gave rise to such

---

4 Washington Irving, *Letters*, vol. 1: *1802–1823*, ed. Ralph M. Aderman et al. (Boston, 1978), 694–5.
5 Ibid., 696.
6 Authors do not admit that there is a connection between their views of the other and their own state of mind. Yet Irving's example cited above suggests that there was such a connection and further examples cited below support my general observation. On the importance of images of the other for the perception, see subsequent discussion.
7 Adams, *Letters on Silesia*, 18.
8 This literature is summarized in Peter J. Brenner, "Die Erfahrung der Fremde: Zur Entwicklung einer Wahrnehmungsform in der Geschichte des Reiseberichts," in Peter J. Brenner, ed., *Der Reisebericht: Die Entwicklung einer Gattung in der deutschen Literatur* (Frankfurt/Main, 1989), 14–49. The best analysis of German perceptions, images, and views of nineteenth-century America as expressed in travel reports and literary productions is Peter J. Brenner, *Reisen in die Neue Welt: Die Erfahrung Nordamerikas in deutschen Reise-und Auswandererberichten des 19. Jahrhunderts* (Tübingen 1991). For German perceptions of America in German journals and magazines, see Volker Depkat, "Amerikabilder in der deutschen Publizistik von 1789 bis 1815," *Staatsexamensarbeit*, History, University of Göttingen, 1992, and his forthcoming Ph.D. diss., "Amerikabilder im politischen Diskurs deutscher Zeitschriften, 1789–1830."

things as Wilhelm von Humboldt's learned descriptions and efforts to come up with systematic observations of nature. Parallel to this trend, which outlived its usefulness in the first half of the nineteenth century, traveling also acquired a new meaning – albeit a meaning that was derived from the noblemen's tour of previous centuries. As Johann Wolfgang Goethe demonstrated, travel for the bourgeois now represented not only an opportunity to learn but also to shape one's personality.

It would be foolish to force all travel accounts into these two categories. For by the early nineteenth century a third type of traveler with a somewhat different purpose had emerged: the traveler who wanted to accomplish a specific mission in a foreign country. Again, there are precedents. The only difference is that the phenomenon now produced a genre, the "secular report" (*weltliche Rechenschaftsbericht*), the account of the traveler's success and doings, a justification addressed to himself as well as to those who had financed his journey and shared his concerns.[9] These "missionaries," clergymen spreading their ideas of the temperance movement, merchants exploring foreign markets as potential recipients of their nation's goods, scholars studying the educational system for the benefit of their own country, all had one thing in common (or so they claimed): Not self-improvement, but betterment of their country served both as their motive and as the rationale of their behavior.

Scholars analyzing the accounts of these travelers speak of "perceptions," "images," and "stereotypes." There is a large scholarly literature on these terms, and it is still growing.[10] Since it is impossible here to deal adequately with their theoretical implications, these remarks are limited to a few observations. On a very general level these terms are used in the sense of reactions to things actually experienced or perceived as "German." These reactions are part of a larger set of ideas and cultural notions, of things learned and heard from others, in short of things belonging to a large, yet always undefinable, context within the individual's mind.[11] Since

---

9 The spiritual autobiography as well as the travel journals of missionaries and ministers were already well established by the early part of the seventeenth century and flourished in the eighteenth century, as journals like those of George Fox, John Woolman, and John Wesley demonstrate. What is new is the report as *Rechenschaftsbericht* to a corporate body like the Temperance Society.

10 See, e.g., John Morris, ed., *Exploring Stereotyped Images in Victorian and Twentieth-Century Literature and Society* (Lewiston, N.Y., 1993); Wolfgang Neuber, *Fremde Welt im europäischen Horizont: Zur Topik der deutschen Amerika-Reiseberichte der frühen Neuzeit* (Bielefeld, 1991), as well as literature cited subsequently.

11 Travelers read traveling accounts in preparing for their trips; before leaving America they likewise sought out those who had been in Europe before and talked to them; thus Motley was a student of Bancroft and Cogswell, former students at Göttingen; Longfellow carried letters of introduction from Washington Irving when he came to Germany; other examples could be given.

contexts, learning experiences, and perspectives and modes of perceiving are thus individualized, it is preferable to speak of "images," "perceptions," and "stereotypes" in the plural rather than of one American "image" of Germany and Germans.[12]

My definition "actually experienced or perceived as German" is, of course, somewhat vague. In theory, it was possible to experience or perceive things as "German" *within* the United States. Indeed, both in the early nineteenth century and in the present Americans regard many goods and products, houses and habits in various parts of the country as genuinely "German." Yet they were also perceived as part of the "other," and thus as part of a construct of "otherness" in the sense of not being truly "American." Moreover, these mental categorizations of objects as "German" tended to be attached to certain regions, such as the Middle Atlantic states or, toward the end of the period under consideration in this chapter, the North Central states. Things perceived as "German" formed part of the image Americans brought over to Europe and Germany; thus regional origin of travelers can reveal important clues about context within which a particular traveler's remarks have to be interpreted.[13]

For clearly the notion of what is thought to be "German" in a region with a large German population would differ from the notions encountered in regions like New England, where Germans were a rarity, where the German language was largely unknown, and where particular items were only rarely described as "German." One can be sure that Pennsylvanians of German stock would not have subscribed to the following words of Henry E. Dwight, Yale President Timothy Dwight's eldest son: "We are accustomed to regard the Germans as a heavy-moulded race, as particularly physical in their character, because the

---

12 Prof. Timothy H. Breen has pointed out to me that cultures construct a shared social reality; if it would not be shared it would be hard to speak of culture at all. That of course is true but sidesteps my point, which is methodological. In approaching a text, one has to read the text not only as a statement of a particular culture but as the individual perception of that culture as well as the individual reflection of one's own culture.

13 Although we speak of American images of Germany as well as of German images of America, we should bear in mind that these images may refer to somewhat less than the whole. Brenner, *Reisen in die Neue Welt*, 298–300, stresses that the German image of America is largely shaped by the German image of New England, and of the Yankee image in particular. I am grateful to Thomas Wimmer for drawing my attention to the problem of the regionalization of images, cf. Thomas Wimmer, "Deutsche Kalifornienbilder in der Mitte des 19. Jahrhunderts," Staatsexamensarbeit, History, University of Göttingen, 1992, 30–56. For the early nineteenth century, I do not perceive such a regionalization of the American image of Germany despite the fact that certain regions, such as the Rhine Valley, Heidelberg, Munich, and the Berlin and Dresden areas, were standard fare, whereas other regions were less often visited, as John Adams had noted.

ignorant peasantry, who have emigrated from this country to the United States, have remained equally ignorant in ours."[14] These remarks reflected the New England experience, which had largely been shaped by books and articles about German farmers in the Middle Atlantic states.[15] Dwight's image – or rather, "stereotype" in Walter Lippmann's sense of that word – probably dates back to the 1740s when, in the heat of a public debate, Benjamin Franklin had made some rash remarks about "German boors."[16]

It is evident that early nineteenth-century American images, stereotypes, and perceptions of other nations and cultures were to a large extent influenced by particular demographic, ethnic, and settlement structures. To give but one further example, although knowledge of German was nothing unusual in the region from southern New York to Maryland and beyond, George Ticknor claimed that in the beginning of the nineteenth century he had great difficulties in finding anyone in Boston who could teach him the rudiments of the German language in preparation for his first visit to Germany. In all of New England, only a few Germans had settled in Maine.[17] George Bancroft, on the other hand,

---

14 Henry E. Dwight, *Travels in the North of Germany in the Years 1825 and 1826* (New York, 1829), 76.
15 Henry E. Dwight was the youngest son of Timothy Dwight, president of Yale University; born and raised in the heart of New England, in New Haven, he received his schooling there; after graduation he was apprenticed to his older brother in New York before he entered Andover Theological Seminary, which he left after serious illness for a four years' stay in Germany where he studied at the universities in Göttingen and Berlin. Upon his return he founded together with his brother the New Haven Gymnasium, most likely modeled on what he had seen in Germany, which both were forced to give up owing to ill health. Henry E. Dwight died in 1832 (American Biographical Archive, sub Henry E. Dwight). The remarks of Dwight suggest that he was not really familiar with the relevant publications. He did not, for example, know Samuel Miller's *A Brief Retrospect of the Eighteenth Century: First Part in Two Volumes, Containing a Sketch of the Revolutions and Improvements in Science, Arts, and Literature During That Period*, 2 vols. (New York, 1803), 2:110–13, 314–30, which offered a detailed, well-informed, and largely positive account of the state of German literary and philological productions. Miller summarized: "No country has ever produced so great a number of authors; and there is no country where a taste for reading more generally prevails, especially in the Protestant provinces. Printing is carried to an excess truly wonderful. Almost every man of letters is an author. Books are multiplied to an incredible extent. Between *six and seven thousand* new works are annually published, besides smaller controversial pieces . . ." (ibid., 2:325). But the author concluded his remarks about Germany on a negative note: "There is no country now on earth (unless, perhaps, we must except France) in which literary enterprise is made the medium for conveying so much moral and theological poison as in Germany" (ibid., 2:330).
16 Hermann Wellenreuther, "Image and Counterimage, Traditions and Expectations: The German Immigrants in English Colonial Society in Pennsylvania, 1700–1765," in Frank Trommler and Joseph McVeigh, eds., *America and the Germans: An Assessment of a Three-Hundred-Year History*, 2 vols. (Philadelphia, 1985), 2:85–105.
17 George Ticknor, *Life, Letters, and Journals of George Ticknor*, ed. George S. Hillard, 2 vols. (Boston, 1876; reprinted: New York, 1900), 2:11–12. Because Ticknor was intimate with the Rev. Joseph Buckminster, who had been in Europe between 1803 and 1806 and who knew German, it is

simply seems to have left for Göttingen without bothering too much about his speaking knowledge of the language.[18]

Yet things did improve in New England. When John Lothrop Motley, who had been a student at Bancroft's and Cogswell's Round Hill School, left for Germany in emulation of his mentors in 1832, he was able during his crossing to Hamburg, to "learn a good deal of German, by talking and reading and writing, and I have been talking all day with the German pilot . . . so that I think I shall not have much difficulty in speaking the language pretty soon" – an observation that suggests some prior grounding in German.[19] Although Motley does not say so, it seems likely that as a preparation for his trip the young man had received advice from many individuals, including his teachers Bancroft and Cogswell; twenty years earlier this would have been more difficult. To illustrate these observations in greater detail, the next section of these remarks sketches the regional, social, and educational background of American travelers.

Since it is impossible to do justice to the richness of what Americans had to say about Germans, the third part of this chapter is restricted to a short analysis of American reactions to and perceptions of Germans, understood not so much as descriptions of what Germans really *were* in those days but as reflections of the American travelers' cultural and conceptual concerns *as Americans*. The central thesis here is that these concerns of Americans were shaped by the early nineteenth-century debate in America about the nature of that country as a democratic, egalitarian, and republican society much in need of continued improvement and reform.[20] Most of the rest of this chapter is based on an analysis of the accounts, letters, and journals of Americans who traveled through Germany between 1800 and 1840 as well as on the findings of a 1991 master's thesis by Dirk Voss.[21]

---

likely that Ticknor exaggerated a bit. Yet the gist of his story, that things German and the German language were largely unknown in Boston, seems true.

18 There is no mention of Bancroft trying to acquire some knowledge of German in preparing for his stay in Göttingen, cf. Howe, *Bancroft*, 1:28–9, although Bancroft seems to have acquired a reading knowledge of German sometime before his departure.

19 George William Curtis, ed., *The Complete Works of John L. Motley: The Correspondence of John Lothrop Motley*, 3 vols. (New York, ca. 1889), 1:15.

20 This debate is described in Rush Welter, *The Mind of America, 1820–1860* (New York, 1975).

21 Dirk Voss, "Das Stereotype Bild der Deutschen in Amerikanischen Reiseberichten, 1800–1839," M.A. thesis, University of Göttingen, 1991. Diaries pose different methodological problems than travel acounts. For a summary of the discussion of the nature of diaries and problems of interpretation, see Ralph Rainer Wuthenow, *Europäische Tagebücher: Eigenart, Formen, Entwicklung* (Darmstadt, 1990).

Anyone who has worked with these sources quickly finds that travelers offer stereotypes while on the move. Moreover, many of these stereotypes are not unique, but are shared by travelers from other nations. As soon as American travelers decided to stay in one place these stereotypes disappeared, because the traveler became, like Clara Crowninshield, part of a particular American-German social setting whose values and concepts gradually transcended imported stereotypes. Accordingly, those stereotypes that *did* persist under changed or new conditions – such as Crowninshield's strictures about smoking, the hard physical work of country women, and the social utility of women's knitting – deserve special attention.

II

There are essentially three different types of American travelers who visited Germany in the early nineteenth century. The first group went abroad for educational and scholarly purposes. Bancroft, Cogswell, Dwight, Everett, Motley, and Ticknor are early representatives. Their focus was the world of scholarship and culture, more especially literary culture, which invariably required a pilgrimage to the venerable Goethe himself. They returned with a high regard for German academic life and scholarship, a deep knowledge of things German and European, and, above all, a greater intimacy with ancient and classical languages. They also brought back definite notions about how to improve the American system of higher education.[22] In short, they represented a definite perspective, a particular interest which in turn shaped their approach to German institutions and German society.

Closely connected to this group, but sharing a larger perspective and purpose, was the second group of travelers who braved the ocean, mostly after 1825. These Americans did not specifically come to Germany, but to Europe in general in a search for intellectual stimulation, to rediscover classical and modern European culture, and to gain firsthand experience of European scholarship. Above all, though, they were determined to search out and meet Europe's greatest academic minds. This group includes people like Charles Sumner, Henry Wadsworth Longfellow, George Washington Greene, James Fenimore Cooper, and William

---

22 See esp. Dwight, *Travels in the North of Germany*, passim, which demonstrates Dwight's deep interest in German institutions of higher education; Bancroft and Cogswell, to name two other Americans, upon their return to America opened a school, the already mentioned Round Hill School, to which Motley went.

Cullen Bryant.[23] These individuals shared a perspective that embraced all of Europe. Finally, a third group consists either of curiosity seekers, tourists in the sense of people who accompanied others (like Clara Crowninshield), or of mercantile travelers such as Richard Jeffry Cleveland (1773–1860).[24]

The three groups have distinctive features. The first were young, typically came from New England,[25] spent most of their time at a German university, and used their leisure time to seek out celebrities like Goethe. In those days Göttingen tended to be the university of choice, with Berlin a distant second. The second group – literati in the proper sense – shared similar backgrounds as well as similar purposes and questions, all of which lent a certain sameness to their wanderings in Europe and Germany. Yet they roamed over wider areas and were less bent on studying than on exploring, meeting, and collecting impressions, knowledge and information.

Members of the third group did not necessarily share similar cultural and educational experiences; nor were shared interests responsible for bringing them to the Old World. Thus their movements and attitudes cannot be easily fitted into a single pattern. Two representatives of this group, Crowninshield and Cleveland, can serve as illustrations. Crowninshield, the illegitimate daughter of a wealthy New England merchant, was brought up in modest surroundings in which she was

---

23 Edward L. Pierce, *Memoir and Letters of Charles Sumner*, 2 vols. (London 1878); James Franklin Beard, ed., *The Letters and Journals of James Fenimore Cooper* (Cambridge, Mass., 1960), vol. 1; Andrew Hilen, ed., *The Letters of Henry Wadsworth Longfellow*, vol. 1: *1814–1836* (Cambridge, Mass., 1966); Samuel Longfellow, ed., *Life of Henry Wadsworth Longfellow, with Extracts from his Journals and Correspondence*, 3 vols. (Boston, 1886), vol. 1; Parke Godwin, *Prose Writings of William Cullen Bryant*, ed. Parke Godwin, 2 vols. (New York, 1884; reprinted: New York, 1964), 2:215–21, 287–91, 335–43; William Cullen Bryant II and Thomas G. Voss, eds., *Letters of William Cullen Bryant*, vol. 2: *1836–1849* (New York, 1977).

24 Andrew Hilen, ed., *The Diary of Clara Crowninshield: A European Tour with Longfellow, 1835–1836* (Seattle, Wash., 1956); Richard Jeffry Cleveland, *A Narrative of Voyages and Commercial Enterprises*, 2 vols. (Cambridge, Mass., 1842), reprinted under the title, *Voyages and Commercial Enterprises of the Sons of New England* (New York, 1857; reprinted: New York, 1968). I have used the reprint edition. I have classified American travelers before 1840 on the basis of who published accounts of their travels or whose extant correspondence allows me to say something about their attitudes and motivations. Clearly, there were many other American travelers touring Europe; some of them are mentioned in the published travel accounts I have read. An example would be Theodore O. Fowler, a retired merchant from New Orleans, whom James Fenimore Cooper met at Spa in early August 1832 (Cooper, *Letters and Journals*, 2:293–7). I have found no further biographical information about Fowler than those given by Cooper.

25 There is a curious correspondence between the German image of the American as "Yankee" and the fact that most early American visitors came from New England; it will be evident that this had some influence on American perceptions of Germany.

never allowed to forget that socially she was not respectable. Her guardian did, however, provide her with what could be called a decent education, which in turn enabled her to move in the rather staid society of New England. In school she became an intimate friend of Mary Storer Potter; when Mary's husband, Henry Wadsworth Longfellow, decided that his intellectual development required a stay in Europe, Mary requested that Crowninshield accompany her as a companion. And thus Crowninshield was enticed to Europe and Germany. This is not to suggest that she was not interested in Europe; it does, however, point to circumstances that cannot have been without influence on how she viewed and experienced the Old World.[26]

Richard Jeffry Cleveland is cut of altogether different material; raised at Salem, Massachusetts, in a seafaring family, he left school at age fourteen to become an apprentice with a merchant. Four years later he joined the merchant marine, where he quickly learned the arts of navigation. At barely the age of twenty-four, he had already become captain of his own vessel and, swashbuckler that he was, soon began to impress others with his daring voyages around the world. He reported his exploits in his *Narrative* in 1842.[27] His bland disregard for other nations' navigation laws won and lost him more than one respectable fortune until he managed to settle down as a member of the U.S. customs establishment.[28] Again, it is obvious that a freebooter of Cleveland's type viewed Europe and Germany much differently from the poet Longfellow. For Cleveland, Germany was synonymous with the harbor facilities and the market opportunities of Hamburg and Kiel.[29]

These three groups viewed and approached Europe and Germany with different cultural, religious, as well as moral notions and experiences. Different individuals would be startled by different phenomena and would

---

26 Hilen, ed., *Diary of Clara Crowninshield*, xiii–xxii. To state the obvious, Crowninshield visited places her employers decided to visit, was much dependent in what she did in a given place on what Mary wanted to do – unfortunately Mary was not very enterprising to the dismay of Clara. Even after Mary's death in Amsterdam this pattern did not change. Her prolonged stay in Heidelberg was forced on her because Longfellow wanted to be in Heidelberg and meet and argue with famous people, such as Thibaut.
27 See Cleveland, *Voyages and Commercial Enterprises*.
28 Of course Cleveland had a different perspective. In his introduction he obliquely referred to this in the following words: "If success attend his enterprise, when returning home with ample compensation for his labor, he runs the risk of having it all snatched from him by some hungry satellite of that great high-sea robber, termed 'His,' or 'Her Majesty,'" Cleveland, *Voyages and Commercial Enterprises*, 13. The biographical informations are based on the article in the *Dictionary of American Biography*.
29 Cleveland, *Voyages and Commercial Enterprises*, 154–5, 270–5.

get excited by different things. And yet there was always a common ground upon which all members of these groups would base their images, notions, and reactions.

Of the fifty-one American citizens who visited Europe between 1800 and 1839 and published accounts of their exploits, more than half were born in New England,[30] and another ten hailed from New York and two from New Jersey.[31] The remaining five travelers came from four different states, three Southern and one Western.[32] They thus shared different regional identities, each of which provided them with certain notions about proper behavior, including such things as the role of religion in daily life.

There are, of course, other classificatory systems than the one just offered. Of the fifty-one travelers almost two-thirds belonged to three categories: clergymen (thirteen),[33] students (ten)[34] and scholars/writers (eleven).[35] Most of the rest at least shared a similar economic, social, and educational background with the members of these groups. This is true for politicians like John Quincy Adams, Aaron Burr (who of course lived in exile in Europe), and Jonathan Russell. It is equally true for Samuel Gridley Howe, who visited Europe's institutions for the blind,[36] and for George Palmer Putnam, who finally spent most of his time in England as a publisher. Whether Cleveland and George Coggeshall, both captains

---

30 George Burgess, Jonathan Russell (Rhode Island); George Coggeshall, Henry E. Dwight, Wilbur Fisk (Connecticut); Baron Stow (New Hampshire); John Quincy Adams, Martha Babcock Amory, George Bancroft, Joseph Stevens Buckminster, Richard J. Cleveland, Joseph Green Cogswell, Clara Crowninshield, Orville Dewey, Edward Everett, Samuel Hadlock, Samuel Gridley Howe, Henry W. Longfellow, John L. Motley, Thomas H. Perkins, Edward Robinson, Catherine M. Sedgwick, Jared Sparks, Charles Sumner, George Ticknor, Samuel Topliff, Nathaniel P. Willis (all Massachusetts).
31 William C. Bryant, Aaron Burr, James Fenimore Cooper, Stephen Grellet, Washington Irving, Henry B. McLellan, Valentine Mott, George P. Putnam, David Sands, William B. Sprague (all New York); Robert Baird, Robert Breckinridge (New Jersey).
32 George H. Calvert (Maryland); Henry Hiestand, Stephen Olin (Virginia); Hugh Swinton Legaré (South Carolina); and Calvin E. Stowe (Ohio).
33 Robert Baird, Mathias Bruen, John Stevens Buckminster, Orville Dewey, Wilbur Fisk, Stephen Grellet, Henry Hiestand, Stephen Olin, Thomas H. Perkins, David Sands, William B. Sprague, Baron Stow, Hezekiah Hartley Wright.
34 George Bancroft, George Burgess, George H. Calvert, Joseph Green Cogswell, Henry E. Dwight, Edward Everett, Hugh Swinton Legaré, Henry Blake McLellan, John Lothrop Motley, and George Ticknor.
35 William C. Bryant, James Fenimore Cooper, Washington Irving, Isaac A. Jewett, Valentine Mott, Edward Robinson, Catherine M. Sedgwick, Jared Sparks, Calvin Ellis Stowe, Charles Sumner, and Nathaniel P. Willis. The persons I have named in this as well as the other notes do not of course comprise all American travelers to Germany but only those whose letters and printed travel accounts are available. For a full bibliography of the writings of these people, see Dirk Voss, "Das Stereotype Bild der Deutschen," appendix.
36 Laura E. Richards, ed., *Letters and Journals of Samuel Gridley Howe*, 2 vols. (Boston, 1909).

and world travelers, had enjoyed the high quality education characteristic of the others can be doubted. The same skepticism can be extended to Samuel Hadlock, the third sea captain in the group. He traveled through Europe, including Germany, with a group of performing Eskimos who demonstrated their skills to curious Europeans willing to pay for the spectacle.[37] Nor is any information available concerning the educational and cultural backgrounds of Martha B. Amory and Charlotte B. Bronson, who honeymooned in Europe, or of Fanny W. Hall, who visited Europe (again including Germany) and reported her experiences at some length.[38]

III

All these visitors, whatever their backgrounds, came to Germany with images of their own country as well as with more or less definite notions about what awaited them in Europe in general and in Germany in particular. They experienced almost instinctively the new things as contrasts to or confirmations of what they cherished. Their experiences largely took the form of comparisons.[39] On a fundamental level they frequently found in Germany a certain confirmation of their own distinctive American nationality, which, according to Cooper, was still too insecure and too much influenced by British models.[40] Yet these comparisons were always colored by individual perspectives.

To illustrate, let us juxtapose two statements about the advantages of American republican government over German monarchy. Henry E. Dwight of New Haven, Connecticut, observed: "While looking at such an exhibition of tyranny, my heart always feels grateful to God for giving

---

37 Rachel L. Field, *God's Pocket: The Story of Captain Samuel Hadlock Junior, of Cranberry Isles, Maine* (New York 1934). I am doubtful about George Rapelje who published *A Narrative of Excursions, Voyages, and Travels, Performed at Different Periods in America, Europe, and Africa* (New York 1834). According to the National Union Catalogue, Rapelje was born in 1771. The *American Biographical Archives* list a sizeable Rapelje family in New York for the Revolutionary period. My guess is, without having seen the *Narrative*, that Rapelje was a sea captain.
38 Fanny W. Hall, *Rambles in Europe: A Tour Through France, Italy, Switzerland, Great Britain, and Ireland in 1836*, 2 vols. (New York, 1838).
39 Only a few were aware of this, cf. the not too serious remarks of Irving, *Letters*, 1:167: "It is my misfortune, perhaps, to be forever drawing comparisons between the Women of Europe and the fair beings I have left behind me in America and the balance turns heavily in favor of the latter – Not but that I confess I have experienced a little wandering of the head among the fair ones of Italy and some transient attachments that are necessary to give a flavor to existence – but my heart still points towards New York as the quarter from whence it feels the most powerful attractions."
40 Cooper, *Letters and Journals*, 2:293–4.

me my birth in the land of freedom."[41] This is more than just rhetoric. Dwight evoked key terms of the American Revolution. The sentence expresses the pride of a young man from Connecticut who in his view had experienced a confirmation of his own American identity. At the same time the remark's vagueness indicates a certain youthful openness and lack of personal experience. He is still unable to tie his concept of "freedom" to particular examples.

The physician Valentine Mott expressed the same feeling, yet within a more definite context: "From the comparison I have made of the conditions of the populations of other countries, I feel still more deeply impressed with the convictions that our republican form of government is infinitely and immeasurably preferable to that of any other that has ever existed."[42] Mott links his sense that his country's republican form of government is superior to his professional comparisons of health conditions in different European countries: The healthier world of North America is to him a result of the superior American constitutional system, and this in turn serves to confirm him in his own identity.

Comparing as a method is even more evident in American reactions to daily activities. Most travelers' comparisons of German and American food found the former lacking in quality, taste, and wholesomeness. Henry E. Dwight stated categorically: "As their cookery is less healthy than ours, we have rather the advantage of them in this respect."[43] This is a general statement largely meant to confirm American superiority in this important field. Once one looks for specifics, though, the picture changes: Ticknor noted in his diary that the dinner on October 19, 1816, to which he had been invited by the chancellor of Halle University, "was better than German suppers want to be," whereas Bancroft three years later described his invitation to a supper by the prorector of Göttingen University thus: "Conversation flagged, but as the supper was good, the jaws were not idle. By and bye the wine began to operate, and the learned body began to buzz with great animation.... A little after 11 o'clock, our wine was ended, the skins of the Professors pretty full."[44] Bancroft noted the German professors' dedication to wine; others added that Germans hated to leave food untried, or even worse, untouched on the table.

---

41 Dwight, *Travels in the North of Germany*, 96.
42 Valentine Mott, *Travels in Europe and the East in the Years 1834–1841* (New York, 1842), xii.
43 Dwight, *Travels in the North of Germany*, 83.
44 Ticknor, *Life and Letters*, 1:111; Howe, *Bancroft*, 1:57.

The enjoyment of wine and good food formed part of a larger context, a view of a particular German lifestyle that was based on a notion totally foreign to the New Englander; that is, that Germans were guilty of wasting time and lacking a determination to get on in the world. Thus, Catherine M. Sedgwick observed that, to Germans, eating was actually something approaching a leisurely exercise: "A German eats as long and as leisurely as he pleases at one thing; and they are the most indefatigable of eaters; not a meat, not a vegetable comes on the table which they do not partake."[45]

New Englanders, of course, saw little merit in celebrating eating as such; if at all, it had to fulfill a function within a larger social context. Celebrating a leisure activity without a higher purpose, like Washington's birthday, was bad because it implied a waste of time. After all, time had been given by God to be used to good and useful purposes and not frittered away at the table or with senseless as well as useless things. This sense that wasting time was not legitimate extended even to literary objects. When the librarian of the Basel Public Library showed Washington Irving a common prayer book that had been "written with a pen but so closely in imitation of printing that the deception could not be perceived," a book that the librarian considered a great treasure as well as a curiosity, Irving added the comment in his journal: "a great deal of time thrown away."[46]

American travelers in Germany found to their surprise that their concept of time was somewhat different from the German idea. Washington Irving cried out in exasperation: "I grow heartily weary of this *langsam* country."[47] Earlier he complained bitterly: ". . . and such roads, – and such delays, – and such impassive phlegm and absolute stupidity! Yesterday we were in constant exertion to get on from four o'clock in the morning until eleven at night and accomplished what in England would have been a half day's journey. Really it requires all the *menschliche Tugend und Empfindsamkeit* of a German to bear with these people."[48]

---

45 Catherine M. Sedgwick, *Letters from Abroad to Kindred at Home* (New York, 1841), 37.
46 Washington Irving, *Journals and Notebooks*, vol. 1: *1803–1806*, ed. Nathalia Wright (Madison, Wis., 1969), 404.
47 Irving, *Letters*, 1:765. However, his impatience may have had something to do with the fact that Irving was quite infatuated with a German lady whose letters were coming so slowly due to the slowness of those "tedious Germans." On another occasion, Irving reports: "We have called in a physician, who appears to be rather one of the *langsams*" (ibid., 757).
48 Ibid., 1:754. As with all these complaints they can of course be matched by cursory remarks indicating that trips went smoothly, cf. ibid., 701; what distinguishes this particular comment from those cursory remarks is the fact that Irving comments on the slowness much more extensively.

Yet it was not just time and the waste of it, or the sheer thought of what could be gained by moving faster that irritated American observers; nor was it just the urgency to exploit to the utmost the time given by God for one's own advancement and accomplishments. It was in fact the different German lifestyle that annoyed them. Germans' "impassive phlegm and absolute stupidity" drove Irving to despair; it irked the gentle New Jersey clergyman Robert Baird to see Germans "content to jog along, with pipe in mouth – a practice which is eminently German – at the rate of five or six miles per hour."[49]

The women, however, disagreed. They were less impatient, and thus felt more comfortable with the slower pace of life in Germany: "Our driver went at a slow pace but I liked it all the better," Crowninshield confided to her diary on one occasion.[50] And Sedgwick remarked: "There is no fast driving – that would be perfectly un-German – but far more to my liking; it is cautious, safe, and uniform."[51]

Indeed, as American travelers saw it, the German concept of time shaped every aspect of German life. If the carriage was delayed, people did not complain even if it meant hanging about for some ten hours, as Aaron Burr noted with astonishment.[52] Politics and administration reflected the same sense of time, Hugh Swinton Legaré thought.[53] Cooper, pondering the political consequences of France's upheavals in 1830, went so far as to establish a hierarchy of nations according to their ability and willingness to do things fast, and then linked his hierarchy to a grandiose explanation of military success and political stability:

Germany is not quiet, though the people are sluggish and far from enterprising. I am thoroughly convinced that the whole secret of Bonaparte's success is to be found in the method and slowness of the Germans. He broke through the

---

49 Robert Baird, *Visit to Northern Europe, or Sketches Descriptive, Historical, and Moral of Denmark, Norway, Sweden, Finland, and the Free Cities of Hamburg and Lübeck*, 2 vols. (New York, 1841), 1:179. It is worth noting here that German travelers made similar observations in America about the different lifestyles of Germans and Americans. J. G. Büttner wrote in 1846: "So weit nun ist der amerikanische Materialismus der gemeinste und niedrigste, den man sich nur denken kann, und der deutsche erscheint als ein feiner und edler. Denn bei uns treibt man Geschäfte und erwirbt, um zu leben. Es paart sich zu dem Erworbenen Lebensgenuss; man weiss das Verdiente anzuwenden und lebt und geniesst" (cited after Brenner, *Reisen in die neue Welt*, 312, and in general ibid., 308–21, on German perceptions of the American concept of "time," "life," and "work").
50 Hilen, ed., *Diary of Clara Crowninshield*, 193.
51 Sedgwick, *Letters from Abroad*, 50.
52 Aaron Burr, *Private Journal [of Aaron Burr, During His Residence of Four Years in Europe, with Selection from His Correspondence]*, ed. Mathew S. Davis (1838; reprinted: Upper Saddle River, N.J., 1970), 379.
53 Hugh Swinton Legaré, *The Writings of Hugh Swinton Legaré . . . Consisting of a Diary of Brussels and Journal of the Rhine*, 2 vols. (Charleston, S.C., 1846), 1:126.

restraint of antiquated rules himself, and conquered them by hazarding all. We should harness a pair of horses in America in half the time they would harness them in France, and in France, they do it in half the time it is done in Germany.[54]

This slowness, which Americans experienced as the key element in the German way of life, encompassed other features that left Americans literally gasping. Not only did Germans enjoy food as long as anything was on the table, not only did they enjoy wine as long as the supply kept up, but they did it all "pipe in mouth – a practice which is eminently German," as the Reverend Baird from New Jersey noted. Crowninshield reported that she had found "Herr von Ramm ... sitting snuggly in one corner, ensconced in *Mantel und Mütze*, and with his long pipe in his hand and the tobacco bag suspended round his neck." This elicited an additional comment: "It is laughable to see the tenderness with which a German handles his pipe as if it were a child."[55]

Even George H. Calvert, the Catholic tobacco-seasoned traveler from Maryland, caustically noted: "The Germans do not smoke, they are smoked."[56] But at least smoking was more acceptable in Maryland than in New England. It is thus not surprising that especially New Englanders noted the overarching social function of smoking in Germany:

The remarkable exhibition of female industry is only equalled by that of the other sex in smoking. The students, I have before observed, smoke most of the time, when not eating, or sleeping, or in their lecture rooms. The peasantry smoke while at work in the fields, as well as at home; and the other classes of Germans, not a small part of their lives. Though the young peasants do not puff while in the waltz, they resume their pipes as soon as it is ended.[57]

Germans were in many ways the antidote to what Americans considered proper. Germans were slow, they loved to eat, they enjoyed sitting around talking, they were united not as republicans but as smokers. Indeed, some Americans believed, these were the only bonds that linked the low with the high, the mighty with the humble. Or to view them through Cooper's ironic words: "The Germans are a kind, but beyond a question, a people who are not yet at the top of civilization. They make too much noise, and no man is a man until he can smoke, sputter dutch and ride a hardtrotting horse at the same time."[58]

54 Cooper, *Letters and Journals*, 1:420.
55 Hilen, ed., *Diary of Clara Crowninshield*, 228.
56 George H. Calvert, *Scenes and Thoughts in Europe* (New York, 1846), 54; for a similar remark by Irving, see *Letters*, 1:765.
57 Dwight, *Travels in the North of Germany*, 325–6.
58 Cooper, *Letters and Journals*, 2:309.

American travelers could bear all this, although smoking was trying indeed, and more than once Crowninshield complained that it would drive her "crazy,"[59] but what really tested American and especially New England forbearance was its combination with three further vices: the German males' treatment of their women, German nonobservance of Sundays, and German love of alcohol.

There was universal agreement among American travelers that German men enjoyed their leisure at the expense of their women; their *Gemütlichkeit*, their ability to sit together and talk was possible because, so one gets the impression, German women worked. The Reverend Stephen Olin put it most succinctly: "Women are the beasts of burden for wood, hay, and potatoes, etc. men walk by their side smoking." And Anna Eliot Ticknor fumed with indignation when she saw the following scene near Dresden: "A day or two ago, I saw a sight, which seemed to capture the climax of the degradation of our sex here; which was a woman drawing an empty coal cart, without the small assistance of a dog; and a man sitting *in the cart*, entirely at his ease, with his arms folded in great dignity."[60] Indeed, concluded Washington Irving: "Germans make cows & old women work – Women seem in this country to be among the beasts of burden & it appears to be computed that a healthy peasant woman can carry as much as a Donkey. They are of course broken down, destitute &c when old."[61]

Crowninshield even thought that the women in the Heidelberg region owed their goiters to an "overstraining of the muscles while they are growing."[62] That such heavy work did nothing to improve the looks of German women Clara Crowninshield also noted on her excursion from Heidelberg to Schwetzingen:

Here and there were groups of women to be seen hoeing the land, with apparently only one garment on their backs and a handkerchief tied over their heads. Their bending posture, which exposed the nudity of their lower extremities, and the vehemence with which they wielded their instruments of agriculture gave them the look of wild creatures.[63]

Moreover, the sight of women working in the fields did not lead some travelers to think simply of "wild creatures." It was natural that certain Americans would also be reminded of a phenomenon even closer to their

---

59 Hilen, ed., *Diary of Clara Crowninshield*, 229, 232.
60 Cited after Voss, "Das Stereotype Bild der Deutschen," 76.
61 Irving, *Journals*, 3:172. Irving wrote this while he stayed at Prague on June 10, 1823.
62 Hilen, ed., *Diary of Clara Crowninshield*, 251.
63 Ibid., 265.

own experience: slavery. Jared Sparks, whose knowledge of the South had began with his first call as pastor to a Baltimore congregation, was not the only one who drew the parallel when he wrote:

> It was not a pleasant sight to see fifteen or twenty women at work in the fields, with a man at their head as an overseer who did nothing. This is the case on larger estates. Except in the color of the laborers, it resembles exactly what you see among the slaveholders in Carolina and Georgia. The women bear burdens of enormous weight; they use the scythe in cutting grass, and in short seem to perform the drudgery and the severest labor.[64]

The Reverend Henry Hiestand, who hailed from Ohio but shepherded congregations in Virginia, also noted the comparison, and aptly concluded: "Females could never have been intended for such employments, and thus to enslave them is a disgrace to any civilized nation."

Americans from the North like Mrs. Ticknor observed that German women worked much harder than their counterparts in America – indeed, this had been a subject already discussed in Christopher Sauer's *Almanac* back in the 1740s – but since slavery was not part of their experience, they did not draw the parallel. Indeed, Crowninshield, while disapproving of the hard work of German farmers' wives, thought it a commendable thing that in the cities women occupied themselves with knitting while enjoying the polite conversation of their husbands and their guests:

> ... altho' it was Sunday evening the ladies all had their work, and I think it is just as well to sew and chat as to chat with idle hands, and I shall introduce the fashion in America, for what is more tedious than our Sunday evenings at home where families meet together to talk about clothes, expenses, and to relate gossip, and the younger members of the family must sit yawning and longing for it to be time to go to bed.[65]

These two attitudes illustrate a peculiar dilemma within American society. On the one hand, American condemnation of how German farmers treated their women reflected a status security and a respect for the opposite sex unknown, so it seemed to the American observer, in German villages. The sight was so shocking that those who had had firsthand experiences with Southern slavery, compared it to the Peculiar Institution. Yet this reaction was not directed against female work as such.

---

64 Herbert Baxter Adams, *The Life and Writings of Jared Sparks, Comprising Selections from His Journals and Correspondence*, 2 vols. (Boston, 1893), 2:86.
65 Hilen, ed., *Diary of Clara Crowninshield*, 206, cf. 219.

To be useful and not idle, to combine leisure with useful work was so eminently American, and so central to the struggle of New England women for their concept of domesticity that Clara Crowninshield decided that she would introduce this custom into American society.[66] Yet what Crowninshield approved of was work eminently fit for women; like her compatriots, she disapproved of work degrading to women. Heavy work was degrading not only because it mixed male and female spheres of work, but because it established a hierarchical pattern of work in the field, thus robbing farmers' wives and daughters of their equal status in rural society. In short, it was unrepublican.

Crowninshield, however, was less enthusiastic about another German habit because it offended her New England sensibilities: German disregard of the religious observance of Sunday. "We think it is almost wicked to sew on a shoestring on Sunday and here the ladies work as much on Sunday as any other day and seldom go to church."[67] Yet Crowninshield slowly got used to the idea; and although she still felt a bit uncomfortable at the thought of starting a journey from Heidelberg to Frankfurt on a Sunday, she and Longfellow nevertheless overcame their scruples, since in Germany "Sunday is the spare day when people can most conveniently put their plans in execution," as she justified her decision in her diary.[68] Others, foremost among them traveling clergymen, were less amused. When a Berlin theology professor suggested to William Sprague that they visit the theater on a Sunday, Sprague politely declined, yet noted sternly in his diary: "I did not suppose that those who professed to be evangelical Christians would attend the theater on the Sabbath."[69] The Reverend Hiestand objected to a similar proposal on more fundamental grounds. He told his German colleague: "I might as well cut my own throat, as go [to the theater], and report the same in America. At this he [the German pastor] was astonished, and asked if clergymen in America did not go to the theatre. I said, 'Christians do not go to the theatre in any

---

66 Paul Goodman, *Towards a Christian Republic: Antimasonry and the Great Transition in New England, 1826–1836* (New York, 1988), 80–102; Barbara Leslie Epstein, *The Politics of Domesticity: Women, Evangelism, and Temperance in Nineteenth-Century America* (Middletown, Conn., 1981), 45–88.

67 Hilen, ed., *Diary of Clara Crowninshield*, 206.

68 Ibid., 227; Goodman, *Towards a Christian Republic*, 80ff, and Robert L. Hampel, *Temperance and Prohibition in Massachusetts, 1813–1852* (Ann Arbor, Mich., 1982), 28, have noted the "feminization" of religion as well as the temperance movement in New England. Except for Bancroft and clergymen, male American travelers did not take particular notice of German religious nonobservance of Sundays probably, as women in New England complained, because they themselves neglected to go to church on Sundays. Again German travelers commented – mostly with negative overtones – on the rigid religious observance of Sundays in America (Brenner, *Reisen in die Neue Welt*, 337–9).

69 William Buell Sprague, *Visits to European Celebrities* (Boston, 1855), 131.

Country.' "[70] To Hiestand, going to the theatre was anathema, and the suggestion that one should go on a Sunday was even worse; and so other Americans also thought.[71]

Religious observance clearly was stricter in America than in old Europe. This was true for all of America as well as for all of Germany. Where, at least according to many historians, religion was fast losing ground in Germany, it was gaining ground in America. Religion, indeed, was probably the most important force fueling early nineteenth-century American social reform efforts. The battle against alcohol was one such effort.[72]

In the United States, the temperance movement had slowly spread since the days when John Woolman and other Quaker reformers in the mid-eighteenth century had firmly if meekly denounced the sinfulness of drinking.[73] By the third decade of the nineteenth century, some Americans were ready to carry the good message abroad to other sinning nations. The Reverend Baird from New Jersey was such a self-proclaimed apostle of the Temperance Movement who toured Germany. He was disgusted with what he saw.[74] Others shared that feeling, often linking it to that other vice, to smoking: "The vice of drunkenness from which France is in a great measure free, is deplorably common in Germany, and one cause perhaps is the vile practice of Smoking; every Man we meet, and even boys of 14 have long pipes hanging from the mouths."[75] Bancroft had reported that after a dinner the Göttingen professors went home with "their skins . . . pretty full" of wine; others commented on the prevalent custom of drinking beer.[76]

It is easy to prove that these Americans were deceived by appearances; it is easy to show that these reports were, at least as far as beer consumption is concerned, based on a misunderstanding. Those who stayed longer in the country, like Cooper, realized that things were not so bad. In fact, they even went further and claimed that Europeans or Germans did not

70 Henry Hiestand, *Travels in Germany, Prussia, and Switzerland* (New York, 1837), 61.
71 Dwight, *Travels in the North of Germany*, 230; Sedgwick, *Letters from Abroad*, 35.
72 The literature on the reform movement in America is large. I found helpful Welter, *Mind of America*, passim; Hartmut Lehmann, "Secularization, Dechristianization, and Rechristianization in Modern Europe and in North America," in Hartmut Lehmann, *Alte und Neue Welt in wechselseitiger Sicht: Studien zu den transatlantischen Beziehungen im 19. und 20. Jahrhundert* (Göttingen, 1995), 247–60.
73 Hermann Wellenreuther, *Glaube und Politik in Pennsylvania, 1681–1776: Die Obrigkeitsdroktrin und das Peace Testimony der Quäker* (Cologne, 1972).
74 Baird, *Visit to Northern Europe*, 1:36.
75 Isaac Carow, *American Backlogs: The Story of Gertrude Tyler and Her Family, 1660–1960*, comp. Edith Kermit Carow Roosevelt and Kermit Roosevelt (New York, 1928), 223.
76 Dwight, *Travels in the North of Germany*, 256.

drink more or less than Americans, but simply had different drinking habits. Although New Englanders stuck to hard stuff like applejack and drank cider instead of beer, Europeans preferred, so Cooper noted, the less potent beer and wine.[77] American irritation with German alcohol consumption thus says less about German alcohol intake than about American concern with American alcohol consumption.[78]

Critical observations about these and other matters reflected issues which at the time were greatly agitated in America. It was true of American reactions to alcohol and smoking, both of which were slowly falling out of fashion in New England's polite society. It was true of American reactions to what were considered Germans' loose morals in general. The latter even prompted George Bancroft to indict Goethe himself:

I am only more and more astonished at the indecency and immorality of the latter [i.e., Goethe]. He appears to prefer to represent vice as lovely and exciting sympathy, than virtue, and would rather take for his heroine a prostitute or a profligate, than give birth to that purity of thought and loftiness of soul, which it is the peculiar duty of a poet to raise, by connecting his inventions with the actions of heroes, and embodying in verse the merits of the benefactors of mankind.[79]

It took the relaxed attitude bred by long experience of Old World customs of Captain Samuel Haddock Jr. of Cranberry Isles in Maine to record the following scene in Hamburg with mild amusement instead of moral outrage:

---

77 Cooper, *Letters and Journals*, 1:429; W. A. Rorabaugh, *The Alcoholic Republic: An American Tradition* (Oxford, 1979), 111–13.

78 Annual consumption of alcohol increased in the United States until about 1830, then slowly fell to a low point in the 1920s. At the time American observers were commenting on German drinking habits, American consumption of distilled spirits was reaching an annual peak of about five gallons of distilled spirits per person (Rorabaugh, *Alcoholic Republic*, 8–9). Similar figures for German consumption are not available.

79 Howe, *Bancroft*, 1:38. It is clear that Bancroft was objecting to Goethe's Gretchen in Faust. Bancroft echoes Samuel Miller's remarks: "It must be granted, however, that some of the most popular German novels are highly mischievous in their moral tendency; and that no small number of their mercenary writers are constantly engaged in diffusing, through the medium of fictitious history, the most corrupt and poisonous principles, both in religion and morals" (Miller, *Brief Retrospect of the Eighteenth Century*, 2:323). The prudishness of American travelers is truly remarkable. Clara Crowninshield's diary is full of indications that exposing any part of the body (except head and hands, of course) was considered indecent. In her diary, which clearly was never meant for publication, she carefully avoids mentioning that the cause of the death of her friend Mary, the wife of Longfellow, was miscarriage. Note, too, her remarks about women exposing themselves while working in the fields, which made them look like "wild creatures," cited previously. Exposing part of one's skin in the initiation rites of freemasonry was one of the important arguments of the Antimasons, whereas in general nudity or anything approaching it was considered highly improper and indecent (Goldman, *Towards a Christian Republic*, 84–5).

On Sunday Evnings [people visited] a fashneable plais for most all sortes of peple, gentull and simpill, hors [whores] and roges. The Dans begines at dusk and is kept up tell one o'clock. I have counted one hundred hors in the Saloon at one time, drest like queans, or rather like venesses [Venus]. Also Gentlemen with fair families resort this interesting plais, if we may so coll it.[80]

American complaints about German slowness reflected American impatience and their desperate efforts to get things done and get on in life. Some American observers themselves occasionally observed the connection. After rushing onto a Rhine boat and surviving a scramble for a seat Catherine Sedgwick reported that the conductor came to check their tickets: "[He] said, 'Ah, ladies, you are placed; I had alloted better seats for you.' Was not this," so Sedgwick asked herself, "an appropriate punishment for our selfish and truly national hurrying? I could give you many instances of similar offences committed by ourselves and other travelers among these 'live-and-let-live' people."[81]

Europeans themselves experienced Americans' inordinate craze to get things done as a crude concern for nothing but money. In November 1836, for example, Heinrich von Gagern wrote his brother who had been thinking of emigrating to North America: "This money, banking, railroad, and canal civilization in America does not appeal to me."[82] At about this same time Alexis de Tocqueville popularized this image of the materialistic American by contrasting it with the refined European styles. Whereas Americans experienced the relaxed attitudes of Germans as silent criticism of their impatience as well as a terrible waste of time and energy, Europeans, including Germans, seem to have misunderstood American dedication and concentration on their own individual material progress as proletarian and democratic, as further proof that republicanism unfailingly led to decadence in public as well as private life. In the final analysis, American visitors perceived a clash between individuality versus collectivism: The notion that all had or should have an equal chance to pursue their particular kind of happiness in a democratic society was confronted in Germany with the notion that social groups collectively accepted their social status as God's calling and were content to pursue their versions of happiness not as individuals but as a social group both in their secular as well as in their religious worlds.

80 Cited in Field, *God's Pocket*, 60.
81 Sedgwick, *Letters from Abroad*, 40.
82 "Diese Geld-, Bank-, Eisenbahn-, Kanalzivilisation in Amerika kann mich nicht ansprechen." *Deutscher Liberalismus im Vormärz: Heinrich von Gagern: Briefe und Reden, 1815–1848*, ed. Bundesarchiv and Hessische Historische Kommission, with the assistance of Paul Wentzcke and Wolfgang Klötzer (Göttingen, 1959), 169–70; Brenner, *Reisen in die Neue Welt*, 321–9.

IV

Yet things were even more complex than that. For in a curious way, American perceptions of Germany and Germans were intertwined with a larger and more fundamental search for an American identity. The dilemma was this: How does one reconcile republican virtues like equality and equal opportunity for all with the ideal of a genteel lifestyle that is affordable not for the many but only for the few? This ideal of a genteel lifestyle was still valid in early nineteenth-century America; it had retained its salient feature as a mimesis of the English genteel lifestyle. It is this paradox that Cooper wanted to convey to the merchant from New Orleans:

> Went up the mountain as usual, and met our American on the hill. Had a long conversation on the effects of different forms of government. Found my countryman, as is the case with half of those who read English books, republican in all his practices and innate principles, but deeply imbued with arguments against all his habits. The prodigious influence that England has and still exercises over American thought is both amazing and mortifying. I gave my acquaintance a few arguments, which he seem'd really glad to receive, like a man who rejoices to find that his own side of the question was not as bad as he had fancied it.[83]

At least according to Cooper, Americans had yet to reconcile their republicanism as a political form and theory with their concept of culture and style of life. Republicanism threw people back onto themselves; it implied that people had to fend for themselves. But it also implied a concept of property devoid of social obligations and a new sense of community based on the pragmatic participation of individuals who did not have to fall back on overarching theories of proper "spheres," "estates," or traditional roles in societies.

What Cooper complained about was that, fifty years after their revolution, Americans were still unable to accept the practical consequences of that event. They were still identifying with English forms of civilized and cultured life, were still hankering after basically gentry modes of living, and thus were still violating the sacred precepts of republican "equality."[84] Even worse: In some parts of the country, especially in New England, new types of prudishness and snobbish exclusiveness had developed that seemed to outdo Old World elitist lifestyles. The observation and criticism of degenerate, uncivilized, crude modes of living in Germany – especially of habits like smoking, drinking, or idleness, or the disgusting

---

83 Cooper, *Letters and Journals*, 2:293–4.
84 See Welter, *Mind of America*, 77–104, for a discussion of these concepts.

sight of children playing in dirt and women undertaking hard physical labor – served to reinforce those genteel American ideas of self and identity that Cooper thought were essentially unrepublican. At the same time, however, these observations reinforced the American sense of national destiny, the conviction of living in a society with superior values, a grander destiny, and greater freedom. Traveling in Germany revealed a fundamental conflict between American republican ideology and American preference for unrepublican yet decent and refined lifestyles. In only one respect did American notions of republicanism and lifestyle coalesce: in the critique of how German farmers treated women. To make "cows & women work" was unrepublican because it violated North American notions of equality and decency.

3

Weary of Germany – Weary of America
Perceptions of the United States in Nineteenth-Century Germany

HANS-JÜRGEN GRABBE

Near the end of the eighteenth century the field of *Amerikakunde* – a distant relation of present-day American Studies – made its appearance in German academic circles. *Amerikakunde* typically combined history, political science, economics, and geography, but it also included the study of such things as botany and mineralogy. The new field was represented by scholars like Dietrich Hermann Hegewisch, a professor of philosophy at the University of Kiel who, with Christoph Daniel Ebeling, co-edited the *Amerikanisches Magazin*, Germany's first scholarly journal devoted to the United States.[1] As Hegewisch put it, he preferred to state facts without argumentation. His texts remained mostly descriptive, and their faulty judgments derived from biases in his sources.[2]

The preeminent representative of *Amerikakunde*, though, was Hegewisch's Hamburg collaborator, Christoph Daniel Ebeling (1741–1817). Indeed, for contemporaries and posterity alike, Ebeling was the most distinguished German scholar of the United States. His *Erdbeschreibung und Geschichte von Amerika* (Geographic description and history of America) appeared over a time span of twenty-three years but remained incomplete.[3] Still, before 1834, when the first volume of George Bancroft's monumental *History of the United States* was published, no other work of comparable scope and learning existed in the field. Ebeling admired the American polity, in particular the prevailing measure of individual liberty that, as he saw it, contrasted so favorably with French *libertinage*. But he was averse to

---
1 *Amerikanisches Magazin* (Hamburg, 1795–7).
2 Eugene E. Doll, "American History as Interpreted by German Historians from 1770 to 1815," *Transactions of the American Philosophical Society*, ns, 38 (1948): 472–3.
3 Seven vols., Hamburg, 1793–1816.

hagiography. In a letter to the American Philosophical Society, Ebeling pronounced his aim to speak of America "as it is, and that is to say, very much to its advantage." He went on: "I am partial to your country whose felicity I admire, but not prejudiced."[4]

The views expressed by some of Ebeling's contemporaries were less balanced. Dietrich von Bülow, scion of an eminent Prussian family, wrote a sharply critical account, *Der Freistaat von Nordamerika in seinem neuesten Zustand* (The free state of North America in its present condition).[5] Like several other self-proclaimed German experts on America, Bülow had met with commercial disaster in the United States. During his stay in the country in the late 1790s he lost his patrimony by investing in glassware and extending credit to persons who defaulted in their payments. It was no wonder, then, that Bülow admitted to being stimulated by hatred. The hatred was directed against vice and not against individuals, Bülow insisted, yet Americans typically appear in his book as hypocritical, materialistic, and bigoted.[6] It is also evident that the German aristocrat had little sympathy for the gradually emerging political participation of the lower classes. Since Bülow was a gifted satirist his book makes good reading. Also, some of his observations were quite to the point. He looked at the United States, in the words of an American reviewer, through a smoked but polished glass.[7]

Ebeling, whose writings were far more sound, suffered from other weaknesses. He was admired by many, but probably read by few. His works resembled quarries from which great slabs of information were cut for years to come. His pedestrian style, overburdened by facts, and his microscopic approach limited his influence on contemporary views of America. Indeed, the seven volumes of Ebeling's magnum opus deal with only ten of the original thirteen states! Furthermore, critics could, with some justification, point to his Achilles' heel: Unlike Bülow, he had no firsthand knowledge of his subject, never having set foot on American soil. It is thus understandable, though unfortunate, that it was not the scholar Ebeling who established new standards in American Studies; rather, it was the polemicist Bülow who set the tone for the continuing discussion on the merits of American society. Bülow's conservatism was unspecific; that is, it was not based on sophisticated ideological beliefs.

4 Ebeling to Ezra Stiles, June 26, 1794, and Ebeling to the American Philosophical Society, Oct. 14, 1793, quoted in Doll, "American History," 477.
5 Dietrich von Bülow, *Der Freistaat von Nordamerika in seinem neuesten Zustand*, 2 vols. (Berlin, 1797).
6 Ibid., 1: iv; Doll, "American History," 493–501.
7 *Philadelphia Magazine and Review* (1799): 226, quoted in Doll, "American History," 500.

However, his anti-American observations and inferences were used as evidence by conservatives of the post-1815 Restoration era in their fight against the remnants of the Enlightenment, the adherents of which had idealistically depicted the United States as a progressive utopia.

The Göttingen-based scholar Johann Georg Ritter von Hülsemann took up Ebeling and the Enlightenment in his *Geschichte der Democratie in den Vereinigten Staaten von Nord-America* (History of democracy in the United States of North America), published in 1823.[8] While acknowledging his indebtedness to the "highly meritorious" *Erdbeschreibung*, the source of much of his own information, he nevertheless questioned Ebeling's fundamental epistemological assumptions. Impartiality concerning facts Hülsemann could accept, but about principles he felt that scholarly disinterest was impossible and not even desirable. Moreover, Hülsemann insisted that Ebeling's treasured impartiality was not genuine, since the Nestor of *Amerikakunde* implicitly regarded the principles of universal toleration and universal enlightenment as axioms, and thus seemed inclined toward democracy and religious indifference.[9] Indeed, there was something to Hülsemann's assertion. One might well claim that Enlightenment scholars rationalized the political events in North America after 1776 into an ideology that, in turn, became a pillar of European and, in particular, German liberalism in the first half of the nineteenth century. The constitution of the United States provided the core of this ideology. It could be understood as the first practical example of a political and social order derived entirely from reason – an order, furthermore, that guaranteed the unfettered development of man's natural talents. The Enlightenment canonized the American constitution in order to refute the feudal order of the European anciens régimes.[10]

A follower of Metternich, Hülsemann felt duty-bound to fight such subversive ideas, which ran counter to the essential doctrines of the Holy Alliance. Since the secular, democratic spirit was still confined to alien and distant lands, it might be conceivable simply to leave it alone; still, its possible infiltration into Europe must be thwarted. Like his political opponents in Germany, Hülsemann mainly regarded American democracy as a foil for the ideological clash in Europe. In his writings, he evoked the specter of a battle formation that pitted the United States,

---

8 Johann Georg Ritter von Hülsemann, *Geschichte der Democratie in den Vereinigten Staaten von Nord-America* (Göttingen, 1823).
9 Ibid., vi–vii.
10 Rolf Engelsing, "Deutschland und die Vereinigten Staaten im 19. Jahrhundert," *Die Welt als Geschichte* 18 (1958): 141–2.

French liberals, and English radicals against the conservative forces of Europe. The latter should therefore endeavor to preserve or create institutions in other parts of the New World with goals akin to those of the Holy Alliance.[11] Although these ideas may seem far-fetched, it should be remembered that Hülsemann's design was considered real enough to make President James Monroe pronounce the doctrine that bears the American statesman's name.

The founding of the United States had been wholeheartedly welcomed by liberals and the *Sturm und Drang* (storm and stress) literary movement; it had been greeted guardedly even by some conservatives. In 1800, Friedrich von Gentz, later to become one of Metternich's associates, could still assert his partial admiration for the American Revolution. In a similar vein, Arnold Hermann Ludwig Heeren, professor at Göttingen and one of the foremost historians of the day, emphasized the status quo character of the Revolution.[12] However, when the Age of the Common Man was dawning, conservative sympathies for the United States tapered off. Only liberals (and not many of them) approved of the modernization and democratization processes that began in the early nineteenth century. Conservatives loathed popular sovereignty. They were also irritated by its obvious appeal to those lower strata of society who were about to provide the mass basis for emigration to the United States.

Fear of revolution and misgivings about emigration led the authorities in Germany to support or even sponsor books, in particular travel accounts, that depicted life in America unfavorably. Even some liberals of the *Vormärz* period who had gone to the United States but later wished to be repatriated offered their services. Ludwig Gall, for example, was readmitted into the Prussian civil service after he had published an extremely critical account of life in America, *Meine Auswanderung nach den Vereinigten Staaten von Nordamerika im Frühjahr 1819 und meine Rückkehr nach der Heimath im Winter 1820* (My emigration to the United States of North America in the spring of 1819, and my return home in the Winter of 1820). Characterized by Edward Everett as a man of "Olympian self-

---

11 Hülsemann, *Geschichte der Democratie in den Vereinigten Staaten*, viii–xii. Hülsemann subsequently became Austrian minister to Washington. For later ideas to create a kind of ideological bloc on both sides of the Atlantic see Güter Moltmann, *Atlantische Blockpolitik im 19. Jahrhundert: Die Vereinigten Staaten und der deutsche Liberalismus während der Revolution von 1848–49* (Düsseldorf, 1973).
12 Friedrich von Gentz, "Der Ursprung und die Grundsätze der Amerikanischen Revolution, verglichen mit dem Ursprunge und den Grundsätzen der Französischen," excerpts reprinted in Ernst Fraenkel, ed., *Amerika im Spiegel des deutschen politischen Denkens* (Cologne, 1959), 79–81. Arnold Herrmann Ludwig Heeren, "Entwickelung der politischen Folgen der Reformation für Europa" (1802), *Historische Werke* (Göttingen, 1821), 1:1–112.

conceit..., the sternest simpleton we ever met with," Gall found himself deceived, defrauded, or otherwise betrayed by just about everybody during his two-year migration from Trier via Antwerp and New York to Philadelphia and Harrisburg, Pennsylvania. However, general deductions from this unhappy experience only took the form of massive criticism of the United States.[13]

Those individuals who had grown weary of their native Germany inevitably held stereotypical views of the United States when taking the decision to emigrate. Gall grew weary of America after months of firsthand experience; yet his views remained stereotypes. Like other authors of books on the United States during the period of Romanticism, he drew from two different, though interrelated, sets of clichés. The first set provides the intellectual underpinning of the novel *Die Europamüden* (The Europe-weary), written by Ernst Willkomm and published in 1838. The second furnishes the groundwork for Ferdinand Kürnberger's 1855 novel *Der Amerika-Müde* (The America-weary).[14] Both writers have been largely forgotten; but their books remain important, for they present, in almost encyclopedic fashion, both positive images of early nineteenth-century America and an accompanying negative image that has persisted since 1800.

The "Europe-weary" were a group of stock German characters from Cologne. They felt that the sacred natural beauty of the Old Continent, as the hero of the novel puts it, had been "crushed under the elegant burden of convention, culture, artificial civilization." On the other side of the Atlantic, however, "the land of promise lies imbedded in the sacred shade of the primeval forest which embraces and caresses it with alluring hope, like a mother her smiling, vigorous child."[15] Willkomm does not follow his characters to the New World and so there is no need to depict America's emerging middle-class society or its mass-market economy.

Kürnberger, in contrast, portrays a romantic hero who is broken in spirit because the reality of the United States does not conform to his idealistic expectations. Since the soundness of his romantic yearnings

---

13 Trier, 1822; Alfred Vagts, *Deutsch-Amerikanische Rückwanderung*, Beihefte zum Jahrbuch für Amerikastudien, no. 6 (Heidelberg, 1960), 157; [Edward Everett], "Schmidt and Gall on America," *North American Review* 17 (1823): 92, 104.
14 Ernst Willkomm, *Die Europamüden: Modernes Lebensbild*, 2 vols. (Leipzig, 1838; reprinted: Göttingen, 1968); Ferdinand Kürnberger, *Der Amerika-Müde: Amerikanisches Kulturbild* (Frankfurt/Main, 1855).
15 Willkomm, *Die Europamüden*, 1:167, 353–4. The translation follows Paul C. Weber, *America in Imaginative German Literature of the Nineteenth Century* (New York, 1926), 211–12.

remains unquestioned, there can be only one solution: The United States must be denounced as a materialistic, superficial, and crude place that a cultured human being had best flee as quickly as possible. This is precisely what happens in Kürnberger's novel. Its hero tires of the United States and finds the flaws of America even more repulsive than those of Germany.

When *Der Amerika-Müde* was published, its author lived the uneasy life of a political refugee, having participated in the abortive Vienna uprising of 1848. Kürnberger never got closer to the United States than the port cities of Hamburg and Bremen. Still, his portrayal of life in America is not wholly fictitious, since he plagiarized travel accounts and other contemporary works on America. Kürnberger later referred to his book as a political and literary document of mid-century German views on the United States.[16] Although this is perhaps overstated, it may safely be said that *Der Amerika-Müde* exemplifies the Hegelian tradition of anticapitalism, which denounced the modern age as the embodiment of particularistic and hedonistic interests.

Kürnberger's central figure, Moorfeld, drew its inspiration from the poet Nikolaus Lenau who had emigrated to the United States in 1832 – not for political reasons but because he suffered from world-weariness and saw himself haunted by demons that he hoped to banish by relocating to America. He also hoped to regain some of his squandered fortune by land speculation. Lenau assumed that five years would suffice to get rich and to cure his *Europamüdigkeit*. He spoke no English and had little practical sense. Having bought an unprofitable farm in western Pennsylvania, the poet neither lived on his land nor cultivated it. After a sojourn of only five months Lenau fled back to Germany from what he called the "swinish states" (*verschweinte Staaten*).[17]

Scholarly works about the United States mainly dealt with the country's political, constitutional, and legal history, or its economy and geography. Its society and culture tended to be neglected. Works of fiction, though, often treated societal themes, but mostly in negative terms. This was at least in part a simple reaction to the way in which America had been presented during the Enlightenment. To adherents of Romanticism,

---

16 Hans-Joachim Lang, "Ferdinand Kürnberger One Hundred Years Later," *The Harold Jantz Collection*, ed. Leland R. Phelps (Durham, 1981), 61–2; Hildegard Meyer, *Nord-Amerika im Urteil des Deutschen Schrifttums bis zur Mitte des 19. Jahrhunderts: Eine Untersuchung über Kürnbergers "Amerika-Müden"*, Übersee-Geschichte, no. 3 (Hamburg, 1929).

17 Vagts, *Deutsch-Amerikanische Rückwanderung*, 105. The pun "verschweinte Staaten – Vereinigte Staaten" cannot be reproduced here.

America appeared as a cerebral construct, built on rationalism and materialism and lacking national uniqueness as well as traditions that had evolved over time.[18] Moreover, the Romantics' love of nature, always in danger of degenerating into cliché, became little more than a pale cipher as the nineteenth century progressed. Industrial society, nature's antithesis, was encoded as the epitome of modernity, thus becoming a cipher as well. Industrialization did not gain momentum in the United States until after the War of 1812. Yet as early as 1811, the prominent Romantic writer Ludwig Tieck complained in the introduction to *Phantasus* about the "clattering and rumbling manufactures" in the Franconian city of Fürth: "This North America of Fürth I could not like next to Nuremberg with its traditional, Germanic, artistic burgherhood."[19]

Romantics cherished the United States as long as they could convince themselves that they should believe in the country's oneness with nature. Thus, they could figuratively contrast American nature with European unnaturalness. To those who longed to preserve a premodern, static way of life, emerging American industrial society seemed quintessentially gain-oriented and highly speculative. Contrasted with a society based in farming and traditional crafts, an economy built on commerce and industry could be stylized as the prototype of mechanized society.

To those Germans who took pride in a traditional sense of culture, the confrontation with America became, as political scientist Arnold Bergstraesser put it, a "general attack on their inner life." Writing in 1963, during the halcyon days of the West German "economic miracle," Bergstraesser asked whether German intellectuals tend to stress those traits as genuinely American which they particularly dislike in their own society.[20] Even today, catchwords like the "Coca-Colonization" or the "McDonaldization" of Germany and Europe, and criticisms voiced against commercialized media or market-oriented leisure patterns, readily come to mind. For Nikolaus Lenau, the American "general attack" on his inner life had truly devastating results. Eight days after his arrival in Baltimore he wrote to a friend: "Brother, these Americans have the souls of small shopkeepers that reek to the heavens. They are dead, stone-dead as far as intellectual life is concerned. . . . A Niagara-voice would

---

18 Engelsing, "Deutschland und die Vereinigten Staaten," 142–3.
19 Ludwig Tieck, ed., *Phantasus: Eine Sammlung von Mährchen, Erzählungen, Schauspielen und Novellen*, 3 vols. (Berlin, 1812–16), 1:8–9.
20 Arnold Bergstraesser, "Zum Problem der sogenannten Amerikanisierung Deutschlands," *Jahrbuch für Amerikastudien* 8 (1963): 15, 21.

be needed to teach these rascals that there are higher goods than those struck off at the mint." Lenau considered American education mercantile and technical; in the United States, "functional man unfolds in fearful banality."[21]

It was not only America's alleged lack of culture that irritated German observers. Some liberals likened democracy to mob rule and were repelled by the advance of universal manhood suffrage. Heinrich Heine spoke of a "gigantic liberty prison, where the most despicable of tyrants, the rabble, exercises his crude powers."[22] A poem of 1851, *Jetzt wohin?* (Now where?), contains these lines: "Sometimes I have in mind / to sail to America / to the great stable of liberty / populated by churls of equality."[23] The "dear German peasants," however, were heartily encouraged by Heine to remove themselves to this boorish land.

Other writers critical of the United States were motivated primarily by intense nationalism. They envied the country where the only successful democratic revolution had taken place, but their patriotism made them insist that in certain areas, at least, Germany surpassed America. Culture and language were deemed cases in point. One such writer was Franz von Löher. According to him, the Pennsylvania Germans of the revolutionary period had wanted to cast off not only English rule but the language as well. Löher deplored their failure "to make the English stock bow out, starting in Pennsylvania," since otherwise "a new German fatherland in America would have been secured."[24] In a similar vein, Ernst Ludwig Brauns, a journalist who wrote several books on the United States and on emigration, contemplated the possibility of a *Neudeutschland* in America. By this he meant an ethnically and linguistically homogeneous German state within the United States of America or Brazil.[25]

Authors who invoked a positive and generally realistic image of America were few and far between. Two names should be mentioned: Karl Postl, a Moravian of German ancestry better known under his penname Charles Sealsfield, traveled extensively through the South, the Southwest, and Mexico. Sealsfield wrote several ethnographic novels such

---

21 Lenau to Anton Schurz, Oct. 16, 1832, and Lenau to Joseph Klemm, March 6, 1833, Anton Schurz, *Lenaus Leben* (Stuttgart, 1855), 199, 204.
22 Heinrich Heine, *Ludwig Börne* (1840), quoted from excerpts printed in Wolfgang Helbich, ed., "*Alle Menschen sind dort gleich . . .*": *Die deutsche Amerika-Auswanderung im 19. und 20. Jahrhundert*, Historisches Seminar, no. 10 (Düsseldorf, 1988), 62.
23 "Manchmal kommt mir in den Sinn / Nach Amerika zu segeln / Nach dem grossen Freiheitsstall / Der bewohnt von Gleichheitsflegeln . . ."
24 Franz [von] Löher, *Geschichte und Zustände der Deutschen in Amerika* (Cincinnati, 1847), 193–4 and passim.
25 Meyer, *Nord-Amerika im Urteil des Deutschen Schrifttums*, 37.

as *Das Cajütenbuch* (The cabin book, 1847), which deals with the Texan struggle for independence.[26]

Friedrich Gerstäcker, one of nineteenth-century Germany's most popular writers, emigrated to the United States in 1837 chiefly because he had read scores of adventure stories by authors ranging from Defoe to Sealsfield. Gerstäcker arrived in New York dressed in a backwoodsman's garb ready-made to specifications gleaned from Sealsfield's novels. Like so many German men of letters, he lost his money in an imprudent investment. Unlike most of them, however, Gerstäcker remained unruffled by this and later misfortunes. He moved to Cincinnati, which served as a base for excursions into the Mississippi River valley.[27] In 1843 Gerstäcker returned to Germany and began a prolific literary production drawing on his American experience. His more than forty volumes of collected works treat subjects such as emigration and German-American life. Gerstäcker is chiefly remembered for his thrilling and realistic frontier novels, for example, *Die Regulatoren in Arkansas* (The regulators in Arkansas, 1846) and its sequel, *Die Flusspiraten des Mississippi* (The Mississippi River pirates, 1848).[28]

The revolutionary Frankfurt National Assembly considered Gerstäcker an expert on emigration and granted the writer a thousand taler with which to visit German overseas communities and inspect possible settlement sites.[29] Indeed, as early as 1846 the third annual meeting of *Germanisten* (Germanists) had set up a committee to study the means by which German civilization and language might be maintained among expatriates. Sigismund, the hero of Willkomm's novel *Die Europamüden*, expresses this notion quite clearly. He wants to preserve his Germanness in America. Indeed, in the New World "a race shall arise with German blood, German perseverance, German soul, and German power of faith."[30] These were not merely poetic eccentricities. It was a great aim of

---

26 Stuttgart, 1847; first English translation London, 1852. For a detailed discussion of Sealsfield's work, see Doll, "American History," 120–51.
27 Vagts, *Deutsch-Amerikanische Rückwanderung*, 112.
28 Three vols., Leipzig, 1846; 3 vols., Leipzig, 1848.
29 Gerstäcker traveled around the world from 1849 to 1852. See Günter Moltmann, "Überseeische Siedlungen und weltpolitische Spekulationen: Friedrich Gerstäcker und die Frankfurter Zentralgewalt 1849," in Alexander Fischer et al., eds., *Russland–Deutschland–Amerika: Festschrift für Fritz T. Epstein zum 80. Geburtstag* (Wiesbaden, 1978), 56–72.
30 The committee was chaired by the Hamburg archivist and historian Lappenberg. See Rainer Postel, *Johann Martin Lappenberg: Ein Beitrag zur Geschichte der Geschichtswissenschaft im 19. Jahrhundert*, Historische Studien, no. 423 (Lübeck, 1972), 210–15. A lengthy report is printed in *Verhandlungen der Germanisten zu Lübeck am 27., 28., und 30. September 1847* (Lübeck, 1848), 21–45. At that time the term *Germanisten* encompassed not only philologists but also lawyers and historians. For the quotation, see Willkomm, *Die Europamüden*, 1:356–7.

liberal nationalism to support *Deutschtum* in America. Two courses of action seemed to hold some promise: the establishment of ethnic enclaves and the preservation of language skills to ease remigration. Even Johann Wolfgang von Goethe had ostensibly recommended that Germans should remain in or come back to their native country, letting the character Lothario in *Wilhelm Meisters Lehrjahre* exclaim after his return: "Here or nowhere is America."[31]

It may be helpful to look at the fate of Karl Follen if one wishes to understand how an intense German nationalism might prevail, even among those who claimed to have grown weary of their native country. Follen had taught at the University of Jena and had been the fatherly friend of Karl Ludwig Sand, a student who killed the writer and Russian secret agent August von Kotzebue in March 1819. Following the assassination, Metternich used the Carlsbad Decrees to clamp down on German universities. Many patriotic intellectuals were repressed as "demagogues" and lost their positions. Given this unhappy state of affairs, Follen despaired of his political and professional future in Germany and set about to write a memorandum on the founding of a German model state in America. The United States, Follen argued, should serve as a retreat for the German opposition, a bastion from where a later rejuvenation of the fatherland could perhaps be initiated. If one could transplant German culture to the New World, the emigrants would not become uprooted, and at the same time one could also help the German-American element preserve its civilization. Even Americans of other ethnic stock might profit from the experience, since Germany, as the center of modern erudition, would thus elevate the land of freedom and equality.[32]

In 1834, another member of the *Vormärz* opposition, Friedrich Münch, gathered a group of like-minded friends and left Germany to establish a settlement on the Missouri. He drew his inspiration from a book by Gottfried Duden, *Bericht über eine Reise nach den westlichen Staaten Nordamerika's und einen mehrjährigen Aufenthalt am Missouri* (Report on a journey to the western states of North America and a sojourn on the Missouri of several years).[33] This author not only looked favorably on the United States but even set about to remove anti-American prejudices

---

31 Book 8, chap. 3.
32 Hermann Haupt, "Karl Follen und die Giessener Schwarzen," *Mitteilungen des Oberhessischen Geschichtsvereins* 15 (1907): 145–7. Follen first found refuge in Switzerland and arrived in New York in 1824. He later became professor of German at Harvard and ended his days as a Unitarian minister.
33 Elberfeld, 1827.

from Europeans. Unfortunately, he, too, exaggerated, particularly in his depiction of the western country, which he pronounced to be void of beggars, vice, forest fires, and rattlesnakes. Friedrich Münch, however, found himself so inspired that he exclaimed: "Onward, bravely and confidently / firmly and brotherly united / let us look ahead / and build huts on the Missouri / where the sun of freedom shines."[34] Duden of course never dwelt in a hut; as a man of means he had led the comfortable life of a gentleman farmer.

Excessive sensitivity might precondition some observers, such as Lenau and Münch, to become weary of America, although in the case of the latter no lasting disappointment resulted. However, Münch remained on the Missouri frontier only for a short time. He had hoped to found his "model republic" in Arkansas but failed miserably; most members of the Giessen Emigration Society, founded by Münch with Karl Follen's brother Paul Follenius, dispersed soon after their arrival in the United States.[35] In other cases, too, group migration projects fell short of the high-minded expectations that had been nourished by the intellectual leadership. The rank and file had joined emigration societies out of functional considerations, were for the most part genuinely weary of Germany, and chose to seek individual happiness rather than pursue utopian projects.

The economist Friedrich List knew more than most about the motivation of emigrants, having questioned scores of them for the Württemberg authorities in 1817. Yet, he also championed the idea of a German-American ethnic settlement. After List had lived in Pennsylvania for several years he changed his mind, but only about the location of such a colony. Emigrants who sought and found happiness in the United States forever lost their Germanness, List argued. The "Germanic race" would therefore be well advised to establish colonies in areas where its civilizing mission could be economically and politically beneficial for the mother country.[36]

---

34 "Auf in mutigem Vertrauen, / fest und brüderlich vereint! / Vorwärts, vorwärts lasst uns schauen, / am Missouri Hütten bauen, / wo der Freiheit Sonne scheint." Quoted from Meyer, *Nord-Amerika im Urteil des Deutschen Schrifttums*, 34.
35 Stefan von Senger und Etterlin, *Neu-Deutschland in Nordamerika: Massenauswanderung, nationale Gruppenansiedlungen und liberale Kolonialbewegung, 1815–1860* (Baden-Baden, 1991), 178–85. Münch later became a leading journalist in the German-American press and – as the Sage of Missouri – was among the founding members of the Republican Party. See Carl Wittke, *Refugees of Revolution: The German Forty-Eighters in America* (Philadelphia, 1952), 207.
36 Günter Moltmann, ed., *Aufbruch nach Amerika: Die Auswanderungswelle von 1816–17* (Stuttgart, 1978; reprinted: Stuttgart, 1989), 120–87; Senger und Etterlin, *Neu-Deutschland in Nordamerika*, 36–7.

Patriotic liberals were loath to let go of emigrants. At the 1847 meeting of Germanists, only Friedrich Christoph Dahlmann and the mayor of Bremen, Johann Smidt, flatly opposed schemes to further the preservation of German nationality abroad and promote return migration. Dahlmann saw the intended enlargement of the German national base merely as a sign of growing self-deception among liberal nationalists. Those who crossed the Atlantic to flee from misery should accept the advantages of the New World without remorse. If they confidently relinquished their language, they could fully embrace the new fatherland.[37]

Before mid-century, the notion that the emigrants might be needed to win the fight for emancipation of the *tiers état* at home was widespread among liberals. Berthold Auerbach, an author associated with the Young Germany movement, expressed this idea in the 1847 novel *Luzifer*: "One should not emigrate like the selfish raven from Noah's Ark, which doesn't reappear when it thrives outside; one should emigrate like the dove, which returns with an olive branch, announcing that the Flood has drained away."[38] List had declared before his departure that he left Germany against his will and would return when possible. Not even Francis Lieber, an eminent German-American jurist who emigrated to the United States in 1827, really tired of Germany.

It is true that Lieber found the American political system congenial. Like his mentor, Barthold Georg Niebuhr, he felt that liberty not only derived from the constitution of a country but also from its administrative structure. What Niebuhr and Lieber sought were safeguards against the bureaucratic encroachment that stifled personal liberty and civic culture in Germany. Yet, when Lieber returned to Germany for a visit in 1844, he would have been happy to stay if only the king of Prussia had offered him a better post than that of an official in the administration of prisons. Lieber returned again in the summer of 1848, hoping to take part in the revolution. He came to comprehend, however, that he was out of step with people and events.[39] At heart, Lieber did not make choices dictated by political preferences, pursuing instead a lifelong quest for self-

---

37 *Verhandlungen der Germanisten zu Lübeck*, 46–8.
38 "Man soll nicht auswandern wie der eigensüchtige Rabe aus der Arche Noah, der draussen bleibt wenn's nur ihm wohlergeht; man soll auswandern wie die ausgeschickte Taube, die heimkehrt mit dem Oelzweig, verkündend: dass die Sündflut sich verlaufen." *Berthold Auerbachs Schriften*, vol. 11 (Stuttgart, [1895]), 246; Vagts, *Deutsch-Amerikanische Rückwanderung*, 157.
39 Franz Lieber, *Erinnerungen aus meinem Zusammenleben mit Georg Berthold [sic] Niebuhr, dem Geschichtsschreiber Roms* (Heidelberg, 1837), 82. On Lieber, see Frank Freidel, *Francis Lieber: Nineteenth-Century Liberal* (Baton Rouge, La., 1947); Peter Schäfer and Karl Schmitt, eds., *Franz Lieber und die deutsch-amerikanischen Beziehungen im 19. Jahrhundert* (Weimar, 1993).

realization. He held a modest professorship at Columbia, South Carolina, which caused him to become despondent; and only a position at Columbia University in New York City reconciled him to his career. Perhaps the very absence of missionary ardor that made him contemplate seriously a permanent residence in Friedrich Wilhelm IV's Prussia also contributed to Lieber's effectiveness as an interpreter of American society.[40]

In some ways, Lieber's experience resembled the life of Carl Schurz, the individual who is usually regarded as the most successful German-American of the nineteenth century. What propelled him to the United States? At the outset, he obviously shared the feelings of liberal activists who couched their political disappointment in the cliché of weariness. After Louis Napoleon's liquidation of the French Republic, Schurz believed that democrats had no future on the European continent. What should a young man do who felt the "passionate urge," as he phrased it in his memoirs, not only to work for a living "but to contribute something really, truly valuable to the welfare of humankind?" Germany was impervious to his zeal, England he did not like, and so America beckoned: "It is a new world, a free world, a world of great ideas and purposes. . . . 'Ubi libertas, ibi patria.'"[41]

Schurz differed from other political emigrants not because he attached no strings to his decision. There is some evidence that he, too, at first believed that his stay in the United States would only be temporary. Soon, however, he embraced the new country without reservation and gradually became tired of Germany. In this respect, he had much in common with the masses of immigrants who would have described themselves as unpolitical. The consequences for Schurz's view of America were clear: "Since I had decided to make the United States my permanent home, I also resolved to see everything in the most favorable light and to let no disappointment discourage me."[42]

Carl Schurz had left Europe as a student. In the New World he became a politician, journalist, diplomat, soldier, U.S. senator, secretary of

---

40 The Committee on Emigration created at the 1846 meeting of Germanists had asked Lieber for advice on the preservation of Germanness in the United States. His dispassionate discussion of America's English heritage in law, political ideas, religion, language, and literature, and in particular his postscript that a genuine American nation had developed, probably made the Germanists realize that they had better drop the issue. Lieber's report is printed in *Verhandlungen der Germanisten zu Lübeck*, 40–5. His writings are listed in Freidel, *Francis Lieber*.
41 Carl Schurz, *Lebenserinnerungen*, 3 vols. (Berlin, 1906–12), 1:410.
42 C.J. Friedrich in Adolf E. Zucker, ed., *The Forty-Eighters: Political Refugees of the German Revolution of 1848* (New York, 1950), 17; Schurz, *Lebenserinnerungen*, 2:1.

the interior, and a speculator on the real estate and stock markets – in short, a quintessentially American career. In 1868, Schurz wrote to his former political mentor Gottfried Kinkel that his life was deeply rooted in America and that his loyalty belonged to the reform movement there. Still, this German-American paragon never completely lost some traits that derived from his German background. It is a case in point that in later years he distanced himself from the nitty-gritty of party politics, thus reducing his effectiveness within the Republican Party.[43]

During the latter part of the nineteenth century, Schurz had some influence on German elite opinion about the United States. Another "Forty-Eighter," Friedrich Kapp, virtually charted a career as mediator between the two countries. He went to America in 1850, hoping, as he wrote to Ludwig Feuerbach, "that the fatherland might one day benefit from the mature man's experience."[44] Kapp contributed to German newspapers and journals, wrote biographies of generals Steuben and Kalb, produced a monograph on the German mercenaries in the War of Independence, and became the first historian of the German element in New York. His objective as a writer was threefold: He wanted to educate the German public about the United States, open its eyes to the ills of particularism (hence his book on *Soldatenhandel*, or trade in soldiers), and he wished to instill filiopietistic pride into German-Americans. In 1870, Kapp returned to Germany, joined the National Liberal Party and was elected to the Reichstag. He continued his writing career, now as a contributor on German affairs to the New York weekly *The Nation*, had a business relationship with the Northern Pacific Railroad, and was among the founders of the Deutsche Bank. Like other political return migrants. Kapp could not be labeled *amerikamüde*, since he had never been *europamüde* in the first place. Germany's "pull" had simply proved stronger than that of the United States. However, unlike Lenau and the fictional return migrants modeled after him, Kapp did not attribute his remigration to the repulsive forces allegedly inherent in American life.[45]

Elite opinion, and in particular published opinion, concerning American society and culture was divided in nineteenth-century Germany. On the whole, a negative assessment prevailed. The political system of the

---

43 Schurz to Kinkel, Feb. 24, 1868, Schurz, *Lebenserinnerungen*, 3:303–4; Friedrich in Zucker, *Forty-Eighters*, 23.
44 Vagts, *Deutsch-Amerikanische Rückwanderung*, 183.
45 Ibid., 184–6. See also Wolfgang Hinners, *Exil und Rückkehr: Friedrich Kapp in Amerika und Deutschland, 1824–1884* (Stuttgart, 1987).

United States – that is, the constitution and the institutions of the federal union – was, however, admired by all but die-hard conservatives. Whether this admiration was based on a genuine understanding of the American polity warrants closer inspection.

Liberals interested in constitutional questions held the federal system of the United States in high regard. The members of the Frankfurt National Assembly in the Paulskirche were acquainted with pertinent studies of the United States by Karl von Rotteck and Karl Theodor Welcker (co-editors of the famous *Staatslexikon*), Robert von Mohl, and Francis Lieber. They also took note of American constitutional commentaries. Under the revolutionary circumstances of 1848, furthermore, interest in the United States grew: America was the only potential ally of European liberalism, and its political order seemed particularly relevant now that a German constitution was under discussion. An American observer who had traveled widely in Germany during 1848 commented: "Of all the astonishing revolutions in Europe the most extraordinary one, certainly, is that of public opinion with regard to the United States."[46] For a short moment in history, all liberal factions were united in a positive assessment of America. The secretary of the American Legation at Berlin, Theodore S. Fay, reported to Secretary of State James Buchanan: "They who before admired, now despair of being able to imitate, and they who used to sneer, at last acknowledge the superiority of our institutions and will probably, by thousands, seek repose, and security for life and prosperity under our government."[47]

Despite much mutual sympathy, differences remained. Friedrich von Raumer, one of the leading liberal intellectuals, said that European liberalism was "incomplete," because its sole aim appeared to be the abolishment of monarchical rule.[48] The liberal press celebrated the United States as the land of progress in which citizens could realize their aspirations for self-determination and social advancement. Such praise obscured the crucial question of whether the proposed German constitution would aim at the development of an egalitarian, participatory democracy. Liberals and adherents of the so-called early constitutional movement (*Frühkonstitutionalismus*) regarded the United States not so much as a model for political solutions but as an arsenal of arguments for their own ends. As has already been noted, such usage was also

---

46 A. Dudley Mann to James Buchanan, July 1, 1848, quoted from Moltmann, *Atlantische Blockpolitik*, 57.
47 Fay to Buchanan, Oct. 16, 1848, quoted ibid., 57.
48 Meyer, *Nord-Amerika im Urteil des Deutschen Schrifttums*, 45.

characteristic of the Romantic movement. The ambivalent attitude of liberal politicians and the entire German middle class, or *Bürgertum*, to popular sovereignty precluded a genuinely positive response to the American constitution.[49] If one browses through the writings of early nineteenth-century liberalism, a clear preference for Alexander Hamilton and a deferential society becomes evident; Jeffersonian democracy was much less popular.

The German left also painted an often blurred portrait of America. Here, too, opinions were equivocal, and on closer inspection they say more about ideas centered on Germany than about views of the United States. The inaugural document of German Social Democracy, Ferdinand Lassalle's open letter of March 1, 1863, to the Committee for Convening a Workers' Congress at Leipzig, demanded the abolition of entrepreneurial profits. Lassalle rejected all individual efforts for economic and social betterment in favor of collective endeavors. Until well after World War I the Social Democratic Party was characterized by authoritarianism, anti-individualism, anti-liberalism, and an ambivalence toward representative democracy (*Parlamentarismus*). Thus handicapped, Social Democrats seldom found the intellectual key to an understanding of American society.[50] It is also important to note that German socialists intended to export their model of society. Liberals, in contrast, debated the viability of American concepts for Germany, whereas conservatives were determined to forestall all foreign innovations. In the late nineteenth century the social democratic press and party functionaries even expressed their hope that the socialist model might supersede the model of Americanism in the United States.[51] Such notions were not so far removed from the nationalistic fantasy of implanting the German language and German civilization in the New World.

Marx and Engels, the patron saints of socialism, studied the United States their entire lives but never fully understood the autonomy of American developments. They believed that they had empirically and thus conclusively deduced the key idea of the proletarian revolution from

---

49 Erich Angermann, "Der deutsche Frühkonstitutionalismus und das amerikanische Vorbild," *Historische Zeitschrift* 219 (1974): 4, 21.
50 "Offenes Antwortschreiben an das Zentralkomitee zur Berufung eines Allgemeinen Deutschen Arbeiter-Congresses zu Leipzig," reprinted in Heinrich Potthoff, *Die Sozialdemokratie von den Anfängen bis 1945*, Kleine Geschichte der SPD, vol. 1 (Bonn-Bad Godesberg, 1974), 171–3; Werner Kremp, *In Deutschland liegt unser Amerika: Das sozialdemokratische Amerikabild von den Anfängen der SPD bis zur Weimarer Republik*, Politikwissenschaftliche Perspektiven, no. 6 (Münster, 1993), 35.
51 Kremp, *In Deutschland liegt unser Amerika*, 36, passim.

the particulars of European industrialization. The revolution would necessarily propel Europe again to the vanguard of civilization and economic well-being. Now, however, England and France stood in danger of reverting to the status of Venice, Genoa, or the Netherlands. The United States, Marx and Engels wrote in the *Neue Rheinische Zeitung* for January 1850, was about to take over the number one position.[52] Yet if Europe, and in particular England, required a proletarian revolution to secure its supremacy, as Marx and Engels reasoned, it is curious that they did not divulge how the United States could have become a serious contender without having itself experienced a revolution in the Marxist sense. Only the discovery of gold in California and the impact of mass immigration are called upon to explain America's progress. Marx and Engels do not even consider the specifics of the American political and economic system. The American threat was simply conjured up to make the European revolution appear more urgent.[53]

Marxist hopes later took a different turn. In 1882 Engels predicted that the United States would soon be ripe for a social revolution since the economy could no longer cope with the continuing pressure of immigration. If immigration came to a standstill German workers faced the alternative of "death from hunger or revolution."[54] In this scenario, in other words, America was to provide the spark by which the European powder keg could be ignited.

How significant were the views expounded by writers from the literary and political spheres? So far, only elite opinion has been considered. To what extent did these sentiments and judgments influence mass opinion?

Duden's account of his immigration to Missouri was probably the most widely disseminated German publication on the United States in the nineteenth century if one disregards works of fiction such as Gerstäcker's. Only about five thousand copies were printed. Other books came off the press in editions of no more than a thousand copies.[55] These publi-

---

52 "Revue," *Neue Rheinische Zeitung*, no. 2 (Feb. 1850), in Karl Marx and Friedrich Engels, *Werke*, ed. by Institut für Marxismus-Leninismus beim ZK der SED, 42 vols. (Berlin, 1967–83), 7:220–1.
53 Kremp, *In Deutschland liegt unser Amerika*, 420–1.
54 Friedrich Engels, "Über die Konzentration des Kapitals in den Vereinigten Staaten," *Der Sozialdemokrat*, no. 21 (May 18, 1882), in Marx and Engels, *Werke*, 19:307; Kremp, *In Deutschland liegt unser Amerika*, 432. Such hopes were anachronistic. In 1848, however, they corresponded to the apprehension of state officials for instance in Saxony. See Günter Moltmann, "Auswanderung als Revolutionsersatz?" in Michael Salewski, ed., *Die Deutschen und die Revolution* (Göttingen, 1984), 274–5.
55 Eckhart G. Franz, *Das Amerikabild der deutschen Revolution von 1848–49: Zum Problem der Übertragung gewachsener Verfassungsformen*, Beihefte zum Jahrbuch für Amerikastudien, no. 2 (Heidelberg, 1958), 36–7.

cations were mostly purchased by the educated middle classes, the *Bildungsbürgertum*. This is not to imply that the impact of ideas was limited. Members of the intellectual and political elites are, so to speak, multipliers of opinion. Thus, the stereotyped views of America discussed here have had repercussions down to the present. However, realistic views must also have circulated, or else the phenomenon of mass German immigration in the nineteenth century cannot be explained.

Ernst Ludwig Brauns was one prominent author of books on America, including some which were designed to provide advice to emigrants. As Brauns saw it, the educated public chose to ignore his writings because it was either uninterested or prejudiced. Those, however, "who longed to read and listen about America" were "either too poor or too ignorant and obtuse" to become acquainted with his works.[56] The farmers, artisans, and workers who contemplated emigration may well have been too poor to buy books, but ignorant and obtuse they were not. Almost the contrary is true.

Gottfried Kinkel, the teacher and mentor of Carl Schurz, visited the United States in 1851 and met President Millard Fillmore, whom he described as a "friendly and well-meaning old man." (Fillmore's age then was fifty-one years!) The two major parties, Whigs and Democrats, were, so the visitor believed, firmly under control of the slaveholders. The information that Kinkel passed on to Schurz was superficial at best. He was uncertain about the interpretation of political events. So was Schurz when he arrived in New York the following year. For both men, coverage of the United States in European newspapers had been a major source of information. Such reporting, as Schurz later recognized, was almost useless for someone who was not directly in touch with American affairs.[57]

Ironically, those with little or no access to published information were often the best informed. Since the 1830s, knowledge of the United States increased rapidly among the lower classes. Five and a half million Germans emigrated to the United States between 1820 and 1920 because they had grown tired of their native land. A certain number returned, having in the meantime wearied of America. Many of these, of course, had never intended to stay in the first place. The return migration rate for nineteenth-century German immigration has been estimated at between 2 and 10 percent. But as Walter D. Kamphoefner has shown, a figure

---

56 Ibid., 37.
57 Schurz, *Lebenserinnerungen*, 2:5.

closer to the minimum seems probable for the 1840s and 1850s.[58] Since it is inconceivable that most emigrants simply leaped into the dark, they must have possessed a fairly accurate notion of what to expect in America.

According to Wolfgang Helbich's daring but plausible estimate, at least 250 million letters were sent to Germany from the United States between 1820 and 1914. The bulk consisted of business mail, but about 100 million private letters may have been sent home. Since most letters were preceded or followed by queries, transatlantic communication must have been heavy. The large amount of letters is all the more remarkable when one considers that nine out of ten emigrants from Germany belonged to the lower classes (including the lower middle class) and that their schooling had been rudimentary.[59]

I beg of you, dear Anton, please write some time in answer to this letter and tell me; you have been on my mind often and I wished to be with you if only I knew whether I shall obtain more there than here, if I can eat my bread more peacefully there than here, then I would leave everything behind me and would follow you. Please write to me about these things ... dear brother.

This is an excerpt from a letter written in 1849 by a woman from the Oldenburg region in northwest Germany to her brother in Cincinnati.[60] The question is whether she will be better off in America than in Germany. Expectations concerning material well-being could not have been high. A little more security in life is her only aspiration.

What did these people find repulsive in Germany? And what drew them to the United States? "In some parts of Europe there is more wealth," wrote Edward Everett in the *North American Review* of 1819, "in most there is more artificial refinement, and more learning, than in America; but in none is there much freedom either of soul or body."[61] German emigrants of the nineteenth century often stated the primary

---

58 Walter D. Kamphoefner, "Umfang und Zusammensetzung der deutsch-amerikanischen Rückwanderung," *Amerikastudien/ American Studies* 33 (1988): 291–307; Günter Moltmann, "American-German Return Migration in the Nineteenth and Early Twentieth Centuries," *Central European History* 13 (1980): 378–92.
59 Wolfgang Helbich, "The Letters They Sent Home: The Subjective Perspective of German Immigrants in the Nineteenth Century," *Yearbook of German-American Studies* 22 (1987): 1–2.
60 "Eine grosse Bitte hab ich an Dich, lieber Anton, schreibe mir wieder einmal auf Post auf diesen Brief und beantworte mir; ich habe schon viel an Dich gedacht, ich wollte mir wohl auch wünschen, bei Dir zu sein, wenn ich nur wüsste, ob ich dort mehr erhalte als hier, dass ich das Brot dort geruhiger essen kann als hier, dann wollte ich hier alles verlassen und wollte Dir nachkommen. Darüber schreibe mir ... lieber Bruder." Printed in Wolfgang Helbich, ed., with Ursula Boesing, *"Amerika ist ein freies Land ...": Auswanderer schreiben nach Deutschland*, Sammlung Luchterhand, no. 541 (Neuwied, 1985), 27.
61 "German Emigration to America," *North American Review* 11 (1820): 19.

motivation for leaving the country thus: that they wished to devote their lives as best they could, unobstructed by the authorities, to the quest for material and immaterial goods. This is what the Declaration of Independence calls the "pursuit of happiness."

In 1817, Friedrich List, as royal commissioner in the Kingdom of Württemberg, questioned several hundred emigrants about their motives for leaving the country. The minutes of the examinations clarify that – even in a year of unparalleled misery – it was not sheer necessity that caused these people to flee from their homes.[62] They emigrated, rather, because of the lack of perspective provided by a life in which they felt harassed by petty officials and overburdened by high taxes and feudal obligations. The causes of emigration still resembled those that a member of the German Society of Maryland had identified in 1786, namely "offences against freedom of religion, constraints of all kinds against the enjoyment of natural rights such as free thinking and free speech, an unfair administration of justice, repression by small and great despots, impediments against free enterprise, and so forth."[63] In the years 1817 to 1820, 80 percent of the Württemberg emigrants questioned by the state about their reasons for leaving mentioned declining incomes and the lack of food along with "hope for better luck." This catch-all formula suggests that most emigrants were unable to explicate the numerous, interwoven motives and causes relevant to their decision making.

The anthropologist Ina-Maria Greverus has developed a theory of "territorial behavior" to explain the emigration decision: to be satisfied with life, one must be able to satisfy one's needs for an area of peace and shelter (*Friedensraum*), action (*Aktionsraum*), and identification (*Identitätsraum*).[64] Although they might have set out looking for "freedom of soul or body," "hope for better luck," or "territorial satisfaction," German immigrants did in fact encounter better living conditions, as their letters clearly show. They tried to characterize the American experience by reporting, for instance, that taxes were low and other contributions unknown, that food was sufficient if not plentiful, or that expressions

---

62 See John D. Post, *The Last Great Subsistence Crisis of the Western World* (Baltimore, 1977).
63 "Gekränkte Religionsfreiheit, Gewissenszwang mancher Art in Hinderung der Ausübung angeborner Menschenrechte, als des freien Denkens und Mittheilens der Gedanken, ungerechte Justiz, Druck kleiner und grosser Despoten, Erschwerung der Mittel des Erwerbs, u.s.w." [Christian Mayer], "Deutsche Gesellschaft in Nordamerika," *Berlinische Monatsschrift* 8 (1786): 392–3. For the List protocols, see Moltmann, *Aufbruch nach Amerika*, 120–87.
64 Ina-Maria Greverus, *Der territoriale Mensch: Ein literaturanthroplogischer Versuch zum Heimatphänomen* (Frankfurt/Main, 1972), 51–5.

of submissiveness were not necessary. Distinctions of status were less clearly marked, and upward mobility was possible. Women in particular commented on the absence of dress regulations as a clear indication of their new-found freedom. As social historian Rolf Engelsing once put it, "The petty bourgeois understood that in the United States, too, he would not belong to the ruling classes, but at least to the valid members of society."[65]

In his seminal essay of 1927, "The History of American Immigration as a Field for Research," Marcus Lee Hansen named "freedom to move" as a necessary precondition of emigration.[66] Freedom to move was directly linked to the loosening of feudal attachments. The rapid disappearance of traditional agrarian society weakened communal solidarity and uprooted many individuals from customary ways of life, but it also eased mobility. Everybody had to change, and many welcomed the chance to provide for themselves in the United States. The risk of failure was seldom denied or overlooked in immigrants' letters. Those who succeeded in the New World became and remained weary of Germany, while many, perhaps most, return migrants had from the beginning planned or at least hoped to make their stay temporary.

In sum, Germans whose friends and relatives lived in the United States had access to a wealth of data contained in the immigrants' letters. It was generally superior to the information available in print. Letters often helped people find correct answers to crucial questions concerning social and economic conditions – unless unforeseen strokes of fate invalidated predictions and shattered hopes.

Intellectuals' views on America oscillated between disappointment with Germany and Europe and disappointment with America. Many of those who disapproved of America did not respond to the realities of life on the other side of the Atlantic. Their affinity to the United States (or lack of it) must be seen as a dependent variable of intellectual and political developments in Germany. Anti-American feelings (here also subsumed under weariness of America) often resulted from the fear that negative facets of modern life might spread to Germany. Where such forces were already at play, some writers deplored the Americanization of German society. In this context, it was unimportant whether or not these negative

---

65 "Der Kleinbürger begriff, dass er in den USA zwar auch nicht zur herrschenden, aber zur geltenden Klasse gehören werde" (Engelsing, "Deutschland und die Vereinigten Staaten," 148).
66 *American Historical Review* 32 (1927): 501. The other conditions were "desire to move" and "means to move."

phenomena were truly typical of the United States. It also mattered little where in the German political spectrum an observer was placed. With some exceptions, nineteenth-century German intellectuals lacked an idiomatic awareness of developments in American society and politics.

4

"Auch unser Deutschland muss einmal frei werden"

The Immigrant Civil War Experience as a Mirror on Political Conditions in Germany

WALTER D. KAMPHOEFNER

I

In this chapter, evidence from immigrant letters is used to address the following question: How did German immigrants in the era before 1871 regard the political situation in their homeland? How widespread was the "spirit of 1848," and, above all, how deeply did it extend down into the rank and file? How were political opinions and preferences concerning the United States, on the one hand, and Germany or Europe, on the other, interrelated, particularly in the Civil War era? This question extends to political partisanship, disposition toward the war effort itself, and toward the race issues that emerged from it. What effect did the confession, education, and social origins of immigrants have on their views? All these questions are closely interwoven with another issue, the degree to which emigration was politically motivated in the first place.

There are a number of works that skirt around the edges of these questions, but none that really gets at its center. Peter Marschalck has estimated that only a few thousand of the emigrants in the aftermath of 1848 were politically motivated. But as other scholars and I have argued, economic and political grievances were often closely intertwined, and at least a rudimentary political consciousness was much more widespread among immigrants than is often realized. Carl Wittke restricted his account of the "48ers" almost entirely to bourgeois elements, and the same can be said of the other standard work on the subject edited by Adolf Zucker. Jörg Nagler has abundantly documented the ideological continuity of these bourgeois elements in their response to the Civil War, and he shows their prominence in the radical unionist movement and the Frémont presidential candidacy of 1864. But he gives less attention to the size of their following among rank and file German voters, despite indications that they were often chiefs without Indians.[1]

Bruce Levine has broken important new ground and uncovered a significant component of plebeian radicalism alongside the bourgeois elements who take center stage in Wittke's account and most other works on 1848 and the "Forty-Eighters" in America. Still, Levine is more successful in documenting the predominance - at least numerically – of plebeians among the German radicals than of radicals among the German plebeians in America.[2]

There is a whole literature on German-American voting in the Civil War era, but some controversial points still remain. According to the old filiopietistic interpretation, the freedom-loving Germans, opposed to slavery and inspired and led by Forty-Eighters such as Carl Schurz, voted as one man for the Republican Party and provided the margin of victory for Lincoln's election. More recent scholarship has challenged this viewpoint, pointing out that the Republicans in many areas were too tainted by nativism and prohibition to be acceptable to most Germans. Doubts have also been raised about the influence of Forty-Eighters, most of whom were vocally outspoken freethinkers, among their more pious compatriots, especially those of conservative Catholic or Lutheran confession.[3]

A historical consensus does exist on several points. There is no doubt as to the zeal of most Forty-Eighters and their allies for the Union, emancipation, and the Republican Party. In fact, if they opposed Lincoln, it was usually from the left rather than from the right. Nor is there any doubt that most Forty-Eighters were freethinkers, though not all of such

---

[1] A pathbreaking, bottom-up perspective from the German side is presented by Jonathan Sperber, *Rhineland Radicals: The Democratic Movement and the Revolution of 1848–1849* (Princeton, N.J., 1991). Peter Marschalck, *Deutsche Überseewanderung im 19. Jahrhundert* (Stuttgart, 1973), 57–8; Walter D. Kamphoefner, *The Westfalians: From Germany to Missouri* (Princeton, N.J., 1987), 58–69; Carl Wittke, *Refugees of Revolution: The German Forty-Eighters in America* (Philadelphia, 1952); Adolf E. Zucker, ed., *The Forty-Eighters: Political Refugees of the German Revolution of 1848*, 2d ed. (New York, 1967); Jörg Nagler, *Fremont contra Lincoln: Die deutsch-amerikanische Opposition in der Republikanischen Partei während des amerikanischen Bürgerkriegs* (Frankfurt/Main, 1984). Even if one doubles the conservative estimate of 4,000 Forty-Eighter emigrants made by Zucker (p. 269), they come to less than 1 percent of the roughly one million Germans who immigrated to the United States in the eleven years from 1850 to 1860.

[2] Bruce Levine, *The Spirit of 1848: German Immigrants, Labor Conflict, and the Coming of the Civil War* (Urbana, Ill., 1992).

[3] A convenient collection and historiographic overview on politics is provided by Frederick Luebke, ed., *Ethnic Voters and the Election of Lincoln* (Lincoln, Neb., 1971).

a radical vein as one St. Louis editor who attempted to reassure his readers that he did not eat little Catholic children for breakfast. What is still under dispute is the degree to which everyday German-Americans without any higher education shared the political views of the Forty-Eighters.[4]

Quantitative electoral analysis is of limited value in disentangling various confessional groups and virtually useless for uncovering class differences among German voters. And merely knowing *how* a group voted hardly tells us *why*. The party platform was sufficiently ambiguous in 1860 that even voting Republican was no guarantee of racial idealism. Rather than rely on self-serving statements of the immigrant political or religious elite, or from aggregate-level voting data which largely precludes any religious or class differentiation, this chapter draws its evidence directly from the German-American rank and file.

The main source of this investigation is letters collected at Ruhr Universität Bochum from roughly seventy-five immigrants writing in the antebellum and Civil War era. Background research in Germany and America has in most cases ascertained the educational level and social position as well as the confessional affiliation of the writers in both their old and new homelands. As important as what is said is often who is saying it.[5] While these letter writers by no means form a random cross-section of immigrants, of greater significance is the fact that we have any letters at all from working-class Germans, and can compare their outlook with that of the liberal bourgeoisie. Notwithstanding difficulties of interpretation, particularly from a sole surviving letter, immigrant correspondence adds more than just nuances to our understanding of German-American political loyalties and the ideology that lay behind them.[6]

---

4 Walter D. Kamphoefner, "German-Americans and Civil War Politics: A Reconsideration of the Ethnocultural Thesis," *Civil War History* 37 (1991): 226–40.
5 The Bochumer Auswandererbriefsammlung (hereafter cited as BABS) is housed in the history department of Ruhr Universität Bochum and contains over 5,000 immigrant letters, largely written by ordinary individuals and mostly collected from private sources. Prime sources of background information were German parish registers and emigration permits, and the manuscript census and city directories in America. Additional sources for military participants were the service and pension records, the latter often including information on the subject's marriage, which was useful in determining confession. Unless otherwise specified, all letters quoted and information on writers is contained in the holdings of BABS. For more information on the BABS collection and sources of background information, see Walter D. Kamphoefner, Wolfgang Helbich, and Ulrike Sommer, eds., *News from the Land of Freedom: German Immigrants Write Home* (Ithaca, N.Y., 1991), 36–50. Unless otherwise noted, all translations are my own. No attempt was made to reproduce the often-deficient grammar and spelling of the original German.
6 Does silence on a subject indicate disinterest of the writer, or perhaps of the recipient? How important was the gender of the writer or addressee? Obviously, letters do not provide a simple "Gallup poll" of immigrant political opinion, which may also change over time.

II

Comments on the political situation in Germany are scarce and restricted almost entirely to persons of bourgeois background among immigrants before 1848 – and they are almost entirely negative. A good example is the university-educated Blümner brothers, whose family were leaseholders of royal estates east of the Elbe. One brother, August, writes from his Missouri farm in 1838 denouncing German censorship, and in 1841 expounds on a friend's remark "that I had an awful vicious tongue when it came to preachers, princes and nobles." None of August's reactions to the revolution of 1848 have survived, but in 1852 his brother Carl, now a Santa Fé merchant, wrote to request information on "the political situation in Prussia and in Germany in general." In his next letter of 1854 he laid out his republican political creed more clearly, hoping that if another revolutionary storm should break forth in Europe, "may Heaven grant that rapid destruction fall on those crowned heads, so that only the *guilty* must suffer, and the people, mankind, may safely, rapidly, and victoriously emerge from this holy battle!"[7]

A Catholic university student from Westfalia who fled to America in the aftermath of the Frankfurter *Attentat* (assassination) expounded on his republican principles in an 1839 letter to his father, "Besides, I believe that the guilt falls less on me than on those who forced me into voluntary flight; for who gives those in power the right so to restrict the personal freedom of mankind and to cast in fetters the human spirit..." In another letter of 1840, he distinguishes between the German people and their rulers; although an American citizen, he still preferred Germany, but did not regret the cause of his emigration.

> ... on the contrary, here I have become all the more aware of what is lacking in Germany, have been reinforced in my opinions on freedom and right, which no one will take from me. But the disgrace which is burdened upon Germany through its government really only came to light for me here; in foreign countries they know very little of the great people [*Volk*] that calls itself German.

Obviously this writer was disappointed by the failure of the 1848 revolution, writing his brother in September of that year that his plans of return had been overturned by "reactionary measures of the governments, particularly Prussia's, and widespread persecution and imprisonment of Germany's liberal men," making it dangerous for someone with his background "to expose himself to the miserable police

---

7 Kamphoefner et al., eds., *News from the Land of Freedom*, 102, 110, 115–16.

state of Prussia." Consequently, he remained in America for the rest of his life.[8]

The only pre-1848 writer who gives a slightly different tone was a merchant's clerk in New York, who later returned to his hometown of Hamburg and who probably planned to do so from the beginning. He took a diplomatic approach with family members whom he depended on for future employment, writing to his uncle in 1845, "I well understand your warning not to get too carried away by the 'Yankeemania'; ... as much as I love the republic and find it appropriate for the land and people here, I remain just as much conservative minded for *Europe*, and I find the outcry over 'Oppressed Germany' etc. laughable."[9]

A letter from the same writer to his father in 1846 finds the English and German language press in America similarly anti-German, and mostly "poor and base beyond contempt, simply because it is a free press." But even these shortcomings had their bright side in that a few good papers, "not hindered by any fearful censors," brought the truth to light, so that everyone knew not to believe the bad papers. This writer returned to his uncle's shipping business in Hamburg in 1847, so his reactions to 1848 have not found their way into letters.

The revolution of 1848 appears to have enjoyed almost universal support among German-Americans, at least among those who took an active position on the issue. Wittke reports that there "was not a single voice raised in the whole German-language press in defense of kings and the *status quo*," with most commentators favoring republicanism in Germany. Subscription rates boomed along with interest in the revolution, and many papers promoted fundraising appeals for the revolutionaries. Rallies were held throughout the major immigrant communities. Whereas the failure of the revolution brought a certain amount of disillusion and criticism of the revolutionaries, German-American newspapers continued for a half decade to report on the fate of refugees and the suppression of the press in Europe. And disillusion notwithstanding, the 1852 American tour of revolutionaries Gottfried Kinkel and the Hungarian Lajos Kossuth was reported enthusiastically not only in the big cities but also in small German settlements such as the county seat town of St. Charles, Missouri.[10]

---

8 Letters of Lorenz Degenhart, BABS. Excerpts from Degenhart's letters have been published in Wolfgang Helbich, ed., *Amerika ist ein freies Land* (Darmstadt, 1985), 29–30, 112–13, 117–18, 122–3, 162–3, 213–14.
9 Beinecke letter collection, BABS. See also excerpts in Helbich, ed., *Amerika ist ein freies Land*, 124, 178–9, 181.
10 Carl Wittke, *The German-Language Press in America* (Lexington, Ky., 1957), 61–71, quotation on 63; *St. Charles Demokrat*, Jan. 1, Feb. 7, Mar. 13, and Apr. 3, 1852.

Letter writers in the Bochum collection confirm these impressions. In general, reactions to 1848 came mostly from the same type of people who had offered political commentary in the two decades before. In fact, we have already heard from several of them. But there was at least a mild degree of interest further down on the socioeconomic ladder.

A saddler and *Turnverein* (gymnastics club) member of petit bourgeois background draws upon German analogies to describe the nativist controversy in St. Louis in 1853: "The Wichs [Whigs] are now trying all sorts of tricks to get back in, like the big wheels tried to do with the people in '48, but flattery doesn't get you anywhere here." The letter then turns to Europe, wishing success for the democrats in Germany and for Kossuth, and ending with the observation that "it is easier to recognize what someone is really like when you are free like over here, as long as you live in servitude to preachers and princes they try to keep you in ignorance."[11]

An immigrant metalworker from the Sauerland wrote at the end of 1848:

There are now three German newspapers being put out in St. Louis alone, and every German here certainly is more or less concerned with the weal or woe of his motherland.... You ask what I think of Germany in case you obtain a republic?... That hardly needs an answer, for a good government is good for any country, and the republican is not only a good, but indisputably the best of all, especially for an enlightened people like the Germans.

He did not survive to comment on the Civil War, but a nephew of similar background, who had enlisted in a Union militia, wrote in 1862:

... when we have survived the revolution here, you'll have over there, unless all the newspaper reports are mistaken, a 48 N[umbe]r two. Here you really see what a military dictatorship it is in Prussia which drains the poor folks dry. Here the standing army is 12,000 man in peacetime..., here a person fights for his own existence and over there for the despots, that is a great difference.[12]

Even one son of a Westfalian peasant asked the home folks in 1848, "When you write again write about the *Rewelutsiohn* too," although he finished the sentence by requesting that they send him three pipes. There are quite a number of writers like him who are frustratingly cryptic about their political activities or sympathies, for example, writing that there was a presidential election without telling who won, whom they favored or voted for, or indeed whether they had voted at all.[13]

11 Kamphoefner et al., eds., *News from the Land of Freedom*, 325–6.
12 Letters of J. H. Spannagel and Wilhelm Zimmermann, BABS.
13 Kamphoefner et al., eds., *News from the Land of Freedom*, 89, also 77.

But in an 1853 letter, another rural Westfalian emigrant, poorer and less literate than the previous one, expressed his support for the revolution of 1848 in unambiguous if humorous terms.

It's too bad that a healthy Germany is ruled by such a bad nation. In terms of [climate] Germany would be preferable to America, if the working class there were not begrudged their life, if only the honorable men who called themselves democrats had issued their appeal under another name, namely Liesebett, then I don't doubt they would have received a great following, because that was a well-known name for everyone, but the word democrat sounded dangerous to them, and no one dared call himself by such a name, even if he carried it in his bosom.

This writer later converted to the Swedenborgian religion and was somewhat unusual for someone of his background in his degree of political awareness. Nevertheless, he implies that at least a latent sympathy for the cause of 1848 was more widespread, even in rural Germany. Not surprisingly, when the Civil War broke out he wholeheartedly backed the Union and Republican cause, grasping many of its political nuances, and saw in the end of slavery evidence of divine justice.[14] Another immigrant who went from being a village weaver in Hesse to a factory worker in Connecticut, found fewer problems with the name "Democrat" but similar connections between Forty-Eighter and antislavery sympathy in his reactions to the 1856 election.[15]

In general the Civil War elicited political commentary from a broader socioeconomic range of writers than ever before. Quite often, perhaps in a majority of cases, these comments included implicit or explicit comparisons with political events in Europe. In addition, there was almost always a congruence between the political principles espoused on both sides of the Atlantic.

The mutual antipathies between Forty-Eighters and orthodox Catholics and Lutherans do indeed show through in some of the letters. Dietrich Gerstein, a Westfalian Forty-Eighter, wrote from a backwoods farm in Michigan before the outbreak of hostilities with a venom unsurpassed by any freethinking big city editor:

The North... can exist by itself..., since by far the greater proportion of its inhabitants are Republicans. Naturally it would be necessary that the northern Democrats be driven to the South, then I would also be rid of my dear neighbors, the Old Lutherans.

14 Dietrich Korthals, "Johann Hermann Sudbrack: Ein Jürnjakob Swehn aus Ravensberg," *Wittekindsland* 1 (1987): 75–104.
15 Kamphoefner et al., eds., *News from the Land of Freedom*, 356–7.

... isn't it strange to see all the pious people voting for slavery. Of course they prove from the Bible that slavery is a divine institution, but also the Catholics, who want nothing to do with the Bible, are wild for slavery, especially the dumbest and most beastly of all nations, the Irish.[16]

Many Catholics, however, knew to reply with equal measure. Joseph Dünnebacke, like Gerstein from Westfalia and now a farmer in Michigan, but unlike him, of peasant origins, complained in May 1862 about high costs and low farm prices and asked: "Who is to blame for it? Unfortunately the abolitionists among them many European Forty-Eighters, they have done a lot to help instigate the war, ... then there is the southern slavery, which they can't agree on." Even this writer expected and hoped for a Union victory, although an 1864 letter shows exasperation at the conduct of the war and sympathy for the Democratic general and presidential candidate George McClellan.[17]

Dünnebacke's grammar and syntax show evidence of minimal education, and his opinion of German radicals was shared by another ordinary Catholic, Nicholas Pack, a surprisingly articulate coal miner from the Saarland living near Pittsburgh.

The source of this war is mostly a nice present from Europe, which the dear Forty-Eighters, the heroes of freedom, who have broken with God and their respective monarchs, have brought into this land. The main cause was the excessive pride of the whole American people. The dear Lord blessed them in abundance.... There were no empty stomachs, and where there are no empty stomachs, there are no cool heads.... This brother's war of the North with the South is a punishment of God. Thousands upon thousands ... have already shed their blood and the matter is still just the same as at the beginning. The Negroes are still not free and just as black as they ever were, and the mark of Cain will not be washed from them.

Surprisingly, not even this writer was devoid of democratic tendencies, complaining about the "despots of Europe," although he did not mention any Germans among them.[18]

16 Dietrich Gerstein, born in 1828 into the Protestant *Bildungsbürgertum* of Rheda, Westfalia, attended *Gymnasium* but was denied *Abitur* because of his revolutionary activities and arrest in 1848, emigrated in 1850, and was married in 1853 by a justice of the peace. The 1860 census of Denmark Township, Tuscola Co., Mich., shows him as a propertyless farmer. Quotation from letter of Apr. 7, 1860.
17 Joseph Dünnebacke, born in 1818 to a peasant family in Niedermarpe, Westfalia, emigrated in 1845 and appears in the 1860 census of Clinton Co., Mich., as a farmer worth $2,025.
18 Nicholas Pack, born ca. 1809, emigrated ca. 1853 from Schiffsweiler in the Saarland and is listed in the 1860 census of Lower St. Clair, Allegheny Co., Pa., as a coal digger worth $950. Quotation from letter of Oct. 12, 1863. His son Jacob was a war casualty, but only entered the army in Feb. 1864, suggesting that he was a draftee or reluctant recruit. Additional information from letter of daughter Elisabeth Pack Weinheimer, May 23, 1895.

Dünnebacke and Pack appear fairly typical of Catholics with little education, but better educated Catholics were on the whole much more friendly toward the Republicans and their program. The most striking case was Westfalian physician Bernhard Bruns, an early immigrant to Missouri, who helped nominate Lincoln as a delegate to the 1860 Republican convention. This former owner of a female black domestic characterized slavery already in 1848 as a "brand-mark for the United States," placing himself in the same letter on the side of the revolution in Germany: "By God, I am sorry to hear the idea expressed that you are not yet suited for a republic." His reactions to the 1858 congressional elections echo the accusations of the freethinking Forty-Eighter press in St. Louis.

The intelligent German population voted as one man for emancipation candidates. The . . . Negro-Democracy, with the might of the Catholic vote, primarily the Jesuits, voted unanimously for slavery – fine Christian brothers – so that this time, in spite of all humane and philanthropic arguments, we had to lose. . . . In general the Catholic clergy revealed itself this time in its true light, or better said, darkness.[19]

Dr. Bruns saw a clear interaction between the struggles for freedom in America and Europe, as his resume of the 1860 election shows.

We Republicans have worked faithfully since the Chicago convention and elected our candidates. For that the German element deserves the honor. Unfortunately the arch-Catholics were against us. Now they are on the side of the disunionists. Now, you have a similar scene with Italy. According to reports, even the people of Münster have sympathy for the rabid proslavery people in Italy.

Bruns's brother-in-law Franz Geisberg, from a solidly bourgeois Catholic family in the Münsterland, expressed similarly liberal views in a letter of 1857. "In St. Louis the whole ticket of the slavery emancipation party was elected and this will have solid repercussions on the rest of the state." His indictment of the authoritarian behavior of the local Catholic clergy toward the immigrant youth goes a long way in explaining the church's limited political influence.

This brusque demeanor of our Catholic clergy, before whom everyone is supposed to humble himself, who want to dominate everything, who immediately

---

19 Bernhard Bruns was born in 1798 near Lingen, Hannover, to a prosperous peasant family that saw another son become a priest. He emigrated in 1835 to Osage Co., Mo., where the 1850 census shows him with property worth $8,000. Additional information on the family is found in Adolf E. Schroeder and Carla Schulz-Geisberg, eds., *Hold Dear, As Always, Jetta, a German Immigrant Life in Letters* (Columbia, Mo., 1988). Quotations from letters of Oct. 28, 1848, and Sept. 21, 1858.

damn everyone who thinks differently, has the effect on many that they are very little bothered with religion and only very seldom seen in the church. Where kindness would accomplish much, they ruin everything through their repulsive manner. Old customs, which one hundred years ago were perhaps appropriate, reemerge again here, but they're not to most people's taste. . . . These men can't stem the tide of progress and only hurt themselves, so that they increasingly lose their influence.

So much for the deference of the Catholic laity. The Bruns family followed their course unerringly throughout the Civil War. A son and a stepson both gave their lives for the Union on the battlefield; Dr. Bruns himself served as a military physician and Republican mayor of Missouri's capital city until his death in 1864. "Too bad that Bruns did not live to see this," was his wife's reaction when a radical Republican took over the governor's office in 1865.[20]

To take another case, Edward Treutlein was perhaps not a conventional Catholic, being the grandson of a priest and his housekeeper, but he was nevertheless a practicing one, and later served as a parochial school teacher and director. Abandoning his *Gymnasium* studies, he learned lithography and then came to America as a sailor. He volunteered for the Union army, transferred to the navy, and appeared to identify fully with the Republican program. In a letter from Illinois in 1868 he painted the contrasts between the Republican and Democratic parties in very similar colors as Bruns: "The former the party of progress, of equal rights for all and everyone without distinction of station or color – the latter if no longer exactly reactionary still very conservative; that is, they would like to leave everything the old way like it was before the war." He goes on to characterize Republican supporters:

. . . all the educated property holders, all the sanctimonious religious fanatics and most of the Germans[;] for the other party are all the dumb farmers and uneducated artisans, the credulous Irish of Catholic faith and practically the whole south. How it comes about that the Catholic element always goes hand in hand with conservatism, also here in America, I don't know.[21]

Although Bruns and Treutlein were both practicing Catholics, one could raise doubts about how devout they were. The same is true of three

---

20 Quotation from letter of Apr. 4, 1865. Widow Bruns ran a boardinghouse for state legislators and would have none but "radicals" as her guests, according to a letter of May 31, 1868.
21 Born the son of a teacher in 1838 in Ittenschwand, Baden, Edward Treutlein joined the Union army in Apr. 1864 and then transferred to the navy the next month. He served as parochial school teacher and organist in several Catholic congregations in St. Clair Co., Ill., in the 1870s. Quotation from letter of Oct. 22, 1868; by 1873 Treutlein was complaining that Catholics were suffering political discrimination, and in 1877 he decried the "presidency swindle," suggesting a switch to the Democrats.

other bourgeois Catholics from whom letters have survived.[22] However, the letters of John Dieden, scion of the Palatinate bourgeoisie and the son and employee of merchants in Chicago, leave no doubt as to his orthodox, indeed ardent Catholicism. Nevertheless, Dieden was well-disposed toward liberalism on both sides of the Atlantic. It shows through in a bit of doggerel he wrote for his uncle in 1855, contrasting American freedom with familiar complaints about Germany. Here, the immigrant is not plagued by the police, he is free from the force of princes, gendarmes are unknown here and he can travel throughout the land without a pass. Even the much-maligned Forty-Eighters enjoyed his admiration, as he indicated in a letter of 1860: "Since the revolution in Germany of 1848 there has been a marked improvement in the position of the Germans in the United States, because since that time many intelligent and educated people have left the old fatherland, and very many had to leave on account of their sovereigns." Dieden naturally welcomed the election of Lincoln, "the man of freedom, the fighter of slavery, the man of equal rights." It is also interesting to see how Dieden applies his same egalitarian, democratic principles to Germany. As he wrote in 1862, "there are a lot of German states that wouldn't be hurt if they had on their thrones instead of their little petty sovereigns [*Zaunkönige*] such a carpenter or tailor or farmer as our current president A. Lincoln."[23]

All seven members of the German Catholic bourgeoisie here cited displayed full sympathy with the Republicans, but this had little to do with the official separation of church and state in America. In fact, American public life in general and the reform elements of the Republican Party in particular had a decidedly and sometimes militantly Protes-

22 Viktor Klausmeyer, son and brother of Catholic schoolteachers and himself a future insurance executive in Baltimore, worked for the War Department in Washington, D.C. In a letter written in Apr. 1865, he refers to blacks as "woolheads," but comments favorably on their fighting ability and goes on to state, "We have but one goal: Establishment of the Union and abolition of slavery." He shows no trace of deference to the Catholic church, characterizing a circular by the Bishop of Paderborn as "not true" and "secessionist reports." Two other bourgeois Catholic Republicans and Union officers with letters in BABS are similarly characterized by lack of orthodoxy: Wilhelm Niedenhofen, a lieutenant from Minnesota, and Magnus Brucker, a surgeon from Indiana, a state legislator and radical Republican. Brucker was a Freemason; Niedenhofen was also a lodge member and was married the second time by a priest after having been divorced – evidence that the Catholic church may been less stringent when dealing with its more prominent parishioners.

23 John Dieden was born in 1836 in Ebernburg, Palatinate, where his grandfather had been *Bürgermeister*. He emigrated in Mar. 1848 along with his stepfather and the rest of his family, and worked during the 1850s as a clerk for an Anglo-American firm. He appears in the 1860 census of Chicago in the household of his stepfather John Herting, a provisions store owner worth $20,000. Quotations are from letters of Mar. 15, 1860, Nov. 29, 1860, and Feb. 21, 1862. Dieden married in Aug. 1860 and did not serve in the war. During the war decade, his stepfather was elected to the city council and his brother to the state legislature, both as Republicans.

tant tone. But with the more enterprising Catholics, as with anticlerical Forty-Eighters, this factor was outweighed by the Republican program of social and economic progress.

Those left behind in the process, the bulk of Catholic immigrants who were less educated and less prosperous, showed considerably more skepticism toward the starry-eyed idealism of the Republicans. But even among the lower ranks of German Catholics, defenses of slavery can hardly be found, much less sympathy for the cause of southern independence. Rather, there is a passivity with regard to politics and the war, and a general silence regarding causes and higher principles, even from some in the Union Army. For many ordinary Catholics, and not only for them, the Civil War was accepted with a passive, peasant stoicism, much like a harvest failure or a natural disaster. But for Prussian military service they had no more sympathy than the most radical Forty-Eighter.[24]

One "poor nailmaker's son" and devout Catholic from the Eifel who had emigrated clandestinely in 1857 wrote his sister in 1860 that "the mere thought of the Prussian authorities arouses my anger, how would that work if I, used to the free life in America, was a Prussian soldier, ordered around by everyone. It would certainly be the greatest misery for me." In an 1877 letter he states baldly, "In Germany there is nothing but oppressors of humanity and slaves." His lone Civil War letter (1862) shows him to be proud of America and up to date on the Trent affair and relations with England, but silent on any higher causes in the war.[25]

Occasionally one discovers also among ordinary Catholics a trace of the idealism expressed by the better educated of their faith. An artisan's son who emigrated from Baden in late 1860 and enlisted a few months after the war began, characterized himself as a "soldier for right and freedom." In the same letter of August 1863 he expressed his support for emancipation as a matter of republican principle: "Trade and sale of human beings must be suppressed in a land like America, for in a true republic there can be no slavery."[26] A poor Catholic immigrant from Rhineland Prussia analyzed the situation in February 1865 from the nation's capital thus:

---

24 A good example is Nicholas and Angela Heck, whose letters are published in Kamphoefner et al., eds., *News from the Land of Freedom*, 367–82.
25 Loewen's letters are published in ibid., 187–9, 192.
26 Hansmartin Schwarzmaier, "Auswandererbriefe aus Nordamerika: Quellen im Grenzbereich von Geschichlicher Landeskunde, Wanderungsforschung und Literatursoziologie," *Zeitschrift für die Geschichte des Oberrheins* 126 (1978): 342–8. The writer, born in 1841 as the son of a dyer, emigrated on a sailing ship, suggesting that his finances were limited. He served in the 4th Ohio Artillery and, when he died of illness in Oct. 1863, was given a Catholic burial.

Sooner or later America will have no more slaves, Freedom takes its course with giant steps. And that's good. That it ends, this shameful stain upon America. I saw it in Virginia. It is horrifying... yesterday I was in the Senate where President Lincoln was reelected, I am very interested in hearing the debates, what the ruler by divine right does over there, the people do here.

Here too one sees the linkage of democratic aspirations for America and Europe, and that from someone who could hardly write a line without a grammar or spelling error.[27]

On the whole, however, such sentiments were much less common among uneducated Catholics than among German who were of a different educational level or confession. When we shift our focus to Protestants (including freethinkers of a Protestant background), we find a similar spectrum of opinion as with Catholics, but several contrasts as well. The Protestants also had a couple out-and-out racists and a goodly number of "passives" on the subjects of war and emancipation. As a rule, however, the ideology of freedom permeated much more strongly into the lower social strata than with Catholics. In fact, the views of the liberal bourgeoisie and those of the common people often show striking parallels. The linkages between views on America and Europe were if anything clearer than among Catholics. A few examples illustrate this point.

Albert Krause, an educated young man from a good family in Posen was not even subject to conscription when he enlisted in a Buffalo regiment in 1862:

[A]s far as I'm concerned, I go courageously and gladly into the fire. The States took me in, I had an income, and now that they're in danger, shouldn't I defend them with flesh and blood?!

I don't want to go back to Germany and especially not back to Prussia. I have tasted freedom and it tastes too good to trade it again for the dungeon.[28]

As Krause's letter of February 27, 1863, makes clear, he is concerned with more than just his own freedom: "shame and disgrace be on those who deal in human flesh!"

Ludwig Kühner, a Badenese artisan and farmer in Ohio, explained with words that match Krause's in idealism if not in eloquence why he,

---

27 Matthias Leclerc, born in 1820 in Vallendar, Rhineland Prussia, emigrated alone in late 1862 because of economic problems. Citation from letter of Feb. 15, 1865. There was some liberal Catholic support for the 1848 revolution in the Palatinate and Rhineland Prussia, as is shown in Sperber, *Rhineland Radicals*, 47–8, 281–3, 451–4.
28 Albert Krause was born in 1841, son of an estate owner in Posen, and had attended a *Gymnasium* before emigrating in 1861 to avoid the Prussian draft. He enlisted in the Union army in Aug. 1862 and served for the duration of the war. The quotation is from letter of Sept. 11, 1862. See also excerpts in Helbich, ed., *Amerika ist ein freies Land*, 121–2, 181–3, and passim.

his brother, and three brothers-in-law had enlisted: "We were not drafted, nor did money or greed bring us to it, it is a hard task to leave wife and children behind and to go into battle. . . . the cause of this war is slavery . . . freedom and slavery cannot live with one another, one will be abolished, my hope is that the right wins."[29] When the South in early 1865 considered the desperation move of putting blacks under arms, the similar reactions of Kühner and Krause reflected not only confidence but racial idealism as well.[30]

Krause and Kühner could stand for at least two dozen other letter writers of various educational levels who commented positively on the Republican program of union *and* freedom. Half of them also showed clear sympathies for the black race, its military role, or above all the granting of equal civil rights. Included were several who were merchants' clerks or had attended a *Gymnasium*, but the majority had not gone beyond an elementary education.[31]

At least one letter writer converted as a result of the war from a zealous Douglas Democrat to an enthusiastic campaigner for union and freedom.

[A]s you know, there exists in our southern realms slavery in all its horrors, but now in order to suppress and exterminate it, the northern men last fall elected a president who advocated anti-slavery policies, and the revolution was there . . . . I enlisted on the first day, namely 4 months back, and am now a sergeant.

. . . Teach my nephews to hate tyrants, to abhor oppressors, and teach them to value and to love freedom, true freedom, because our Germany too must someday be free. . . . O truly there lives a God, and God does not desire servants but free men.[32]

---

29 Ludwig Kühner was born in 1834 in Schefflenz, Baden, emigrated following his brother around 1852, married in 1854, and had three children by the time he enlisted Nov. 1861 in the 15th Ohio Lt. Artillery, serving for three years. The 1870 Census of Geauga Co., Ohio, lists him as a farmer worth $4,800. It is worth noting that he was living in the heavily Republican Western Reserve district of Ohio, had been married by an Anglo-American pastor Collins, and had apparently anglicized his name to Lewis Keener. His spelling and grammar suggest limited education.

30 See Krause's letter of Feb. 1 and Kühner's letter of Feb. 24, 1865, in BABS.

31 Besides Zimmermann, Gerstein, Kühner, Krause, and Weitz cited above and Martens, Jürgens, and John and George Bauer cited below, the BABS collection includes the following examples of Germans in the north expressing Republican sympathies: August Horstmann, Paul Petasch, Conrad Weinrich, Wilhelm Barthel, Louis Miller, John Penzler, Adolph Frick, Heinrich Mattinger, Otto Albrecht, Friedrich Booch, Emile Dupré, Julius and Karl Wesslau, as well as Cornelius Knoebel and his two brothers, whose letters were published in Paul Priesner, *Die Auswanderung aus Ehrenstetten und Kirchhofen nach Nordamerika* (n.p., 1981), 220-38.

32 Frederick Martens was born in 1838, the son of a peasant farmer in Heide, Schleswig-Holstein, which was then Danish. Besides elementary school, he had received some private instruction from the local Deacon, and though his spelling is imperfect he cites Schiller and Heine. The 1870 census shows him as a sign painter worth $4,500; he was married in 1864 by a Lutheran pastor. He enlisted on Apr. 20, 1861, rising to 2nd Lieutenant before resigning because of illness in Aug. 1863.

As this citation shows, religion did not always serve as a prop for the existing social order, and aspirations for America and Germany were intimately connected.

Another good example is John Bauer, a Badenese peasant's son with some secondary education who emigrated in 1854 and became a Missouri farmer and a born-again Methodist. From 1856 to 1877 he consistently stood up for the Republican Party and its program, including emancipation and political rights for blacks. In a letter of 1860 he draws several explicit contrasts to Germany:

> When I speak of a hot campaign, however, you mustn't imagine that there are soldiers everywhere and that anyone who speaks out is grabbed by the hair or the coat. . . . I also will be taking part in this campaign & this for the first time. . . . I thought, by the way, that if I were in danger of being stuck as a soldier in Germany, I'd rather be in America, even if it is not the best just now.

Because of a bad eye, he did not serve in the Civil War, but his brother George, already a husband and father, volunteered and died for the Union. Idealism was not always put into practice, but nearly two-thirds of this group of "verbal Unionists" backed word with deed and served in the Union Army, a militia or home guard unit.[33]

As with the "idealists," so also with the "passives," one finds parallels among people of quite different social and educational levels. Robert Rossi, who had completed secondary education in Schwerin, called himself a merchant on his arrival in 1858, and was engaged in commerce after immigrating, served in a New York German regiment. His letters hardly mention war aims, but he complains about Union leadership and the removal of German and Democratic generals, and in the 1864 election he also favored the Democrats.[34] Totally different from Rossi in social status, but just as unconcerned with any higher purpose of the war, was the aptly named Christian Lenz, a pious but struggling cooper from Indiana. Two of his letters, written more in Hessian dialect than in High German, tell nothing more of the war than conscription, hardships, and

---

33 Bauer's letters are published in Kamphoefner et al., eds., *News from the Land of Freedom*, 149–81, quotations from 158–9, 161–2. Of the Union supporters listed in note 31, Gerstein, Kühner, Krause, Zimmermann, Horstmann, Martens, Bauer, Petasch, Weinrich, Miller, Penzler, Frick, Mattinger, and Cornelius Knoebel served at least in a Union militia.

34 Robert Rossi was born in 1831 in the city of Schwerin, Mecklenburg, the son of a physician. He received a good secondary education and trained as a merchant in Hamburg and, after emigrating in 1858, continued in the same line of work before enlisting in the 8th New York Artillery in the Fall of 1861. His political statements are contained in a letter of June 19, 1863. Excerpts from other letters are published in Helbich, ed., *Amerika ist ein freies Land*, 172–5, 183.

battles – about slavery, or anything on origins of the war, not a word.[35] One could add four or five other Germans in the North to this list, mostly farmers or artisans, whose letters about the war report only of its economic impact and conditions of draft eligibility.[36]

This passive, uninvolved attitude was particularly apparent among Germans in California during the Gold Rush. The main thing that six letter writers from there had to report was that the war was far away, and as one put it, "here ... everyone just wants to make money, that is everybody's ambition."[37] The most astute analysis of the war, showing much in common with Levine's plebeian radicals, came from an illiterate miner from the Saarland.[38]

To be sure, there were among northern writers a couple of voices that expressed thoroughly racist viewpoints. For example, an Illinois wagonmaker recently arrived from Hesse quoted a piece of doggerel obviously taken from the 1864 campaign and complained that "in order to uplift the Negro/they plunge us in slavery" and wished victory to Lincoln's opponent. Even among Union volunteers there were isolated sentiments like those of a peasant's son from Württemberg serving in the Michigan cavalry, who seemed to be more indignant at the opponents of slavery than at the rebels: "as soon as we're done here we'll come north well armed and drive the *Blackleg* abolitionists to the devil along with their niggers."[39] None of the better-educated Germans – regardless of political persuasion – left any similarly racist remarks, although the reference to the "mark of Cain" by the Catholic coal miner cited above shows similar tendencies. But these three citations were the only ones among about sixty writers, the majority with no more than elementary education, who expressed outright hostility to the black race. Disparaging remarks against the Irish were more common, even from some Catholics.

---

35 The Lenz letters are published in Kamphoefner et al., eds., *News from the Land of Freedom*, 122–48.
36 See the letters of John Walz, Ihnke Kleihauer, and Christian Monn, and the ambiguous cases of the Kessel and Ruckles family and David Böpple. A typical example is also the Klinger family in Kamphoefner et al., eds., *News from the Land of Freedom*, 532–68.
37 George Heubach, a miller's son from Thuringia, emigrated in 1849, possibly for political reasons, and came to California in 1852. He comments favorably on Germans in the Union army and also shows sympathy for Polish freedom. The 1870 census of Nodaway Co., Mo., shows him as a miller worth $12,000. Compare the apolitical letters of Hermann Krooss, Sophia and Fritz Meinecke, A. I. Lafontaine, and August Strohsahl, the latter of whom enlisted, but only for economic reasons.
38 See the Peter Klein letters in Kamphoefner et al., eds., *News from the Land of Freedom*, 402.
39 First citation from Christian Boensel, Jan. 29, 1865, also published in Helbich, ed., *Amerika ist ein freies Land*, 158; second from Friedrich Schmalzried, July 11, 1862. The latter had been a propertyless farmhand before enlisting.

Overall, a slight majority of the letter writers supported the Republican program of both union and freedom; the rest were divided among conservative unionists or the uninvolved. There were no blatant defenders of slavery or proponents of southern independence among these German letter writers in northern or border states.

But the unionist and emancipationist sentiments of Germans in the north would count for little if it turned out that they were merely conforming to their surroundings, and that Germans in the south took a totally different position. Because communication with the homeland was virtually cut off by the Union blockade, most surviving correspondence from German men in the Confederacy is with wives in America, with whom they had no doubt discussed beforehand the issues involved in enlisting, being drafted, or fleeing conscription. In the little evidence we have, often between the lines, such writers seldom expressed approval of Confederate war aims, even when coercion or opportunism led them to serve under the Stars and Bars. Just as German letter writers in the North showed only support of the Union cause or indifference, those in the South showed only opposition to the Confederate cause or indifference. The one writer who comes closest to being a Confederate supporter, a captain in the Rebel army, hints that he would not have enlisted had he expected to gain exemption through his postmaster's job. The men in his overwhelmingly German company were even less enthusiastic about the Confederate cause, while his home county was so "unpatriotic" that it was put under martial law. But active, as opposed to passive resistance (especially involvement in the attempted escape via Mexico that led to the Nueces Massacre), was largely restricted to persons of bourgeois origins, especially those with Forty-Eighter connections.[40]

One individual who did serve reluctantly in the Rebel army seemed pleased with the outcome of the war. In 1866 he wrote his brother-in-law that "the existence of the United States stands more firmly than ever before, the stumbling block of slavery is cleared out of the way," an opinion that most of his German neighbors shared: "No element of the population rejoiced more about peace than the Germans, since they never had any interest in the cause anyhow."[41] This view is further bolstered by

---

40 For examples of reluctant Confederates, see the letters of Capt. Robert Voigt to his wife, Oct. 21, 1862, and Feb. 10, 1863. Regarding bourgeois refugees from Texas, see the letters of Dr. Hermann Nagel and the account of his son Charles Nagel, *A Boy's Civil War Story* (Philadelphia, 1935). On the Nueces Massacre, see the letters of Ernst Cramer and Ferdinand Simon (both merchants before the war).

41 Louis Lehmann was born in 1824 in Havelberg, Brandenberg, where he took his *Abitur* and emigrated to Texas with his parents and siblings in 1849. By 1860 he was a farmer worth $3,400

the high levels of German support for the Republican Party in post-Civil War Texas.[42]

No doubt some of the humanitarian principles of immigrants had been acquired in America. (Missouri Germans, where the press was overwhelmingly Republican, were especially strong and radical Unionists, whereas those in Michigan, where the German Republican press was weak, showed much more racist inclination.) But an important strain of republican egalitarianism had also been brought along from Germany; immigrants in Texas were certainly exposed to a very different system of American values than those settling in the North.

There were several other ideological litmus tests that emerge from these letters. Not surprisingly, French intervention in Mexico earned Maximilian the unanimous opprobrium of the four writers who commented upon it.[43] At stake was one of the principles of both American and European republicanism, that of national self-determination. However, this may have been clouded and overlaid by other motives: German nationalist rivalries with France and Austria, and anti-Catholicism. But the fact that two of the four critics were Catholic suggests that republican principles were paramount. An assertive American self-confidence is also unmistakable – none of the writers had the least doubt that the European meddlers in Mexico would be eaten up for breakfast should it come to a showdown.

One case where the principle of self-determination was unmixed with German or American self-interest was the matter of independence for Poland. Five writers, four of them Protestant, commented on the Polish cause, one in 1846 in relation to Austria, and four others in the wake of 1863, all in sympathy with the Poles (their Catholicism notwithstanding). The prime target of criticism was of course Russia: "The polar bear should go to Poland and do justice to them first before he sets his paws upon American soil." But at least one correspondent offered the opinion that "Prussia must be taught a good lesson because she suppresses the freedom of Germany and also Poland."[44]

---

and was married with three children. He was one of the founders of a liberal Lutheran parish near Brenham in Washington Co., Tex. Citations from letter of Jan. 1866.

42 For more detail on the Texas German situation, see Walter D. Kamphoefner, "Texas Germans and Civil War Issues: The Evidence from Immigrant Letters," *German-Texan Heritage Society Journal* 9 (1991): 16–23; Donald G. Nieman, "Black Political Power and Criminal Justice: Washington Co., Texas, 1868–1884," *Journal of Southern History* 55 (1989): 391–420. Gillespie Co., perhaps the most heavily German in all Texas, voted Republican in every presidential election from Reconstruction through 1960.

43 The writers involved were Gerstein, Klausmeyer, Horstmann, and Pack.

44 Quotations from Pack, Oct. 12, 1863, and Heubach, July 1, 1863; the other persons commenting on Poland were Benecke, Köster, and Wesslau. For evidence of Polish sympathies and Russian antipathies in the 1848 Revolution, see Sperber, *Rhineland Radicals*, 268–9.

Two other elements of a liberal critique of Germany that are pervasive in the correspondence are the issues of censorship and Prussian military service. A couple of writers went so far as to suggest that German-Americans, because of their free press, were better informed about what was going on in Germany than the folks back home. One otherwise rather apolitical artisan wrote from Michigan in 1854, "I believe that we find out everything much quicker and in more detail than you do, for they speak very freely in our newspapers, we find out a lot of things about Germany that aren't even mentioned over there."[45]

Prussian conscription and the large standing army were perhaps the most universally condemned features of the German state. A number of writers whose clandestine emigration was probably designed to avoid military service later volunteered for the Union Army; other Union soldiers wrote brothers back home advising them to emigrate before they became draftees. Even a devoutly Lutheran blacksmith in Minnesota, who had escaped the Union draft because of his recent arrival, saw an important contrast between German and American military service in an 1867 letter:

Above all I regret the condition of the German population when they fight about crown and dominion and shed blood . . . and for what? That, they are hardly in the position to say themselves, and when peace comes it is still no peace and not the peace that our God has given us in order to enjoy, and then the poor man with all his labor and toil can never get ahead. . . . Even if it did come to bloodshed here we have something for it, a hope and prospect of the enjoyment of freedom.[46]

Albert Krause, who had fled the Prussian draft only to enlist for the Union, was if anything more adamant in his 1866 assessment:

Things look very warlike with you over there now, and I'm really glad that I don't need to wash my hands in brothers' blood – It's really horrible how far the all-discerning governments have let things come! I have made it through my war time here, and I am proud of it, because I know for what, I know that I have fought for freedom.

Sometimes it is difficult to tell where idealism shades into self-interest, and liberal republicanism into German nationalism. One wonders to what extent the support for American union was related to the frustration with German disunion, which immigrants often associated with the disrespect they experienced in America. Only one letter writer, a Protestant from

---

45 Letter of Christian Mann, July 17, 1854; Gerstein made a very similar statement in a letter of Jan. 1, 1861. See also the 1864 letter of August Horstmann.
46 Letter of Heinrich Jürgens, Mar. 15, 1867.

Baden, draws a direct connection in an 1867 letter: "I'm happy that the war in Germany turned out so well and that it's almost all united, I hope that Baden, Württemberg, and Bavaria will also still join Prussia, they pick up a lot from America in their lawmaking." Even more surprising is the fact that two south German Catholics expressed quite similar sentiments. John Dieden wrote early in the Civil War:

[A] Prussian bread is rather hard, but when the issue is turning Germany into a *Reich* and giving it power, honor, and strength, and it isn't otherwise possible without Prussia as the head, then I would nevertheless rather subject myself to the spiked helmet [*Pickelhaube*] than be a servant of Napoleon III.

For Treutlein in 1869, Austrian opposition to German unity weighed heavier than its Catholicism or Prussia's reactionary tendencies:

If only the Germans would swear off that miserable and petty particularism, which brings a contemptuous smirk from every foreign observer. . . . When *all* of Germany is subsumed in Prussia and Prussia has become Germany, then the junkerdom will be in the minority and the people will give themselves their rights. . . . I'm not speaking up for Prussia as it now is, but how it, through the cooperation of all Germans, will become or at least should become.

Surprisingly enough, the greatest reservations against Prussia were expressed by a pious Protestant from Baden, Bauer. He was also practically the only writer to temper his jubilation at German unification in 1871 with admonitions against Prussian hubris. In contrast, various writers who were otherwise totally apolitical, even during the Civil War, offered congratulatory words at the events of 1870–1.[47]

III

What is the overall picture of political consciousness that emerges from the letters of German-Americans? First, a clear linkage can be seen between republican idealism on both sides of the Atlantic. Its core values were popular sovereignty, freedom of thought and expression, and an egalitarian belief in universal human dignity, extending also to the black race. Slavery was opposed less on economic grounds than because it was seen as incompatible with a true republic – the one glaring flaw of America up to that point. These values were present to some extent already before emigration, but they were undoubtedly intensified in the New World, where an unfettered press was dominated by political refu-

---

47 Kamphoefner et al., eds., *News from the Land of Freedom,* 169; cf. 141–2, 430, 585–6.

gees.⁴⁸ Moreover, republican idealism (with a small or capital "r"), also as it applied to the race question, was by no means restricted to liberal freethinkers or Protestant bourgeoisie, although it was understandably strongest there. Common farmers, artisans, and the small strata of industrial workers, especially those who were Protestant, often expressed sympathies for such ideas. Freethinkers of a Forty-Eighter background aroused the most indignation among the less educated Catholics; such Catholics, in turn, were the chief targets of the Forty-Eighters. But bourgeois Catholics proved to be quite receptive to the ideology of progress which the Republican Party represented. Moreover, the struggle for freedom in America was perceived by many German-Americans at various levels of society to be closely related to the ideals of 1848 and aspirations for a democratic Europe, corroborating Lincoln's characterization of the American republic as "the last best hope of earth."⁴⁹

---

48 Already during the 1848 Revolution, the United States was often pointed out as a positive counterexample. Sperber, *Rhineland Radicals*, 267.

49 Quotation from Annual Message to Congress, Dec. 1, 1862, in Andrew Delbanco, ed., *The Portable Abraham Lincoln* (New York, 1992), 270. Similar sentiments were expressed more often by Lincoln, for example in his *Gettysburg Address* (p. 295), and in his reply to an address of the International Workingmen's Association, stating that "the United States regard their cause in the present conflict with slavery-maintaining insurgents as the cause of human nature" (Karl Marx and Frederick Engels, *The Civil War in the United States* [New York, 1961], 283).

5

Different, But Not Out of This World
German Images of the United States Between Two Wars, 1871–1914

WOLFGANG HELBICH

In 1858 a young man in the Saarbrücken area wrote to his brother who worked in Pennsylvania as a coal miner:

Dear Peter, I must let you know that we were firmly decided to join you, but then there was very bad news from America everywhere, that everything had stopped and there was no work, me and my wife still want to go to America but you must write telling me exactly if we are to join you, and how it is now.[1]

This quotation from a letter to a German emigrant in the United States and many similar ones reveal two points in our context. Whereas it is plausible to assume that a fair number of Germans had no image of America at all, since they either had no chance to learn about it or simply did not care, the letter writer quoted must have had such an image. But he and many others like him apparently felt that it was so vague or incomplete or contradictory that a truly vital decision could not be based on it. The missing keystone was the personal opinion of a relative who lived in America.

One may also infer that an image had an entirely different weight and quality for people seriously considering emigration from that of their contemporaries who did not. For the former, it was an existential proposition and the basis for a crucial decision; for the latter, it may have held

---

1 "Lieber Peter, ich muss dier auch zu wissen thun dass wir fass gesonnen waren für zu dir zu kommen, aber das hörten man überall sehr Schlechte Nachrichten, aus Amerika, dass alles still Gingen thät und wäre kein verdienst, vorfanden, Ich und meine Frau wier sind noch immer gesonnen nach Amerika zu kommen aber Du must mir eine genauen nachricht schreiben ob wir nachkommen, wie es jetzt zufällig ist" (unsigned letter fragment from a brother of Peter Büch to the latter, Güchenbach/Saar to Pottsville, Pa., about April 1858. Saarbrücken/Klein series, Bochumer Auswandererbriefsammlung [hereafter abbreviated as BABS]).

some intellectual attraction, or entertainment value, or at most some enticement to social, political, or commercial action, but constituted neither a powerful magnet nor a potential threat to their previous and future existence. Whereas emigrants' images of the United States is addressed here, more attention is paid to the less existential images of people who did not intend to emigrate.

Images – whether of an individual, a group, an institution, or a nation – have long been the object of study by several disciplines: history, literature, social sciences, and psychology. Even a grotesquely oversized footnote could not hold the references to all the books and articles published on various aspects of the "German image of the United States" for our period, but a few examples might be in order. In history, three dissertations seem fairly typical with regard to topic and scope,[2] whereas in literature, another dissertation, a sixty-three column encyclopedia article and two massive collections of articles can serve as examples.[3]

Virtually all of those authors define the term "image" in a distinctly or at least slightly different way. I shall steer clear of any comment on the validity of different definitions, and this goes even more decidedly for the terminological debate having been carried on without interruption ever since the publication of Walter Lippmann's classic.[4] But I wish to explain briefly why I use the term and which meaning I attribute to it.

1. Though generalizations or abstractions may be legitimate, an image as a realistic concept can be held only by individuals.
2. Yet there were not only eight or eighteen million individual images of America in late nineteenth-century Germany, but a virtually unlimited number. From year to year, possibly day to day, at least whenever a new item is incorporated into the image or an older one dropped from it, it changed somewhat. It may also have been affected by a specific mood at a specific moment.

---

2 Gertrud Deicke, "Das Amerikabild der deutschen öffentlichen Meinung von 1898–1914," Ph.D. diss., University of Hamburg, 1956; Notker Hammerstein, "Deutschland und die Vereinigten Staaten von Amerika im Spiegel der führenden politischen Presse Deutschlands 1898–1906," Ph.D. diss., Johann von Goethe University, Frankfurt/Main, 1956; Ursula Schottelius, "Das Amerikabild der deutschen Regierung in der Ära Bülow 1897–1906," Ph.D. diss., University of Hamburg, 1956.
3 Samuel Schroeder, "Amerika in der deutschen Dichtung von 1850 bis 1890," Ph.D. diss., University of Heidelberg, 1934; Harold Jantz, "Amerika im deutschen Dichten und Denken," in W. Stammler, ed., *Deutsche Philologie im Aufriss*, vol. 3 (Berlin, 1962); Sigrid Bauschinger, Horst Denkler, and Wilfried Malsch, eds., *Amerika in der deutschen Literatur: Neue Welt – Nordamerika – USA* (Stuttgart, 1975); Alexander Ritter, ed., *Deutschlands literarisches Amerikabild: Neuere Forschungen zur Amerikarezeption der deutschen Literatur*, Germanistische Texte und Studien, vol. 4 (Hildesheim, 1977).
4 Walter Lippmann, *Public Opinion* (New York, 1922).

3. An individual image is not simply the sum of the bits of information made available. Whatever information is conveyed has to pass the test of plausibility, and the degree of acceptance depends very much on the trustworthiness of the conveyor. Moreover, which data are incorporated into an image depends not only on the individual's level of education and generally on his or her type of personality, but also on specific social circumstances
4. I use "image" rather than the popular term "stereotype," since the latter would be too close to "cliché" or "prejudice," both clearly negative by denotation or connotation. My "image" is meant to be decidedly free from any value judgment and also from any notion of correct or incorrect. I do use *image*, however, rather than "the whole of the relevant information available," since while I mean precisely that, I also attempt to include the irrational element beside the rational, to admit the affective angle, or in short, include both what is *known* and what is *felt* about America.
5. I prefer "image" to "perception" for largely subjective reasons. While there appears to be little difference in denotation, the connotations are such as to render "image" more appropriate for my purposes. "Perception" to me evokes more strongly the process rather than the result, more a purely rational basis than one that is also voluntaristic and emotional, and more a part than the whole of the panoramic image.

From the wide spectrum of groups and media that might hold images of the United States, I have selected a few segments, mainly on the basis of the availability of sources. On the following pages, I present (1) some findings on the "images" of German literature, (2) emigrant guides, (3) more general books describing the United States, (4) the press, (5) school textbooks, and (6) prospective or actual emigrants to America.

I

German literature's image of the United States has been studied more thoroughly than any other medium or group in our context. In fact, among the disciplines involved in "imagery," it is only philology or literary history that has elevated such endeavors to the rank of a subdiscipline with a label of its own. "Imagology" or, slightly more narrow, "comparative imagology" are terms commonly used at least in German-language literary scholarship, and there is even the luxury of a second technical term for more or less the same thing: iconics.[5]

---

5 Hugo Dyserinek, *Komparatistik: Eine Einführung* (Bonn, 1977), 5, 125–33; Peter J. Brenner, *Reisen in die Neue Welt: Die Erfahrung Nordamerikas in deutschen Reise- und Auswandererberichten des 19. Jahrhunderts* (Tübingen, 1991), 2; Kenneth E. Boulding, *The Image* (Ann Arbor, Mich., 1961), 148–9.

But for all the efforts devoted to theorizing about this line of research (which includes the massive controversy around René Wellek's 1958 anathema)[6] and to interpreting novels, poems, or plays, the result is a crazy quilt in constant motion. By the beginning of the last third of the nineteenth century, the colors had lost some of their shrillness, the changes some of their violence. Spectacular conversions like Lenau's or Heine's from praise to disdain as well as the juxtaposition of extremes like Willkomm's *Europamüde* and Kürnberger's *Amerika-Müde*[7] belong to the earlier period, and the validity of the observation that America served as "a screen for the projection of wishful thinking and nightmares,"[8] strikingly obvious into the 1860s, recedes somewhat toward the end of the century. The approach becomes more subdued, more sophisticated, and frequently the theme of America is more marginal.[9]

Of course, there was also some continuity, like the numerous books published before 1870 that kept spawning new editions. One example that also illustrates the variety of literature dealing with America is a 144-page book "for children and people who like children" that was first published in 1837.[10] It tells the story of the shortsighted emigration of a cabinet-maker's family, their exciting adventures with Indians, abductions and wild nature in the American West, and their well-advised return home – emigration had been a big mistake. The same text appeared in 1897 (14th edition) and in 1906 (15th edition), and only in 1907 was a *revised* edition published.[11]

---

6 At the Second Congress of the International Comparative Literature Association in Chapel Hill, N. C., Welleck asked: "It may be all very well to hear what conceptions Frenchmen had about Germany or about England – but is such a study still literary scholarship?" He provides clear answers in saying that it is "national psychology, sociology," instead, and by warning of "dissolving literary scholarship into social psychology and cultural history" (quoted in Peter Boerner, "Das Bild vom anderen Land als Gegenstand literarischer Forschung," in Ritter, ed., *Deutschlands literarisches Amerikabild*, 28–36, quotation on 29).

7 Ernst Willkomm, *Die Europamüden: Modernes Lebensbild* (Leipzig, 1838); Ferdinand Kürnberger, *Der Amerika-Müde: Amerikanisches Kulturbild* (Frankfurt/Main, 1855).

8 Reinhold Wagnleitner in a paper presented at the annual meeting of the Organization of American Historians in Chicago, Apr. 1992: "The Problem of America as an Artifact of European Expansion," p. 2 of the manuscript he kindly sent me.

9 On the works of Lenau and Heine, Willkomm and Kürnberger, see also Hans-Jürgen Grabbe's chapter in this book, "Weary of Germany – Weary of America." While there is some slight overlapping here and on his concluding pages between his paper and mine, they differ both in the periods and the groups examined. Grabbe deals with the nineteenth century as a whole, with particular emphasis on the first half, and he concentrates on "members of the intellectual and political elites."

10 Gustav Nieritz, *Die Auswanderer: Eine Erzählung für Kinder und Kinderfreunde* (Berlin, 1837).

11 Data on editions from: *Gesamtverzeichnis des deutschsprachigen Schrifttums 1700–1910*, vol. 103 (Munich, 1984), 170.

American themes were touched upon by many of the serious German novelists of our period – and some not all that serious. For Herman Grimm, the United States served as a medium for his criticism of German conditions in the sense of his "liberaldemokratischer Amerikakult," with antitheses like "dreamer" versus "man of action," or "bound" versus "free."[12] Fontane held no firm ideological position pro or con, but for all his admiration for the vitality of the New World, he clearly preferred German culture to American lack of same, sensitivity and warm feeling to American coldness and aloofness.[13] Gustav Freytag set his *Heimath* myth against American modernism.[14] Liliencron appreciated American liberty, but deplored the dominant materialism and greed.[15] Gerhart Hauptmann's antithesis seems to be materialism versus culture, Möllhausen's, on the other hand, the destruction of the Indians versus railroads and factories, and Spielhagen's liberty versus repression.[16]

Thomas Mann, in *Königliche Hoheit* (1909), may be interpreted as claiming that the better sort in Europe were even more materialistic than their opposite numbers in America,[17] thus standing a cliché on its head, while Gottfried Keller strikes an uneasy and problematic balance between unfree, narrow bourgeois society, decadence, and an idyllic way of life on the one hand, liberty and materialism on the other.[18] For Wilhelm Raabe, it is authoritarian German society with, on the other hand, a quiet bourgeois life and reliable happiness, versus liberty, adventure, modernity, and heartless rushing about (*herzloses Getümmel*).[19]

Whether one tries to distill a collective image of the brief sketches above or establish five or six different ones – it is quite clear that all of the

---

12 Helmut Kreuzer, "Herman Grimms 'Unüberwindliche Mächte'. Deutschland und die Vereinigten Staaten in einem Adelsroman des bürgerlichen Realismus," in Bauschinger, Denkler, and Malsch, eds., *Amerika in der deutschen Literatur*, 205–217.
13 Manfred E. Keune, "Das Amerikabild in Theodor Fontanes Romanwerk," in Ritter, ed., *Deutschlands literarisches Amerikabild*, 338–62.
14 Ibid., 342.
15 Ernst L. Loewenberg, "Liliencron und Amerika," in Ritter, ed., *Deutschlands literarisches Amerikabild*, 363–71.
16 Siegfried H. Muller, "Gerhart Hauptmann's Relation to American Literature and His Concept of America," in Ritter, ed., *Deutschlands literarisches Amerikabild*, 372–8; Samuel Schroeder, "Amerika in der deutschen Dichtung von 1850 bis 1890," Ph.D. diss., University of Heidelberg, 1934, 52–6; 67–78.
17 Harald Jantz, "Amerika im deutschen Dichten und Denken," in Stammler, ed., *Deutsche Philologie im Aufriss*, 357.
18 Fritz Martini, "Auswanderer, Rückkehrer, Heimkehrer. Amerikaspiegelungen in Erzählungen von Keller, Raabe und Fontane," in Bauschinger, Denkler, and Malsch, eds., *Amerika in der deutschen Literatur*, 178–204, quotation on 181–8.
19 Ibid., 188–96.

characteristics attributed to America had originated earlier in the century, or putting it more bluntly: Nothing new was diagnosed or invented after 1870.

Yet whether it is one literary image of America or several, German literary historians have a hard time making a convincing case: Too many dubious or random decisions stand in the way. What counts? Books that appeared after 1870 only, or the continuing editions of earlier years as well?[20] Only "serious" literature or also mass audience writing? How about German-American authors? And did not translations of American (and British) authors influence the German reading public significantly? Should they be ignored? Are works dealing with German emigrants, return migrants, and immigrants, in a different category from those describing "genuine" Americans?

I have no intention to unravel these problems and complexities. But I wonder whether René Wellek was not right, after all, when he urged his colleagues not to get entangled in images.

II

Moving on from literary works and works of scholars about them to the books written expressly for potential and actual emigrants, one reaches more stable ground. Though here the problem of later editions of earlier works exists as well, it is attenuated by the fact that emigrant guides – books providing information for prospective emigrants[21] – seem to age, or become outdated, faster than fiction. Compared to the guides of the 1830–70 period,[22] the later ones show significant changes.[23]

---

20 Among the works Juliane Mikoletzky selected for her *Die deutsche Amerika-Auswanderung des 19. Jahrhunderts in der zeitgenössischen fiktionalen Literatur* (Tübingen, 1988), 58, are those the last edition of which appeared before 1871. Forty-nine of those were re-edited after 1870, and thirty-four still had new editions after 1900. Even of the fifteen of that group published before 1851, eleven were still being printed after 1870, and no less than eight even after 1900 (calculation on the basis of Mikoletzky's figures, 325–30).

21 Stephan W. Görisch, *Information zwischen Werbung und Warnung. Die Rolle der Amerikaliteratur in der Auswanderung des 18. und 19. Jahrhunderts*, Quellen und Forschungen zur hessischen Geschichte, no. 84 (Darmstadt, 1991), is not only the most comprehensive study of the genre, but also a remarkable work. Unfortunately for our purposes here, it is briefest on the content, especially those aspects that might serve to construct an image of America.

22 I have analyzed twenty-five of them, mainly with regard to their comments on American "national character," in "The 'Trained Observer' and the Common Immigrant: Differences in the Perception of 'the Americans,'" in Eberhard Reichmann, LaVern J. Rippley, and Jörg Nagler, eds., *Emigration and Settlement Patterns of German Communities in North America*, Max Kade German-American Center, vol. 8 (Indianapolis, Ind., 1995).

23 The selection of the following ten titles, on which this discussion is based, was initially mine: I ordered some thirty, from standard bibliographies, by interlibrary loan. But then the vagaries of a creaking system took over and made the final selection. These ten are what I received within

The most striking one, perhaps, concerns the attitude toward emigration as such. Hardly any of the later guides failed to assure the reader that it did not want to persuade anyone to leave his home country; guidance was provided only for those who had definitely decided to leave. Most of them now carried a list of categories of people who should *not* emigrate. The following may be the most restrictive of them, but it illustrates the trend: Don't emigrate if you can somehow make ends meet at home; if you're older than thirty; if you're not healthy and adventurous; if you cannot work, work, work.[24] The themes behind such admonitions are not entirely new, but the emphasis is: Things are not as easy as they were in the old days; America is anything but a paradise where one gets rich quickly; one has to work a lot harder than in Germany to get anywhere.

The guides have become far less philosophical and far more practical. There were not only hints about buying tickets and protecting luggage from damage, but the question of the relative earning and purchasing power was pursued with long lists of wages, prices, exchange rates and comparisons between Germany and the United States. Some of them did and some did not point out the crucial facts that could make all the wage tables virtually meaningless: business cycles, and especially unemployment. All emphasized the high appreciation of labor or rather the person who labors, no matter in what capacity.

Emigrant guides had next to nothing to say about American imperialism, the protective tariff, or the economic potential of the country. But much space was devoted to the purchase of land – qualities, prices, conditions, locations – even long after 1890, that census date frequently misunderstood as marking the end of agrarian immigration.

The old theme of the lack of culture, and the superiority of *Kultur* as well as the concomitant diatribes against Americanization have receded;

---

three months from placing the orders. One consolation is that availability on interlibrary loan might have some relation to availability or popularity at the time. J. J. Sturz, *Die Krisis der Deutschen Auswanderung und ihre Benützung für Jetzt und Immer* (Berlin, 1862); Albert Gloss, *Das Leben in den Vereinigten Staaten, zur Beurtheilung von Amerika's Gegenwart und Zukunft: Theilweise für Kapitalisten und Auswanderungslustige in Deutschland*, 2 vols. (Leipzig, 1864); Eduard Pelz, *Über Auswanderung* (Bremen, 1864); *Führer für deutsche Auswanderer nach den Vereinigten Staaten von Nord-Amerika* (Würzburg, 1877); Adolf Ott, *Handbuch für Auswanderer mit besonderer Berücksichtigung der Vereinigten Staaten von Amerika und Argentinien*, 2d ed. (Basel, 1881; Basel, 1882); Richard Lesser, *Über's Meer. Taschenbiliothek für deutsche Auswanderer*, vol. 1: *Wegweiser von der alten zur neuen Heimat* (Leipzig, 1883); F. Cuntz, ed., *Ratgeber für Auswanderer nach den Vereinigten Staaten von Nordamerika* (Bremen, 1889); Paul Kanzleiter, *Der Auswanderer und die Vereinigten Staaten von Nord-Amerika* (Nürtingen a. Neckar, 1895); Kurt Aram, *Mit 100 Mark nach Amerika. Ratschläge und Erlebnisse* (Berlin, 1912).

24 Aram, *Mit 100 Mark nach Amerika*, 7–9.

only one or two authors still hoped that German language and culture could be preserved; the others settled for adding some German ingredients to the melting pot. As one author had it, "there will come a time in the foreseeable future when the boring, joyless Anglo-American Sunday turns into one of an entirely German character."[25] But the dominant cliché of the earlier period was still going strong: Americans are dollar-oriented, materialistic, and cold; they lack the German's warmheartedness, idealism, and *Gemüt*. And on this point at least one can find agreement with many authors of fiction as well as those who wrote general descriptions of North America.

III

According to a standard bibliography,[26] ninety-one books containing accounts or descriptions or travel impressions of the United States appeared in Germany between 1870 and 1914. There were certainly more, but here we can refer to only a fraction of them, including some that were considered among the most important during the period and afterward, like the works of Goldberger, Münsterberg, and Sombart.[27] Of all of them, including the less prominent,[28] one may state that the attitudes common in the earlier nineteenth century, like breathless admiration, fascination with the exotic, abrasive condescension or even brusque dis-

---

25 "... und in absehbarer Zeit wird es dahin kommen, dass der langweilige, freudenleere, englisch-amerikanische Sonntag einen vollständig deutschen Karakter annimmt." Kanzleiter, *Der Auswanderer und die Vereinigten Staaten*, 146.
26 Henry A. Pochmann and Arthur R. Schultz, eds., *German-American Relations and German Culture in America: A Subject Bibliography, 1941–1980* (Millwood, N.Y., 1982).
27 Ludwig Max Goldberger, *Das Land der unbegrenzten Möglichkeiten: Beobachtungen über das Wirtschaftsleben der Vereinigten Staaten von Amerika* (Berlin, 1903). According to Georg Büchmann, *Geflügelte Worte* (Berlin, 1964), 651–3, Goldberger coined the term "land of unlimited possibilities" in 1902. Hugo Münsterberg, *Die Amerikaner*, 2 vols. (Berlin, 1904). Werner Sombart, *Warum gibt es in den Vereinigten Staaten keinen Sozialismus?* (Tübingen, 1906). Because the considerable number of calculating errors of the original have been corrected in the English translation, using the latter is advisable: *Why Is There No Socialism in the United States?*, ed. C. T. Husbands and trans. Patricia M. Hocking (London, 1976).
28 Gustav von Struve, *Diesseits und Jenseits des Oceans*, Zwanglose Hefte zur Vermittlung der Beziehungen zwischen Amerika und Deutschland, nos. 1–4 (Coburg, 1863); Philipp Schaff, *Der Bürgerkrieg und das christliche Leben in Nord-Amerika* (Berlin, 1866); Eduard Pelz, *Die Deutschen in den Vereinigten Staaten von Nordamerika: Eine Beleuchtung* (Gotha, 1870); Ernst von Hesse-Wartegg, *Mississippi-Fahrten: Reisebilder aus dem amerikanischen Süden, 1879–1880* (Leipzig, 1881); Arthur Salomonsohn, *Reise-Eindrücke aus Nordamerika* (Berlin, 1903); Hugo von Knebel Doeberitz, *Besteht für Deutschland eine amerikanische Gefahr?* (Berlin, 1904); Cd. M. von Unruh, *Amerika noch nicht am Ziele! Transgermanische Reisestudien* (Frankfurt/Main, 1904); Karl Lamprecht, *Americana: Reiseeindrücke, Beobachtungen, geschichtliche Gesamtansicht* (Freiburg/Breisgau, 1906); Wilhelm von Polenz, *Das Land der Zukunft oder Was können Deutschland und Amerika voneinander lernen?* (Berlin, 1909).

dain, have largely disappeared and made room for less extreme, more balanced, more "normal" accounts. Though many authors claim that most of their predecessors published wildly misleading accounts and that they are setting the record straight, most books of our period turn out to be reports from a country that has apparently come very close to being like a European one, with economic and social problems as well as promises, very few black-and-white issues, and a number of peculiar characteristics. Among the most popular themes are the economy, labor, race relations, immigration, German-Americans, women, equality, the spoils system and the political corruption associated with bossism and machines, and – under whatever guise or label – national character.

I would like to single out one book that deals with all of them (and many more, like schools, universities, science, literature, art, religion, etc.), but in a rather unique fashion. Münsterberg's work, for all its many flaws, misunderstandings and misinterpretations, is outstanding in that the author accords the central role in his work to the correction of what he considers previous mutual misconceptions. He tests, for example, the old cliché of the young land without any culture; since he does so from the vantage point of a Harvard professor, his conclusions are predictable – and convincing.

Since Münsterberg spent many years in the United States, since he did so in a position that facilitated accurate observation, and most of all since German-American understanding and friendship at all levels – government, scholarly, and popular – was his main concern, the result is a uniformly calculable work that offers few surprises in value judgments. Thus one can be certain that Münsterberg saw issues in a sympathetic light, that his interpretation was the friendliest possible (within the bounds of empirical facts and plausibility), and largely also that he had immersed himself in the mainstream of optimistic American intellectuals reflecting upon American society. With most other works, the tendencies, prejudices, or ultimate aims were rarely so obvious or rarely so consistent, and thus more difficult to identify and evaluate.

With regard to American industry and trade, the realization was growing, toward the end of the nineteenth century, that a formidable economic power as well as an actual and potential competitor was developing at a breath-taking pace. The abundance of raw materials, Yankee (and German-American!) engineering ingenuity, the marvels of American business acumen and several other factors added up to Goldberger's "Land der unbegrenzten Möglichkeiten," a term that for all its being misunderstood as meaning individual rags-to-riches careers was clearly referring to the opportunities and possibilities of industrial or business enterprises or whole industries, even of regions.[29] No one denied the economic success story; the range of reactions reached from awed admiration to grudging acknowledgment. Similarly, the debate, mainly during the first decade of the twentieth century, between those who warned of the "amerikanische Gefahr," and others who endeavored to prove that there was no such thing, had a lowest common denominator in the sense that if worst came to worst such threat to the German economy might exist, but one side claimed that it would never come to that and the other considered it very likely. While all of this was obviously highly speculative, matters became even more complicated by the reasonable assumption that the pessimists were in some way allied with those branches of German business that clamored for protection and the optimists with free-trade interests.

The condition and the future of labor in the United States were of particular interest to German authors in two respects: the comparative standard of living of American and German industrial workers (the central issue for Werner Sombart, but ignored by virtually no one), and the prospects of the struggle between capital and labor, where the dissimilarities with German conditions were emphasized.

The standard-of-living comparisons are not very sophisticated from a present-day perspective, and the results were not uniform. There was agreement that American workers were better off, especially skilled ones, but there was little accord on how much. And more often than not, the scourge of the American working man, rampant unemployment, was conveniently forgotten in the equations.

Reading what these German authors had to say about slavery, freedmen, and the future place of blacks in American society, one is rudely reminded of the fact that "Birth of a Nation" represented the views not of an unreconstructed rebel minority, but of much of educated America, North and South. Not all authors claim that it had been a terrible mistake to simply set the slaves free, though some actually do; but the sorrow about these hopelessly inferior creatures, the condescending scorn and biting ridicule, the latter usually of a very cheap sort, are well-nigh ubiquitous. Virtually all authors proclaim the existence of a "Negro problem," and for a few it is *the* most difficult item on the American agenda. Surprisingly enough in view of the important role of Indians in the earlier period, the earliest Americans are no longer an object of particular interest, and the

---

29 It appeared in print originally in *New Yorker Staatszeitung*, June 3, 1902, 1. The catchy term was then used as the title of Goldberger's book, *Das Land der unbegrenzten Möglichkeiten*.

indictment of white Americans for having destroyed the aboriginal nations has either become subdued, or changed into a justification or at least a declaration of inevitability. It cannot come as a surprise, then, that the unanimous attitude toward the "New Immigration" and immigration restriction is, at its very mildest, that of the Dillingham commission.

Whether Negroes, Indians, or South-East Europeans, the German authors seem to have fully absorbed the contemporary conventional wisdom. I would tend to grant them that what they could personally observe did not seem to clearly contradict those views. And I would also claim that it would be unfair to label them "racist." Racism, if the term is to have any meaning at all, clearly refers to heredity and genes; while some authors did not differentiate between inherited and acquired traits, others, like Münsterberg, stated quite clearly that "the quality of immigrants ... depends on the cultural condition of their home country."[30]

German-Americans and their culture, their politics, and their chances of survival as a distinct group drew considerable interest. With one or two exceptions who keep hoping against all reasonable evidence, the German observers admitted that language and culture will disappear within a generation or two, and comforted themselves with the expectation that many German ingredients will be fed into the melting pot. All of them repeated that German-Americans were failures in politics, a cliché that does not seem to survive serious inquiry if one looks closely.[31] Similarly, they claimed that German-American culture was just derivative and not original or innovative. Overall, there was more condescension than solidarity, if one excepts the respect paid to Carl Schurz and some other historical figures. There was full agreement that German-Americans were Americans first, not a pressure group for the old country, and definitely not a potential Fifth Column.

Women in America had been a fascinating topic for German writers ever since the early nineteenth century, and it kept its popularity far into the twentieth. Both the enthusiasm and the bitterness of the earlier period had disappeared. What had remained is facetiousness, envy, discomfort, or satisfaction about that famous privileged position of women in America.

---

30 "... die Qualität der Einwanderer, die von dem Kulturzustand ihres Heimatlandes abhängt" (Münsterberg, *Die Amerikaner*, 1:271).
31 For instance, in the case of mayors in American cities, Walter Kamphoefner, Wolfgang Helbich, and Ulrike Sommer, eds., *News from the Land of Freedom: German Immigrants Write Home* (Ithaca, N.Y., 1991), 20.

Equality, or the lack of deference on the part of social inferiors, or even the nonexistence of any social inferiority, had been a very prominent theme around the middle of the century.[32] After 1870 it had lost some of its prominence, and certainly most of its novelty. But it was still worth mentioning. From 1893 through 1909, Baedeker's various editions carried the advice to the tourist that he "should from the outset reconcile himself to the absence of deference or servility on the part of those he considers his social inferiors."[33]

The spoils system and political corruption, especially in the cities with their bosses and machines, had become a major target of German criticism around the middle of the century, and remained so through its end. Thereafter it receded, without disappearing entirely. It was always a worthwhile line of attack, since it could easily be contrasted with the honesty of German municipal government and especially the incorruptibility of German *Beamte*.

National character was not as weighty a topic as it used to be, but it was still there, and it is amazing to see how little it had changed. At best the extremes like money-orientation or deficiency of culture (or lack of *Gemüt*) had been toned down or set in a more favorable light, but the Yankee of 1830 is still clearly recognizable in the description of 1913.

What had been missing before 1870, except in speculations that usually paired Russia and America in a somewhat distant future, was present after 1890 and especially 1898, though not very prominently: the role of the United States as a world power, a military rival, an imperialistic state. These aspects were primarily seen as an entirely normal indication of increasing maturity and America's becoming more like Europe, to be taken seriously but not to be particularly worried about.

IV

With regard to images reflected by the press, we have to tread on very thin ice; though on one side of the pond it is thicker, even there it is full of cracks and bumps. German press reactions to foreign and foreign economic policy moves of the United States have been reliably if not

---

32 See, e.g., my "Letters from America: Documents of the Adjustment Process of German Immigrants in the United States," *Anglistik und Englischunterricht* 26 (1985): 205–6.
33 Quoted from C. Vann Woodward, *The Old World's New World* (New York, 1991), 111 and n. 15.

exhaustively recorded in three solid diplomatic history studies[34] and are given considerable attention in three German Ph.D. dissertations.[35] Unfortunately, these best-researched aspects are among the least exciting, because they are the most predictable. Almost unfailingly, the position of German papers from the far right to the left toward the Spanish-American War, the Venezuela crisis or the Monroe Doctrine were dictated by their specific aims and predilections: The papers of *Alldeutsche*, conservative and *Zentrum*-oriented papers tended to be anti-American, the *Freisinn* and Social Democratic ones pro-American in the foreign-policy field. Deicke's attempt to cover other areas as well – national character, culture, religion, education, labor, government, politics, economy – is spread so thin and raises so many more questions than it answers that the only conclusion to be drawn from it is that the image of the press *seems* to resemble somewhat that to be gleaned from the books on America. This is not too surprising owing to the fact that book authors also wrote in newspapers and that journalists dealing with America read the books written about it. But much significant work remains to be done with the national and some of the regional and local newspapers, e.g. in Southwest Germany with a population of whom a majority had relatives in the United States.

I would like to add two items that might be considered part of the "press" category, one article from the most low-brow or popular variety of the genre, a *Volkskalender*, and pictures of American scenes in German illustrated magazines. In one of the rare instances that *Volkskalender* deal with America during our period, the *Evangelischer Württembergischer Kalender für 1871* (Reutlingen) carried a story entitled "To America." Among German immigrants, the author found nothing but wickedness, murder, and adultery; Turners were insolent godless people; bloodthirsty Indians killed and tortured hundreds of people; America was "the gold land of liberty and profit" ("das Goldland der Freiheit und des Gewinns").[36] The message was a strong admonition not to emigrate.

---

34 Otto Graf zu Stolberg-Wernigerode, *Deutschland und die Vereinigten Staaten von Amerika im Zeitalter Bismarcks* (Berlin, 1933); Alfred Vagts, *Deutschland und die Vereinigten Staaten in der Weltpolitik* (London, 1935); Reinhard R. Doerries, *Washington – Berlin 1908/1917: Die Tätigkeit des Botschafters Johann Heinrich Graf von Bernstorff in Washington vor dem Eintritt der Vereinigten Staaten von Amerika in den Ersten Weltkrieg* (Düsseldorf, 1975).

35 Deicke, "Das Amerikabild der deutschen öffentlichen Meinung von 1898–1914"; Joseph Werner Gerhards, "Theodore Roosevelt im Urteil der deutschen öffentlichen Meinung (1901–1919)," Ph.D. diss., University of Mainz, 1962; Hammerstein, "Deutschland und die Vereinigten Staaten von Amerika."

36 *Evangelischer Württembergischer Kalender für 1871* (Reutlingen, 1871), 8–12, quotation on 12.

Illustrations of American life and scenery were to be found frequently in German mass media after the middle of the nineteenth century. Preferred subjects were "Indians, technology, the Wild West, violence, blacks, architecture, and women" and most of them illustrated "typically American traits" like a "pioneering spirit, mobility, speed, courage, efficiency, modernity."[37] The illustrations were highly unfavorable toward African Americans, Native Americans, and feminist Americans, whereas achievements like the *Merrimac*, Brooklyn Bridge, or skyscrapers are depicted as symbols of progress and the future in store for Europe as well. Apart from the above, the images of America to be found in the German press of our period offer a wide-open field for research.[38]

V

Textbooks used in schools reflect images held by their authors, or at least the images they want to convey to teachers and students, and probably also make a contribution, possibly a decisive one, to creating images in the minds of those who study them. There is no use looking at the elementary schools in our period, since practically all through the nineteenth century, and with little variation among the German states, they taught the three Rs, plus the capital R of Religion; exceptionally, there might be a smattering of *Vaterlands- und Naturkunde* (studies of patriotism and natural history) and drawing. In secondary schools, pupils might have one or two hours of geography and history per week. But less than 5 percent of Prussian children between six and fourteen attended secondary schools, as opposed to 94 percent in elementary ones. One may thus safely assume that most of the schools, at present certainly one of the most influential image makers with regard to foreign countries,

---

37 Hartwig Gebhardt, "Die Neue Welt für alle – Amerikabilder in den deutschen Illustrierten des 19. Jahrhunderts," in Peter Mesenhöller, ed., *Mundus Novus: Amerika oder die Entdeckung des Bekannten: Das Bild der Neuen Welt im Spiegel der Druckmedien vom 16. bis zum frühen 20. Jahrhundert* (Essen, 1992), 124–40, quotation on 124.

38 Similarly, despite the existence of such excellent studies as those by Stolberg-Wernigerode, Vagts, and Doerries as well as a considerable number of others, much remains to be done with regard to the images of America held by German foreign policy decision-makers in our period. A worthwhile analysis would involve reexamining a large part of the diplomatic correspondence and would particularly have to make use of the tools developed by the proponents of the cultural system approach to international history. Cf. Akira Iriye, "Culture and International History," in Michael J. Hogan and Thomas G. Paterson, eds., *Explaining the History of American Foreign Relations* (Cambridge, 1991), 214–25; Michael H. Hunt, *Ideology and U.S. Foreign Policy* (New Haven, Conn., 1987); Enrico Angelli and Craig Murphy, *America's Quest for Supremacy and the Third World: A Gramscian Analysis* (London, 1988).

made no significant contribution to the students' image of the United States.[39]

With regard to secondary school textbooks, a truly "scientific" approach would involve investigating which books were most widely used where, when, and how long; what changes were made over time, what the influence of government departments were, and the differences among various German states. That would mean a book-length study. What I can offer here are some tentative conclusions based on a sizeable collection of history and related textbooks accumulated over the past fifteen years at the University of Bochum. It includes two twentieth-century elementary school history textbooks,[40] but with regard to the United States the nineteenth-century situation of "no relevant instruction offered" had not changed: they contain not a word on America (though Hoffmann writes about Napoleon and France), and entirely ignore the emigration of five million Germans (though Kabisch treats social history extensively).

Out of the nineteen textbooks for secondary schools in the collection, nine did not even mention the United States, or German emigration to America.[41] Two of them dealt with emigration, but not with the United States,[42] four with the United States, but not emigration,[43] and finally four

---

39 Anita Mächler, "Aspekte der Volksschulpolitik in Preussen im 19. Jahrhundert," in Peter Baumgart, ed., *Bildungspolitik in Preussen zur Zeit des Kaiserreichs* (Stuttgart, 1980), 224–41, 227–9, 234–40. Hartmut Titze, *Die Politisierung der Erziehung* (Frankfurt/Main, 1973). Peter Lundgreen, *Sozialgeschichte der deutschen Schule im Überblick*, pt. 1: *1770–1918* (Göttingen, 1980), 91, 94.

40 C. Hoffmann, *Handbuch für den Geschichtsunterricht in preussischen Volksschulen* (Langensalza, 1903); Richard Kabisch, *Erziehender Geschichtsunterricht: Versuch einer preussisch-deutschen Staatsgeschichte für Volksschulen* (Göttingen, 1913).

41 Jakob Karl Andrae, *Grundriss der Geschichte für höhere Schulen*, pt. 2: *Deutsche Geschichte bis zur Gegenwart für Tertia und Untersekunda* (Leipzig, 1902); Karl Biedermann, *Deutsche Volks- und Kulturgeschichte für Schule und Haus* (Wiesbaden, 1891); Joseph Dahmen, L. Hoffmeyer, and W. Hering, *Quellenbuch für den Geschichtsunterricht im Seminar* (Breslau, 1908); L. Hoffmeyer and W. Hering, *Lehrbuch für den Geschichtsunterricht in Lehrerbildungsanstalten: Hilfsbuch für den Geschichtsunterricht in Präparandenanstalten* (Breslau, 1905); Karl Kauffmann, Johannes Berndt, and Walther Tomuschat, *Geschichtsbetrachtungen: Hilfsbuch für den Geschichtsunterricht insbesondere in Lehrerseminaren und für die Fortbildung des Lehrers* (Leipzig, 1909); David Müller, *Geschichte des deutschen Volkes in kurzgefasster übersichtlicher Darstellung für höhere Schulen und die Selbstbelehrung* (Berlin, 1894); Friedrich Neubauer, *Lehrbuch der Geschichte für höhere Lehranstalten*, pt. 1: *Lehrbuch der Geschichte für die mittleren Klassen* (Halle/Saale, 1900); Gustav Rusch, Alois Herdegen, and Franz Tiechl, *Elementare Staats- und Gesellschaftskunde auf kulturgeschichtlicher Grundlage: Ein Hilfsbuch für den geschichtlichen und bürgerkundlichen Unterricht* (Vienna, 1909).

42 C. Spielmann, *Der Geschichtsunterricht in ausgeführten Lektionen für die Hand des Lehrers*, pt. 3: *Preussen-Deutschland [Befreiungskrieg bis zum Anfang des 20. Jahrhunderts]* (Halle/Saale, 1902); Emil Wolff, *Grundriss der preussisch-deutschen sozialpolitischen und Volkswirtschaftsgeschichte von 1640–1900* (Berlin, 1904).

43 Jakob Karl Andrae, *Grundriss der Weltgeschichte für höhere Lehranstalten: Ausgabe für Real- und Bürgerschulen sowie Lehrerseminare* (Leipzig, 1892); Joseph Dahmen, *Leitfaden der Geschichte für Höhere Mädchenschulen und verwandte Anstalten*, pt. 3 (Leipzig, 1907); Anton Gindely, *Lehrbuch der All-*

with both.[44] Spielmann devoted a page to German emigration, stating that mass emigration could not stop overall growth. He continued with a remarkably sympathetic account which suggests that not only diseases, high food prices, unemployment, and the desire to get rich fast caused emigration after 1830, but also "the repression of freedom" (*Unterdrückung der Freiheit*).[45] For Wolff, Germany's "loss" or the fatherland's being deprived of the capital invested in the emigrants' upbringing and education as well as their labor was the salient message to be brought home, while the reasons for emigrating (workers' and peasants' striving to become self-employed) were hardly an afterthought.[46]

An entirely neutral stance toward emigration was taken by Hoffmeyer and Hering ("most of them endeavored to improve their economic situation"), and Neubauer, who simply stated that the US received most of Europe's and Germany's emigration.[47] Wolff noted nothing but the "loss" of 5.2 million, 1820–1900, and offered a fascinating balance sheet showing that only 68 percent of the German nation lived within the borders of the *Reich*; not quite eleven million were to be found in Switzerland, Belgium and the Netherlands, but fully eleven million in the United States. The loss from emigration to America, however, amounted to "about twenty million," counting the second and third generations.[48] Schanze and Schanze tried to have the best of both worlds. Claiming 20 million (out of 86) to be first and second-generation Germans and emphasizing their amazing contribution to the success of the country, they categorically stated that things had changed and unemployment was rampant, so that no one should emigrate any longer.[49]

Neubauer also included a sympathetic page on the American colonies and the Revolution, Wolff a neutral thirty lines on American government, Schanze and Schanze three pages on the contemporary United States, and Hoffmeyer and Hering brief remarks on colonial history, a

---

gemeinen Geschichte (Prague, 1865); F. Rossbach, *Hülfsbuch für den Unterricht in der deutschen Geschichte in den oberen Klassen höherer Mädchenschulen und in Lehrerinnen-Bildungsanstalten* (Berlin, 1895).

44 L. Hoffmeyer and W. Hering, *Lehrbuch für den Geschichtsunterricht in Lehrerbildungsanstalten: Hilfsbuch für den Geschichtsunterricht in Seminaren* (Breslau, 1905); Friedrich Neubauer, *Geschichtliches Lehrbuch für Lyzeen und höhere Mädchenschulen* (Halle/Saale, 1915); J. Schanze and W. Schanze, *Lesebuch für städtische und gewerbliche Fortbildungsschulen (sowie zum Gebrauche in Handelsschulen und kaufmännischen Fortbildungsschulen* (Wittenberg, 1905); Heinrich Wolf, *Angewandte Geschichte und Erziehung zu politischem Denken und Wollen* (Leipzig, 1911).

45 Spielmann, *Der Geschichtsunterricht in ausgeführten Lektionen*, 407.

46 Wolff, *Grundriss der preussisch-deutschen sozialpolitischen und Volkswirtschaftsgeschichte*, 179.

47 Hoffmeyer and Hering, *Lehrbuch für den Geschichtsunterricht in Lehrerbildungsanstalten*, 329; Neubauer, *Geschichtliches Lehrbuch für Lyzeen und höhere Mädchenschulen*, 95.

48 Wolf, *Angewandte Geschichte und Erziehung*, 181, 185.

49 Schanze and Schanze, *Lesebuch für städtische und gewerbliche Fortbildungsschulen*, 493–4.

page on the War of Independence, a slightly longer, very pro-Union account of the Civil War, and finally the statement that U.S. trade and industry had reached such heights that it "threatens the entire Old World with its competition."[50]

Finally, a few remarks might be added about the four authors who had nothing to say about the controversial topic of emigration, but at least a few words about the United States and its history. The fewest were offered by Dahmen, who devoted one page to the War of Independence – a "rebellion against British plans of taxation" – complete with references to Franklin and Washington. Similarly, Andrae has a rather friendly page on the *Freiheitskrieg* (war of independence) of the United States, also focusing on Franklin and Washington, and one strictly neutral page on the Civil War. A highly sophisticated and positive account of the American *Freiheitskrieg* was presented by Gindely, but there history ended for him. Rossbach not only repeated the Franklin-and-Washington-centered brief account of the War of Liberation, admiringly called "a great popular movement" (*grosse Volksbewegung*) with such major consequences for world history as the spreading of the idea of freedom. He noted that the United States became a maritime rival of Britain and added, without mentioning any tension or problems, that Germany's trade profited from the growth of the United States.[51]

The extreme scarcity of material on America has led me to go into considerable detail. The conclusion is simple: In the world as depicted by German history textbooks, the United States hardly existed, and if it did, it rarely appeared in a favorable light. Yet the few exceptions where a surprisingly liberal attitude prevailed show that there were a few cracks in the wall behind which America was hidden. One might go so far as to say that the tendency to simply ignore the United States was so strong that no authority even bothered to issue a directive on how it should be dealt with.

VI

At the beginning of this chapter, I claimed that the image of potential emigrants has a quality significantly different from those held by people

---

50 Neubauer, *Geschichtliches Lehrbuch für Lyzeen und höhere Mädchenschulen*, 95; Wolf, *Angewandte Geschichte und Erziehung*, 264–5; Schanze and Schanze, *Lesebuch für städtische und gewerbliche Fortbildungsschulen*, 490–3; Hoffmeyer and Hering, *Lehrbuch für den Geschichtsunterricht in Lehrerbildungsanstalten*, 329, 425.
51 Dahmen, *Leitfaden der Geschichte für Höhere Mädchenschulen*, 74–5; Andrae, *Grundriss der Geschichte für höhere Schulen*, 119, 167–8; Gindely, *Lehrbuch der Allgemeinen Geschichte*, 237–9; Rossbach, *Hülfsbuch für den Unterricht*, 545–7.

who would never seriously think of settling outside their country. Returning to this group now, I would like to add some remarks and then sketch some of the salient traits of such images.

Owing to the nature of the sources available to me – the Bochumer Auswandererbriefsammlung or BABS (Bochum Emigrant Letter Collection) contains westbound letters only in the order of two percent – but also because letters *from* America are so much richer in "image" content, I had to build a bridge between the eastbound letters and their recipients. I cannot prove, but I do claim that the latter's images of America did not differ widely from those conveyed by the letter writers. For one thing, even by the eve of World War I, there were few competing sources of information about the United States for the broad base of the educational pyramid; for most of this group, certainly no less than two thirds of the population, the letters written by their sons and sisters, uncles and good friends or neighbors contained far more news from the land of freedom than the occasional newspaper that found its way onto the kitchen table. But the qualitative aspect is even more important than the quantitative: Whereas the lower strata of society nurtured a healthy distrust of information emanating from the government and by extension of anything in print, they trusted the reports of their relatives very largely, if not absolutely. Close to five million German chain migrants in the nineteenth century attest to that.

With about 2.7 million German-born people living in the United States during the decade of the 1890s,[52] and some four million letters sent from America to Germany every year,[53] it would appear to be a very conservative estimate that an equal number of persons in Germany were direct recipients of letters from America over a five year span, while the number of people to whom the news was spread by village or family networks may have been twice or three times that number. If this sounds plausible – and in view of the statistical material we possess it can never be more than that – the conclusion is almost inevitable that those people in Germany who were in direct or indirect letter contact with emigrants in America not only had a more vital connection to their images of America but also were by far the largest single group that held any meaningful images of America.

---

52 1870: 1.691 million foreign-born, country of birth: Germany; 1880: 1.967 million; 1890: 2.785 million; 1900: 2.663 million; 1910: 2.311 million. *Foreign-Born Population (1850–1970): Historical Statistics of the United States, Colonial Times to 1970*, 2 vols. (Washington, D.C., 1975), 117, 118.

53 See my "The Letters They Sent Home: The Subjective Perspective of German Immigrants in the Nineteenth Century," *Yearbook of German-American Studies* 22 (1987): 1–20.

With such an abundance of weight attributed to the letters and their readers, was the content of the resulting images equally significant? Rather than basing the following conclusions on the whole of the relevant BABS material, I have confined myself to the sample represented by the Civil War through World War I letters printed in the two scholarly editions of BABS materials[54] in order to at least mitigate the major drawback of such source material: that the reader has to trust the author rather blindly except for an occasional quotation. By limiting our corpus to the printed letters, we should not lose too many insights but might gain in credibility.

Generally speaking, the basic character of the letters does not change compared with the pre-1870 ones; but a very different picture – and "image" – emerges. What remains the same is the basic factual accuracy and reliability against all temptations to exaggerate or to put oneself or America in a brighter light than is justified. So where is the change? The letters very distinctly reflect the fact that America had changed, or rather was changing at an accelerated rate.

Almost gone are the enthusiastic reports and the gloomy accounts, even the letters centered on the family that hardly take notice of society at large. Black-and-white has given way to different shades of grey, the "yes" and "no" to a whole variety of "yes, but." While there is no doubt that the general tendency of the sample letters' evaluation of the United States was positive, the number and weight of the caveats and liabilities is impressive. Of the twenty-nine items commented upon, places two (fourteen times) and three (twelve times) are held by "things are better than in Germany" or "we are better off than in the old country," and "one earns more money in the U.S.," respectively. But unemployment of the letter writer was mentioned seventeen times and thereby easily holds the top quantitative spot among comments on America.

As to rural immigrants, the advantages of cheap land, land appreciation, and machinery are praised nine times, but complaints about agricultural depression and the voicing of Populist criticism occurred almost as frequently (eight times). Apart from some of the themes just mentioned and the description of strikes (not always in a favorable light) as well as complaints about machinery destroying crafts, practically all the other

---

54 The whole or part of the Dumsch, Treschwig, Scheuermann, Matthies, and Gille-Mentges series in Wolfgang Helbich, *"Alle Menschen sind dort gleich . . ." Die deutsche Amerika-Auswanderung im 19. und 20. Jahrhundert* (Düsseldorf, 1988), as well as of the Lenz, Bauer, Löwen, Möller, Probstfeld, Witten, Dorgathen, Kirst, Dilger, Klinger, Winkelmeyer, and Wiebusch series in Kamphoefner, Helbich, and Sommer, eds., *News from the Land of Freedom*.

points written about sound strikingly familiar to someone acquainted with the letters of the middle of the century.[55] The following had been partly more prominent one or two generations earlier, but here they showed up again, in very similar wording and appreciation: America is a free country, with no certificates or exams; it is a free country politically; it is a free country with no conscription and few taxes; women are privileged; working hours are longer and work harder than in Germany; medical costs are high, political corruption is rampant; Germans are discriminated against, crime levels in the cities are high, and there is no social security.

Thus much had remained the same since the 1830s. The changes that had taken place are significant, however. Unemployment, the most prominent topic now, had rarely been mentioned before 1870. On the other hand, three characteristics at the very top of the agenda of earlier letters had retreated to back-bench positions: the handicap of not speaking English, good food ("meat three times a day"), and "materialism," frequently defined as money-grubbing without restraint, conscience, or culture. Among the most frequently mentioned and praised points of the earlier period, one had receded in importance, but still made a respectable showing: social equality.

As in 1835 or in 1863, the reporting of most emigrant letters, and the images of America thus conveyed or modified, would seem to justify the claim that prospective emigrants trusted them more than anything else, even though the letter writers were generally quite selective as to the aspects they described and simply omitted many that appeared important in most emigrant guides.[56] But the point is that the images produced by emigrant letters were functionally accurate, concentrating on precisely those points the recipient really wanted to know about.

The five groups or media I have commented on, plus the two I have hardly more than mentioned, certainly do not represent a complete list of items relevant for images of America. Songs, cartoons, paintings, children's books, scholarly books and journals, and popular magazines could

---

55 For texts, see the editions mentioned in notes 31 and 54 to this chapter. For analysis and interpretation, see Helbich, "Letters They Sent Home," 1–20, and "Stereotypen in Auswandererbriefen: Die USA im 19. Jahrhundert aus der Sicht deutscher Einwanderer," in Anselm Maler, ed., *Exotische Welt in populären Lektüren* (Tübingen, 1990), 63–80; "'Die Englischen': German Immigrants Describe Nineteenth-Century American Society," *Amerikastudien/ American Studies* 36 (1991): 515–30.

56 Cf. Helbich, "The 'Trained Observer' and the Common Immigrant," in Reichmann, Rippley, and Nagler, eds., *Emigration and Settlement Patterns of German Communities.*

be added – and certainly several others. While detailed studies could be fascinating and would certainly yield new and perhaps surprising insights, I believe they would not significantly alter the images of America I have tried to sketch here when raised to a high level of abstraction – or simplification:[57]

1. Most strikingly, America had become a real country, almost a "normal" one, though with many differences.
2. Of the two elements that go into images, information and projection, the former had gained more weight, though the latter held its own.
3. The images of mid-century were still present, though partly weakened. Only the extreme romantic and idealistic traits – majestic nature and noble savages – had almost disappeared.
4. The new elements – world power and imperialism, massive economic growth and competing trade, triumphant technology – were making their way into various images at very different speeds.
5. Generally, however, it is the persistence of older images and the slowness of change that stands out.
6. The old antithesis of German idealism, culture, depth, *Gemüt*, and *Gemütlichkeit* versus American utilitarianism, lack of culture, profit orientation, superficiality and coldness had become somewhat less stark, but had greatly gained in weight and credibility by the addition of technological marvels, skyscrapers, and the breath-taking progress of civilization on the American side of the scales.
7. Slowly, and only in books and parts of the press, a novel idea was becoming part of the image. Its presence in German media dates back further, but earlier it was only of minor importance: America as the land of the future, which has surpassed Europe and is showing the way to the Old World – for better or worse.

---

57 In the preceding text as well as in the following summary, I have confined myself to a factual account of images as they appear in the sources used. Trying to explain the processes by which such images were shaped in the different media and the reaons why images changed in the course of the nineteenth century would be an essay by itself, and a highly speculative one at that. These questions are too difficult and important to be dealt with in passing.

6

From Culture to Kultur

Changing American Perceptions of Imperial Germany, 1870–1914

JÖRG NAGLER

I

In January 1871, shortly before the proclamation of the Second Reich at Versailles, the American poet Charles Goethe Baylor dedicated a poem to Germany that illustrates the prevailing sentiment in the United States toward Germany during this time. "America to Germany" begins

All hail! O Bible Land/Grand 'mid the nations stand/by God's degree/For thru the cloud that lowers/Deep 'neath the blood that pours/We see their cause as ours/Dear Germany.¹

In the poem's four verses, Baylor celebrated German achievements and emphasized the communality of both nations. Indeed, the years following each nation's respective struggle and quest for nationhood – the Civil War in the case of the United States and the wars of unification in the case of Germany – witnessed the high point of German-American relations.²

Germany had fought for national unity against an imperial French aggressor, and it had been one of the few friends of the North during the American Civil War. German immigrants had participated, particularly in the Northern armies, in numbers disproportionate to their percentage of the total population, and in so doing had partially liberated themselves from the "foreign" stigma that American nativists attached to them before

1 Charles Goethe Baylor, "America to Germany," *Boston Daily Journal*, Jan. 1871, cited in Clara Eve Schieber, *The Transformation of American Sentiment Toward Germany, 1870–1914* (New York, 1923), 36.
2 For a comparative view of both wars, see Stig Förster and Jörg Nagler, eds., *On the Road to Total War: The American Civil War and the German Wars of Unification, 1861–1871* (New York, 1996).

the war. In 1871 most Americans considered Germany a world leader in cultural pursuits, a land of poets, musicians, writers, philosophers, and scholars.³

Not quite fifty years later, however, one heard the following devastating American comment on German culture:

> In the vicious guttural language of Kultur, the degree B.A. means Bachelor of Atrocities. Are you going to let the Prussian Python strike at your Alma Mater, as it struck at the University of Louvain? The Hohenzollern fang strikes at every element of decency and culture and taste that your college stands for.⁴

This excerpt from a Committee on Public Information poster distributed widely on the American home front during World War I sets the tone and emphasizes certain points raised in this chapter. The eminent role and function of *Kultur* in the anti-German propaganda struggle on the American home front during World War I suggests that it had prewar origins.⁵ Although "culture is the source of a people's reality . . . and the way people think and behave at very sophisticated levels is driven by culture," historiography has neglected the American prewar perception of Germany and its culture.⁶ An analysis of the cultural dimension, however, clarifies our understanding of the growing alienation of the two countries between 1870 and 1914.

Several factors no doubt contributed to the growing cultural antagonism between the United States and Germany that culminated in emotional outbursts on the American home front during World War I. One might point, for example, to the ways in which diplomatic and commer-

---

3 See Hans W. Gatzke, *Germany and the United States: "A Special Relationship?"* (Cambridge, Mass., 1980), 32; Henry M. Adams, *Prussian-American Relations, 1775–1871* (Cleveland, 1960), 105; Melvin Small, "The American Image of Germany 1906–1914," Ph.D. diss., University of Michigan, 1965, 455.
4 The poster is depicted in Stephen L. Vaughn, *Holding Fast the Inner Lines: Democracy, Nationalism, and the Committee on Public Information* (Chapel Hill, N.C., 1980), 167.
5 I thus concur with Arthur Marwick's hypothesis that war is a catalyst for trends that had already existed in peacetime. See Arthur Marwick, *War and Social Change in the Twentieth Century: A Comparative Study of Britain, France, Germany, Russia and the United States* (London, 1974), 10.
6 Michael Vlahos, "Culture and Foreign Policy," *Foreign Policy* 82 (1991): 59. On the subject of culture and foreign policy, see also Morell Heald and Lawrence S. Kaplan, *Culture and Diplomacy* (Westport, Conn., 1977); Akira Iriye, "Culture and Power: International Relations as Intercultural Relations," *Diplomatic History* 3 (1979): 115–28; Ruth Emily McMurry and Muna Lee, eds., *The Cultural Approach: Another Way in International Relations* (Chapel Hill, N.C., 1947). For an analysis of Germany's image in America over the course of three centuries, see Konrad H. Jarausch, "Das amerikanische Deutschlandbild in drei Jahrhunderten," in Klaus Weigelt, ed., *Das Deutschland- und Amerikabild: Beiträge zum gegenseitigen Verständnis beider Völker* (Sankt Augustin, 1986), 10–20, as well as his "Huns, Krauts or Good Germans? The German Image in America, 1800–1980," in James Harris, ed., *German-American Interrelations: Heritage and Challenge* (Tübingen, 1985), 145–59. Studies on German cultural policies include Kurt Düwell and Werner Link, eds., *Deutsche Auswärtige Kulturpolitik seit 1871* (Cologne, 1981).

cial factors helped arouse American fears and suspicions toward Imperial Germany. In this essay, however, I look primarily at changing patterns of American perceptions of German culture over the course of four decades.[7] How were these images transmitted, by whom were they perceived, and with what possible consequences? I consider four issues that together deal with the processes by which perceptions are transmitted. First, how did certain sectors of the American cultural elite – primarily academicians – perceive German culture, especially those who had experienced Germany first-hand? Second, how did Germany react to these perceptions, and how was this reaction, in turn, perceived in America? Third, in what ways did German-Americans serve to transmit images of Imperial Germany? Finally, how might elite perceptions have differed from those of the general American public?

Although every propaganda effort has to base its approach on certain elements that preexist in the public mind, it can also create new emotions where no previous national stereotype existed or only very little was known about a national character. Robert H. Wiebe has stated that in 1914 Germany could not counteract "the natural pull toward Britain" since there existed no real profile of Germany in the public American mind.[8] Although Wiebe is right in emphasizing "the natural pull toward Britain," his assertion that there was an absence of opinions on Germany is questionable. In fact, as noted previously, for the majority of Americans in 1871 Germany represented a land where culture flourished and where universities were of the highest standards. In order to examine national perceptions, national images, and national stereotypes, one has to be aware that the diverse processes of perception and stereotype formation are dynamic and selective.[9] One also has to consider the role of the political and cultural changes in the respective nations. In historical writing the curious reader often encounters a tendency to regard the "other" nation in a rather static fashion, either from the point of view of the "image perceiving" or "image reflecting" society. This approach neglects the changes in the country that reflects the images of the other.

---

7 For a good introduction into the problematics of the perception of other nations, see Knud Krakau, "Einführende Überlegungen zur Entstehung und Wirkung von Bildern, die sich Nationen von sich und anderen machen," in Willi Paul Adams and Knud Krakau, eds., *Deutschland und Amerika: Perzeption und historische Realität* (Berlin, 1985), 9–18. The study of national perceptions of other nations naturally always includes the application of comparative history.
8 Robert H. Wiebe, *The Search for Order, 1877–1920* (New York, 1967), 264.
9 See Knud Krakau, "Einführende Überlegungen zur Entstehung und Wirkung von Bildern, die sich Nationen von sich und anderen machen," in Adams and Krakau, eds., *Deutschland und Amerika*, 9–18; H. C. J. Duijker and N. H. Frijda, *National Character and National Stereotypes* (Amsterdam, 1960).

In other words, even if the attitudes in the one country stayed relatively stable, the attitudes of the reflecting nation might change dramatically during this period, and so too will its perception of the other country.

Between 1870 and 1914, a time of nationalist and imperialist competition for world power, an aggressive concept of "culture" was instrumentalized, both consciously and subconsciously. At the turn of the century and increasingly before World War I, German ambitions for more global power included the cultural penetration or annexation of other countries. In a sense it was the equivalent of the American idea of "mission" or, as it was put in the well-known if untranslatable German phrase, "am deutschen Wesen soll die Welt genesen" (the German character shall make the world a better place).

In the 1870s, a relatively noncompetitive decade between America and Germany, many Americans perceived German culture in admiring terms. As a symptom of this "era of good feelings," in 1877 the head of the U.S. legation to Berlin could think of nothing more important than to send a detailed report to Washington describing the Berlin museums and recommending the establishment of similar institutions at home.[10] It should be noted, however, that this "happy" relationship was "somewhat more artificial than the natural one that had existed and flourished for many years between England and America . . . while cultural relations between Germans were cordial, they never approached the intimate level reached by the Anglo-Saxon powers."[11] Moreover, American interest in and enthusiasm for the German cause and culture as celebrated by Charles Baylor was short-lived. The pressing problems of America's post-Civil War years, that is, Reconstruction, industrialization, and urbanization, accompanied by a massive influx of new immigrants, transformed the United States from an agrarian into an industrial society. For a certain period of time these developments kept Americans focused more on internal matters than on foreign countries and foreign affairs. The United States from 1870 to 1914 has been aptly characterized by Wiebe as a nation engaged in a "search for order."[12] The Gilded Age, with its crass materialism, and the so-called Progressive Era, with its attempt to remedy the ills of social dislocation caused by industrialization, symbolize these developments, which in turn encouraged a martial spirit within certain strata of American society.[13] Indeed, there were striking similarities be-

10 See Manfred Jonas, *The United States and Germany: A Diplomatic History* (Ithaca, N.Y., 1984), 34.
11 Small, "American Image of Germany," 281.
12 Wiebe, *Search for Order*.
13 See Nell Irvin Painter, *Standing at Armageddon: The United States, 1877–1919* (New York, 1987), esp. 253–82.

tween the United States and Imperial Germany in terms of these socioeconomic developments and transformations, which in turn had repercussions in the cultural realm.[14] Once America had regained its self-confidence after the trauma of its Civil War, its economic achievements encouraged a quest for a national culture independent of older and still prevalent European influences. American diplomatic and economic interests also began to diverge from those of the European powers, particularly as the United States became increasingly caught up in imperialist competition and rivalries.

Beginning in the 1880s, both Germany and the United States started to look abroad for new markets and colonies. But as newcomers to the arena of world imperialism, they could collect only "leftovers." German colonial ambitions nettled American expansionists and led to strained diplomatic and economic relations between the two countries. This increasing competition spread to the cultural realm, and for Americans the German Empire subsequently lost its reputation as a cultural leader. In the Progressive Era – with its emphasis on moralism – American intellectuals lamented the decline of German idealism and the emergence of a more materialistic culture. To a large extent, however, such writers projected their own American cultural criticism onto German culture. The autostereotypes and heterostereotypes produced were influenced by this projection process. All the same, some of the older American admiration for German philosophy survived even after "the soldier substituted the philosopher as the national symbol."[15]

In the decade or so before the Great War, occasional newspaper editorials and magazine articles warned of a German naval buildup and speculated about Germany as a potential enemy.[16] At the turn of the century, the United States was given new cause for questioning the motives of Germany owing to the Reich's increased activity in South America and the Caribbean. To the general American population, it seemed that the kaiser was determined to test the Monroe Doctrine and secure naval bases in the West Indies. From 1897 to 1900 friction between the two countries reached an intensity greater than at any other point in the previous four decades. Over the course of these few years, grave problems arose concerning the new American tariffs, German gunboat diplomacy, the German prohibition of American cattle ship-

---

14 For a good survey on American cultural changes during this time, see John Higham, "The Reorientation of American Culture in the 1890s," in John Weiss, ed., *The Origins of Modern Consciousness* (Detroit, 1965), 25–48.
15 Small, "American Image of Germany," 455.
16 Vaughn, *Holding Fast the Inner Lines*, 63.

ments, and German aggressiveness during the punitive expedition against the Boxers in 1900. These difficulties, together with the Manila Bay incident, brought forth an outpouring of anti-German sentiment in the newspapers and magazines of the day. For the first time, epithets such as "Hun" began to appear in articles on Germany as frequently as did references to Goethe and Beethoven.[17]

II

The perception of German culture in the United States was generated or transmitted through various information channels. Primarily these were newspapers, in which foreign correspondents and editorials commented on contemporary issues. Literature and travelogues also played an important role in reflecting and reproducing perceptions of German cultural characteristics. In other words, different producers of images and different audiences for these images existed, and it may be hypothesized that some of the perceptions contained in these written documents were actually read and then stored in the reader's subconscious.[18] In the absence of public opinion polls, we are forced to look for different paradigms that could indicate patterns of a national image of Germany. Accordingly, it is necessary first to examine how certain sectors of the American elite perceived Germany's culture and then to consider how German-Americans were perceived as image-bearers of their fatherland.

Henry F. May correctly asserts that the people he calls "the professional custodians of culture," the leading writers, editors, publishers, university presidents – often widely traveled – were much more instrumental in shaping American opinion, and possibly even policy, toward Germany than the emotional attachment to their country of origin of the millions of German-Americans.[19] From the very outset of World War I, these cultural custodians were instrumental in influencing and shaping public opinion, and when America entered the conflict, many of them became involved in the war of the words to influence the general public regarding the Teutonic enemy. It is crucial, then, to look at members of this elite when attempting to come to a better understanding of mechanisms of public opinion and the consequent shifts in attitudes toward Germany.

17 Jonas, *United States and Germany*, 57–60; Gatzke, *Germany and the United States*, 43–5; Small, "American Image of Germany," 4–6.
18 Apart from the written documents, pictures are important vehicles for image building and for conveying ideas. See Walter Lippmann, *Public Opinion* (New York, 1922), 162.
19 Henry F. May, *The End of American Innocence: A Study of the First Years of Our Own Time* (New York, 1959), 363.

It is difficult to pinpoint the role played and the opinions held by the intellectual elite. This somewhat amorphous group, ranging from populists to elitists, included Germanophiles, such as John W. Burgess and H. L. Mencken, as well as members of the more Anglophilic and anti-German New England intellectual establishment, such as Henry and Brooks Adams. The personal attitudes of these individuals were indeed powerful, and, in the new forum of international cultural interaction, they were the leaders of opinion. Although several of these authors, scholars, artists, and editors were not specifically concerned with German culture, their general views of Germany affected many Americans.[20]

Because people form stereotypes based on very limited information we have to differentiate between those members of the elite who had indirect knowledge of Germany and those who had visited Germany at length and had thereby gained an intimate knowledge of the country and its culture.[21] The latter included scholars who, for a variety of reasons, were particularly interested in the politics, history, and culture of Germany. Although we still lack a systematic analysis of this influential group as image builders, it is necessary to examine them rather closely; in their careers at universities and as political administrators they became important leaders of opinion in American society and thus were in a position to shape and influence images of Germany. As academic, cultural, and political "opinion makers" they painted a certain image of Germany, colored by academic admiration for the German system of higher education – effectiveness combined with a sense of idealism – and darkened by a critical attitude toward German political culture, which was regarded as too rigid and unfriendly to foreigners. As the academic standards and the reputation of American universities improved, and with them the growing self-confidence of American academicians, the critical attitude toward Germany's political culture began to be directed toward the education system as well. It came to be viewed by American academics as just one more element of the overall Prussian definition of *Kultur*, which they saw as an attempt to generate a state-sponsored culture, and which they criticized as an attempt to control cultural and educational activities.[22]

---

20 A valuable survey of leading American intellectual and cultural figures of the last two decades of the nineteenth century is George Cotkin, *Reluctant Modernism: American Thought and Culture, 1880–1900* (New York, 1992); also on the specific East Coast situation, see Thomas Bender, *New York Intellect: A History of Intellectual Life in New York City, from 1750 to the Beginnings of Our Own Time* (New York, 1987), esp. his chapter on "Academic Culture," 265–93.
21 On national stereotypes, see Lippmann, *Public Opinion*, esp. chap. 5; Duijker and Frijda, *National Character and National Stereotypes*.
22 See Bender, *New York Intellect*, 284.

There can be little doubt that Friedrich Althoff, one of the main organizers of the Prussian and German university system and well-known promoter of an active *Wissenschaftspolitik*, symbolized for them this German notion of *Kultur*.[23]

Despite all this criticism, however, it is important to recognize that a large proportion of the American intellectual community continued to regard Germany favorably as the model of excellence in academic training. Several generations of American scholars and scientists were educated in Germany, and these German-trained intellectuals probably felt a loyalty toward Germany comparable to that which American undergraduates feel toward their alma mater and the surrounding countryside.[24] But there were also important exceptions.

Although negative comments on German culture increased noticeably in the 1880s, critical voices had already been raised by those who came back from earlier studies in Imperial Germany. For example, John Sharp Williams, long-time Democratic U.S. senator from Mississippi, was already ambivalent about Germany in the early 1870s. He had spent a year (1873–4) studying in Germany, and came back with a genuine admiration for German scholarship and the land itself, but with a dislike for the country's militarism and rigid caste system, which he described as "utterly abominable – an abject cringing to superiors, with an arrogant domineering tyranny over inferiors." Nevertheless, he enjoyed outings and picnics with German-American constituents throughout his political life.[25] One American doctor who "like most Americans, saw no connection between German scientists and German society," recounted with displeasure the rigidity and repression of everyday German life.[26] In general, however, during the 1870s and partly into the 1880s, American academicians and students continued their educational pilgrimages to Germany's educational institutions. Representative of this group were well-known scholars such as Herbert Baxter Adams, John W. Burgess, James Harvey Robinson, and Andrew D. White (U.S. ambassador to Germany from 1897 to 1903).[27] German universities served as cultural symbols and even

---

23 On Friedrich Althoff, see Bernhard vom Brocke, "Hochschul- und Wissenschaftspolitik in Preussen und im Deutschen Kaiserreich, 1882–1907: Das 'System Althoff,'" in Peter Baumgart, ed., *Bildungspolitik in Preussen zur Zeit des Kaiserreiches* (Stuttgart, 1980), 9–118.
24 See Thomas Neville Bonner, *American Doctors and German Universities* (Lincoln, Neb., 1963), 64–5.
25 See George C. Osborn, *John Sharp Williams* (Baton Rouge, La., 1943), 254; Small, "American Image of Germany," 117.
26 Bonner, *American Doctors*, 50–2.
27 Adams was a student of Johann Bluntschi at the University of Heidelberg, where he received his Ph.D. in 1876; on the influence of German historical scholarship on Adams, see Raymond J.

into the 1880s furnished the only model for a genuine graduate institution. By the close of the nineteenth century, however, most American universities had become self-sufficient.

Two other major factors contributed to the development of a more negative attitude toward German culture in general. First, a heightened American nationalism and self-confidence carried with it the desire to be more competitive in terms of education. As a result, criticisms of the German educational system came to be directed not only against the institutions but also against German scholarship itself, which had come to be identified with the country's undemocratic structures. Second, the changed perception of Germany's academic and cultural merit resulted not merely from an improvement in American academic standards, but from the generational change of scholars that took place in the 1880s and 1890s. The generation that had considered a German education the *sine qua non* for academic achievement had passed, and among younger academics there was a growing distrust of German degrees and German scholarship. In other words, on the eve of the war younger and middle-aged intellectuals did not necessarily follow the Germanophile Burgess's path as defender and lover of German scholarship and Germanic culture. Some of these younger scholars, such as historians Guy Stanton Ford and Charles D. Hazen, worked for the Committee on Public Information or CPI during World War I, drafting pamphlets about the "German menace" and writing texts for posters such as the one mentioned previously. In this way they became opinion makers in the true sense of the term. In these pamphlets the authors contemplated the nature of German *Kultur*, which for them had become synonymous with Prussian militarism, autocracy, and a rigid political atmosphere. There can be little doubt that their own direct exposure to German culture, in many cases, later influenced

---

Cunningham, "The German Historical World of Herbert Baxter Adams: 1874–1876," *Journal of American History* 68 (1981): 261–75. On Burgess, see Bernhard E. Brown, *American Conservatives: The Political Thought of Francis Lieber and John W. Burgess* (New York, 1951); Hans-Ulrich Wehler, "Nachwort zu 'Uncle Sam' von John W. Burgess," *Jahrbuch für Amerikastudien* 8 (1963): 261–6; cf. John W. Burgess, *Reminiscences of an American Scholar* (New York, 1934). On Robinson, see Hartmut Lehmann, *Martin Luther in the American Imagination* (Munich, 1988), 227–39. On White, see most recently Wolfgang Drechsler, *Andrew White in Deutschland: Der Vertreter der USA in Berlin 1879–1881 und 1897–1902* (Stuttgart, 1989); though Glen C. Altschuler's study, *Andrew D. White – Educator, Historian, Diplomat* (Ithaca, N.Y., 1979), provides more information on White's notion of German historiography. Examples of other academicians with an extensive direct German experience include Albert B. Hart (who had studied under Treitschke), Arthur Hadley, Henry Farnman, Robert McElroy, and James Henry Breasted. See Walter P. Metzger, *Academic Freedom in the Age of the University* (New York, 1955), 93; Carol S. Gruber, *Mars and Minerva: World War I and the Uses of the Higher Learning in America* (Baton Rouge, La., 1975), 70–80; George T. Blakey, *Historians on the Homefront: American Propagandists for the Great War* (Lexington, Ky., 1970), 28–31.

their work and their readiness to work for the CPI. Ford's experience as a student in prewar Germany may be illustrative. Having arrived in Berlin too late to study with Prussian historian Heinrich von Treitschke, Ford enrolled in the seminar being offered by the military-political historian Hans Delbrück while in Germany. Ford kept a diary of his travels in the summer and autumn of 1899, and in addition to giving a fascinating picture of Marburg and Berlin, the diary shows that even then Ford was concerned about the spirit of militarism that he encountered in parts of Germany. He noted with distaste the "ever-present uniformed official . . . , crowds following marching soldiers, and the potential dangers of standing armies. . . . You felt in it all the difference between the German character and spirit and the American."[28] Time and time again we find remarks from similarly skeptical Americans on the incompatibility of the German national character with American democratic ideology, and on the merits of democracy versus autocracy.[29] This incompatibility was transferred to the cultural realm, as growing numbers of critics began to suspect that the German equation of autocracy and culture would lead them to posit a superior culture. There was, furthermore, an aristocratic air about German universities that was more or less antagonistic to the democratic spirit of American educational institutions. There came to be a feeling that, even in the endeavor of learning, Teutonic methods were ill-suited to the instruction of American citizens. Kuno Francke emphasized that German "slowness" and "dependence upon authority" were equally distasteful to the "self-reliant and agile American" who is "instinctively distrustful of any decision which he has not made himself."[30]

Many other academicians who wrote critically on Germany for the Committee on Public Information had either spent time studying there or had at least taken graduate degrees from universities strongly influenced by German scholarship. In addition to Ford, Hazen, Elmer E. Stoll, Charles Altschul, and Dana C. Munro had also studied in Germany.[31] Hazen, for example, had spent two years in the early 1890s at the universities in Göttingen, Berlin, and Paris; he had returned from his studies concerned about the growth of militarism in Germany and the undemocratic nature of its government.[32] As a result, he was blunt in his

---

28 Vaughn, *Holding Fast the Inner Lines*, 66, cited Ford.
29 See Gruber, *Mars and Minerva*, 21, 23.
30 Kuno Francke, *The German Spirit* (New York, 1916), 12.
31 See Small, "American Image of Germany," 430.
32 See Vaughn, *Holding Fast the Inner Lines*, 69.

condemnation of German autocracy, as his subsequent work for the Committee on Public Information demonstrated.

One can detect from these pamphlets the experiences and perceptions that these scholars had picked up during their stays in Germany. One of the most effective CPI pamphlets, entitled *Conquest and Kultur*, was more than 1,500 pages long and had a very high distribution of 1.25 million copies. It was written by two professors of English, Wallace Notestein and Stoll. The latter had studied in Berlin in 1902, took a doctorate at Munich two years later, and thereafter taught at Harvard and Case Western Reserve. Stoll translated most of the German passages in *Conquest and Kultur*, and both authors argued that Germans thought themselves to be a chosen people whose mission was to establish a new, superior culture and impose it on the world.[33] They used quotations from German authors and leaders to prove their point. While these two men and many others like them may have been impressed by German scholarship and artistic culture, they were at the same time disturbed and even repelled by other aspects of German society, particularly the high esteem accorded to the military establishment and the authoritarianism that characterized German political and social life. As the American journalist Price Collier commented in 1913: "In Germany there are more men of culture per thousand of the population than in any other land, but they rule not by 'sweetness and light' but by force."[34]

It was not only the younger generation of students and scholars returning from Germany that had become skeptical about German education and German culture in general. The German scholars themselves who came to the United States were increasingly greeted with reservation by the American academic establishment. When German constitutional historian Hermann von Holst,[35] who had specialized in American history – a rare phenomenon among German historians – accepted an invitation to become one of the University of Chicago's first history professors, he was met with skepticism and cool reserve. In a revealing remark, Harry P. Judson, dean and later president of the university, expressed his concern not so much with Holst's personal qualifications as with the possibility that he might become a representative of the German Reich: "Of course there was a time when German notions were a valuable leaven in

---

33 Ibid., 66–9.
34 Price Collier, *Germany and the Germans from an American Point of View* (New York, 1913), 263.
35 On Holst, see most recently Jörg Nagler, "Mediator Between Two Historical Worlds: Hermann von Holst and the University of Chicago," in Henry Geitz, Jürgen Heideking, and Jurgen Herbst, eds., *German Influences on Education in the United States to 1917* (New York, 1995), 257–74.

America – German enthusiasm for pure knowledge and careful specialization. But I think that day has about gone. We have learned the German lesson – quite too thoroughly. . . . I should be hopelessly out of accord with a fragment of the German empire transplanted to Chicago."[36] The major criticism of Holst's work grew out of a general American skepticism about German historians, who had come to be identified with the interests of the autocratic German-Prussian state.[37] Holst's allegedly false interpretations of American institutions were perceived as a lack of experience with "free institutions," since "these things are mysteries to German professors, because they are mysteries to German statesmen also. The German scholar simply reads in a book of things which we [Americans] are always looking at and acting in."[38] Only a few years later, in 1898, E. A. Fuerts, dean of the College of Civil Engineering at Cornell University, made a revealing remark to Andrew D. White: "Every day I am less and less reconciled with the teutonizing wave in educational matters . . . and I do not believe [it] contains the proper seeds for the intellectual growth of our republic."[39] These comments and many others in the same vein indeed reflect the growing tendency to identify German scholarship with authoritarianism and antidemocratic hierarchical structures, and they anticipate a growing reservation regarding the German (Prussian) state and everything attached to it. (It also should be mentioned in this context that a nativist and antihyphen mentality, the result of new waves of immigration, existed in parts of American society and was accompanied by a growing suspicion of foreign ideas and culture.)[40] When von Holst died in 1904, the American ambassador attended his funeral in Freiburg and spoke on "Friendly Relations between German and American Scholars and Thinkers."[41] This speech was more an exercise in rhetoric and politesse than an accurate reflection of the cultural and political relations of the two countries at that time. Indeed, Holst's case clearly illustrates what Jurgen Herbst once called "the rise and decline of

---

36 Judson to Samuel Rainey Harper, Dec. 5, 1891, cited in Richard J. Storr, *Harper's University: The Beginnings: A History of the University of Chicago* (Chicago, 1966), 159.
37 James J. Sheehan, *German Liberalism in the Nineteenth Century* (Chicago, 1978), 234.
38 John Alexander Jameson, *A Treatise on Constitutional Conventions*, 4th ed. (Chicago, 1887), 658. For a similar view, see W. L. Penfield's review of vols. 4 and 5 of Holst's *Constitutional History*, in *American Law Review* 20 (1886): 123–4.
39 E. A. Fuerts to Andrew D. White, Aug. 10, 1898, cited in Alfred Vagts, *Deutschland und die Vereinigten Staaten in der Weltpolitik*, 2 vols. (New York, 1935), 2:2004n.3.
40 See Vagts, *Deutschland und die Vereinigten Staaten*, 1:435. Vagts misinterprets Holst's call from the University of Chicago as a conscious antinativist decision.
41 See Hans-Günter Zmarzlik, "Hermann Eduard von Holst," in Johannes Vincke, ed., *Freiburger Professoren des 19. und 20. Jahrhunderts* (Freiburg/Breisgau, 1957), 75.

the German historical school" in the United States between 1876 and 1914.[42]

This growing antagonism also reflected significant shifts that were affecting the writing of history within the United States. Among other things, the criticism of Holst's work was indicative of a move away from the New England-dominated school of historians, who were strongly influenced by German historiography, to a more self-reliant, confident, and genuinely American school of historiography. This in turn coincided with a strong American nationalism that called for self-definition. Frederick Jackson Turner exemplified that tendency. A student of Herbert Baxter Adams (one of the strongest advocates of German historical scholarship), Turner nevertheless gave high priority to social history in place of more traditional kinds of political history.[43] This new trend in American historiography also indicated the failed attempt by German-trained American historians, such as Adams, to transplant German historical thinking to the United States. But it was precisely through this German concept of *Ideengeschichte* (history of ideas) that Holst, who viewed history through the lens of contemporary political interests, tried to manifest the moral dimension of history and the human actions involved in the historical process. Even Herbert Baxter Adams was not an uncritical disciple of German scholarship. As early as 1886 he proudly compared the best of the American universities with German universities and stated that it was no longer the *sine qua non* for American history students to attend German universities for training in European and American history.[44] He also gradually changed his positive perception of the German historical profession and increasingly orientated himself toward the English "democratic" historians.[45]

The overwhelming majority of the 9,000 American students who studied in Germany between 1820 and 1920 did so in the years from 1870 to 1914. In 1880, for example, there were 1,088 Americans in German universities, but these numbers gradually decreased to 338 in 1912.[46] This decline in the number of American students at German

---

42 Jurgen Herbst, *The German Historical School in American Scholarship* (Ithaca, N.Y., 1935), viii.
43 Higham states that Adams "did more than anyone else to Germanize American historical scholarship" (John Higham, *History: Professional Scholarship in America* [Baltimore, 1983], 11).
44 Herbert Baxter Adams, *The Study of History in American Colleges and Universities* (Washington, D.C., 1887), 41.
45 Herbst, *German Historical School*, 127.
46 See *Foreign Relations*, 1880, no. 1, pt. 1, 424; Gruber, *Mars and Minvera*, 17; Higham, *History: Professional Scholarship in America*, 19; Barnes, "German Influence on American Historical Studies," 68. More recent studies on American students in Germany are Cristopher J. Bernett, "Die Wanderjahre: The Higher Education of American Students in German Universities, 1870 to

universities suggests that a once-admired educational system could not effectively counter the growing chorus of American criticism directed against an undemocratic, autocratic political system. American students were coming to realize that German universities were not effective vehicles of democratic political education.[47]

III

In Germany the kaiser and the cultural administrators were well aware of the generational shift in opinion that was taking place in the United States. They realized acutely that the once-lauded German system of higher education was losing its hold on the imaginations of the younger generation of scholars, who were starting to look toward England and France for advanced research. Kaiser Wilhelm II realized that the opinion of the United States was a factor to be reckoned with in his theory of *Weltpolitik*, and he also knew that the growing criticism on the part of American opinion leaders was observed and keenly felt by German leaders.[48] Wilhelm himself interpreted this trend as a possible indication of a more general American disregard for German culture. To counteract these tendencies and once again spur interest in German culture, the German academic and cultural institutions established an exchange program for German and American professors in 1905.[49] Although informal routes of exchange already existed, this was the first official attempt to bring "the men of learning of one country into other countries and by comparison of fundamental ideas to arrive at a world-philosophy and world-morality upon which the world's peace and the world's civilization may finally and firmly rest."[50] How did Americans perceive these German attempts to counteract the growing cultural alienation between the two

---

1914," Ph.D. diss., State University of New York, Stony Brook, 1984, and Konrad H. Jarausch, "American Students in Germany, 1815–1914: The Structure of German and U.S. Matriculants at Göttingen University," in Geitz, Heideking, and Herbst, eds., *German Influences on Education*, 195–211.

47 See Schieber, *Transformation of American Sentiment*, 256.

48 See Ernst von Halle, "Deutschland und die öffentliche Meinung in den Vereinigten Staaten," *Preussische Jahrbücher* 107 (1902): 189–212.

49 For this subject, see Bernhard von Brocke, "Der deutsch- amerikanische Professorenaustausch: Preussische Wissenschaftspolitik, internationale Wissenschaftsbeziehungen und die Anfänge einer deutschen auswärtigen Kulturpolitik vor dem Ersten Weltkrieg," *Zeitschrift für Kulturaustausch* 31 (1981): 128–82; Willi Paul Adams, "Die Geschichte Nordamerikas in Berlin," in Reimer Hansen and Wolfgang Ribbe, eds., *Geschichtswissenschaft in Berlin im 19. und 20. Jahrhundert: Persönlichkeiten und Institutionen* (Berlin, 1992), 608–12.

50 William Shaw, *William of Germany* (New York, 1913), 273.

countries?[51] It is sufficient to mention only the most prominent individuals involved in these exchanges, which primarily took place between the University of Berlin in Germany and Harvard and Columbia universities in the United States. They included the psychologist Hugo Münsterberg, the historian, political scientist and economist Burgess, the theologian Francis Peabody, and Nicholas Murray Butler, president of Columbia University and an acquaintance of the kaiser.[52]

Other efforts to counter the rising tide of antagonism took the form of elaborate gifts to the newly founded German Museum at Harvard, which had been initiated by German-born academic Kuno Francke several years earlier. Charter directors of the museum included a number of intellectually and politically distinguished individuals, including Carl Schurz, Andrew D. White, and Theodore Roosevelt.[53]

In a rather different kind of fence-mending effort, Wilhelm II sent his brother, Prince Henry, on a friendly visit in 1902, just as the Venezuelan episode was beginning to arouse American suspicions of German designs in the Western Hemisphere.[54] According to official instructions, the prince came to America to "reach out the friendly hand of Germany over the ocean." Henry's final instructions from his brother were: "Keep your eyes and ears open and your mouth closed." During this visit, American cultural institutions, such as libraries and universities, were high on the prince's priority list. He easily won the sympathies of some Americans by virtue of his surprisingly nonautocratic simplicity and frankness of manner. American intuition, however, seemed to be suspicious of the kaiser's good-will efforts, with the result that public opinion was almost equally separated into two groups, one of which believed that the visit was prompted by honest motives, while the other group either regarded the visit with great apprehension or made fun of it. Moreover, the kaiser's gift of the statue of Frederick the Great as a gesture to improve cultural

---

51 On the cultural exchange programs in general, see Frank Trommler, "Inventing the Enemy: German-American Cultural Relations, 1900–1917," in Hans-Jürgen Schröder, ed., *Confrontation and Cooperation: Germany and the United States in the Era of World War I, 1900–1924* (Providence, R.I., 1993), 99–125.
52 See Small, "American Image of Germany," 273–5.
53 Francke considered the founding of the museum as a necessity against the British and French cultural influence in the United States. See Henry J. Schmidt, "The Rhetoric of Survival: The Germanist in America, 1900–1925," in David P. Benseler et al., eds., *Teaching German in America: Prolegomena to a History* (Madison, Wis., 1988), 167.
54 For a detailed analysis of the confrontational situation between Germany and the United States in Latin America, see Ragnhild Fiebig von Hase, *Lateinamerika als Konfliktherd der deutsch-amerikanischen Beziehungen, 1890–1903: Vom Beginn der Panamerikapolitik bis zur Venezuelakrise von 1902/03*, 2 vols. (Göttingen, 1986).

relations could hardly pacify those who had already been critical of the German symbiosis of militarism and *Kultur*. As Hans W. Gatzke has fittingly remarked: "The statue of Frederick the Great was hardly a statue of liberty."[55]

As this episode demonstrates, it was difficult to counteract the suspicion that had been aroused between two countries that were competing for world-power status. Indeed, even well-meaning attempts to achieve better cultural understanding often failed to achieve their objectives.[56] Moreover, the World Exposition that took place in St. Louis in 1904, a unique opportunity for countries to present their national image, proved to be problematic for Germany since there existed no consensus on how to present German culture to an American audience.[57]

In a noncompetitive situation, individuals and nations tend to regard each other more or less positively. However, once a competitive situation prevails, closer contacts may in fact prove counterproductive, only increasing the antagonism they were intended to overcome. This finding, emphasized by social psychology, is certainly applicable to the bilateral national perceptions between the United States and Imperial Germany in the era before World War I. It is also important to recognize that American perceptions of Imperial Germany affected new cultural policies, specifically, German attempts to change prevailing American attitudes. Here we can observe the development of a complex process of multiple perceptions that included auto and heterostereotypes, the cultural projections onto the respective nation's processes of self-identification. The presence of a substantial contingent of German immigrants in the United States further complicated this binational perception process.

Since Wilhelm II's accession to the throne in 1888, the American perception of German culture had tended to focus on the person of the kaiser, who in fact liked to see himself as the guardian of German *Kultur*. For many Americans, Germany became synonymous with "the kaiser" and with the personality of Wilhelm II in particular. The association of kaiser and *Kultur* presented a troublesome equation. Images of Wilhelm were among the most important aspects of the composite perception of Germany, its citizens, and its culture, much like Saddam Hussein is for contemporary Iraq.[58] We should not be deceived by the images of the

---

55 Schieber, *Transformation of American Sentiment*, xiii–xiv, 240; Gatzke, *Germany and the United States*, 45.
56 Schieber, *Transformation of American Sentiment*, xiii–xiv.
57 See Peter Paret, "Art and the National Image: The Conflict over Germany's Participation in the St. Louis Exposition," *Central European History* 10 (1978): 175–83.
58 See Small, "American Image of Germany," 361.

kaiser produced later on the American home front; the prewar images of the kaiser were not necessarily as unfavorable as those promoted during the war years by George Creel and British propagandists, which depicted the kaiser as the bloodthirsty beast of Berlin. On the contrary, some American prewar commentators called Wilhelm II "the greatest and most interesting personality now on a European throne." Other Americans even considered him a renaissance man, much like a Yankee. *Harper's Weekly* wrote that the kaiser was made up "of stuff that would have made a first-rate American."[59]

The kaiser's much-touted role as the guardian of German culture led, however, to controversy. His inordinate love of uniforms and his penchant for saber-rattling speeches strengthened the impression of German militarism and the notion that the army continued to hold the central place in German society.[60] Indeed, between 1886 and 1894, the German military budget doubled and the German army increased by approximately 30 percent. Thus, the physical presence of the military increased, for example, on the streets of Berlin, where American visitors often noticed them.[61] To the American mind, militarism and *Kultur* were an odd mixture, and the wide difference in connotation between the German word *Kultur* (which encompasses all aspects of German life – social, military, scientific, etc.) and the English word "culture" (which focuses primarily on the arts and humanities) resulted in misinterpretation at many levels. Assuming the words to be identical, many Americans could not understand why German and German-American remarks on *Kultur* usually started or ended with references to German military efficiency and strength. Consequently, it was often remarked with humor that "when a German talked of *Kultur* he first cocked his pistol."[62]

Wilhelm II's well-publicized speech to the German soldiers as they departed to quell the Boxer Rebellion in China seemed to support this charge: "Give no quarter, spare nobody, take no prisoners. ... Be as terrible as Attila's Huns." It also presented the world with its favorite epithet for the Germans – "Huns" – which was later exploited fully by British and American propagandists.[63] German and German-American opinion leaders, however, continued to admire the kaiser, even as they overly idealized his own role. Even Francke, normally an opponent of

---
59 Ibid., 367.
60 Gatzke, *Germany and the United States*, 41.
61 Michael Geyer, *Deutsche Rüstungspolitik* (Frankfurt/Main, 1980), 51.
62 Cedric C. Cummins, *Indiana Public Opinion and World War, 1914–1917* (Indianapolis, Ind., 1945), 48.
63 Gatzke, *Germany and the United States*, 44–5.

ethnic extremists, was moved to confess that he thought the kaiser to be a combination of Richard Wagner's Parsifal and the Nietzschean Superman.[64]

IV

America's unique history as a land of immigrants gave rise to a very different kind of image transmission process; namely, perception as acquired via the substantial number of Germans living in the United States. As Frederick C. Luebke has rightly emphasized: "While images of Germany, its people, and institutions must be distinguished from ideas about German-Americans, the former were rarely separated from the latter except in rigorous, analytical thought."[65] Indeed, for many other Americans, German-Americans served as a lens for viewing Imperial Germany. This direct human experience probably established a much more tangible image of Germany than those transmission processes described so far. German-Americans were stereotyped as industrious, honest, efficient, and sturdy.[66] However, after the Haymarket Riot of 1886, when it became known that five of the six rioters sentenced to death were German-Americans, the image and perception of German immigrants began to change dramatically, and the American fear of imported ideologies increased.[67] Of course, there was no uniform or consistent content to the stereotype of the German-American. It depended on the social and cultural background of the perceiver and the social environment in general. Here again it is important to realize that the "custodians of culture" in America – its "highbrow culture" to use Van Wyck Brooks's term from his seminal work *America's Coming of Age* – generally perceived German-Americans more favorably than did the representatives of the "lowbrow culture" (again, Brooks's term).[68] The first group's exposure to German-Americans seldom extended to ordinary, working-class German immigrants, but was usually limited to their well-educated, elite, German-American counterparts who had, in most cases, assimilated into American society and culture. By the turn of the century, however, as relations

---

64 Kuno Francke, *A German-American's Confession of Faith* (New York, 1915), 6.
65 See Frederick C. Luebke, *Bonds of Loyalty: German-Americans and World War I* (DeKalb, Ill., 1974), 58.
66 For the American perception of immigrant groups, see Herbert A. Strauss, "Changing Images of the Immigrant in the USA, " *Amerikastudien/American Studies* 21 (1976): 119–37.
67 John Higham, *Strangers in the Land: Patterns of American Nativism, 1860–1925* (New Brunswick, N.J., 1955), 54.
68 For "highbrow" versus "lowbrow" in American culture, see also Lawrence W. Levine, *Highbrow/Lowbrow: The Emergence of Cultural Hierarchy in America* (Cambridge, Mass., 1988).

between the two countries deteriorated and the number of immigrants from Germany declined, German-Americans became much more defensive and nationalistic than in any previous period, and their leaders much more vociferous and aggressive. In fact, extreme differences in attitudes polarized the German immigrants themselves; there were those who advocated complete assimilation, and others who maintained an "ardent identification with the German empire which precluded any adoption of worthwhile American ways and culture."[69] This type of nationalism could sometimes be extreme, and was increasingly accompanied by the rhetoric of cultural superiority – a typical defense mechanism against the often alienating forces of assimilation.

The cultural chauvinism of German-Americans contributed to a generally negative perception of Germany's *Kultur*. It also reflected the crisis of identity of German-Americans at the end of the nineteenth century, when German immigration was waning. The banner of cultural superiority was carried mainly by the German-American mandarins of high culture. For example, Charles J. Hexamer, the American-born president of the National German-American Alliance (*Deutsch-Amerikanischer National-Bund*), an organization intended primarily to promote German culture, once asserted: "No one... will ever find us prepared to step down to a lesser *Kultur*; no, we have made it our aim to draw the other up to us."[70] This kind of rhetoric further incited those American representatives of high culture who already nurtured anti-German feelings. It supported their suspicion that Germany and its "fifth column," that is, German-American leaders, aimed at cultural penetration and the consequent subversion of American culture. To be sure, connections between the National Alliance and the Pan-German League did exist.[71] Although Hugo Francke charged that the National Alliance and the Pan-German League further alienated Americans from German culture, he himself had described the German struggle for cultural dominance in terms of a holy war.[72] Because German-American intellectuals increasingly looked to their counterparts in the fatherland and did not consider the majority of their German fellow immigrants to be worthy representatives of German *Kultur*, their American colleagues became even more suspicious of Ger-

---

69 Guido A. Dobbert, "German-Americans between New and Old Fatherland, 1870–1914," *American Quarterly* 19 (1967): 665.
70 At the outbreak of World War I the German literature scholar Heinrich Hermann Maurer hoped for a German victory, since it would bring German-Americans the victorious influence of a superior German *Kultur*. See Schmidt, "The Rhetoric of Survival," 167.
71 Dobbert, "German-Americans," 679.
72 Schmidt, "The Rhetoric of Survival," 167.

man efforts to carry out plans for a cultural mission in the United States.[73] Seen in this context, the efforts to bring German culture to America by means of exchange programs, fellowships, and gifts to Harvard could only prove counterproductive, since it amplified the fear of German cultural imperialism and expansionism.

Exactly how much of the kind of provocative rhetoric of German-American cultural chauvinism reached the general American public is hard to assess, but most information indicates that it was primarily limited to the American "academic mandarins" who were especially sensitive to it.

V

But what precisely were the differences in perception between the elite and the general population in America? As we know from public opinion research, the gap in opinion between the public and the political and social leaders can be vast. According to a poll conducted in the United States in 1990, only 32 percent of the general population considered the Soviet Union stronger in terms of military power than the United States, whereas 71 percent of the leaders believed that the Soviet Union was militarily stronger than the United States.[74] Such a wide gap in opinion may also have existed with respect to images of German culture, even prior to 1914.

For the majority of the population, foreign affairs and foreign cultures were certainly not the major concern. In a study on public opinion and the image of Germany from 1906–14, Melvin Small has found that "all evidence available in magazines and books of nonfiction points unmistakably to the conclusion that the general public probably had a much more favorable image of Germany than the elite."[75] American school books from this period provide interesting evidence in support of Small's observation. Textbooks, especially grammar-school books, are crucial in shaping lifelong images of other countries or peoples. Grammar-school books have a far greater readership than all other books and magazines com-

---

73 The Imperial German Ambassador in Washington, Johann Heinrich Count Bernstorff, reflected the disparaging attitude of German-American intellectuals to fellow Americans of German origin when he wrote that, "as representatives of German culture, because coming from the lower classes, they had not brought any culture with them" (Bernstorff to Bethmann Hollweg, Apr. 7, 1913, cited in Reinhard R. Doerries, *Imperial Challenge: Ambassador Count Bernstorff and German-American Relations, 1908–1917* [Chapel Hill, N.C., 1989], 22).
74 John E. Reilly, "Public Opinion: The Pulse of the '90s," *Foreign Policy* 82 (1991): 88.
75 Small, "American Image of Germany," 462.

bined, and thus every American who spends a few years in school is exposed to and very likely influenced by their content. Interestingly enough, "Germany occupied a small but choice position" in the textbooks. Most presented the German immigrant favorably and depicted the German national as an honest, hard-working, industrious citizen, quite similar to the Yankee. There was evidence of some concern for the military character of German society, but this concern was not great, particularly since German militarism was usually associated with efficiency, not brutality. In general, Germany and Germans were treated favorably in American grammar-school texts; few derogatory images were either articulated or reproduced.[76] When he criticized these "pro-German" texts he had seen in America's schools, former American ambassador to Germany James W. Gerard confirmed that school books generally depicted Germany and German-Americans positively. In a propagandistic, anti-German book published during the war, Gerard warns against these texts "cleverly compiled to impress children at a youthful age with a favorable idea of kings and emperors." The embittered diplomat attacked American school books that lauded Goethe without mentioning his hatred of Prussia.[77]

Supportive of and linked to the predominantly positive assessment of Germany by most Americans was the teaching of the German language in prewar America. In the late nineteenth century, German had been considered the second language in the United States, and just before America's entry into World War I, approximately one-fourth of all public high school students took German. Today, the high school enrollment in German language classes is merely 1.5 percent. The teaching of German was actively supported by the German-American press, cultural organizations, and churches. Readers of CPI propaganda, which called German the "vicious, guttural language of Kultur," must have been surprised to learn of this hitherto unknown quality of the language they had learned in high school. In conjunction with language lessons, many German teachers before the war felt compelled to emphasize to their students the German cultural heritage and the positive aspects of the "moral idealism of Wilhelmian Germany."[78]

76 See Ruth Miller Elson, *Guardians of Tradition: American Schoolbooks of the Nineteenth Century* (Lincoln, Neb., 1964), 143–6; Ruth Miller Elson, "Deutschland und die Deutschen in amerikanischen Schulbüchern des 19. Jahrhunderts," *Internationales Jahrbuch für Geschichtsunterricht* 7 (1959–60): 51–7; Small, "American Image of Germany," 464.
77 James W. Gerard, *Face to Face with Kaiserism* (New York, 1918), 282–8.
78 Schmidt, "The Rhetoric of Survival," 165. Victor Lange supports this assessment by emphasizing that "the teaching of German [was] motivated by a passionate and unswerving attachment to the

In conclusion, for the general American public the general image of Germany on the eve of the war was mixed, but it certainly was not overwhelmingly unfavorable. If anything, Americans were ambivalent toward that paradoxical country. Although they abhorred militarism and autocracy, they admired orderliness and progress. Images of Kaiser Wilhelm II, Social Democrats, a welfare state, the army, German education, and German culture presented pictures that were both favorable and unfavorable. Not interested in world politics and the balance of power, the vast majority of the public were prepared to give Germany a fair hearing on August 4, 1914. In other words, for members of the "high culture" and "low culture," respectively, perceptions of German culture were characterized by keywords such as "Wagner," "Nietzsche," and "universities," or by images of beer-drinking and yodeling Bavarians, or, as Frederick C. Luebke put it, "soul Germans" and "stomach Germans."[79]

VI

Four weeks after the guns of August 1914 had started the Great War, the eminent German academics Rudolf Eucken and Ernst Haeckel directed a letter to the universities of America in which they expressed their confidence in "the friendly feelings of the American universities" and their members who had been exposed to German academic life and culture. Those people would surely "know what German culture means to the world."[80] The German writers' confidence was ill-founded, as the negative reactions and attitudes of their American colleagues at the outbreak of the war clearly demonstrated. Eduard Meyer, professor of history in Berlin, expressed his shock in 1915 over support for the Allies on American campuses and by old friends, such as Nicholas Murray Butler and Charles W. Eliot.[81] Most academic groups in Germany overestimated the strength of their cultural ties with the United States. Their misjudgment of the situation was perhaps predictable. The latent, sometimes open suspicion of German *Kultur* had already indicated a shift in attitudes. This

---

values – political, philosophical and literary – that were then held in Germany: pride in the Imperial power" (Victor Lange, "Thoughts in Season," in Walter F. W. Lohnes and Valters Nollendorfs, eds., *German Studies in the United States: Assessment and Outlook* [Madison, Wis., 1976], 11).

79 Luebke, *Bonds of Loyalty*, 27.
80 Rudolf Eucken and Ernst Haeckel to the universities of America, Aug. 31, 1914, cited in Gruber, *Mars and Minerva*, 20.
81 Eduard Meyer, *Nordamerika und Deutschland* (Berlin, 1915), 13–14.

shift was also seen in the growing sense of competitiveness and even hostility among American academics. But for the most part, German cultural mandarins were convinced of the superior quality of the German *Kultur*, and they remained convinced that their American counterparts would be ready to accept this superiority. In the age of imperialism, national culture represented a powerful symbolic focus for the pursuit of world power. The more Germany realized that the American rapprochement with Britain was not limited to the political and economic spheres but extended to the cultural realm, the more aggressive German cultural chauvinism and its American counterpart, German-American chauvinism, became. In 1901 the German ambassador in Washington, Theodor von Holleben, spoke of "intellectual annexation" in the United States; and five years later his successor, Herman Speck Sternburg, maintained that Germany still had one field of influence (*Aktionsfeld*) left in the United States; namely, the cultural one.[82] On the eve of the war, however, Speck's successor, Johann Heinrich Count von Bernstorff, had to admit with resignation that "comparatively speaking our American policy had the least success on the cultural level." The ambassador, however, insisted on "the German nation's universal historical duty to insure that the American culture of the future would not become exclusively Anglo-Saxon."[83]

Any assessment of American perceptions of German culture between 1870 and 1914 will differ according to the manner in which one attempts to measure the relative cultural intimacy between the two countries. Although custodians of culture became increasingly critical of German *Kultur* and created heterostereotypes of an autocratic Prussian culture, it seems that the majority of Americans did not consider German culture a threat to their own.[84] Prewar British propaganda in America did inflame suspicions regarding the aggressive designs of a German missionary *Kultur*. The image of the "Hun" already overshadowed other traits in German culture, and the propaganda campaign further contrasted a refined and well-mannered Anglo-Saxon culture with an aggressive German one. As in the case with all other imperialist nations, the concept of culture was intertwined with concepts of race and with the struggle to gain world-

---

82 Theodor von Holleben to Auswärtiges Amt, Apr. 5, June 11, 20, 1901; Sternburg to Auswärtiges Amt, June 26, 1906, cited in Vagts, *Deutschland und die Vereinigten Staaten*, 2:2004n.5, and 2005.
83 Bernstorff to Bethmann Hollweg, Apr. 7, 1914, cited in Doerries, *Imperial Challenge*, 22. In this letter Bernstorff also suggested a cultural exchange program in order to "create an appropriate regard for German culture – something to which it is by all means entitled as the first culture in the world."
84 Small, "American Image of Germany," 469.

wide recognition and prestige. In 1910, James E. Russell, dean of Columbia Teachers College, published a major study on the German higher education system that reflected the ambivalent American attitude toward German culture and institutions. As we have seen, that attitude combined admiration for German efficiency and organization with a thorough dislike of regimentation and the lack of individualism. One passage from Russell's book, *German Higher Schools*, exemplifies these discordant notions: "The foreigner may not admire German ideals, he may even despise German culture and civilization; but if he is an observant schoolmaster, he cannot fail to admire the practical workings of the German schools."[85]

This ambivalence changed almost overnight when the news of the invasion of Belgium reached the United States. The latent and sometimes open stereotypes of the Hun and Prussian soldier now wiped away the positive perceptions of German *Kultur* that still remained. That a nation with supposedly high cultural values could destroy by brutal force the cultural treasures of Louvain was enough evidence of the genuinely militaristic nature of *Kultur*.[86] British propaganda concentrated its efforts on convincing the world, especially the United States, that German *Kultur* posed a threat to the world security and indeed was the actual cause of the war. In 1915 a *New York Times* editorial reflected on the rise and fall of German culture from 1870 to 1914 and the perception of this development in America. It stated that Germans had been "transformed from a nation worthy of the world's esteem and admiration into a people who stand apart from other nations, distrusted and feared, disturbers of the peace.... Their ideals have been abased and their intellectual development stifled, they have been bred away from the 'high and noble things of life.' "[87] The admiration of American writers like Charles G. Baylor for Germany's "culture of high and noble things" had been transformed. American perceptions had come to be focused on the ambiguous term *Kultur*, and therein can be found the prewar roots of the vehement homefront attack against all things German.

85 James E. Russell, *German Higher Schools* (New York, 1910), 421.
86 See Small, "American Image of Germany," 474.
87 *New York Times*, June 1, 1915, cited in Luebke, *Bonds of Loyalty*, 86.

7

The Reciprocal Visions of German and American Intellectuals
Beneath the Shifting Perceptions

JAMES T. KLOPPENBERG

In 1881 a seventeen-year-old boy apprenticed to a mortician in the town of Oldenburg faced conscription into the German army.[1] Like many others in his region, Ignatz felt no particular loyalty to the new German *Reich*, nor did he have any interest in military service, so he decided to leave home for America. Lacking money and papers, his only choice was to stow away on a ship leaving Bremen bound for New York. On board he met a seventeen-year-old girl named Anna, from nearby Nordwalde, who was traveling to America with her parents and her two sisters. When the ship's authorities searched for stowaways, she managed to hide him under her down comforter. Perhaps not surprisingly, by the time the ship reached New York Ignatz and Anna had become good friends, and the girl's family agreed that the boy should accompany them to Hanover, Kansas, where they knew other recent German immigrants and planned to make their home. When they arrived in Hanover, Ignatz found there was already a mortician in the town, so he decided to become a carpenter. Soon he and Anna married, his carpentry business flourished, they had ten children, and their family became a permanent part of the town. Because Ignatz and Anna were my great grandparents, I have always had more than a passing interest in the subject of German immigration to America during these years. But until I read Wolfgang Helbich's contri-

1 This chapter was originally prepared for the conference "Mutual Images and Multiple Implications: American Views of Germany and German Views of America from the 18th to the 20th Centuries," Kalamazoo College, Apr. 15–17, 1993. I would like to thank the conference organizers, and especially Elisabeth Glaser-Schmidt, for bringing together for publication the papers from this fine conference. Parts of my discussion of Max Weber are adapted from my essay "Democracy and Disenchantment: From Weber and Dewey to Rorty and Habermas," in Dorothy Ross, ed., *Modernist Impulses in the Human Sciences, 1870–1930* (Baltimore, 1994), 69–90.

bution on this subject, I knew little about the attitudes of ordinary Germans toward America in the late nineteenth century. If there are, somewhere in northern Germany, letters back home to family and friends from Ignatz and Anna, it seems reasonable to suppose that the themes in those letters correspond to those Helbich has discussed.

Since my own field is intellectual history rather than social history, I concentrate here on a few individuals who occupied positions very different from those of Ignatz Kloppenberg and Anna Ross (to use the spelling their names acquired somewhere between leaving Germany and arriving in Kansas). In the closing decades of the nineteenth century and the first two decades of the twentieth, German and American philosophers and social scientists crossed the Atlantic in increasing numbers and formed their own perceptions of the social systems they encountered. This essay focuses on some of those voyagers who recorded their experiences in private or published form.

I examine four specific cases, two involving German intellectuals' perceptions of American culture and two involving American intellectuals' perceptions of German culture. First, I discuss the experiences and writings of the German sociologist Max Weber; second, the first two generations of American economists, many of whom studied in Germany; third, the German philosophers who wrote about William James and the American philosophy of pragmatism; and fourth, John Dewey's writings about German culture. From this analysis a pattern will emerge.

In 1904, Max Weber visited the United States for the first and last time. Given Weber's reputation for pessimism, and given the tendency of European intellectuals to malign the United States, one might reasonably expect that Weber found little to like about the American version of the flattened, utilitarian *Zivilisation* that German critics were fond of contrasting to their own more refined *Kultur*. When Freud traveled to America from Vienna in 1909, for example, the experience turned his stomach. He later complained that his American journey caused the deterioration of both his digestive system and his handwriting. As he told Ernest Jones, in a judgment expressing the sentiment of countless Europeans before and since, "America is a mistake; a gigantic mistake, it is true, but none the less a mistake."[2]

---

2 Ernest Jones, *The Life and Work of Sigmund Freud*, ed. Lionel Trilling and Steven Marcus (New York, 1961), 270, see also 265–71 on Freud's American visit; and cf. Peter Gay, "Freud's America," in Frank Trommler and Joseph McVeigh, eds., *America and the Germans: An Assessment of a Three-Hundred-Year History*, vol. 2, *The Relationship in the Twentieth Century* (Philadelphia, 1985), 303–14.

Measured against that standard, Weber's response to America seems surprisingly moderate. Of course the smell of New York's streets and the impersonality of its dwellings disgusted him, as did Chicago's stockyards, an "ocean of blood" serving only to break the monotony of the "endless human desert" of the city itself. Characterizing Chicago with an unnerving image that only a student of urban sociology could love, Weber wrote that "the whole tremendous city ... is like a man whose skin has been peeled off and whose intestines are seen at work." Notwithstanding such remarks, though, Weber found his American travels exhilarating and even therapeutic. He embarked on the journey after six years of almost complete mental incapacitation, and the lecture he delivered at the Universal Exposition in St. Louis was his first public performance since the mental collapse that followed his father's death in 1897. In contrast to Freud, whose experience illustrates how travel can narrow the mind, Weber reflected at the end of his stay that the trip had widened his scholarly horizons and improved his state of health. To the surprise of everyone traveling with him, Weber found America to be the tonic he needed. As he put it, in what might serve as the motto of conference goers everywhere, "Stimulation and occupation of the mind without intellectual exertion simply is the only remedy."[3]

In his lecture in St. Louis, Weber sketched several of the explanations historians have offered to account for popular government in America. Weber emphasized the absence of a feudal past, which accounted for the equality that American immigrants described in their letters home. He noted the presence of free land, which lured so many immigrants from Germany and elsewhere. He remarked on the luxury of prosperity and the even greater luxury of safe borders, the absence of which in Germany might be said to account for the militarism of German culture (and thus for the presence of many German immigrants before and after the arrival of my great grandfather Ignatz). But Weber also suggested another argument, which he developed at length in *The Protestant Ethic and the Spirit of Capitalism*. Thanks to its Calvinist heritage and its historical circumstances, America afforded individuals the opportunity to participate actively in small-scale, egalitarian organizations at the community level, organizations that nourished democratic values and institutions. While Weber hoped such "'club' associations," as he called them, would flourish in Germany, he realized that the depth of the authoritarian tradition made such mass participation extremely unlikely. Moreover, he

---

3 Marianne Weber, *Max Weber: A Biography*, trans. Harry Zohn (New York, 1975), 304, see also 279–304 on Weber's American visit.

considered the future of pluralist democracy problematical even in the United States, because he believed that the logic of instrumental rationality, which he believed would dominate the modern world on both sides of the Atlantic, contradicts the logic of democracy. The unpredictability of the electorate is taken for granted in democracy. But that unpredictability undermines the values of consistency and efficiency central to large-scale corporations and large-scale government. For that reason, Weber believed that popular participation in setting goals or determining ends would necessarily disappear Even the United States, which Weber admitted "still bears the character of a polity which, at least in the technical sense, is not fully bureaucratized," was bound to change. "The greater the zones of friction with the outside and the more urgent the needs for administrative unity at home become, the more this character is inevitably and gradually giving way formally to the bureaucratic structure."[4] Faced with a choice between the strict calculability of a professionalized administration or the spirited but capricious will of the people, all cultures operating according to the principles of instrumental reason – that is to say, all modern culture, whether in America or Europe – would inevitably opt for bureaucracy over democracy.

Weber conceded that democracy might succeed in certain circumstances. Democracy requires small, local, egalitarian organizations, staffed by rotating administrations of amateurs, which disappeared as interdependent social and economic organizations of great size and complexity replaced well integrated and harmonious communities. In direct democracies, participation was an end in itself as well as a means, and for that reason efficiency mattered less than maintaining civic virtue. But with a few notable exceptions, such as the Greek and Italian city states and the Swiss cantons, democratic communities quickly collapsed; frequently, as in Switzerland, the appearance of participation masked the reality of elite domination. Even in apparently undeveloped regions of America such as the Oklahoma Territory, Weber reported after his visit, traditional forms of local life of the sort necessary to sustain a democratic culture were

---

4 Max Weber, "Capitalism and Rural Society in Germany," in Max Weber, *From Max Weber: Essays in Sociology*, trans. ed., and intro. by Hans H. Gerth and C. Wright Mills (New York, 1946), 363–85; Max Weber, *The Protestant Ethic and the Spirit of Capitalism*, trans. Talcott Parsons (New York, 1930), 47–78; and Max Weber, *Economy and Society: An Outline of Interpretive Sociology*, trans. Ephraim Fischoff et al., ed. Guenther Roth and Claus Wittich (Berkeley and Los Angeles, 1978), 961, 971; see also Wolfgang J. Mommsen, *Max Weber and German Politics, 1890–1920*, 2d rev. ed., trans. Michael S. Steinberg (Chicago, 1984), 323; David Beetham, *Max Weber and the Theory of Modern Politics* (London, 1974), 152–64; and Guenther Roth's epilogue in Guenther Roth and Wolfgang Schluchter, *Weber's Vision of History: Ethics and Methods* (Berkeley and Los Angeles, 1979), 200–1.

under attack. "With almost lightning speed," he wrote, "everything that stands in the way of capitalistic culture is being crushed."[5]

Weber did not of course believe that socialism offered an alternative to the inevitable domination of popular impulses by a professionalized bureaucracy. To the contrary, "the steel frame of modern industrial work" would impose its logic even if the management of the economy were integrated into the state bureaucracy. Working conditions in the state-owned Prussian mines and railroads, Weber pointed out, did not differ appreciably from those in private industries. Now it is surely true that there are bureaucracies and bureaucracies, and Weber might have begged important questions by offering the notoriously rigid Prussian civil service as prototypical. But his point concerned a structural problem. Whereas in a capitalist economy public and private bureaucracies could, at least in principle, check one another's excesses, in a socialist state they "would be merged into a single hierarchy. This would occur in a much more rational – and hence unbreakable – form." Weber dismissed democratic socialism as a utopian delusion. In the modern world, the pressure of instrumental reason would strangle popular participation in any economic scheme. In small groups, value rational and instrumentally rational action might combine, but the insistence on abstract rules for the sake of equality, together with the prevalence of merely functional interactions characteristic of interdependent society, would gradually displace all forms of democratic participation.[6]

Because he identified bureaucratization with the larger process of rationalization, Weber denied that democracy could control the power of bureaucracy. The demand for specialized knowledge, which replaced the demand for what Weber called "magical means to master or implore the spirit," rendered democracy anachronistic. "Technical means and calculations," Weber wrote, now "perform the service" of providing meaning. One of the paradoxes of this period concerns the contrast between the liberation apparently promised by social science and the control threat-

---

5 Marianne Weber, *Max Weber*, 293; see also Weber, *Economy and Society*, 2: 949–52, 1414–15; and the fine essay by Ernest Kilker, "Max Weber and the Possibilities for Democracy," in Ronald M. Glassman and Vatro Murvar, eds., *Max Weber's Political Sociology: A Pessimistic Vision of a Rationalized World*, Contributions in Sociology, no. 45 (Westport, Conn., 1984), 55–65.

6 Max Weber, "Parliament and Government in a Reconstructed Germany," in Weber, *Economy and Society*, 2: 1401; "Speech for the General Information of Austrian Officers in Vienna," in *Max Weber: The Interpretation of Social Reality*, ed. J. E. T. Eldridge (New York, 1971), 203–4. See also Stephen Kalberg, "The Role of Ideal Interests in Max Weber's Historical Sociology," in Robert J. Antonio and Ronald M. Glassman, eds., *A Marx-Weber Dialogue* (Lawrence, Kans., 1985), 59; Wolfgang Schluchter, *The Rise of Western Rationalism: Max Weber's Developmental History*, trans. Guenther Roth (Berkeley and Los Angeles, 1981), 115–17; and Jürgen Habermas, *The Philosophical Discourse of Modernity: Twelve Lectures*, trans. Frederick Lawrence (Cambridge, 1987), 70.

ened by bureaucratization: On the one hand, the emancipation of knowledge from dogma made possible an increasing emphasis on experience and volition. On the other hand, however, the increasing reliance on bureaucracy, as the institutionalized form of that knowledge, made use of the techniques of social science to usurp power from the individuals whose liberation, both intellectual and political, Weber and other liberals and social democrats wanted to make possible.[7]

Weber nevertheless championed the democratic values that appeared from his description of modern politics to be in such peril. In an address he delivered in 1894, Weber proclaimed that the goal of political and social action must be to cultivate "personal responsibility, the deep aspiration for the moral and spiritual goals of mankind."[8] Although his commitment has seldom been acknowledged, Weber passionately affirmed the importance of struggling against the thrust of history for the values of personal liberty and popular government. Arguing against liberals waiting for the market and orthodox Marxists waiting for the revolution, Weber wrote, "It would be extremely harmful to the chances of 'democracy' and 'individualism' today, if we were to rely for their 'development' on the 'lawlike' operation of *material* interests." For those interests were pointing history in the opposite direction, either toward industrial America's "benevolent feudalism" or toward Germany's "so-called 'welfare institutions,'" both of which in their separate ways threatened individual autonomy. "Everywhere," Weber wrote, "*the casing of the new serfdom* is ready." Merely the continuation of the economic, social, and political processes already in motion would end in that enslavement.

Weber expected the pressures threatening individuality to intensify, but he considered resistance possible. The further "parcelling out of the soul," to use his description of the consequences of disenchantment, could be halted only by "the resolute *will* of a nation not to allow itself to be led like a flock of sheep. We 'individualists' and supporters of 'democratic' institutions are swimming 'against the stream' of material developments. Anyone who wishes to be the weathervane of 'developmental trends' might as well abandon these outdated ideals as quickly as possible."[9] Weber himself, however, emphatically refused to abandon the ideals of

---

7 Max Weber, "Science as a Vocation," in *From Max Weber*, 139.
8 Cf. the contrasting interpretations of Weber's speech before the Protestant Social Congress in Beetham, *Max Weber and the Theory of Modern Politics*, 43–4; Mommsen, *Max Weber and German Politics*, 91–123; and Lawrence A. Scaff, *Fleeing the Iron Cage: Culture, Politics, and Modernity in the Thought of Max Weber* (Berkeley and Los Angeles, 1989), 65–72.
9 Max Weber, "The Prospects for Liberal Democracy in Tsarist Russia," in *Weber: Selections in Translation*, ed. W. G. Runciman and trans. Eric Matthews (Cambridge, 1978), 281–2.

individuality and democracy, despite their slim chances of survival in the face of rationalization.

As a scholar Weber felt obliged to identify the unique constellation of economic, social, political, and intellectual factors that led to the development of the liberal values he cherished, and he felt obliged to point out the differences between those circumstances and the circumstances of his own day. His aversion to wishful thinking did not, however, entail acquiescence in the demolition of freedom and popular government. Indeed, the concept of plebiscitary leader democracy that Weber developed in the wake of World War I must be understood in terms of his conviction that democracy in Germany could survive only in that unstable form. Given the precarious position of any German state in the postwar crisis, given the absence of any democratic tradition in Germany, and given the pressures of bureaucratization, Weber judged the personal charisma of a leader indispensable for a German republic. Of the three forms of legitimate domination, *viz.* traditional, rational, and charismatic, Weber believed that only the latter was appropriate in a postimperial Reich. Tradition had been annulled by the end of the German Empire. Rationality would lead inexorably to bureaucratization. But a charismatic leader – restrained, it must be remembered, by constitutional government, and deriving his authority from the consent of the governed – might be able to prevent the paralysis of the public will that Weber considered otherwise unavoidable in postwar Germany. While his concept of democracy understandably evokes a shudder in the wake of this century's lessons in charismatic domination, I believe Weber was willing to entrust such power to a democratically chosen leader precisely because he feared the numbing effects of bureaucracy more than he doubted the ability of the people to select responsible leaders.[10]

Weber was not disillusioned about the prospects for political action. In fact, he suggested in "Politics as a Vocation" that a unique form of ethical life might be possible in the public realm. He drew a distinction between the ethic of single-minded conviction, which can be equated roughly with Kant's categorical imperative, and the ethic of responsibility, which resembled utilitarianism. Given Weber's dramatic characterization of the conflict between these two approaches as a "death struggle," efforts to

---

10 Weber, *Economy and Society*, 2:1459–60; and cf. Mommsen, *Max Weber and German Politics*, 34–43, 355–6, for Weber's emphasis on the difficulties facing Germany in the postwar period, and 382–89, for Mommsen's controversial and tendentious comparison of Weber with Carl Schmitt. See Stephen Turner and Regis Factor, "Decisionism and Politics: Weber as Constitutional Theorist," in Scott Lash and Sam Whimster, eds., *Max Weber, Rationality, and Modernity* (London, 1987), 334–54, for a thoughtful discussion of these issues.

reconcile them might seem futile. Yet Weber seems to have considered a limited resolution possible in a particular kind of political practice. Although Weber failed to find in history or reason any foundation for ultimate standards, he did not conclude that all values are therefore equally legitimate. Ultimately, he believed, individuals must choose their values on the basis of accumulated social experience, without the consolation of certainty. However attractive the ethic of conviction may be, it is no longer possible for everyone in the modern era, because the absolute confidence that must inform such an ethic is no longer widely available. Neither religion nor science can any longer provide the content for a genuine and universal ethic of conviction.

Weber nevertheless believed passionately that a moral life requires more than simply instrumental adjustment to the world. He thought the clubs and associations he encountered all over America were designed to substitute for the "life-forming" doctrines and institutions formerly provided by religions, but they were too shallow to serve the same purpose. The individual must be responsible for the consequences of his actions, for the religious flight from the world remains open to few in a secular age. Yet unless the individual acts in service to some ideal, he sinks into opportunism and forfeits the chance to give meaning to life. "Some kind of faith must always exist," Weber insisted, or else "the curse of the creature's worthlessness overshadows even the externally strongest political successes." Politics "is made with the head, but it is certainly not made with the head alone." Life must be fired by what William James called a will to believe, a faith in the validity of one's goals – even though that faith can have no foundation beyond individual conviction – if it is to have meaning and ethical significance. "It is immensely moving," Weber proclaimed, when an individual

feels with his entire soul the responsibility for the consequences of his actions and thus acts according to the ethic of responsibility. At some point he says, "I cannot do otherwise. Here I stand." That is something genuinely human and stirring. For each of us who is not spiritually dead, this situation must surely be a possibility. In that sense, the ethic of single-minded conviction and the ethic of responsibility are not absolute opposites but supplements, which together constitute a genuine man, a man who can have the "vocation for politics."[11]

11 Max Weber, "Politik als Beruf," in Max Weber, *Gesammelte Politische Schriften*, ed. Johannes Winckelmann (Tübingen, 1958), 536, 547. In this case I have not followed the translation by Gerth and Mills, because I believe it muddles the distinction Weber wanted to draw; cf. *From Max Weber*, 117, 127. For a fine discussion of Weber's 1919 lectures on *Wissenschaft* and *Politik* as vocations, see Wolfgang Schluchter, "Value-Neutrality and the Ethic of Responsibility," in Roth and Schluchter, *Max Weber's Vision of History*, 65–116.

This was obviously a "virtuoso ethic," whose difficulty made its general adoption impossible. Weber doubted that this desperate form of reason, without the buttress provided by religious faith, could sustain the commitment of any but exceptional individuals to such an ethics. We cannot escape the dilemma of choosing between competing values. Especially if we choose to enter the sphere of political activity, we are forced to decide, as William James put it, which of our ideals to butcher.

Weber concluded that no universally applicable solution could be found in religion, science, or politics for the problem of ethics in an era of disenchantment. Neither the democracy offered by America nor the *Kultur* offered by Germany provided a sure solution to this problem. With the freedom that Weber, like most German observers, associated with America, came a challenge to the instrumental rationality characteristic of modernity. The persistent cherishing of such freedom, exemplified by the Americans he met during his trip to St. Louis, prevented the passage of social legislation that activists such as Florence Kelley assured him was essential. But the persistence of that freedom nevertheless seemed to him endangered by the prospect of bureaucracy that instrumental rationality promised, even in America. With the security that Weber, like most German observers, associated with Germany, came a challenge to freedom and the promise of servitude.[12]

The impressions recorded by the first and second generations of American social scientists to study in Germany reveal changes in American perceptions from the late nineteenth to the early twentieth century. In the 1870s American economists taught classical economics, the economics of laissez-faire. American students who wanted to continue their studies in economics after completing their undergraduate training in America were seldom invited into the clubby world of English universities, but they could attend German universities, which welcomed foreigners. Moreover, even including the cost of transatlantic travel, they were able to study in German universities for a third less than a year's study at Cornell, Harvard, or Johns Hopkins. When American students arrived in Germany in the 1870s, they found not only the *Kultur* that Americans

---

12 Most of Weber's critics have considered his ethical ideas inadequate because he does not resolve the conflict between the ethics of conviction and responsibility. Cf. esp. Wolfgang Schluchter, "The Paradox of Rationalization: On the Relation of Ethics and World," in Roth and Schluchter, *Max Weber's Vision of History*, 50–9; and Mommsen, *Max Weber and German Politics*, 440–5. Efforts to "go beyond" Weber on this point seem to me unpersuasive, for reasons I discuss in *Uncertain Victory: Social Democracy and Progressivism in European and American Thought, 1870–1920* (New York, 1986), 340–8. The contrast Weber drew between freedom and security was consistent with the contrast presented in Helbich's contribution to this volume, but Weber was hardly optimistic about the cultural consequences in either case.

associated with the German world, they also found a new nation apparently alive to a wide range of possibilities.

Their German experience helped turn American economists toward the notion of economic reform. Developments during the earliest phase of the American Economic Association (AEA) reflect the importance of the model provided by the Verein für Sozialpolitik, which challenged the doctrines of laissez-faire and emphasized state action to counter the destructive forces of the market. Not coincidentally, five of the six founding officers of the AEA had studied in Germany, and they hoped to make the AEA an instrument for social reform. For these Americans, the Berliners Adolph Wagner and Gustav Schmoller, the central figures in the Verein, were the most important influences. Wagner emphasized morality as a counterweight to capitalist excess; although he agreed with most of the program of the German Social Democratic Party, he refused to become a member. Garrett Droppers, a Harvard graduate who arrived in Berlin in 1888, contrasted what Wagner offered to the "thinness" of American economic teaching: "German teaching inspires more fervor – gives one somewhat a spiritual sense of the true destiny of man." Economics in Germany was "more saturated with the spirit of social helpfulness, a higher sense of the dignity and functions of the State, an enthusiasm for the welfare of society. It was a new experience and I have never forgotten or lost it."[13] As that passage illustrates, it was the weight of German *Kultur* that most powerfully impressed these American students. Schmoller contributed the historical sensibility to the study of economics: He taught that all economic doctrines change and develop. Schmoller was the central figure behind the Verein, which Daniel Rodgers characterizes as "a factory of social fact finding, building cautiously and professionally the empirical rationale for the interventionist state."[14] Wagner looked for income redistribution through taxation; Schmoller relied mostly on a paternalistic welfare state engineered from above.

But all of these American students were put off by Wagner's and Schmoller's fondness for Bismarck and state authority: a preference for popular sovereignty was evidently an American impulse unaffected by

---

13 Droppers' response to a questionnaire distributed by Henry W. Farnam is quoted by Daniel Rodgers, "The Transatlantic Roots of the American Welfare State, 1870–1945," an unpublished paper delivered at the annual meeting of the Organization of American Historians, Apr. 1992, 32. I discuss the origins of the American Economic Association, and the competing interpretations of its development, in *Uncertain Victory*, 211, 461n.23. See also Dorothy Ross, *The Origins of American Social Science* (Cambridge, 1992).

14 Rodgers, "The Transatlantic Roots of the American Welfare State," 35.

exposure to German *Kultur.* H. C. Adams reported that he was troubled by the banning of books during the period of anti-socialist repression and unsettled by the policeman who silenced him with the stern admonition that in Berlin, "whistling is forbidden."[15]

This first generation returned to America in the late 1870s and early 1880s with a mixed message: They accepted the critique of capitalism's excesses and the immorality of poverty, a critique they associated with German *Kultur* and its respect for restraint and humanistic rather than materialistic values. But they were unwilling to resort to autocratic state socialism as the solution. H. C. Adams, H. L. A. Seligman, John Bates Clark, and Richard T. Ely all shared a certain enthusiasm for what was considered radical democratic reform in America during these years.

After the Haymarket Riot of 1886, however, agitation for reforms such as the eight-hour day took on a different tone. Such activism was seen as dangerous and subversive. Preliminary efforts to establish the American Economic Association had begun in 1885, and showed clearly the influence of German historical economics and the shaping influence of the model provided by the Verein. But during the 1890s, the economics profession shifted away from that early flirtation with radical reform. The popular reaction against radicalism was certainly part of it, as was the emergence during those years of the competing vision of marginalist economics. In Germany, according to Daniel Rodgers, reservoirs of "precapitalist sentiment" sustained the economists' critique, and their high status made them immune to pressure from businessmen. In the United States, in the absence of equally powerful precapitalist sentiments, businessmen did indeed dictate to universities who should teach what. The case of Richard Ely, one of America's most prominent economists, who was charged with teaching socialism and brought to trial before the University of Wisconsin Board of Regents in 1895, demonstrated that lesson. Ely managed to clear his name, and maintain his position at Wisconsin, by distancing his brand of reformist activism from the revolutionary socialism he deplored. But his case, as well as the experience of other academics who espoused unpopular political ideas, had a chilling effect on American social science. American economists resolved their problem by settling for a more or less secure role as policy advisors, which they won by making clear that they were advocating moderate, democratic reform rather than anarchism or revolution. Champions of laissez-faire lost their grip over academic discourse in America during these years,

---

15 Adams quoted in ibid., 40.

but they were replaced by a less self-consciously reformist band of professional economists than at least some members of this generation had initially hoped to become.

When a later generation of Americans arrived to study in Germany in the 1890s, their reaction to German *Kultur* was quite different. First, the novelty had worn off the challenge to laissez-faire, largely through the efforts of the generation of social scientists that preceded them. Germany too had changed: W. E. B. Du Bois, for example, reported that Berlin in 1892–4 was dominated by an ever-present military that set the tone for the city's public life. Berlin marched in a "half military stride," and "German ideals from king to lower orders appear at first sight to be clad in spurs and shoulder straps." To Du Bois, the regular parades through the Brandenburg Gate left an indelible image of a Germany dominated by the Kaiser and his "white and golden troops." To Du Bois and to others of his generation, Germany no longer appeared to be the bastion of attractive precapitalist values that American students could contrast to their own culture of laissez-faire liberalism. Instead it had become something very different, something unattractive.[16] The seeds of that transformation, it might be noted, were already present in the ambivalence the first generation felt toward the autocratic politics that they considered the underside of the Germany they encountered as students.

My third test case is the German reception of America's principal contribution to twentieth-century philosophy, pragmatism. The standard German response to William James's *Pragmatism*, which was translated into German by Wilhelm Jerusalem and published in Germany in 1908, was to characterize his ideas as a typical American expression of the commercial mentality that was "inimical to all philosophy and science."[17] James's critics accused him of reducing philosophy to a mere question of what works. In the words of C. Gutberlet, writing on "Der Pragmatismus" in *Philosophisches Jahrbuch* (1908): "This philosophy degrades the truth to the level of expediency, just as, in days gone by, a similar way of thinking was imported to us from the land of the shopkeepers preaching the reduction of morality to utility."[18] Other German

---

16 Du Bois quoted in David Levering Lewis, *W. E. B. Du Bois: Biography of a Race, 1868–1919* (New York, 1993), 136–7. A quick survey of two generations of American economics students thus confirms the argument of Jörg Nagler in this volume regarding the changing significance of German *Kultur* from the American point of view.
17 See Hans Joas, "American Pragmatism and German Thought: A History of Misunderstandings," in Hans Joas, *Pragmatism and Social Theory* (Chicago, 1993), 97.
18 Ibid., 98. Such misconceptions of pragmatism were common during James's lifetime, and they have persisted despite the efforts of James and other pragmatists. I discuss the continuities and

interpreters treated pragmatism as a species of Mach's positivism, a reduction of philosophy to science.

One of the few German philosophers to understand James's work as an effort to resolve Kant's antinomies was Günther Jacoby, who offered an appreciation of pragmatism as his inaugural lecture at the University of Greifswald in 1909. Jacoby saw pragmatism as an attempt to bring the critical spirit of science to the world of philosophy. His efforts won him James's gratitude and a visiting professorship at Harvard in 1910, the year of James's death. But by 1912 even Jacoby had turned away from pragmatism, and in his later writing on American philosophy he resorted to the sorts of national stereotyping he had earlier rejected as misleading and unhelpful. Whereas German philosophy reflected what Jacoby called the "inexhaustible power of the German people," American philosophy, as reflected in James's work, derived instead from American culture's obsession with "personal qualities having economic value."[19]

Another influential interpretation of James's pragmatism was that expressed by Georg Simmel, who characterized pragmatism as "the part of the [sic] Nietzsche which the Americans adopted."[20] Although there is no evidence of Nietzsche having exerted any influence on American pragmatists, this remark was not altogether off the mark, because James *was* attempting to call into question the basic assertion of a stable, universal human truth and to suggest we open up our inquiries in other directions. But James had another agenda, the desire to replace old absolutisms with more fruitful philosophical and cultural hypotheses, and there he parted company decisively with Nietzsche.

The later use and abuse of pragmatism by German thinkers such as Max Scheler and Martin Heidegger, and the recent appreciation of pragmatism by Karl-Otto Appel and Jürgen Habermas, is beyond the scope of these remarks. I want only to emphasize that the prevailing stereotypes of American thought poisoned the German reception of the most important philosophical development of this century, and it is only within the last two decades that efforts to correct this misunderstanding have begun. Hans Joas's outstanding book *Pragmatism and Social Theory* and his efforts to make available the ideas of John Dewey should go a long way toward advancing that cause.

---

changes in the discourse of pragmatists, and the critical commentary on pragmatism, in "Pragmatism: An Old Name for Some New Ways of Thinking?" *Journal of American History* (forthcoming, 1996).
19 Ibid., 100.
20 Ibid., 99.

Late nineteenth- and early twentieth-century American philosophers, for their part, largely returned the favor of their German contemporaries, misunderstanding German thought by filtering it through a set of equally distorting stereotypes. James's writings about German philosophy were almost uniformly critical, either of the dogmatic rigidity or the obsession with lifeless abstractions that he associated with the German philosophical tradition descended from Kant and Hegel. Although James's own philosophy resonated with themes strikingly similar to those developed in Wilhelm Dilthey's hermeneutics, James never addressed the similarities himself; instead he persisted in criticizing what he considered the unhealthy inheritance of earlier idealists in German philosophy.[21]

John Dewey, the other most prominent American pragmatist, was deeply engaged with German philosophy. He wrote his doctoral dissertation on Kant, and he often confessed his lifelong debt to Hegel and to the historical sensibility that he associated with Hegelian thought. But when he tried to characterize the German cultural tradition in his 1915 book *German Philosophy and Politics*, he relied on stereotypes as wooden as those employed by the German interpreters and critics of pragmatism. Dewey argued that the autocratic and militaristic dimensions of Wilhelmine Germany had their roots in an unlikely source, the transcendental philosophy of Kant. By separating the noumenal and phenomenal spheres, Kant demarcated realms for spiritual freedom and for ruthless efficiency. Since Kant's categorical imperative was purely formal, ethical constraints did not check the development of a power-hungry *Realpolitik*. Dewey pointed out, accurately enough, that Kant's ethics requires men to do their duty but does not specify what that duty is. In Dewey's words, "a gospel of duty separated from empirical purposes and results tends to gag intelligence. It substitutes for the work of reason displayed in a wide and distributed survey of consequences in order to determine where duty lies, an inner consciousness, empty of content, which clothes with the form of rationality the demands of existing social authorities."[22] To provide moral guidelines, the German state autocratically imposed specific duties and justified them according to a grand vision of the historical role of the German nation.

Dewey's portrait might seem to be drawn more plausibly from an ungenerous reading of Fichte and Hegel than from the writings of the author of *Perpetual Peace*. After all, in one formulation of the categorical

---

21 I discuss James's critique of German thought in greater detail in *Uncertain Victory*, 46–63.
22 John Dewey, "German Philosophy and Politics," in John Dewey, *The Middle Works, 1899–1924*, vol. 8: *1915*, ed. Jo Ann Boydston, with intro. Joe R. Burnett (Carbondale, Ill., 1979), 164.

imperative, Kant specified "Treat humanity as an end in itself, and never as a means only," which would seem to rule out absolutely wars of conquest for reasons of state. But Dewey insisted that Kant, by severing the link between ideals and the consequences of action, had set Germany down the road toward the autocratic politics, the imperialism, and the militarism that Dewey believed characterized the late nineteenth- and early twentieth-century *Reich*.

Clearly, misconceptions about the other culture abounded during these years on both sides of the Atlantic: German philosophers misinterpreted and dismissed American pragmatists; American pragmatists misinterpreted and dismissed German philosophers. Nevertheless – and this is an awkward question to raise, since it shifts the inquiry from the misty atmosphere of perceptions to the perhaps even more elusive atmosphere of ostensibly verifiable historical reality – one might ask whether these perceptions were altogether inaccurate. After all, American reformers such as Ely, or Dewey, were indeed judged unrealistic if not dangerous when they challenged the dominance of American culture by businessmen. Does their fate suggest that America was becoming just as much a commercial culture as German critics assumed? James's German interpreters surely misunderstood his pragmatism, but they nevertheless might have understood his America all too well. Their critique of American culture not only resembled that of Thorstein Veblen – and prefigured that of C. Wright Mills and other mid-twentieth-century American radicals – it was also similar to James's own critique of American culture and its worship of what he called "the bitch goddess success."[23]

By the same token, were the second generation of American graduate students, and Dewey, altogether mistaken about the absence of popular sovereignty, the anemic liberalism of the German bourgeoisie, and the autocratic and militaristic tendencies of Wilhelmine Germany? If Dewey overstated the role played by Kant, did he not identify precisely the fatal bargain made by German liberals when they repeatedly justified the presence of autocracy by idealizing the historical mission of the German nation? Dewey's exaggerations notwithstanding, there are striking similarities between Dewey's argument and Leonard Krieger's still provocative analysis in *The German Idea of Freedom*.[24]

The point I want to suggest in conclusion is that Americans' percep-

---

[23] I discuss James's social and political criticism in *Uncertain Victory*, 145–95; see also George Cotkin, *William James, Public Philosopher* (Baltimore, 1990), 73–176.

[24] Leonard Krieger, *The German Idea of Freedom: History of a Political Tradition from the Reformation to 1871* (Chicago, 1957).

tion of German *Kultur* changed in part because Germany changed, because it did indeed become more militaristic and autocratic from 1870 to 1914. German perceptions of America likewise changed in part because America also changed, because it did indeed become more materialistic, more commercially oriented, during this period.

The reason for those changes lies in the cultural transformations noted by Weber in his analysis of rationalization and by Dewey in his analysis of what happened to Kantian ethics in German public life during the course of the nineteenth century. As instrumental rationality, means-ends reasoning, and an obsession with calculations of efficiency replaced the traditional religious and moral values that underlay both German *Kultur* and the Christian and republican virtue prized in eighteenth- and early nineteenth-century America, both nations changed.[25] The shifting perceptions of intellectuals on both sides of the Atlantic, despite undeniable exaggerations and distortions, reflected that profound cultural transformation.

25 I examine this complicated process in greater detail in "The Virtues of Liberalism: Christianity, Republicanism, and Ethics in Early American Political Discourse," *Journal of American History* 74 (1987): 9–33; and in "The Republican Idea in American History and Historiography," *La Revue Tocqueville/The Tocqueville Review* 13 (1992): 119–36.

8

Germany and the United States, 1914–1933

The Mutual Perception of Their Political Systems

PETER KRÜGER

Some years ago Octavio Paz wrote:

There is no country better informed than the United States; its journalists are excellent and they are everywhere, its specialists have all the data and background facts needed for each case – yet what comes forth from this gigantic mountain of information and news is, almost always, the mouse of the fable.[1]

There is indeed a widening gap between the ever increasing wealth of detailed information and the ability to make adequate use of it, to digest and to integrate it into a larger context.

This leads to an interesting point worth noting in regard to images and perceptions. The sheer amount and the complex character of information might indirectly become a source of misperception; if the details are hard to follow, their interpretation becomes ambiguous. Most people tend to dismiss thorough analysis, if it becomes too difficult, lengthy, and wearisome. Whether they are unable or merely unwilling to cope with the unwieldy bulk of modern information, the consequences will be that they tend to relapse into their familiar views of other countries and into traditional patterns of explaining the attitudes of foreign nations. Moreover, today it seems necessary to distinguish between misperception and misunderstanding. "Misperception" is a mistaken perception of a more or less obvious phenomenon, of a certain behavior, action, or institution – in the comprehensive sense of the word –, whereas "misunderstanding"

I would like to express my thanks to the Wilson Center in Washington, D.C., for supporting part of the research for this chapter and to Prof. Paul W. Schroeder for his helpful comments during preparation of this manuscript.
1 Octavio Paz, "Notes on the United States," *Wilson Quarterly* 10 (Spring 1986): 90.

may include all this but implies still more, for instance, a wrong interpretation or utilization of perceptions, even if they are correct. Furthermore, misunderstandings may arise from a biased emphasis, generalization, or exaggeration of a correct perception as well as of the results of scholarly research. Whether a misunderstanding will become popular depends on the national tradition, the public atmosphere, and the media. Consequently, the borders toward "misinterpretation" are imprecise, "misinterpretation" referring mainly to a miscarried analysis.

Such a vast field of research must be limited. Because constitutional principles and governmental power have an increasing impact even on international relations this chapter concentrates on the mutual American and German evaluations of each other's political systems, considering the political system in a broader sense as the place where the characteristic structure, the issues, and the main tendencies of a society are manifest. There is no doubt, however, that in the United States as well as in Germany it was only a small, though sometimes influential minority that really observed the constitutional development in the other country.[2] This fact intensifies, in contrast, the vagueness of the mutual perceptions in the general public, since that minority was both, only selectively influential as well as often not interested very much in educating a broad variety of less-educated opinion. Therefore, my study is concentrated on a few groups – politicians and diplomats, jurists, and publicists – and on public statements that influenced public opinion or at least certain segments of it. In a first stage of research these groups had been analyzed extensively but separately; in a second stage their views had been compared and linked along lines of common historical development as well as contemporary arguments and political affiliation; and in a third stage, presented in this chapter, the source material was condensed to a few prevalent strands

---

2 There is a growing literature dealing with the image of the United States in Germany and vice versa; see, e.g., *Amerikastudien/American Studies* 31, no. 2 (1986); Frank Trommler, ed., *Amerika und die Deutschen: Bestandsaufnahme einer 300jährigen Geschichte* (Opladen, 1986). On constitutional matters, see Hermann Wellenreuther, ed., *German and American Constitutional Thought* (New York, 1990). Although they deal with different areas of research, the contributions in this volume by Jörg Nagler (on mutual cultural images) and Philipp Gassert (on industrial rationalization and technically oriented modernization) add important dimensions of mutual images between 1870 and 1939. Jörg Nagler's chapter paves the way for discussing mutual American-German images during World War I; the current chapter follows the course he has laid out. Additional studies are Phyllis Keller, *States of Belonging: German-American Intellectuals and the First World War* (Cambridge, Mass., 1979); James R. Mock, *Words That Won the War: The Committee on Public Information, 1917–1919* (New York, 1968); Jürgen Möckelmann, "Das Deutschlandbild in den USA 1914–1918 und die Kriegszielpolitik Wilsons," Ph.D. diss., University of Hamburg, 1975; Fred A. Sondermann, "The Wilson Administration's Image of Germany," Ph.D. diss., Yale University, 1953; and Philipp Gassert, *Amerika im Dritten Reich: Die Kritik der amerikanischen Moderne in Ideologie, Volksmeinung und Propaganda, 1933–1945* (forthcoming).

and positions across the groups in order to gain on that higher level of public discourse a basis for the development of common as well as conflicting images and attitudes in correlation to different political orientations. The more ambiguous and complicated German perception of the political system of the United States has acquired more emphasis than vice versa.

I

World War I became a basic determinant of the strange relationship and the precarious understanding between the United States and Germany during the short-lived Weimar Republic. Under the influence of the war German-American tensions, which had been growing continuously during the prewar period, erupted into fierce ideological warfare. At the same time the war revealed in an unexpected way and accelerated dramatically the process of both countries becoming particularly important to each other, a process already discernible in the two decades before 1914, above all in their growing, extraordinary economic strength. Obviously, the defeat of Germany created new conditions. However, although now dependent on the rising American world power, the United States still needed Germany – at least since they wanted to stabilize Europe for the sake of their economic and political interests.[3]

Particularly during the war a special kind of nationalist feeling arose in Germany that can be characterized as the "besieged nation syndrome," a nationalist phenomenon that has proved its force again and again, most recently in the case of Serbia. Many Germans, especially in the educated classes, were propagating a war-minded, anti-Western mission to the world – and this basically defensive mood developed before 1914, too, although standing out far less prominently and aggressively then. At the same time they wanted to protect themselves against dangerous influences

---

3 On American-German relations, see Werner Link, *Die amerikanische Stabilisierungspolitik in Deutschland 1921–32* (Düsseldorf, 1970); Hans W. Gatzke, *Germany and the United States: A "Special Relationship?"* (Cambridge, Mass., 1980); Manfred Jonas, *The United States and Germany: A Diplomatic History* (Ithaca, N.Y., 1984); Klaus Schwabe, *Woodrow Wilson, Revolutionary Germany, and Peace-Making* (Chapel Hill, N.C., 1985); Manfred Berg, *Gustav Stresemann und die Vereinigten Staaten von Amerika: Weltwirtschaftliche Verflechtung und Revisionspolitik 1907–1929* (Baden-Baden, 1990); Elisabeth Glaser-Schmidt, "Von Versailles nach Berlin: Überlegungen zur Neugestaltung der deutsch-amerikanischen Beziehungen in der Ära Harding," in Norbert Finzsch et al., eds., *Liberalitas: Festschrift für Erich Angermann* (Stuttgart, 1992), 319–42; Hans-Jürgen Schröder, ed., *Confrontation and Cooperation: Germany and the United States in the Era of World War I, 1900–1924* (Providence, R.I., 1993), and Hans-Jürgen Schröder, ed., *Deutschland und Amerika in der Epoche des Ersten Weltkriegs, 1900–1924* (Stuttgart, 1993), with a detailed bibliography.

from abroad in politics and culture, against a tide of changes in a changing world. Under these circumstances, the image of the United States became a touchstone of the political tendencies and the attitude toward modernization within Germany. Not only modernization in general was at stake but in particular the question of how to organize society adequately – in both countries.

Finally, American war propaganda and condemnation of Prussianized Germany, of its autocracy, militarism, and inhumanity, also has to be placed within its historical context. From 1866 on most American commentators, although not uncritical, had been pro-Prussian and welcomed Germany's being united by Prussia and the constitution of the Reich as well.[4] Remarkable, however, was the gradual move from optimism to skepticism in the United States. It was not only due to the evolution of the German system of government, to the changing political and social conditions in the United States, and to political tensions between both countries in the age of imperialism, especially since the turn of the century. From the very starting point of Prussia's German career there had always been in the United States a current of outright disapproval, opposition, and distrust of Prussia and Prussian Germany as well. This attitude became obvious among former Confederates, in the pro-French and pro-democratic press during the Franco-Prussian War. They accused Prussia of perpetrating atrocities. It is from this period that all those catchwords dominant in World War I date – militarism, despotism, Prussianism, etc. – including the comparison with the Huns.[5] These were definite patterns that were not unique and typical of World War I but rather cliches that could be reactivated quickly.

Thus, World War I compressed and drew to an extreme certain negative images of the other nation, in the United States as well as in Germany, that did not originate in the war. This may be briefly illustrated by referring to the interlaced American perception of Prussia and of the interventionist German notion of the state as well as of the German perception of American political mechanisms and mass democracy. Especially during the Wilhelmine era comments on the American political system were more conventional and less stimulating than

---

4 Peter Krüger, "Die Beurteilung der Reichsgründung und der Reichsverfassung von 1871 in den USA," in Finzsch et al., eds., *Liberalitas*, 263–83.
5 John G. Gazley, *American Opinion of German Unification, 1848–1871* (New York, 1926; reprinted: New York, 1970), 398; Clara E. Schieber, *The Transformation of American Sentiment Toward Germany, 1870–1914* (New York, 1923).

vice versa.⁶ Nonetheless, in both countries fundamental topics of major concern stood their ground over long periods, especially from the late nineteenth century to 1933, regardless of sympathy or antipathy; they did not change together with a positive or negative basic mood. The image of Prussia is one of the best examples; it remained important, for better or worse. Moreover, in both countries those preferred topics directed the mutual perceptions of the masses on the political level in general. Again, Prussia as the epitome of certain German characteristics and with a deep mobilizing effect on the masses during World War I provides an impressive example.⁷

To start with German perceptions under the reign of William II, knowledge and understanding of the complicated political system of the United States was poor, even among educated Germans. There was less motive or inclination among Germans than in other periods to look across the ocean for constitutional models or advice. Toward the end of the nineteenth century well-known stereotypes were spreading in Germany. They denounced and misunderstood cases of political corruption, bad administration, and arbitrary presidents as the very essence of the American political order and as telling examples of what befell republics based on unrestrained mass democracy.

To many Germans, particularly in the nationalist movement and in certain economic interest groups, the United States was becoming a nightmare in the late nineteenth century, an ascending, irresistible world power constricting Germany and dominating world markets. Its strength was said to be based on ruthless capitalism and on a political system that concentrated its energy on rational organization, mechanization, and economic success. No bulwark existed against unbounded capitalism and against the enormous danger of economic and hence political concentration of power. This development was seen as the consequence of a serious

---

6 There are exceptions, e.g., Georg Jellinek, *Allgemeine Staatslehre*, 2d ed. (Berlin, 1905), or Heinrich Triepel, "Die Kompetenzen des Bundestaats und die geschriebene Verfassung," in Wilhelm van Calker and Fritz Fleiner, eds., *Staatsrechtliche Abhandlungen: Festgabe für Paul Laband zum fünfzigsten Jahrestage der Doktor-Promotion*, 2 vols. (Tübingen, 1908), 2:247–335; but cf. James H. Robinson, *The German Bundesrath* (Philadelphia, 1891); Jean DuBuy, *Two Aspects of the German Constitution* (New Haven, Conn., 1894); A. Lawrence Lowell, *Governments and Parties in Continental Europe*, 2 vols. (London, 1896); Walter J. Shepard, "Tendencies Toward Ministerial Responsibility in Germany," *American Political Science Review* 5 (1910): 57–69; Robert Ludlow Fowler vs. Roscoe Pound, "New Philosophies of Law," *Harvard Law Review* 27 (1913–14): 718–35.
7 Cf. the change from *The Nation*, Aug. 16, 1866, to Thorstein Veblen, *Imperial Germany and the Industrial Revolution* (New York, 1915). In general, see Otto Büsch, ed., *Preussen und das Ausland: Beiträge zum europäischen und amerikanischen Preussenbild am Beispiel von England, den USA, Frankreich, Österreich, Polen und Russland* (Berlin, 1982).

lack of culture and an equally serious lack of a well-trained, impartial civil service with a long tradition and a strong sense of duty. A deep-rooted misunderstanding in a double sense: In their failure to appreciate the facts, most Germans were convinced of the superiority of their lauded civil service as being able to control modern economic, technical, and social processes by bureaucratic regulation; and they were likewise convinced that effective political control by parliament and self-government could not work.[8]

During World War I all Germans, especially the political and economic elites, had to decide for or against the United States in a debate that culminated in the question of returning to unlimited submarine warfare in spring 1917. Especially the conservatives felt a hitherto unknown combination: The American Government was striving for a new international order as well as for democratic reform in the world. Moreover, the traditional fears of a disunited and helpless Europe at the mercy of the overwhelming power of the United States seemed to be materializing and frightened not only conservatives. The American political system as a whole became a vital threat to German conservatives and was denounced as a seedbed of all the evils of modern society. But even during the war a minority among the Germans did not accept such war-prolonging views. Hence, the dividing line between Germany and the United States also ran through German society. As a result it was apparent that the United States had become a kind of battleground for the fighting out of fundamental controversies not only over siding with or against American – and Western – political and economic principles but over the future of Germany's constitution.[9]

On the American side the benevolent, pro-German comments from the 1870s, culminating in the emphasis of similarities between the American and German constitutions, had changed in the two decades preceding World War I. This period prepared the ground for the American attitude during the war. Optimism faded away when a liberal development of the Reich did not take place and the interests of both countries began to clash. The American experts in constitutional law, however, did not run into the other extreme. They produced some excellent pieces of penetrating judgment and critical understanding with a remarkable emphasis on

---

8 Fritz Blaich, "Die Rolle der amerikanischen Antitrust-Gesetzgebung in der wirtschaftspolitischen Diskussion Deutschlands zwischen 1890 und 1914," *Ordo* 22 (1971): 229–54.
9 Peter Krüger, "German Disappointment and Anti-Western Resentment, 1918–19," in Schröder, ed., *Confrontation and Cooperation*, 323–35; Ernst Fraenkel, "Das deutsche Wilsonbild," *Jahrbuch für Amerikastudien* 5 (1960): 66–120.

the peculiar course and legacies of German history. This process of deeper analysis and of learning how to evaluate the complicated elements of the German political system and their interrelation was continued into the Weimar Republic, although it influenced only a small part of the American people.

The German notion of the state attracted the greatest attention in the United States and has not lost its prominent position since then. It touched the core of the self-image in both nations and marked the fundamental difference in their principles of how to organize society: American individualism versus the German belief in comprehensive regulation by the state. And yet despite strong American rhetoric some lingering doubts could not be suppressed that the state-oriented German pattern on the road to modernity might become influential or even unavoidable in the United States, too. Such fears came to the fore when American war efforts were to be organized effectively, and they were emphatically repudiated in the strenuous "back to normalcy" politics of the 1920s, only to materialize for many people in the New Deal era. A few hints may suffice to illustrate this development of American perceptions and to explain the American attitude during the war, when the image of the German state was merged with that of Prussia.

A certain starting point, a new challenge to the Americans who distrusted state intervention and rejected governmental organization of society, was provided by the epochal social security acts, inaugurated by the imperial message of 1881. They fascinated American observers from the beginning as a bold experiment in handling social problems critical to every industrialized nation and its political system. Although several commentators recognized the great importance of the German initiatives, soon the opinion prevailed that "the idea ... is socialistic," a kind of state socialism, because the state forged ahead and there would be "no logical end short of that which the extreme socialists have advocated as the 'organization of labor.'"[10]

The next stage, in a worsening public atmosphere between the United States and the Reich, was characterized by thoughtful analyses of the development of Germany's governmental system. In view of Germany's political and social cleavages, its territorial divisions, and its level of political culture, the political scientist Walter Shepard, in 1910, thought

---

10 White (Berlin) to Department of State, Feb. 21, 1881; National Archives, Washington, D.C., DNA, SDR, RG 59, M 44, roll 46. Peter Krüger, "Gesellschaft und Verfassung – ihr Spannungsverhältnis im Kaiserreich von 1871 aus amerikanischer Sicht," in Ferdinand Seibt, ed., *Gesellschaftsgeschichte: Festschrift für Karl Bosl zum 80. Geburtstag* (Munich, 1988), 105–20.

the "adoption of the outward forms of parliamentary government" premature and delaying liberal progress because this incited reactionary forces and the one-sided priority given to achieving national unity:

> The nature of constitutionalism, culminating as it does in democracy, is dispersive, centrifugal, disintegrative. Unification could only be accomplished by the absolutist agencies of iron and blood. The priority between these two movements belonged logically to that for national unity. The constitutional propaganda undoubtedly interfered with, and probably somewhat delayed, the achievement of a united Germany; but the dominant note throughout the period from Jena to Sedan was national unity. This movement has left a heritage of crass materialism, a worship of force, which constitutes one of the striking characteristics of present-day Germany.[11]

Nevertheless, Shepard and others recognized remarkable indications of transition to more representative government and ministerial responsibility. The eminent and decisive role of Prussia in Germany was generally emphasized.

These well-informed perceptions of a small minority paved the way for Thorstein Veblen's pioneering, penetrating analysis of the socioeconomic fabric of the Reich[12] and John Dewey's inquiry into the philosophical aspects of German political thinking.[13] Both books appeared in 1915, with new editions in World War II, a fact that demonstrated the conviction that Hitler's Germany was only the continuation of a distorted historical development in Germany already discernible before World War I. Veblen's book in particular gained extraordinary influence and publicity when American government agencies distributed selected parts of it "as a telling attack on the character of German society" in 1917.[14]

Dewey stressed the separation between state and society in Germany, the dominance of the state as a higher moral entity, and the responsibility of German philosophical and political thinking since Kant for the outcome, the justification of war and sacrifice for "the realization in the Germanic state of the divine idea [of the state]."[15] Veblen set out to explain how it could happen that Germany, a modern society, was embedded in a preindustrial feudal, dynastic state. During a long historical development the concept of an omnipotent state that organized society and the economy and devoted the economic surplus to the expansion of

---

11 Shepard, "Tendencies Toward Ministerial Responsibility in Germany," 58.
12 Veblen, *Imperial Germany*.
13 John Dewey, *German Philosophy and Politics* (New York, 1915; 2d ed., 1942).
14 David M. Kennedy, *Over Here: The First World War and American Society* (New York, 1980), 77–8.
15 Dewey, *German Philosophy*, 113.

its power had been accepted by the people. A tradition of war, bureaucratic surveillance, and "subservience of the community to dynastic ends and dynastic management"[16] had come to prevail in a more and more Prussianized Germany, accustomed to take advantage of any innovation from abroad. This method was applied with remarkable success in the case of modern industrialization. Yet even the United States seemed in danger at the turning point of World War I, when critical American commentators were irritated by the dismal outlook of only being able to fight Prussianism with Prussian tools and of a threatening loss of individualism and freedom.[17]

II

After 1918 all Germans were forced and, to some extent, willing to conform to changed conditions, and particularly the leading political and business circles in their majority were convinced of the necessity of seeking close cooperation with the United States. The United States seemed to be in the position of a more neutral power with a certain distance to European antagonisms and clashes, as a counterweight to France or Great Britain. In Germany, expectations of American assistance flourished continuously. The unbalanced German attitude, often superficial and impaired by thoughtless misunderstandings, was soon discussed in the United States. In 1925, in his preface to Sidney Brooks's *America and Germany, 1918–1925*, George Baker noted:

All through this record appear traces of serious-minded German expectations of finding in America a friend, or even a champion to aid and protect Germany against what the majority of Americans are apt to regard as the consequences of her own acts. One of the principal ingredients for nourishment of those hopes began to show itself, from a certain point in 1918, throughout all classes in Germany in a dependence upon America resembling something akin to childlike faith and forgetfulness of past national acts.... War hatreds have passed, yet many Americans express impatience at what they are likely to term the curious mentality that misconceives America's motives.[18]

World War I had caused a sharpening of the negative German image. It was difficult to forget this, a precarious state of affairs. To a certain degree it depended on the Germans in the Weimar Republic themselves: If they did not behave as they were expected to do, accusations were quickly

---

16 Veblen, *Imperial Germany*, 80.
17 Kennedy, *Over Here*, 43.
18 Sidney Brooks, *America and Germany, 1918–1925* (New York, 1925), ix–x.

revived. Moreover, simplifying images gained a new quality as a way to deal with the increasing complexity of modern political and social processes. It was difficult to understand what the Germans – or Americans – did and why, and how to solve the enormous complexity of problems after the war. There was a growing need for simplification and for selective understanding that favored going back to well-known characteristics and cliches.

The Americans showed their traditional dislike of Prussia as well as of the German state and its social policy. The failure, for instance, to dissolve Prussia in the constitutional decisions of 1919 caused many American commentators to blame the founding fathers of the Weimar constitution for thus preserving the embodiment of a dangerous tradition and a seedbed of reaction.[19] Obviously, it was difficult to understand that after 1919 Prussia had remained not only the backbone of German unity, but above all, under Social Democrat leadership, the backbone of democracy in the Weimar Republic. As to the pattern of the interventionist state, after 1918 the German government reinforced its concern with social policy. The new constitution extended the social responsibility of the state and firmly established recently improved labor legislation. Several American observers commented on this fact with some reservations. In their dislike of state interference and the welfare state, and in their disgust for socialism, they misunderstood German tradition and social necessities.

However, as was usual in periods of good American-German relations, the superficial American emphasis of political affinity and constitutional similarities appeared again and sometimes outweighed cautious analysis in the 1920s. A telling example was the Steuben Day address in New York in 1927, when the American ambassador to Berlin, Jacob Gould Schurman, hailed a unique harmony:

Never in our history have the political institutions and international ideals of Germany and the United States been as much in agreement as they are today. Both nations believe in government of the people, by the people, and for the people. Both are instinctively and unalterably opposed to dictators, no matter whether the dictator is an individual or a class.[20]

---

19 For instance, see Walter J. Shepard, "The New German Constitution," *American Political Science Review* 14 (1920): 34–52; Peter Krüger, "Zwei Epochen. Erfolg und Misserfolg amerikanischer Einwirkung auf den Verfassungswandel in Deutschland nach dem Ersten und Zweiten Weltkrieg," in Helmut Bernsmeier and Hans-Peter Ziegler, eds., *Wandel und Kontinuum: Festschrift für Walter Falk zum 65. Geburtstag* (Frankfurt/Main, 1992), 295–322.
20 Gatzke, *Germany and the United States*, 1.

Sympathetic Germans echoed the theme. Ernst Jaeckh, for instance, the liberal politician and scholar, stressed the congeniality of the two countries' political and social ideals and suggested an alliance of ideas between the United States and Germany, since both nations had in principle the same political orientation.[21]

No doubt, there was a sometimes intimate understanding in the 1920s, and Germany did make some progress toward becoming a democratic state and a society of the Western type, but that advance was supported only by a minority and ended in a failure with terrible consequences. The fact that German politicians, diplomats, or businessmen were eager to win the benevolence of the Americans and to establish the best relations possible and that, moreover, all the interested or well-meaning, openminded Germans, trying to modernize their country, looked to the United States as a model and largely endorsed the American political and economic system, may have created a seductive atmosphere of accord and friendship. Business connections, political relations, and all other contacts worked satisfactorily: a state of affairs very agreeable to pragmatic people.

The actual state of the Weimar Republic received less attention in the United States. In general, there was no adequate comprehension of Germany's undetermined, bitterly controversial way into the future nor of the precarious balance between antagonistic forces in German politics and society. Hence, American misperceptions derived from the often ignored discrepancy between a fascinating facade of modern culture, good will, and temporary success, on the one hand, and, on the other, a deeply shaken, unstable society – a political system without roots and with little popularity.

Like most Americans, the majority of Germans were strongly determined by their own tradition in their views of the other country, but German debates concerning the United States were notably different from American debates on Germany. They were far more extensive and controversial, thus reflecting the inner strife and dissatisfaction of German society. A defensive mood and resentment toward the Americans after 1918 intermingled with the desire for cooperation. Additionally, widespread inability to understand the conditions and the essence of President Wilson's peace policy contributed substantially to the negative attitude toward the United States and its political system. To denounce the American constitution and political practice as deceit and as a superficial performance of an inorganic, "soulless," mechanistic, and atomistic politi-

---

21 Ernst Jaeckh, *Amerika und wir: Amerikanisch-deutsches Ideenbündnis* (Berlin, 1929).

cal machine had become popular in a wide range of conservative and rightist groups. The refusal to discuss seriously and to understand such a complex system reflected in part a long tradition of different political values. After 1918 and throughout the Weimar Republic it was kindled by the vigorous domestic struggle about the right way to reconstruct the German constitution and government. However, liberal groups, and to a certain degree the Social Democrats, welcomed the liberal constitutional standard of the United States. Finally, there was a small but influential group of moderately liberal politicians, businessmen, and political advisers, such as the well-known banker Max Warburg, who for tactical reasons suggested stressing the importance of the American constitution for the creation of the new German constitution, just to please the Americans at a point where they were traditionally susceptible.[22]

In this process Max Weber played a central role. During World War I and immediately thereafter he contributed some of the most penetrating thinking about the reconstruction of Germany's political system. His essays reveal a good knowledge of the American system, but in order to substantiate some fundamental premises and ensuing proposals for a new German constitution, he used his knowledge of American politics to obtain examples of a systematic, typological, and comparative analysis of the functions of political forces in general. This meant that, being basically interested in the structure and functioning of indispensable bureaucracies and their political control within a democratic constitutional framework, he isolated certain elements of American practice and neither took into account their position within the whole system nor raised the question of whether their shortcomings were temporary and accidental phenomena.

Max Weber concentrated on three vital points in American politics: the presidency, the party system, and the problem of the bureaucracy. Above all, he stressed the patronage and the spoils system and their effects, characterizing the parties as completely without principles, as pure majority and office-seeking organizations that changed their meaningless programs according to their only guideline: the best means of getting votes and winning elections. Hence, he described the party system as inevitably addicted to corruption, a welcome contribution to the conservatives' denunciation of any modern party system. Besides this, Max Weber emphasized the formative influence of a combination of three elements

22 Politisches Archiv des Auswärtigen Amts, Bonn, Geschäftsstelle für die Friedensverhandlungen, Protocol of the meeting of Mar. 15, 1919.

on the American political system: the strict separation of powers, the popular election of the president (he omitted the role of the electoral college), and the fact that no parliamentary system existed. Especially the strict separation of powers was not carefully analyzed within the wider framework of the American system of checks and balances but rather quickly declared a defect of the United States' constitution that caused political corruption.

As is well known, Max Weber influenced public opinion in Germany as well as the deliberations of the Weimar National Assembly. Therefore, the effect of his statements was not limited to the academic field. He was apparently impressed by the scandalous events in American politics during the last decades of the nineteenth century, by party bosses, party machines, and corruption. He passed over the changes and countermovements, defined the parties too rigidly, and did not consider the very complex American system of the separation of powers and checks and balances in making his case for parliamentary government as well as strong presidential leadership and a president elected by the people.[23]

In any case, it was no surprise that the National Assembly, which was working on the constitution, decided on the election of a strong president by direct popular vote, but not in the context of a strict separation of powers. Unlike the debate of 1848, there was no profound discussion of the American constitution, neither in this respect nor in others essential to Germany, above all, the substance of a federal structure. Max Weber, considering the German tradition, had pleaded for a federal system that privileged the smaller states in the proportion of votes, but not in such a "radical" way as in the U.S. Senate with its absolute equality of votes for all states. With a rather complicated scheme the National Assembly followed the same principle as Max Weber did. Whenever in constitutional discussions the term "American system" was used, this term was used not to describe the actual American system but merely as a synonym for a federal alternative to the unitarian plans of Hugo Preuss and others. Directly or implicitly this debate revealed that American federalism either was not really understood or that understanding was brushed aside. However, the National Assembly did broach the topic of corruption in

---

23 Max Weber, *Gesammelte politische Schriften*, 3d ed. (Tübingen, 1971), 326–7, 438, 463, 469, 498–500; cf. Wolfgang J. Mommsen, "Die Vereinigten Staaten von Amerika im politischen Denken Max Webers," *Historische Zeitschrift* 213 (1971): 358–81. Mommsen is interested primarily in the general conclusions Max Weber had drawn from his studies of the American political system, particularly his characterization of "leadership democracy with machine" as the future form of democratic rule. He is less interested in analysis of Weber's distortion of the American Constitution and politics.

the American system. The German conservatives condemned the Weimar constitution as "un-German" while it was still being drafted, alleging that it was forced on Germany primarily by the United States.[24]

Thus, German efforts to understand the actual workings of democracy and government in the United States and to compare them with the functioning of German institutions were limited.[25] Nevertheless, Hugo Preuss, first republican minister of the interior and the most important "founding father" of the constitution of the Weimar Republic, was convinced that this constitution stood close to that of the United States or, more generally, the Western constitutional tradition. Its essential characteristics were the same: It established a plan of government, set down a declaration of human and civil rights, and guaranteed these rights by making the very existence of the commonwealth depend on its adherence to these principles. This concept revealed a complex misunderstanding. In most details Preuss did not follow the pattern of the United States' constitution. Not being versed in American politics and constitutional life, he neglected the fact that fundamental principles needed in practice a congenial organization of governmental powers and of the different branches of the political system. He lacked a clear understanding of the close connection between the interdependent elements of sovereignty of the people, separation of powers, and federalism in the United States' constitution, and his own views on these principles were sometimes ambiguous. He was too much bound up in the tradition and the legacy of German constitutionalism. He strove for national unity and misinterpreted the sovereignty of the people as a principle that was effective only on a national level and in the unified state. Federalism in his view was mainly (as was typical of the German tradition) a matter of contract between the states.[26]

The doubts expressed by jurists and by members of the National Assembly about the American model of president, parliament, and the separation of powers were an offspring of traditional German problems with the definition of sovereignty and parliamentary government.[27] On

---

24 Gerhard Anschütz, *Der deutsche Föderalismus: Die Diktatur des Reichspräsidenten*, Veröffentlichungen der Vereinigung der deutschen Staatsrechtslehrer, no. 1 (Berlin, 1924), 22, 24–5; *Verhandlungen der verfassunggebenden Deutschen Nationalversammlung: Stenographische Berichten*, vols. 326–43 (Berlin, 1919–20).
25 See the instructive analysis of changing German interest in the United States by Earl R. Beck, *Germany Rediscovers America* (Tallahassee, Fla., 1968), 135.
26 Above all, see Hugo Preuss, *Reich und Länder: Bruchstücke eines Kommentars zur Verfassung des Deutschen Reiches: Aus dem Nachlass des Verfassers herausgegeben von Gerhard Anschütz* (Berlin, 1928), passim.
27 Rupert Emerson, *State and Sovereignty in Modern Germany* (New Haven, Conn., 1928), 231–6.

the one hand, a strong president elected by direct popular vote was deemed necessary, among other reasons to balance the power of parliament, so that the people in such a dual system would be raised up to the position of a judge over both powers, and could thus make its sovereignty felt. The American concept of sovereignty was not actually considered, or at least not understood. On the other hand, the American presidency throughout the Weimar Republic was often criticized because of the way in which the executive power was not responsible to parliament – again a misunderstanding of the American principle of the separation of powers. It should be added that in general the potential power of the German president escaped the notice of most Americans in the 1920s, and their too optimistic view that the formerly authoritarian state had really been changed by the constitution was often regarded with little sympathy in Germany where the idea of the state as a higher entity did not die.

Another fundamental question, not really dealt with in 1919, was the establishment of a supreme court with the right of judicial review. The National Assembly passed over the idea of a constitutional court rather quickly. It would have been too drastic a change in the German tradition, although some weak seeds existed that produced some surprising growths in the 1920s.[28] But public comments on the problem reveal a profound dislike and misunderstanding of the American institution of a supreme court. Two main objections[29] found a certain resonance in public opinion. First, many commentators, frequently from the conservative ranks, attacked the principle of a supreme court because it subordinated and controlled government. The critics thereby implicitly showed their lack of understanding of the American idea of government as well as of the thorny problems of sovereignty. Second, the Americans were blamed for the difficult procedure for amending their constitution. Such reproaches again demonstrate the problem for Germans of comprehending the fundamental principles of a constitution, of basic and unchangeable rights in a democracy, and of popular sovereignty, which depends on basic rights. In the Weimar Republic the constitution could be changed and constitutional rights set aside by parliament.

Because neither outstanding scholars nor politicians, who were influential both in public affairs as well as in public opinion, paved the way for

---

28 Peter Krüger, "Einflüsse der Verfassung der USA auf die deutsche Verfassungsentwicklung," *Zeitschrift für Neuere Rechtsgeschichte* 18 (1996).
29 See, e.g., *Politisches Handwörterbuch*, 2 vols. (Leipzig, 1923), 2:857; Adolf Halfeld, *Amerika und der Amerikanismus* (Jena, 1927), 15.

a thorough discussion of the American political system, most Germans were little interested in the constitutional structure of the United States. They remained bound by the limits of the German constitutional tradition. The occasional, mostly superficial, use of American examples often merely served political argumentation.[30] This reduced the wealth of American solutions to constitutional problems and constitutional experiences to a matter of political convenience and orientation, a special source of misperception particularly at the lower level of public debate. Some well-known examples may illustrate this.

H. L. Mencken's essay "The American Credo" became popular in Germany, particularly in conservative circles, because of its harsh critique of contemporary American life. It was translated and published in *Die Grenzboten* (1922), an influential conservative journal. Friedrich Schönmann, a well-informed expert on the United States, introduced Mencken in an article with a crushing paragraph on the American character, a malicious collection of contemptuous gibes, obviously a reply to enthusiastic pro-American attitudes. He attacked the Americans for their conceit; they considered their own political system to be the best in the world and others evil and frightening. Their theories should be a blessing to mankind but their political practice was quite different. In his view American idealism was not a passion but a business, and the American himself less free personally than any other part of mankind; even his political liberty was in decay.[31]

Similar views were repeated in other publications. At the bottom of such statements there was generally the accusation that the political system of the United States was neither able to form a real state in the German sense and to produce personalities nor to create a real human community of the people and of common belief, based on many smaller communities. Instead, there was only an association for a common purpose, an election and voting machine, a civilization of masses and machines demanding human beings fit for uniform organization, where the machine dominated men and where equity was only mechanistic, counting miserable human atoms in a grey society without culture, directed by the press and by propaganda. Such a system, which reduced life to a few standardized formulas for all its manifestations, was contrasted with German "organic

---

30 The judgment of Hildegard Meyer, *Nordamerika im Urteil des deutschen Schrifttums bis zur Mitte des 19. Jahrhunderts* (Hamburg, 1929), 6, applies to her contemporaries as well; see also Gesine Schwan, "Das deutsche Amerikabild seit der Weimarer Republik," *Aus Politik und Zeitgeschichte*, B 26/86, June 28, 1986, 3–15.
31 *Die Grenzboten*, 80 (1921): 179–82.

democracy," deep emotion, and a people not merely existing in a constitution but having grown in a long history and "somehow rooted in the irrational realms of the community."[32] These German critics frequently showed no understanding of political opposition within an existing liberal or democratic system and accused the United States of not having a fundamental opposition with a different concept of politics and society (in this the conservatives and the socialist left agreed).

These deep-rooted resentments were combined with a marked aversion to modern big cities, skyscrapers, the strangling net of big business, technical civilization, the dictatorship of the dollar exercised by omnipotent trusts in a rationalized economy, and the "horrible importance"[33] of advanced capitalism. Such phenomena were often traced back to their alleged origins, the destructive enlightenment, modern rationalism, and Jefferson's *Vernunftstaat* (a state founded on reason).[34] The distorted view of American reality was part of a long anti-modern and anti-Western tradition. Besides, Europe was often regarded as totally dependent on the United States. This was the more frightening in a time that was felt to be a period of alienation and threatening moral degeneration of everything that was rooted and indigenous in Germany. Germans might be forced "to borrow from Negroes and Bolsheviks." In particular, the restless acceleration of change by the United States evoked the worst fears. The pernicious combination of rapid technical progress and advanced capitalism seemed to be the driving force; "as if change in itself were precious."[35]

These anxieties, mainly caused by social change, modernization, and alienation as a consequence of modern civilization, were not restricted to the conservatives. But among them more misunderstandings occurred, often presented with obvious political intentions. Those who sympathized with the United States, above all the liberals, sometimes tended to idealize their findings, which caused misunderstandings as well. But usually, they were more sensitive and accurate, and in some cases produced excellent studies on the United States.

---

32 Halfeld, *Amerika*, 32. For the conservative journalist Halfeld and his influential publications, see Klaus Schwabe, "Anti-Americanism Within the German Right," *Amerikastudien/ American Studies* 21 (1976): 96–7.
33 *Politisches Handwörterbuch*, 2:863. Nevertheless, for German big business the takeover of selected parts of American modernization in productivity and rationalized economic organization was often accepted as confirming and improving German efficiency; for the inherent ambiguity of this attitude, see Philipp Gassert's chapter in this volume.
34 Halfeld, *Amerika*, 32.
35 Eduard Wechssler, "Die Generation als Jugendgemeinschaft," in Richard Peters, ed., *Geist und Gesellschaft: Kurt Breysig zu seinem 60. Geburtstage*, 3 vols. (Breslau, 1927–8), 1:85, 96.

Another outstanding analysis, which may represent the views of the socialist left, was published by Charlotte Lütkens and contains a wealth of information and clear-sighted remarks.[36] Her book deserves attention as an achievement in social science and goes beyond mere images or perceptions. Nevertheless, a general source of misunderstanding becomes effective in her basic thesis, of Marxist descent with apparent contributions from Sombart and Hilferding: that there is an unchangeable sequence of stages in the development of industrialized societies, the most advanced capitalistic stage being that of organized capitalism. Measured by this rigidly applied scheme, she concluded, the anarchic capitalism and the individualistic liberal-egalitarian society of the United States were remarkably backward and antiquated compared to Germany, with its organized classes and interests and the advanced position of the state and of social administration. She undervalued the dynamic character, vitality, and adaptability of American society and liberalism. In addition, the well-known patterns of misunderstanding of the American political system were also present (the "excessive" power of the Supreme Court as being incompatible with popular sovereignty; the unacceptable difficulty of constitutional amendment; the absence of fundamental, organized opposition; the "legend" of liberalism and of the prevalence of reasonable compromise; the omnipresent and exaggerated concept of the "frontier"; the indifference to or contempt for the American system of checks and balances, decentralization, and self-government, etc.).

III

The variety of interpretations, above all, reflected the deep cleavages and confrontations within German society. There was neither a consensus about modernization and change nor a satisfactory and accepted notion of constitutional principles and political liberty. In the judgments on the political system of the United States the intention often prevailed to occupy a certain position and to get support in domestic controversies by presenting an intentionally distorted view of the American political system.

When the Great Depression came, German critics of a modern constitution and of the American political system could pretend to be right in the end, with fateful consequences. In both countries, in Germany far more than in the United States, the Great Depression intensified the

---

36 Charlotte Lütkens, *Staat und Gesellschaft in Amerika* (Tübingen, 1929).

struggle for and against modernization. In Germany the national opposition prevailed and America became a synonym for all those developments leading to depression and national catastrophe. The United States took the other path, but there were similar reactions. They confirmed that the image of Germany was embedded in the American image of Europe, although the Germans were temporarily regarded as abnormal.

The image of a decadent, disorderly Europe, plagued by aggressive or plotting governments, struggling for power and in constant internal and external conflict, always on the verge of war, was as old as the United States. This traditional American view, combined with a marked sense of superiority, remained preponderant despite critical voices in the United States blaming the majority of their compatriots for being incapable of understanding the specific problems of Europe.[37] In the 1930s Hoover called the New Deal anti-American and a kind of "European degeneration." For him it was the bad effect of European evils almost overwhelming the United States with something between fascism, socialism, and a bureaucratic octopus, so that the New Deal took the form of "some sort of personal government based upon collective theories."[38] This sounds like a substratum of typical German characteristics and evils and should rather have been applied to the "Third Reich."

To these results I may add some general concluding remarks. In dealing with "images" and "perceptions" – and with "stereotypes" as well – it is a methodological commonplace of historians to want to compare perception with reality. However, this would appear to be one of the generally unreflected pitfalls for historians; at best an imprecise choice of words, such a formulation would seem to reveal imprecise thinking. Do we know for certain what reality is like? What we in fact are doing is comparing perceptions, different classes of perceptions. We should be aware of the fact that we are comparing one set of perceptions from outside a system with the perceptions of those within it and, in addition, with the perception of the particular observer. To mention one example: The American perception of German federalism is compared not with reality but with the perception Germans themselves have of their federal system and with the perception of the observer, a historian or jurist.[39]

37 For an interesting example, see Walter E. Weyl, *The New Democracy* (New York, 1912).
38 Herbert Hoover, *The Challenge to Liberty* (New York, 1934), 88, and idem., *Addresses upon the American Road, 1933–1938* (New York, 1938), 128, 130, 160.
39 This is a general experience; see in particular Robinson, *Bundesrath*, or Emerson, *State*. An outstanding example in a different field, derived from a comparative study and including a thorough evaluation of German jurisprudence is Roscoe Pound, "The Process of the Law – Analytical Jurisprudence, 1914–1927," *Harvard Law Review* 41 (1927–8): 174–99.

This clarification brings us further in our attempt to investigate mutual images and perceptions of the United States and Germany and it implies some consequences we should consider in our research: in dealing with the relations between two nations and their concepts of each other, we are dealing with two different contingent and complex systems. Two nations, each with a characteristic and complex structure, disseminate information and images about themselves; this is like sending messages abroad that are received by the other nation according to its different structure and receptivity. What each can receive is information about the behavior, attitudes, actions, and reactions of the other nation, although it is unable to experience and to comprehend its real structure directly. Consequently, what emerges is a separate system of interrelation and interaction between both nations, as a process and with a life of its own, a system of mutual information, images, signals, perceptions, and reactions to them. This separate system becomes the basis, however imperfect, of any mutual understanding and a prerequisite for actions. Moreover, understanding is never complete but always a simplification of complexity. In the process of mutual perception and understanding, the influence of their own national structure, tradition, and thinking on those who try to comprehend other nations is as important as what they know about other nations and what the sources of their knowledge are. Usually, the image or perception of other nations even depends on the fundamental interests, principles, beliefs of one's own nation. Perhaps, Niklas Luhmann is right – misunderstandings do not really exist.[40]

40 Niklas Luhmann, *Soziale Systeme: Grundriss einer allgemeinen Theorie* (Frankfurt/Main, 1984).

9

Between Hope and Skepticism
American Views of Germany, 1918–1933

ELISABETH GLASER-SCHMIDT

In the years after World War I, Weimar Germany seemed prone to provoke contrasting views from within and without the Reich.[1] American feelings toward Germany had turned from subtle ambiguity to outward hostility during the war. The peace order resulting from World War I led to an intense fight about the ratification of the peace treaty in the U.S. Senate. After the Senate had refused to ratify the peace treaty, the incoming Republican administration opted to conclude a pragmatic peace with Germany that derived in large parts from the precedent of the Versailles Treaty. By the date of the conclusion of the Treaty of Berlin in August 1921, the dominant views among American diplomats and journalists with regard to Germany's position in international politics had changed from animosity to a growing insight that Weimar Germany needed America's help to stabilize its finances as well as to solve the fractious reparations question.

In the scenario that developed in 1923 – growing domestic turmoil, a seemingly uncontrollable hyperinflation, and the Ruhr Crisis – Germany appeared as a republic created more by the force of circumstances than by the higher insights of its citizens.[2] In order to promote democracy, sound financial management, and a nonaggressive foreign policy, postwar Germany would need external encouragement and American assistance. With the adoption of the Dawes Plan in 1924, inspired by informal American intervention, it became clear that Germany's future conduct depended on the maintenance of a pro-Western foreign policy and an enlightened

---

1 See the chapters by Peter Krüger and Philipp Gassert in this book.
2 For a comprehensive assessment of Germany's inner history during the inflation, see Gerald D. Feldman, *The Great Disorder: Politics, Economics, and Society in the German Inflation, 1914–1923* (New York, 1993).

administration of domestic finances.³ Contemporary American accounts of Germany's domestic and foreign policy therefore focused on the question whether Germany's continued adherence to territorial and reparation agreements of 1924–5 could be taken for granted. American views of Germany, largely shaped by Weimar's conflicting foreign policy missions of territorial revision in the East and international cooperation with the West, thus remained ambiguous: Many reports were full of positive future expectations about Weimar's attempts to reform German politics, yet others raised doubts about its capacity to fulfill its financial and diplomatic obligations. As a result, American perceptions of Germany, as this chapter illustrates, changed from more hopeful to more skeptical assessments. The American investigation of German conditions recounted here was administered with a mixture of emphatic understanding of the requirements to maintain a modern capitalist democracy and sober skepticism about Germany's ability to play that role. The paradigm of the modern capitalist democracy, to be sure, derived in large parts from American rather than German concepts of the modern state. Still, America's stabilization policy clearly responded to Germany's evident need for a foreign role model. The American concepts that U.S. diplomats and reporters consciously applied in their analysis of Germany's domestic and foreign policy thus appear as pragmatic reflections of the Reich's real need for American intervention.

In the history of German-American relations, the period from 1924 to 1930 marks an era of unprecedented American control over German affairs. Official U.S. diplomacy, however, remained aloof from overt involvement in the internal affairs of the Weimar Republic. The reason for this was to avoid anxieties in the legislative branch concerning foreign entanglements which might in turn provoke isolation-

---

3 For an assessment of German-American relations in the years of the Weimar Republic, see Werner Link's standard monograph, *Die amerikanische Stabilisierungspolitik in Deutschland, 1921–1932* (Düsseldorf, 1970); William C. McNeil, *American Money and the Weimar Republik: Economics and Politics on the Eve of the Great Depression* (New York, 1986); Stephen A. Schuker, *American "Reparations" to Germany, 1919–33: Implications for the Third-World Debt Crisis* (Princeton, N.J., 1988); Manfred Berg, *Gustav Stresemann und die Vereinigten Staaten von Amerika* (Baden-Baden, 1990); Elisabeth Glaser-Schmidt, "Von Versailles nach Berlin: Überlegungen zur Neugestaltung der deutsch-amerikanischen Beziehungen in der Ära Harding," in Norbert Finzsch and Hermann Wellenreuther, eds., *Liberalitas: Festschrift für Erich Angermann zum 65. Geburtstag* (Stuttgart, 1992), 319–42, which cover German and American diplomacy; international aspects of the reparations questions are examined by Stephen A. Schuker, *The End of French Predominance in Europe: The Financial Crisis of 1924 and the Adoption of the Dawes Plan* (Chapel Hill, N.C., 1976); Melvyn P. Leffler, *The Elusive Quest: America's Pursuit of European Stability and French Security* (Chapel Hill, N.C., 1979); Frank C. Costigliola, *Awkward Dominion: American Political, Economic and Cultural Relations with Europe, 1919–1933* (Ithaca, N.Y., 1985). Peter Krüger, *Die Aussenpolitik der Republik von Weimar* (Darmstadt, 1985), discusses German foreign policy.

ist congressional interference into the conduct of the nation's foreign policy.[4]

Yet, beyond this, American mediation efforts that led to the Dawes Plan and its implementation in Germany demonstrated that by 1924 financial diplomacy had largely superseded traditional intergovernmental ties. Moreover, in the presidential campaign of 1924, the Coolidge administration had linked its fate to that of the reparations plan, which it had secretly sponsored. The choice of Seymour Parker Gilbert as agent general for reparations in Germany made an American citizen the executor of the *dette allemande*, the German obligations arising from the war. In this function he served also as supervisor of the Reichsbank. Gilbert worked in close consultation with American financial circles and the State Department in order to ensure smooth functioning of the plan and with it the financial reconstruction of Germany. American scrutiny of German economic and political affairs had thus become a matter of supreme importance for U.S. diplomacy, be it conducted from inside or outside the State Department.

This chapter evaluates the concepts of Germany held by American specialists who knew more about Weimar's affairs than the average German voter, not to speak of their American counterparts. It examines the views of the reparations agent, Gilbert, the ambassador to Germany, Jacob Gould Schurman (1854–1942), and the head of the Western European Affairs Division in the State Department, William R. Castle. In our discussion of American diplomatic reports, their underlying perceptions, and resulting images of the Weimar Republic, we are dealing with an elite of well-informed specialists, men on the spot or in key decision-making positions. Our main question here is: Did not diplomatic reports constitute the most accurate information obtainable at an international level? In other words, did not the corresponding perceptions provide a more informed knowledge than even national mass images? For example, Gilbert's expertise about German financial policy exceeded that of many German specialists and even finance ministers.[5] Finally, a look at *The New York Times*'s editorial opinions and reports about Germany shows that the image creation by the press directed at a larger, informed public remained a determining factor in foreign policy formation.

---

4 Selig Adler, *The Uncertain Giant, 1921–1941: American Foreign Policy Between the Wars* (New York, 1965).
5 Secretary of the Reichsbank to Hans Schäffer, Dec. 29, 1927, Reichsbank 6694, Bundesarchiv Abteilungen Potsdam; Schuker, *American "Reparations"*, 33–43, 59–60; McNeil, *American Money*, 165–88 and passim.

Research on mutual perceptions in the historical discipline aims frequently at larger social groups and concentrates on the images that shape their views. Findings about the gap between perception, image, stereotype, and reality form the controlling assumption of many students of the field. Others, however, propose that, while not equaling reality, stereotypes still contain a large amount of truth.[6] Similar projects in political science look at decision-making processes at the executive level where access to expert information often tends to generate refined perceptions and stereotypes.[7] The growing interest during the 1960s in sociopsychological analysis of image formation has had surprisingly little impact. Instead, political scientists have often neglected the history and formation of individual views in favor of general theories of political behavior. Moreover, American diplomatic historians have paid little attention to the exercise of impartial observation and foreign-policy reporting that began with the modernization of the American diplomatic service after World War I.[8] Thus, we still face the question how well did American foreign policy analysis function in the interwar years and whether, even if influenced by stereotypes, it could generate more detached analysis and more authentic information than that produced by diplomats of other nations or contemporary domestic observers.[9]

From 1925 to his retirement in 1929, during the largest part of this era of American stabilization diplomacy, Jacob Gould Schurman held the position of American ambassador to Germany.[10] Schurman's achievements

---

6 Knud Krakau, "Einführende Überlegungen zur Entstehung und Wirkung von Bildern, die sich Nationen von sich und anderen machen," in Willi Paul Adams and Knud Krakau, eds., *Deutschland und Amerika: Perzeption und historische Realität* (Berlin, 1985), 9–18; Otto Klineberg, *The Human Dimension in International Relations* (New York, 1964); Charles W. Brooks, *America in France's Hopes and Fears, 1890–1920* (New York, 1987), 3–5.

7 Ole R. Holsti, "Cognitive Dynamics and Images of the Enemy", in John C. Farrell and Asa Smith, eds., *Image and Reality in World Politics* (New York, 1967), 16–39; Richard K. Herrmann, *Perceptions and Behavior in Soviet Foreign Policy* (Pittsburgh, Pa., 1985); more relevant for our purpose of examining international images in the context of interwar diplomatic history is the question of how states can affect and use the images others have of them, which has been put by Robert Jervis, *The Logic of Images in International Relations* (Princeton, N.J., 1970).

8 Claudia Breuer, *Die "Russische Sektion" in Riga: Amerikanische diplomatische Berichterstattung über die Sowjetunion, 1922–1933/40* (Stuttgart, 1995), describes the new scientific diplomatic reporting that was developed after 1921.

9 For an analysis of diplomatic assessments in Germany and the United States during the prewar years, see Ute Mehnert, *Amerika und die "Gelbe Gefahr": Zur Karriere eines Schlagworts in der Grossen Politik, 1905–1917* (Stuttgart, 1995); for another assessment, see Frank Ninkovich, "Interests and Discourse in Diplomatic History", *Diplomatic History* 13 (1989): 135–61.

10 There exist no biographies of the three players described here. The following biographical sketches rely on standard references such as the *Dictionary of American Biography*; obituaries in *The New York Times*, Oct. 14, 1963, 29 (Castle); Feb. 24, 1938, 1, 18 (Gilbert); and Aug. 13, 1942, 19 (Schurman), and the manuscript sources used in this chapter. For an assessment of Schurman that recounts his activities pertaining to academic and cultural relations, see Detlef Junker, "Jacob

as a college student had enabled him to pursue postgraduate studies in philosophy and political science at London, Paris, Edinburgh, Heidelberg, and Göttingen. During his student years, Schurman developed a strong interest in German philosophy that culminated in his critique of Kantian ethics, published as a book in 1881. With the backing of Andrew Dickson White and Henry W. Sage, Schurman obtained a professorship at Cornell University in 1886. In 1890 he became dean of the newly endowed School of Philosophy, and in 1892, again supported by Sage, he became president of the university. As an independent-minded liberal with gifts as a vigorous administrator, Schurman oversaw the successful expansion of Cornell. He supported the conservative wing of the Republican Party of the McKinley-Taft generation and embarked on a public career in 1899 that helped him to nurture his renewed wanderlust. He served as president of the first Philippine Commission in 1899 and as minister to Greece and Montenegro from 1912 to 1913. Schurman resolutely supported American entry into World War I and, later, American involvement with the League of Nations. His appointments as ambassador to China (1921–5) and Germany (1925–30) constituted the apogee of his career as a self-educated diplomat.

Schurman's ambassadorship in Berlin thus formed the last step in his academic and political activities. Without substantial ties to the business community, to the younger generation of the Republican Party, or to the foreign service establishment, Schurman remained in the position of an outsider. His tendency to lecture rather than to listen seems to have contributed to his lack of social ties to his younger colleagues.

In his critical mission to Berlin, this character trait handicapped Schurman in his relationship with Gilbert, the reparations agent and thirty-eight years his junior. The Berlin post figured as Gilbert's first foreign assignment. His academic education had taken place at Rutgers and at the Harvard Law School, where he won all the prizes. His intelligence and diligence as a law clerk in the firm of Cravath and Henderson led to his recruitment as a counsel in war-loan matters in the Treasury Department in 1918. Gilbert became the protegé of Russell C. Leffingwell, who had left Cravath and Henderson to serve as assistant

Gould Schurman, die Universität Heidelberg und die deutsch-amerikanischen Beziehungen," in *Semper Apertus: Sechshundert Jahre Ruprecht-Karl-Universität Heidelberg, 1386–1986: Festschrift in sechs Bänden* (1985), vol. 3; Berg, *Gustav Stresemann*, 228–73, discusses Schurman's nomination as ambassador and his friendship with the German foreign secretary. McNeil, *American Money*, contains a critical description of Gilbert's role in Germany from 1925 to 1930 which will be questioned here. The best source for William R. Castle is his diaries in the Houghton Library at Harvard and his papers at the Herbert Hoover Presidential Library in West Branch, Iowa.

secretary of the Treasury before becoming a partner of J. P. Morgan and Co. after the war. Young Gilbert's performance likewise impressed the incoming Republican Treasury chief, Andrew Mellon, who promoted Gilbert to the newly created post of undersecretary. After a brief hiatus (1923–4), during which he had returned to his old law firm, Gilbert took up his assignment as reparations agent. In light of his brilliant record and his ties to Mellon and Leffingwell, he seemed the logical choice among the younger generation of legal and financial experts once Owen D. Young and Dwight Morrow had become unavailable owing to political and personal reasons. Although Gilbert had to report to the Reparation Commission in Paris, his position as reparations agent appeared in fact independent. He mainly had to deal with the German bureaucracy, but he had also to gain the confidence of the British and French governments as well as their central banks. In the United States, his chief liaison developed with the banking house of J. P. Morgan and Co., which was responsible for floating the Dawes Plan loan.

The task of supervising Schurman and, in an informal sense, Gilbert's activities insofar as they affected American war debt policy fell to William R. Castle Jr. (1878–1963), head of the Western European division of the State Department. Son of the prominent Hawaiian businessman William Richards Castle, the younger Castle went to Harvard and served from 1906 to 1913 as dean of Harvard College, subsequently becoming editor of the *Harvard Graduates' Magazine*. During the war, Castle worked as director of the Bureau of Communications of the American Red Cross, which was established to locate American prisoners of war or missing men in Germany. When Castle resigned from his post in 1919, that agency, which had begun with a staff of two, commanded 450 clerks and had established a well-functioning network of private reconnaissance. He then served until 1921 in his new post as special assistant at the Division of Western European Affairs at the State Department. The incoming secretary of state, Charles Evans Hughes, regarded him as the most competent man in this key division and promoted him to chief.[11] One of the first professional-quality diplomats in that bureaucracy, Castle defies easy classification. He was prepared by his upbringing and education to keep functional ties to foreign diplomats and members and friends of the Republican administration. His correspondence and his diaries show him to have been a detached pragmatic conservative and realist with a pro-

---

11 David I. Danelski and Joseph S. Tulchin, eds., *The Autobiographical Notes of Charles Evans Hughes* (Cambridge, Mass., 1973), 203.

nounced gift for cynical observation. Castle's diplomatic and political talents led to his appointment as assistant secretary of state for European affairs in February 1927 and undersecretary of state in 1931. His subsequent support for Herbert Hoover occasioned his dismissal in 1933.

Emerging from the Ruhr occupation and hyperinflation, the Weimar Republic in the years after 1924 did not constitute an object for easy observation. To this day, historians disagree about the state of the Weimar economy and Germany's willingness and capacity to pay reparations.[12] Meanwhile, the historiography of German-American relations during the Weimar years has produced a consensus about America's preeminence as the dominant partner in a relationship characterized by a willingness for political and economic cooperation on both sides.[13] The functioning of the Dawes Plan and the transformation of the reparations problem from a stumbling block for European reconstruction into a nonpolitical mechanism ensuring economic growth and orthodox monetary policy formed the cornerstone of American financial diplomacy from 1924 to 1930. It likewise created a precondition for the safe investment of American capital. At the same time, the foreign policy of Gustav Stresemann sought to establish a close German-American understanding in order to establish a counterweight to France. Stresemann also wanted to render American economic and financial resources accessible to Germany to prepare for revision of the Treaty of Versailles and the Dawes Plan.[14]

Despite their apparent compatibility, German and American foreign policies differed in their long-term goals regarding reparations and economic policy. For Germany, economic growth and rehabilitation served to prepare it for a revision of the Versailles Treaty. By contrast, the United States viewed German prosperity as a means to an end, namely, fulfilling Weimar's obligations arising from that treaty and thus to solidify political and economic stability in Western Europe. Germany's fear of U.S. economic dominance and business rivalries in third markets formed strong undercurrents during the era examined here. In addition, a reassessment of American foreign policy during the 1920s underscores the one-sidedness of the prevailing view in German historiography to the

---

12 See the contributions in Jürgen Baron von Kruedener, ed., *Economic Crisis and Political Collapse: The Weimar Republic, 1924–1933* (New York, 1990); summaries of the recent historiography on reparations history and assessments reflecting German sources are in Peter Krüger, "Das Reparationsproblem der Weimarer Republik in fragwürdiger Sicht: Kritische Überlegungen zur neuesten Forschung," *Vierteljahrshefte für Zeitgeschichte* 29 (1981): 21–47; and Schuker, *American "Reparations"*, 11–50 and passim, who bases his conclusions on German, French, English, and American sources.
13 Link, *Amerikanische Stabilisierungspolitik*, 545–93; Berg, *Gustav Stresemann*, 418–28.
14 Link, *Amerikanische Stabilisierungspolitik*, 348–57 and passim; Berg, *Gustav Stresemann*, 228–417.

effect that the United States figured as the principal partner of Germany in international postwar policy. By force of its subjection to international controls and close scrutiny, Germany indeed formed a centerpiece of American financial and stabilization diplomacy. Nevertheless, the relationship between the two nations remained asymmetric. American policy and business elites maintained stronger ties to England and France and thus perpetuated a tendency that had been established during the war.

Castle had been firmly committed to American entry into the war against Germany. After the war he remained skeptical about Germany's capacity or willingness to reform its foreign policy. Mistrust about the impact of reactionary nationalism on German foreign policy runs deeply throughout his diaries. For example, Alanson B. Houghton, the first American ambassador to Germany after the war, tended to stress the economic hardship hyperinflation had brought to Germany and strongly questioned the wisdom of trying to impose the London schedule of payments on the Reich.[15] In the light of German obstinacy in the reparations question during the London Conference in March 1921 and Germany's subsequent default that led to the Ruhr occupation, Castle and like-minded State Department officials did not agree with Houghton.[16] In fact the ambassador's anguished letters provoked fear among Castle and his colleagues at home that Houghton's views were marred by a pro-German bias. Despite these conflicting impressions, Castle gradually became a strong advocate of a constructive policy toward the Weimar Republic. As early as 1920 he had called for a continuous revision of policy insofar as the other side justified it. He thought that life must be lived and that for the world, peace was all important. Real peace, however, could not be unless the victors of World War I would deal with the Germans, watchful always, but supporting good intentions as they appeared.[17]

Castle belonged to the first generation of top-level State Department bureaucrats who traveled repeatedly to Europe on official missions of general reconnaissance and information gathering. These trips in 1920, 1922, and 1924 served as opportunities to survey the work of American diplomatic posts, to establish personal contacts with key bureaucrats at the respective foreign offices, and to meet leading politicians. Contacts with

---

15 Hermann-Josef Rupieper, "Alanson B. Houghton: An American Ambassador in Germany," *International History Review* 4 (1979): 490–508.
16 Dieter Bruno Gescher, *Die Vereinigten Staaten von Nordamerika und die Reparationen, 1920–1924* (Bonn 1956), 90–2; Link, *Amerikanische Stabilisierungspolitik*, 148–89.
17 William R. Castle diary, vol. 2, Aug. 30, 1920.

prominent industrial leaders also belonged on the agenda of the trips. The travel program provided occasion for a fresh assessment of the German economy. Castle visited Berlin in the fall of 1920 and again in the fall of 1922, and he witnessed the signs of economic decline and poverty when he walked through the poorer sections of the city. Compassion with the economic plight of the German working class, however, did not lead him to give credence to German propaganda that stressed the economic hardships of inflation in order to excuse noncompliance with reparations obligations.[18]

The Treaty of Rapallo strongly reinforced the assistant secretary's skepticism about the aims of German foreign policy.[19] His opposition to the views of the American ambassador in Germany hardened. During a visit to Berlin in October 1922, he argued with Houghton about the origins of World War I. The result, it seems, was a very vigorous discussion of the whole question of war. Houghton and Castle took opposite sides and the debate became quite heated. The ambassador accused Castle of having fallen under the spell of century-old propaganda, and Castle answered that Houghton was influenced by new German propaganda.[20]

Castle's reactions to the Germans he met while in Berlin in 1922 suggest that he believed in the continuing ability of monarchists and conservatives to control Germany's policy in the midterm. He took a particular liking to President Friedrich Ebert, but he also showed a keen interest to engage in conversations with men he deemed reactionary and therefore influential. He considered Carl von Schubert, soon to become *Staatssekretär* (undersecretary of state) and thus the leading official in the foreign ministry bureaucracy, very intelligent and therefore dangerous. He disliked Ago von Maltzan for his role at Rapallo and accused him of being solely responsible for this treaty with the Soviet Union. Castle thought that the Rapallo Treaty figured mainly as a product of Maltzan's ignorance of Russia's real intentions as well as the diplomat's personal ambitions.[21]

Despite the fact that he had formed critical views of the German politicians he had encountered, Castle stressed the necessity of European stabilization. He departed from Germany in October 1922 firmly con-

---

18 Ibid., vol. 4, Sept. 13, 1923 and passim.
19 Ibid., vol. 3, Apr. 19, 1922.
20 Ibid., Oct. 26, 1922.
21 Ibid., Oct. 18, 1922; regarding Schubert, see particularly Krüger, *Aussenpolitik*, 181, 184, and passim, who has had exclusive access to the Staatssekretär's papers.

vinced that a future solution of the reparations question should rest on an honest estimate of how much Germany could really pay. Nevertheless, he remained suspicious about German *Erfüllungspolitik* (policy of fulfillment) and its German protagonists.[22] Like his boss Hughes, whom he deeply admired, Castle seems to have intuitively favored the Social Democratic Party, which promised to work for a closer understanding with France, but he realized that only a coalition government with conservative participation could marshal enough support for a cooperative foreign policy.[23]

More important for the future of German-American relations, his mission to Germany left Castle a firmer adherent of limited American intervention, and he subsequently emphasized Germany's need for moral leadership and the corresponding imperative for a constructive American role.[24]

In brief, Castle's views of Germany up to 1924 seem to have been shaped by his experiences during World War I and his resulting animosity against the Reich. The assistant secretary, however, did not allow these stereotypes to influence him unduly. Instead, he collected his own information by way of frequent meetings with European diplomats in Washington and his own visits to the continent. Whereas he and Hughes remained unconvinced by Houghton's German sympathies, Castle vigorously supported the secretary of state's initiative for a revision of the London schedule of payments that finally led to the Dawes Plan. Although he feared the influence of pro-monarchist and nationalist elements within Germany, he likewise criticized the hazardous character of Raymond Poincaré's decision to occupy the Ruhr. This step, in Castle's view, endangered France's real interests, since it completed that country's isolation.[25]

Castle's realistic insight into the necessity of a cooperative resolution of the reparations problem thus strongly influenced his thinking on Germany. He subsequently became Hughes's most reliable supporter in engineering diplomatic support for the Dawes Plan, which embodied Castle's ideas about cooperative stabilization. Castle again visited Europe in the fall of 1924 to get personally acquainted with the situation after the London Conference. For the first time, he met the new German cabinet

---

22 Castle diary, vol. 3, Nov. 18, 1922.
23 Ibid., vol. 7, Dec. 11, 1924; Link, *Amerikanische Stabilisierungspolitik*, 188; Castle diary, vol. 3, Nov. 20, 1922. The standard biography of Hughes is Merlo Pusey, *Charles Evans Hughes*, 2 vols. (New York, 1951).
24 Castle diary, vol. 3, Nov. 20, 1922.
25 Ibid., vol. 4, Jan. 10, 1923.

and found himself pleased with Chancellor Wilhelm Marx. His sympathy, however, did not extend to Stresemann, whom he disliked. According to Castle, Germany's foreign minister was a politician rather than a statesman.[26]

In contrast to Castle, the incoming ambassador to Germany developed great admiration for the German foreign minister. In fact, Schurman came to value the leading spirit in Weimar's diplomacy as "more statesman than politician."[27] Since he considered the Center Party to be opportunistic, Schurman almost logically identified Stresemann as the leading statesman of Germany.[28] As has been noted elsewhere, Stresemann showed himself more than willing to respond to the ambassador's friendly gestures and arranged to honor the former student of Göttingen and Heidelberg universities. In May 1928 Heidelberg University awarded Schurman an honorary doctorate after the foreign minister had persuaded the university of the political merits of such a gesture.[29] Given Stresemann's political efforts after 1924 to reach a closer understanding with France, Schurman's positive views of the German foreign secretary were echoed to a considerable extent by American public opinion, if not by the director of the State Department's Division of Western European Affairs. Castle thought that Stresemann in 1925 appeared as a broadminded and clever politician, very well educated, yet not quite dependable.[30]

If one searches for a prevailing assumption underlying Schurman's embassy reports, it seems that he held an unshakable faith in the prospects for the growing political stability of the Weimar Republic. Except for questions touching directly on Weimar's democratic system, the ambassador tended to avoid giving his personal views in his despatches, which to a large extent comprised news summaries compiled by his staff. Although not oblivious to extremist tendencies on both sides of the political spectrum, Schurman compared Germany to France after 1875, hoping that continuing public acquiescence in the republican constitution would incrementally strengthen its hold.[31] And despite his continued apprehension regarding German nationalism, he welcomed the inclusion of the

---

26 Ibid., vol. 6, Oct. 22, 1924.
27 Schurman to State Department, Oct. 4, 1929, National Archives, Washington, D.C. (hereafter cited as NA), Record Group (hereafter cited as RG) 59, Decimal File 862.00PR/52.
28 Schurman to State Department, July 27, 1926, NA, RG 59, Decimal File 862.00/2229.
29 Berg, *Gustav Stresemann*, 263–4.
30 Lecture by Castle to the Fletcher School of Diplomacy, Aug. 1925, NA, RG 59, Decimal File 611.6231/242.
31 Schurman to State Department, Jan. 19, 1927, NA, RG 59, Decimal File 862.00/2295; regarding the question of the authorship of the reports, see Castle-DeWitt C. Poole correspondence, Castle papers, Hoover Library, files G 55–6.

German National People's Party (*Deutschnationale Volkspartei* or DNVP) into the cabinet as a move that would bind the more reasonable elements in that party to the government and thus contain monarchism.[32] Schurman's belief in the integrative power of Weimar's democratic politics extended even to the German military. When faced with Social Democratic attempts to curtail the Reichswehr's power in light of mounting evidence about its illegal activities, the ambassador deemphasized the possibility of aggressive revisionist designs and stressed instead the high-mindedness of advocates of a stronger Reichswehr.[33] Furthermore, he tended to ignore questions about German breaches of the military clauses of the Versailles Treaty.[34] Even more striking seems his inactivity during June and July 1925, when Stresemann threatened to insist on complete evacuation of the Rhineland as a precondition for negotiations on a security pact.[35] Faced with Schurman's passivity, former ambassador Houghton had to intervene through a personal letter in order to persuade Stresemann to moderate his further demands.[36]

In short, partly as a result of his peripheral position and partly owing to his personal inclinations, Schurman preferred to emphasize the ceremonial rather than the diplomatic aspects of his assignment. Thus, he made considerable efforts to take part in Germany's public life and to contribute to the improvement of German-American relations, where his personal contacts seemed to matter.[37] In contrast, he neglected to cultivate political contacts back in the United States. Unlike Houghton and numerous other American diplomats in Europe, he rarely supplemented his official reports with personal letters to Castle. Instead, he limited himself almost exclusively to routine political reports that were likely to escape Castle's attention. This constituted a crucial omission, since the assistant secretary welcomed personal letters that contained more pointed judgments than official reports allowed. The West European Division frequently consigned Schurman's despatches to the files without taking further notice.[38] Yet Schurman's declining influence in the State Department resulted from more than just personal factors. The choice of a less prominent

---

32 Schurman to State Department, Jan. 29, 1927, NA, RG 59, Decimal File 862.00/2295.
33 Schurman to State Department, Jan. 24, 1927, NA, RG 59, Decimal File 862.00/2303; Francis Ludwig Carsten, *The Reichswehr and Politics, 1918–1933* (London, 1966), 254–75.
34 See the reports on the German military in NA, RG 59, Decimal File 862.20.
35 Jon Jacobson, *Locarno Diplomacy: Germany and the West, 1925–1929* (Princeton, N.J., 1972), 54–9.
36 Castle diary, vol. 8, July 6 and 7, 1925.
37 Junker, "Jacob Gould Schurman"; Berg, *Gustav Stresemann*, 246–8.
38 Allen Dulles to Ellis L. Dresel, May 27, 1920, Ellis Loring Dresel papers, Houghton Library, Harvard; see also reports in NA, RG 59, Decimal File 862.00.

figure as ambassador to Germany after 1924 forms just one link in a chain of dissonances in German-American relations that developed during the era of seeming stability.

The quandary created by the lack of communication between Schurman and Castle became more serious owing to Castle's strong personal dislike for Maltzan. Although the German ambassador often conversed directly with Castle, he delegated his attaché to impress the assistant secretary with the need to secure political success in solving trade disputes in order to fend off domestic critics. Maltzan's desire for political success emanated from his wish to appease nationalist opposition to his decision to fly the embassy's flag on Armistice Day.[39] Castle, who valued personal courage and intelligence highly, did not take Maltzan's attempt to curry favor through political maneuvering kindly. He came to prefer the French ambassador, Paul Claudel, to the German diplomat, thus allowing his personal predilections to conform to a predominant cultural mode.[40]

Germany's foreign policy after 1924 irritated Castle even more than did his disdain for Maltzan. He took the ambassador's criticism of the League of Nations, which was meant as an overture for a closer German-American understanding, as a sign of Maltzan's inclinations toward more intimate German-Soviet cooperation.[41] The fact that the baron tried to link German compliance with the Dawes Plan to American handling of tariff rates for German imports did not ameliorate the relationship between the two men.[42] Worse followed. Maltzan visited Castle in early February 1927 to complain about American conduct toward Germany. The release of German property in the United States was still pending, and German imports had been subjected to penalty duties. Maltzan took the excuse of these bureaucratic vicissitudes to let loose a veritable tirade against American policy. The diplomat claimed, rather undiplomatically, that there had been not a single friendly act toward Germany since his arrival in Washington. He again raised the specter of his withdrawal, which to Castle appeared rather as a ray of hope. The diplomat's *furor teutonicus* only enhanced Castle's resentment, who surmised after this perturbation that if it were the people of Maltzan's type who were running Germany, Germany was no different from what it was before the

---

39 Castle to Poole, Dec. 22, 1926, Castle papers, file G 55; Castle diary, vol. 10, Dec. 3 and 10, 1926.
40 Castle diary, vol. 13, July 20, 1928.
41 Ibid., vol. 7, Mar. 16, 1925.
42 Ibid., vol. 9, June 9, 1926.

war.[43] When he recounted the episode to DeWitt C. Poole, attaché at the American embassy in Berlin, Castle used even blunter expressions:

I have never seen him [Maltzan] quite as bitter as he was and I cannot help feeling very strongly that his bitterness largely arises from the fact that he is afraid for his own position. Of course we might get something worse if he were withdrawn, but my personal feeling with regard to the man is so strong that I feel I could stand almost anything.[44]

Whereas Castle's scorn for the German diplomat ended with Maltzan's death on September 23, 1927, and the succession of the more tactful Friedrich von Prittwitz und Gaffron, American fears of German revisionist leanings regarding the Polish border and designs for closer German-Soviet cooperation constituted an ongoing source of controversy.[45] Although officially maintaining aloofness, Castle had personally disapproved of the German-Soviet Neutrality Pact of 1926. To him, that accord constituted a weakening of Germany's obligation to cooperate with the League of Nations against potential Soviet breaches of peace. The assistant secretary thus largely agreed with the Polish interpretation of the Russo-German agreement. He recognized, however, that any serious move through the League of Nations against that treaty would drive Germany into an even closer alliance with the Soviets.[46]

After he was promoted assistant secretary of state for European affairs, Castle became even more concerned about Polish security and more doubtful about the sincerity of Stresemann's foreign policy. The Polish minister, John Ciechanowski, informed him in February 1927 of German propaganda efforts to undermine Polish attempts to get a loan in the United States. In fact the German embassy organized a public campaign to discourage American banks from giving loans to Poland.[47] Castle thought the Polish minister's intimations were exaggerated, but noted nevertheless that the Germans would very much like to eliminate Poland from the map and that the corridor and Upper Silesia remained sensitive issues for the Reich.[48] The American minister in Warsaw, John Stetson, confirmed Castle's fears of German intrigues.[49] The State Department

43 Ibid., vol. 11, Feb. 3, 1927.
44 Castle to Poole, Apr. 4, 1927, Castle papers, file G 56.
45 For an assessment of Prittwitz's role in 1933, see Günter Moltmann, "Ein Botschafter tritt zurück: Friedrich von Prittwitz und Gaffron, Washington, 6. März 1933," in Finzsch and Wellenreuther, eds., *Liberalitas*, 367–86.
46 Castle diary, vol. 9, May 7 and Dec. 12, 1926.
47 This problem will be examined more fully in my forthcoming book, *Germany, the United States and the World Trading System, 1921–1931*.
48 Castle to Poole, Feb. 15, 1927, Castle papers, file G 56.
49 Castle diary, vol. 11, Jan. 17, 1927.

refrained from direct actions to discourage German activities against Polish economic reconstruction and instead quietly supported Poland's currency stabilization and financial reform.[50] In brief, the episodes described here deepened Castle's doubts concerning the good intentions of Germany's foreign policy.

A fundamental disagreement between Schurman and Gilbert exacerbated the conflicts and misunderstandings that had shaped German-American mutual perceptions during the 1920s. That antagonism dashed all substantial prospects for a specific American reparations diplomacy and divested the ambassador of the remaining credibility he might have otherwise enjoyed in the department. The souring relationship between the ambassador and the agent general from 1925 to 1929 reflected their different aims as well as the growing personal animosity between the two men.

The mission of the new ambassador to Berlin consisted of sending political reports and representing the United States diplomatically.[51] This deliberately modest agenda meshed poorly with Schurman's own hankering for publicity. Gilbert, however, controlled and regulated German mark payments and their transfer to the Reich's creditors under the reparation schedule by dint of his chairmanship in the transfer committee for reparation payments under the Dawes Plan. That operation involved a wide range of competencies in order to safeguard the stability of German exchange rates. The agent general nominally had to report to the Reparation Commission in Paris. However, owing to the stake J. P. Morgan and Co. had in furnishing the Dawes loan and in insisting on the appropriate political guarantees for German economic growth, that bank in effect became the plan's nonpolitical supervisory agency. Accordingly, J. P. Morgan and Co. actually nominated the agent general.[52] All the same, Gilbert only accepted the post after having obtained Hughes's personal assurance that he would have the unswerving support from the whole administration.[53] Thus, Schurman's role in his relationship with the agent general was clearly reduced to that of a bit player. For his part, Gilbert would have preferred the American banker Gates McGarrah to

---

50 Neal Pease, *Poland, the United States and the Stabilization of Europe, 1919–1939* (New York, 1986), 81–120; Frank C. Costigliola, "American Foreign Policy in the Nutcracker: The United States and Poland in the 1920s," *Pacific Historical Review* 48 (1979): 85–105.
51 Berg, *Gustav Stresemann*, 247.
52 Link, *Amerikanische Stabilisierungspolitik*, 315–23; Schuker, *The End of French Predominance*, 287.
53 Mssrs. J. P. Morgan to Thomas W. Lamont, Aug. 25, 1924, Thomas W. Lamont papers, 177–6, Baker Library, Harvard University, Cambridge, Mass.

obtain the ambassadorship and, like Houghton, opposed Schurman's nomination.[54]

The public style of the two men could hardly have been more different. Whereas Schurman strove to improve German-American cultural relations and loved public occasions and travel, the agent general maintained a Spartan working schedule. He largely limited his contacts with German officials to necessary consultations and showed no interest in getting personally involved in German reparations or financial politics any further.[55] With only three assistants he commanded the smallest staff of all supervisory bodies of the Reparation Commission.[56] As early as 1926 a conflict developed between Schurman and Gilbert, since the latter tended to stress the growth potential of the German economy and thus Germany's ability to comply with the plan.[57] The chief point of contention between the two men became the evaluation of the German capacity to pay reparations when substantial cash payments of 410 million reichsmark fell due in the third year of the plan.[58] Gilbert reacted with distress to Schurman's tendency to represent the German perspective on the question. When Gilbert saw Castle during a visit to Washington, he used the occasion to criticize explicitly Schurman's reports. Castle recalled that Gilbert had warned him not to take Schurman's despatches too seriously. The reparations agent had surmised that the old man was always quick to take a gloomy view of things.[59]

Matters came to a head in April 1926, when the embassy's economic report about the second annuity year criticized the approved method of an export levy to pay reparations. Gilbert was incensed and tried to forestall publication of the report.[60] Schurman nevertheless continued to throw cold water on future prospects for the Dawes Plan. In September 1926 he stated publicly that Germany might not be able to continue its payments beyond 1928.[61] Further rumors of similar indiscretions subsequently reached the department. Secretary of State Frank B. Kellogg deemed it necessary to remind the diplomat in a formal letter not to make

---

54 Lamont to J. P. Morgan, Mar. 3, 1925, Lamont papers, 108–14; Castle diary, vol. 7, Mar. 11, 1925.
55 Confidential memorandum by Schubert, Nov. 14, 1927, *Akten zur Deutschen Auswärtigen Politik*, series B, vol. 7, no. 100; Krüger, *Aussenpolitik*, 426–7.
56 *Deutschland unter dem Dawes Plan: Bericht des Generalagenten für Reparationszahlungen*, June 19, 1927, Annex IX.
57 *Bericht des Generalagenten*, Nov. 30, 1926, 91 and passim.
58 *Bericht des Generalagenten*, June 10, 1927, 26.
59 Castle diary, vol. 9, Jan. 18, 1926.
60 Schurman to State Department, Apr. 30, 1926, NA, RG 59, Decimal File 862.00/2181.
61 *New York Times*, Sept. 30, 1926, 13.

any such statements to Germans. Schurman denied the corresponding allegations, but kept up his silent obstruction.[62] He let it be known in Germany that he opposed a uniform war debt policy toward France and Britain, one of the State Department's fundamental principles in handling this delicate problem. This time Gilbert flatly contradicted Schurman's utterances in a face-to-face meeting with German *Staatssekretär* Schubert.[63] When Schurman continued to undermine Gilbert, the agent general stopped sending his communications to the State Department via the embassy and began to transmit them instead through the Federal Reserve Bank of New York.[64]

The intertwined history of German reparation payments and fiscal policy during the last phase of the Dawes Plan has been recounted elsewhere and need only be briefly summarized.[65] Although Germany's credit had become temporarily impaired in 1927 because of a large wave of public issues, Weimar's economy was just emerging from the transition crisis of 1925–6 and was starting to boom. For Gilbert the time seemed ripe to fix German reparation liabilities once and for all and thus to end the experimental stage of reparation policy under the Dawes scheme. Moreover, the unwillingness of the German government to limit public spending and to balance the budget – and thus to conform to the spirit of the plan – seemed to make revision of the Dawes Plan increasingly necessary. This step would require curbing, if not abolishing, transfer protection. Gilbert believed it essential to shift responsibility for transferring reparations and implicitly for conducting the Reich's financial policy in a more orthodox manner to the German government.[66] Continued international confidence in German finance seemed to be a precondition to secure the international loan that would function, like the Dawes loan earlier, to smooth the transition phase.

Already in the fiscal year 1926–7, the German budget showed a current deficit of 110 million reichsmarks, as special budget expenditures for subsidized housing and transfers to the *Länder* (federal states) had risen.[67] The lack of a financial settlement between the Reich and the *Länder* on the necessity of cutting expenditures had created another basic

---

62 Kellogg to Schurman, Apr. 11, 1927, Jacob Gould Schurman papers, John Olin Research Library, Cornell University, 3/4/8; Schurman to Kellogg, Apr. 26, 1927, ibid.
63 Secret memorandum by Schubert, Feb. 25, 1927, *Akten zur Deutschen Auswärtigen Politik*, series B IV, no. 192.
64 Castle diary, vol. 11, Sept. 13, 1927.
65 Schuker, *American "Reparations"*, 14–52; McNeil, *American Money*, 97–280.
66 This strategy is clearly stated, see *Bericht des Generalagenten*, May 21, 1930, 114.
67 Ibid., 114–25; Schuker, *American "Reparations"*, 41–3.

problem. Gilbert found himself on the horns of a dilemma: Without any formal competence to intervene in German financial policy, he remained responsible for the functioning of the Dawes Plan and thus implicitly for a modicum of budgetary orthodoxy on the part of the Reich. Therefore he had to find a way to discourage effectively Weimar's profligate spending without impairing Germany's international credit. The agent general opted for discreet but clear criticism in his report of November 1926 and in subsequent conversations with German Finance Minister Heinrich Köhler.[68] Both expedients showed no effect. The Reich budget for 1927–8 postponed the financial settlement between the Reich and the *Länder* and instead increased transfer of Reich's funds to the latter. Ultimately, Gilbert saw himself forced to issue an unmistakable warning about these matters. Through two well-staged public appeals during the next ten months, he called for financial and bureaucratic reforms, spending cuts, and likewise an end to American loans to the states and cities. Furthermore, he linked those issues clearly with German responsibilities under the Dawes Plan.[69] Gilbert arranged publication of his last pronouncement in 1927, a memorandum to the finance minister, and thus finally managed to provoke an interdepartmental debate on budget policy and spending cuts.[70]

The primary motive for Gilbert's action derived from his view of Weimar policies. The agent general perceived that "the present financial tendencies of the Government may appeal to many Germans who would prefer to see their assets squandered at home with bad administration rather than conserved with good administration for Reparations." The Center Party's desire to gain the support of as many political forces as possible for its current policies and the Weimar constitution had emerged, in Gilbert's view, as the underlying political problem. However, as he observed, the present German cabinet formed the driving political force that actively promoted the Reich's deficit and overborrowing.[71]

Gilbert actively promoted revision of the Dawes Plan after the summer of 1927 as an emblem of his resolve to shift responsibility for future

---

68 *Bericht des Generalagenten*, Nov. 30, 1926, 36–41; Sir R. Lindsay to Austen Chamberlain, Mar. 17, 1927, *Documents on British Foreign Policy*, serial I A, vol. III, no. 48.
69 *Bericht des Generalagenten*, June 10, 1927, 25–53; Gilbert to the German finance minister, Dec. 10, 1927, in *Report of the Agent General for Reparations Payments*, Dec. 10, 1927, annex 1 (London, 1927).
70 McNeil, *American Money*, 183–91.
71 Gilbert in conversation with Sir R. Lindsay, Lindsay to Austen Chamberlain, Mar. 17, 1927, *Documents on British Foreign Policy*, serial I A, III, no. 48.

reparation transfers to the German government.[72] In the fall of 1927, he traveled to the United States to confer with Washington officials and with J. P. Morgan and Co. In consultation with Castle, he emphasized that Germany had the ability to pay the Dawes annuities but lacked the willingness to comply.[73] Gilbert had a carefully orchestrated strategy to prepare revision of the Dawes Plan. He would first obtain the backing of the American authorities and J. P. Morgan and Co. He would then contact the British and French governments. To carry out his program, he needed to maintain the authority of his appeal for financial orthodoxy in the Reich.

Gilbert's prospects for maintaining his credibility diminished considerably when Schurman, on his way home for Christmas, stopped in New York on November 26 and publicly denounced Gilbert's criticism of German unproductive spending of the proceeds of foreign loans.[74] Schurman deliberately misrepresented Gilbert's position. In fact, Gilbert had addressed not merely foreign loans, but a whole variety of controversial budget items, such as immoderate salary increases for civil servants and the Reich's failure to screen expenses by the cities and the states.[75] Schurman likewise discounted the importance of secret German military cooperation with the Soviet Union.[76] Kellogg and Castle became infuriated when they learned about Schurman's remarks; they reproached the ambassador, but refrained from taking formal action against him.[77] Schurman nevertheless continued to obstruct Gilbert's attempts to begin revision of the Dawes Plan. When State Secretary Schubert explicitly asked Schurman about Gilbert's intentions in January 1928, the ambassador refused to offer any explanation. Whether out of substantive disagreement or personal pique at his treatment by Washington, he said that he would refrain from further comments on reparations, because these could be misinterpreted as active American interference in that issue.[78]

---

72 Note of Jacques Seydoux, July 6, 1927, Papiers d'Agents, Jacques Seydoux, vol. 39, Archives diplomatiques, Ministère des Affaires Etrangères, Paris; McNeil, *American Money*, 191–5; Leffler, *Elusive Quest*, 182–7.
73 Castle diary, vol. 11, Sept. 13, 1927.
74 See *Lokalanzeiger* article of Nov. 26, 1927, and other press clippings, Schurman papers, John Olin Research Library, Cornell University, 3/4/8.
75 McNeil, *American Money*, 183–5.
76 Hans W. Gatzke, *Stresemann and the Rearmament of Germany* (Baltimore, 1954), 72–88; Francis Ludwig Carsten, *The Reichswehr and Politics* (London, 1966), 275–84.
77 Castle diary, vol. 11, Dec. 1, 3, and 7, 1927.
78 Memorandum by Schubert, Jan. 21, 1928, *Akten zur Deutschen Auswärtigen Politik*, series B, vol. VII, no. 39; McNeil, *American Money*, 221–2.

Through this embittered reaction Schurman let pass an opportunity to reestablish a close German-American understanding to revise the Dawes Plan and likewise to coordinate his actions with Gilbert. This opened the way for numerous German-American misunderstandings and discord during the Young Plan negotiations.[79] On November 22, 1928, Gilbert told Stresemann that Germany had to face annuity demands of 2 to 2.5 billion marks when the Dawes Plan was revised. According to Stresemann, Gilbert did not wholly rule out the happy possibility of a negotiated reduction down to about 1.5 billion marks, which the foreign minister had named as the maximum that Germany could pay under transfer protection. It seems that Reichsbank President Hjalmar Schacht chose to ignore the figures that were named by Stresemann and Gilbert. This enabled him to trigger a serious crisis at the Paris negotiations in April 1929 by maintaining that Germany could pay at most 1.5 billion marks. His further precondition for that offer was the restitution of the Polish Corridor and overseas colonies to the Reich.[80]

Schurman's decision to stay strictly within the official limits of his competence had promoted discord. Had Alanson Houghton acted likewise in 1923–4 the Dawes Plan and the end of the Ruhr occupation would have been impossible. The extent to which Schurman had departed from Washington's policy of upholding Germany's responsibility to pay reparations became clear only after his resignation. In a speech to the annual dinner of the Westchester County Historical Society on October 28, 1931, Schurman described reparations as the financial load that the Paris "Diktat" had imposed on Germany and that Germany was unable to carry.[81]

In sum, the complexity of Weimar's political and economic problems had deterred Schurman from observing dissonant elements that deflected from his positive image of Weimar Germany. Although his analysis of party politics often seemed well-meaning and even sensible, his distaste for reparations politics in general and the work of Gilbert in particular led him to eliminate this essential factor in German-American relations from

---

79 McNeil, *American Money*, 228–32, summarizes these, but wrongly blames Gilbert for the German refusal during the Paris conference to confirm the earlier commitments regarding the size of the reparations annuity. For another assessment of Gilbert's activities in regard to the Dawes Plan revision and German reactions, see Harold James, *The Reichsbank and Public Finance in Germany, 1924–1933: A Study of the Politics of Economics During the Great Depression* (Frankfurt/Main, 1985), 57–94.
80 McNeil, *American Money*; Nov. 22, 1928, memorandum of Stresemann's conversation with Gilbert on the previous Nov. 13, *Akten zur Deutschen Auswärtigen Politik*, series B, vol. X, no. 147.
81 Schurman papers, John Olin Research Library, Cornell University, 3/4/8.

his reports. The resulting lack of communication prevented him from weighing the political and economic determinants of reparations policy correctly. Gilbert's motives in analyzing the German situation reflected his own desire to make the Dawes Plan work. That rendered it necessary not merely to supervise but also to control and to reform Germany. Like Castle, the agent general did not share Schurman's view that Germany had the capacity for political evolution without outside assistance. Consequently, Gilbert acquired a vast amount of data on contemporary Germany and developed an expertise that exceeded that of the ambassador. Gilbert remained skeptical with regard to the will of those in power in Germany to comply with the international regime that governed Weimar from 1924 to 1930. The agent general's personal views themselves suggested a clear sympathy for France. Whatever the substantive effect of these sympathies, he remained steadfast in his goal to make the Dawes Plan work as an instrument for European stabilization. His detailed discussions of the German economy and contemporary policy, however, demonstrated an exceedingly sophisticated understanding of Weimar during the Dawes Plan years; indeed, his remarks remain a valuable historical source. He largely shared Castle's realistic if not sympathetic knowledge about Germany, whereas the well-meaning Schurman remained an outsider with his partial and fuzzy images of the society he was supposed to understand so well.

The New York Times editorials between 1924 and 1933 offer the best example of American journalistic opinion during those years. From 1917 onward The New York Times News Service constituted the biggest newspaper syndicate in the United States.[82] After 1924 it also held the most prominent position in foreign reporting, since its communications chief had built a super-heterodyne receiver for direct reception of press dispatches from Europe.[83] Although nominally independent, under the editorship of Adolph S. Ochs the paper tended to lean toward the Democratic Party. The Times had at least two regular correspondents in Berlin, A. S. Ybarra and Lincoln Eyre. When the latter died in 1929 he was replaced by Guido de Enderis.[84] In addition, Paris correspondent Edwin James covered the theme of reparations and German economic policies on the basis of frequent briefings by Morgan partners and Repa-

---

82 Edwin Emery, *The Press and America: An Interpretative History of the Mass Media* (Englewood Cliffs, N.J., 1972), 485.
83 Meyer Berger, *The Story of the New York Times* (New York, 1951), 270.
84 Robert W. Desmond, *Crisis and Conflict: World News Reporting Between Two Wars, 1920-1940* (Iowa City, Iowa, 1980), 299.

ration Commission officials. His painstaking reports about the occupation of Germany after World War I won him a high reputation. He was then promoted to the post of the chief European correspondent of the *Times*. In 1929 he returned to New York and three years later became the paper's managing editor.[85] Rollo Ogden was responsible for its editorial page. He had joined the paper in 1920 after having served for twenty years as editor for the *New York Evening Post*, most recently owned by Thomas Lamont.[86] Alexander D. Noyes served as the financial editor and in that capacity also covered the issues of war debts and reparations.[87]

Times editorials from the spring of 1924 heaped praise on the Dawes Plan and, when they addressed German politics, often assumed the tone of an experienced if impatient schoolmaster. To skeptical German reactions to the experts' committee's report in April 1924 the paper responded: "It is not surprising that Germany's attitude toward the Dawes report is like that of the irate little girl who was quarreling with a schoolmate and sought to put an end to the discussion by remarking, 'I don't know what you're going to say, but whatever it is, 't aint true.'"[88]

The German elections in May 1924 and the battle between nationalists and moderates over the country's reparation obligations figured as a prominent editorial theme.[89] DNVP Reichstag opposition to the Dawes Plan legislation induced *The New York Times* in late August to address German elite opinion directly. The *Times* recalled Secretary of State Hughes's unofficial visit to Berlin earlier in the month. Hughes had told the German government that compliance with the expert committee's report represented Germany's last chance for American cooperation. The editorial pointedly summarized the importance of the plan for the future of Europe: "It is perhaps not too late for an unofficial reminder to the German nationalist leaders that on their shoulder will rest the catastrophe of a failure of the most promising settlement of Europe's reconstruction problem. Sometimes even a word to the unwise is heeded."[90]

Once the Dawes Plan was ratified in Germany and put into operation, editorial coverage of the Weimar Republic in *The New York Times* was less frequent, and its tone was less critical. Yet the election of Paul von Hindenburg as president of the republic in April 1925 moved the paper to observe that Germany was running an enormous risk by inviting

85 See his obituary in the *New York Times*, Dec. 4, 1951.
86 Obituary, *New York Times*, Feb. 23, 1937, 28.
87 Obituary, *New York Times*, Apr. 23, 1945, 9.
88 *New York Times*, Apr. 2, 1924, 18.
89 Ibid., Apr. 3, 20; Apr. 5, 14; June 5, 1924, 20.
90 Ibid., Aug. 29, 1924, 10.

monarchist unsettlement at home and wide distrust abroad.[91] The Locarno Conference and German readiness for a settlement of its western border, however, signaled a move away from editorial censure.[92] Once the Locarno treaties were signed, the *Times* stressed the declining influence of the DNVP in the context of Germany's reconciliation policy.[93] It likewise commented positively on Hindenburg's endorsement of the agreements and acknowledged that Europe was facing the future with brighter hopes and better feeling than at any time since 1914.[94] Subsequent reports on the Thoiry scheme and Germany's wish to speed evacuation of the Rhineland met with an understanding attitude.[95]

Even after Locarno, though, reparations – and, with them, the Dawes Plan – remained major concerns of *The New York Times* editorial writers. In June 1926 Eyre began a series of three feature articles on the Weimar Republic with a piece on German economic readjustment after inflation that summarized the most recent of Gilbert's reports. The second article was exclusively devoted to counteracting criticism of the Dawes Plan. Growing German prosperity constituted the dominant theme throughout the rest of the series.[96] In December 1926 an editorial recapitulated the report of the agent general after the Dawes Plan's second year of operation.[97] Throughout 1927 editorial opinion on questions related to the plan and the German budget continued to reflect Gilbert's reports.[98] The agent general's visit to the United States at the end of the year to prepare for Dawes Plan revision was acknowledged with a sympathetic comment. The editorial also stressed the interrelatedness of war debts and reparations, which was to become an essential feature of the Young Plan.[99]

In 1928 and during the negotiations that followed in Paris for revision of the Dawes Plan, editorial opinion continued to support Gilbert's position. It shared the agent general's view that a final determination of Germany's reparation debt was essential and that the operation of the

---

91 Ibid., Apr. 27, 1925, 16; see also Berg, *Gustav Stresemann*, 232, 248–51.
92 *New York Times*, July 28, 1925, 12.
93 Ibid., Oct. 27, 1925, 22.
94 Ibid., Nov. 16, 1925, 18.
95 Ibid., Sept. 21, 1926, 28; Aug. 27, 1927, 12; on United States–Germany relations between 1930 and 1933, see Bernard V. Burke, *Ambassador Frederick Sackett and the Collapse of the Weimar Republic, 1930–1933: The United States and Hitler's Rise to Power* (New York, 1994).
96 *New York Times*, Sept. 6, 1926, 3; Sept. 7, 1926, 4; Sept. 8, 1926, 3; Sept. 10, 1926, 3.
97 Ibid., Dec. 7, 1926, 26.
98 Ibid., Feb. 24, 1927, 22; Apr. 8, 1927, 22; June 14, 1927, 26; Oct. 25, 1927, 28; Nov. 21, 1927, 22; Dec. 19, 1927, 22.
99 Ibid., Dec. 21, 1927, 24.

Dawes Plan had demonstrated that Germany could make the required annual payments without upsetting international exchange.[100] Likewise, it refuted Schacht's contention that transfer of the Dawes annuities had been effected only with the help of foreign loans.[101] During the first Hague Conference, when Gilbert published a carefully timed interim report, an editorial emphasized that Germany had an enormous interest in permitting the Young Plan to come into force.[102] Subsequently, it asserted that Alfred Hugenberg's campaign against the plan did not constitute a serious danger.[103]

The daily's comments on political developments in Germany paralleled its inclination to assert confidence in Weimar's stability. The upcoming elections in France and in Germany in the spring of 1928, which would determine the subsequent reparation settlement, evoked the prognosis that continuation of the politics of moderation seemed certain.[104] The editors cheered the victory of the Social Democratic Party and reminded readers that the SPD had initiated the policy of pacification that had led to the Dawes Plan.[105] Under the headline "German Democracy," the paper commended Hindenburg for his steadfast loyalty to the republic and concluded that Weimar's practice of democracy had refuted the fears of those who were concerned about the political incapacity of the German people.[106] When the DNVP increased its anti-Young Plan propaganda after the Paris deliberations had been made public, an editorial underlined Stresemann's support for the plan and the strength of moderate politics.[107]

After Stresemann's death on October 3, 1929, correspondent James eulogized him as the greatest German statesman since Bismarck.[108] In this and all other references to the deceased foreign minister the paper avoided making any comparison with other European politicians, thus suggesting that it still regarded German nationhood and nationality as distinctive phenomena. In a fair assessment, James briefly mentioned Stresemann's ardent support for World War I, but mainly emphasized the German's contribution to reconciliation with France as well as his dignified and

---

100 Ibid., June 13, 1928, 26; Jan. 3, 1929, 26.
101 Ibid., Feb. 6, 1929, 28.
102 Ibid., Aug. 14, 1929, 22.
103 Ibid., Sept. 13, 1929, 13.
104 Ibid., Mar. 30, 1928, 24.
105 Ibid., May 22, 1928, 26.
106 Ibid., Feb. 19, 1929, 24.
107 Ibid., June 26, 1929, 28.
108 Ibid., Oct. 4, 1929, 2.

amicable personal manners.[109] Further comments stressed his moral courage in supporting a peaceful accommodation in Europe in 1924.[110] In its sympathetic commemoration of Stresemann, the paper followed a standard trend in international public opinion. Earlier comments on Stresemann, while praising his political aptitude and readiness for improving German-French relations, also noted that he, like Aristide Briand, had profited from the improvement in European politics that had taken place since 1924.[111]

The sympathy shown for Stresemann paralleled the generally positive tone of reporting on Weimar politics after 1925. This tendency reflected both positive factual developments as well as a need to establish confidence that future German governments would comply with the settlements of 1924. After the death of Stresemann and the emerging discord over the Young Plan, *The Times* continued to show its faith in Weimar's future performance. In the wake of the Reichstag election of September 14, 1930, an editorial anticipated gains for the Communist Party and the NSDAP, yet reminded its readers: "It is not unreasonable to expect a working majority for the Brüning Government, made up of a coalition of middle parties such as has been the rule in Germany almost since the establishment of the Republic."[112]

After more than 6.4 million voters had cast their ballots for the NSDAP and had returned it to the Reichstag as the second largest party, *The New York Times*, while noting French apprehension about the outcome, stressed that the election stopped short of being a disaster for the moderate parties that formed the government.[113] When in early October the SPD promised benevolent neutrality toward Brüning, the editorial page cheered the passing of what it called "fascist clouds."[114] Although a feature article by Joseph Shaplen at the end of September convincingly demonstrated Hitler's appeal to the German working class,[115] editorial opinion called Hitler's rhetoric childish and again stressed the potential of German moderates to contain him.[116] The gravity of the situation emerged clearly only when the paper published an urgent appeal on October 19 that called on Germany to put its politics and finances in

---

109 Ibid., Oct. 4, 1929, 4.
110 Ibid., 26.
111 Ibid., May 22, 1929, 24.
112 Ibid., Sept. 6, 1930, 14.
113 Ibid., Sept. 16, 1930, 26.
114 Ibid., Oct. 6, 1930, 22.
115 Ibid., Sept. 21, 1930, Sec. X, 5.
116 Ibid., Sept. 27, 1930, 6.

order. Concerned about an impending German default on its foreign obligations, the editors reminded Germany "that crashing into bankruptcy now would be more unsettling than a Germany defeated in the Great War."[117]

The New York Times editorials on Germany in the period discussed here followed a middle course between candid documentation and pragmatic persuasion. The tendency to support the reparation regime of 1924 for the joint benefit of the United States and Western Europe created the underlying rationale for the paper's stance. The Times thus reflected the views of the policy-making professionals at the State Department, the Federal Reserve Bank of New York, and J. P. Morgan and Co.

To what extent did these individuals or institutions directly influence editorial opinion and reporting? There can be no doubt that Thomas W. Lamont of J. P. Morgan and Co., who considered press relations his special bailiwick, tried incessantly to furnish reporters and editors with pertinent information pointing to the wisdom of current war debt and reparation policies.[118] Ochs and Noyes, however, did not uncritically adopt the Morgan corner's point of view.[119] The Morgan group and U.S. embassy officials overseas exercised leverage more successfully at the source of information, or possibly through such informal ties as Lamont's association with Ogden.[120] In the final analysis, though, they persuaded by means of the economic facts, namely, the economic recovery of Germany and France after 1924.

This stocktaking of professional perceptions of the Weimar Republic suggests that diplomatic and financial relations between 1924 and 1930 were shaped more by the exercise or absence of communication, and more by the selective use of information, than by stereotypical views on the part of the policy elite. The New York Times at crucial instances succumbed to dominant pragmatic modes in its editorial opinions. Yet two of the three professional diplomats described here, despite their sympathy for France and their skepticism toward Germany, based their political actions on an accurate, hard-nosed, and pragmatic assessment of the facts and on their desire to sustain and develop the politics of West European stabilization.

117 Ibid., Oct. 19, 1930, Sec. III, 1.
118 Ronald Steel, *Walter Lippmann and the American Century* (Boston, 1980), 251.
119 See Lamont's correspondence with *The New York Times*, Lamont papers, 120–20.
120 See Lamont's correspondence on the Dawes and the Young plans in the Lamont papers; and the Castle-Poole correspondence in the Castle papers, files G 55–6.

10

"Without Concessions to Marxist or Communist Thought"
Fordism in Germany, 1923–1939

PHILIPP GASSERT

I

This chapter addresses the German discussion of America during the interwar period in the context of contemporary, reactionary modernist thinking, which promoted technological progress and rationalization while radically rejecting the political ideals of the Enlightenment – freedom, equality, and fraternity.[1] The chapter also investigates long-standing phenomena in the German-American relationship using German images of America as a guide. Although researchers like to describe the German-American relationship in the twentieth century as a dramatic lurching between war and peace, friendship and enmity, confrontation and cooperation,[2] it is by no means clear how or whether German images of America (and American images of Germany) have been affected by the vicissitudes of political relations.[3] Were century-old stereotypes of cultural

---

I would like to thank Pamela Abraham, Manfred Berg, Manfred Boemeke, Elisabeth Glaser-Schmidt, Detlef Junker, and Daniel S. Mattern for their helpful comments on earlier versions of this chapter. Sally E. Robertson of Arlington, Va., provided the translation from German.
1 Jeffrey Herf, *Reactionary Modernism: Technology, Culture, and Politics in Weimar and the Third Reich* (Cambridge, 1984).
2 Cf. Günther Moltmann, "200 Jahre USA: Eine Bilanz Deutsch-Amerikanischer Beziehungen," *Geschichte in Wissenschaft und Unterricht* 27 (1976): 393–408; Hans W. Gatzke, *Germany and the United States: A Special Relationship?* (Cambridge, 1980), vii; Manfred Jonas, *The United States and Germany: A Diplomatic History* (Ithaca, N.Y., 1984); Detlef Junker, *Kampf um die Weltmacht: Die USA und das Dritte Reich, 1933–1945* (Düsseldorf, 1988), 13; Hans-Jürgen Schroeder, ed., *Confrontation and Cooperation: Germany and the United States in the Era of World War I, 1900–1924* (Providence, R.I., 1993); Frank A. Ninkovich, *Germany and the United States: The Transformation of the German Question Since 1945* (New York, 1994), 1.
3 For initial references to this basic problem of perception research, see Knud Krakau, "Einführende Überlegungen zur Entstehung und Wirkung von Bildern, die sich Nationen von sich und anderen machen," in Willi Paul Adams and Knud Krakau, eds., *Deutschland und Amerika: Perzeption und*

anti-Americanism resistant to changes in the political and diplomatic relationship between the two countries? What about the traditional admiration of the Germans for the "land of unlimited opportunity" as an economic superpower? Could National Socialist propaganda be confident that the American model had lost its attractiveness as a result of the Great Depression? How did it define its own relationship to Fordism and Americanism? How did the National Socialist image of America fit into the Nazi ideology?

The following sketch of the economic image of America from the time of the reichsmark stabilization until World War II should provide answers to these questions.[4] Because the main interest of this chapter is in the origins of the National Socialist interpretation of America, it almost entirely disregards the discussion of America by unions and entrepreneurs and by moderate and liberal adherents of Americanism, as well as the contribution of orthodox Marxist criticism. Precisely because the only detailed studies of German images of America stop at the customary epochal boundaries, and because the National Socialist image of America has yet to be systematically portrayed, I believe this approach to be reasonable and necessary. Because this collection also includes Peter

---

historische Realität (Berlin, 1985), 9–18; an essay building on the experiences of cultural studies could help in this regard, e.g., Akira Iriye, "Culture and International History," in Michael J. Hogan and Thomas G. Paterson, eds., *Explaining the History of American Foreign Relations* (Cambridge, 1991), 214–25; and the papers in "Culture, Gender and Foreign Policy: A Symposium," *Diplomatic History* 18 (1994): 47–124.

4 Researchers have paid particular attention to the image of America during the Weimar period; see, e.g., Ernst Fraenkel, "Das deutsche Wilsonbild," *Jahrbuch für Amerikastudien* 5 (1960): 66–120; Peter Berg, *Deutschland und Amerika, 1918–1929: Über das deutsche Amerikabild der zwanziger Jahre* (Lübeck, 1963); Manfred Buchwald, "Das Kulturbild Amerikas im Spiegel deutscher Zeitungen und Zeitschriften, 1919–1932," Ph.D. diss., University of Kiel, 1964; Erich Angermann, "Die Auseinandersetzung mit der Moderne in Deutschland und den USA," in *Deutschland und die USA/Germany and the USA* (Braunschweig, 1968), 53–75; Earl R. Beck, *Germany Rediscovers America* (Tallahassee, Fla., 1968); Helmut Lethen, *Neue Sachlichkeit, 1924–1932: Studien zur Literatur des "Weissen Sozialismus"* (Stuttgart, 1970); Klaus Schwabe, "Anti-Americanism within the German Right, 1917–1933," *Amerikastudien* 21 (1976): 89–107; Eberhard Schütz, *Kritik der literarischen Reportage: Reportagen und Reiseberichte aus der Weimarer Republik über die USA und die Sowjetunion* (Munich, 1977); Theresa Mayer Hammond, *American Paradise: German Travel Literature from Duden to Kisch* (Heidelberg, 1980); Frank Trommler, "The Rise and Fall of Americanism in Germany," in Frank Trommler and Joseph McVeigh, eds., *America and the Germans: An Assessment of a Three-Hundred-Year History* (Philadelphia, 1985), 2:333–42; Sara Markham, *Workers, Women, and Afro-Americans: Images of the United States in German Travel Literature, 1923–1933* (New York, 1986); Ulrich Ott, *Amerika ist anders: Studien zum Amerikabild in deutschen Reiseberichten des 20. Jahrhunderts* (Frankfurt/Main, 1991); Frank Becker, *Amerikanismus in Weimar: Sportsymbole und politische Kultur, 1918–1933* (Wiesbaden, 1993); Dan Diner, *Verkehrte Welten: Antiamerikanismus in Deutschland: Ein historischer Essay* (Frankfurt/Main, 1993); Werner Kremp, *In Deutschland liegt unser Amerika: Das sozialdemokratische Amerikabild von den Anfängen der SPD bis zur Weimarer Republik* (Münster, Hamburg, 1993); Mary Nolan, *Visions of Modernity: American Business and the Modernization of Germany* (New York, 1994).

Krüger's essay dealing with the reciprocal influences of the political systems and constitutional law between 1914 and 1933 and Detlef Junker's overview of the German image of America between 1933 and 1945, I shall limit myself to an interepochal study of socioeconomic aspects of the German image of America. I am well aware, however, that another line of continuity could be drawn to the Third Reich from the cultural-conservative criticism of America.[5] I have concentrated on the ideological current of *reactionary modernism*, which played a significant role in the German discussion of America before 1933, and which determined the attitude of the Nazis toward Americanism after 1933. My sources for the time before 1933 were primarily "America books." For the period after 1933, I traced the assimilation of reactionary modernistic thought by using primary and secondary literature on rationalization measures within National Socialism, as well as reports in the National Socialist press. Only in this way could I glean the "official" Nazi image of America.[6]

My presentation is built on the hypothesis that National Socialism's ambivalent image of America can be understood only when one considers that, between 1900 and 1950, German images of America served to clarify Germany's own viewpoint on modernism, that is, the social structure that developed in Europe in the seventeenth and eighteenth centuries, extended to the entire world in the nineteenth and twentieth centuries, had its ultimate breakthrough and apex during the period between the wars, and is still the essential determining factor of the present.[7] Max Weber characterized this process as the "demystification of the world," defined as rationalization in the most comprehensive sense.[8] In the 1920s, which have sometimes been called the years of "classical

---

5 For details, see Philipp Gassert, *Amerika im Dritten Reich: Die Kritik der amerikanischen Moderne in Ideologie, Volksmeinung und Propaganda, 1933–1945* (forthcoming). Ott, *Amerika ist anders*, 243ff, is working on the continuity of cultural stereotypes from the Weimar Republic to the Third Reich.
6 In terms of my hypothesis, National Socialist publications such as *Völkischer Beobachter* and *Angriff* are almost completely unproductive for the period before 1933. In their place, the speeches of Adolf Hitler are useful and are addressed briefly here. For more details on Hitler's image of America, see the literature cited in footnote 65 and Detlef Junker's chapter in this book.
7 For a definition, see Anthony Giddens, *The Consequences of Modernity* (Stanford, Calif., 1990), 1. There is no room to discuss here the fact that the concept of modernity has become problematic and that modernization theory has been subjected to severe criticism. See, e.g., Geoff Eley, "Die deutsche Geschichte und die Widersprüche der Moderne: Das Beispiel des Kaiserreiches," in Frank Bajohr and Werner Johe, eds., *Zivilisation und Barbarei: Die widersprüchlichen Potentiale der Moderne: Detlev Peukert zum Gedenken* (Hamburg, 1991), 17; on the history of the concept, see Hans Ulrich Gumbrecht, "Modern, Modernität, Moderne," in Otto Brunner, Werner Conze, and Reinhart Koselleck, eds., *Geschichtliche Grundbegriffe: Historisches Lexikon zur politisch-sozialen Sprache in Deutschland* (Stuttgart, 1975), 4:93–131.
8 See Detlev J. K. Peukert, *Max Webers Diagnose der Moderne* (Göttingen, 1989), 30–1, 70ff.

modernism," borrowing a term from art history,[9] America was considered the Mecca of the rationalization movement and was seen as the exact opposite of a traditional agrarian, static, and hierarchically organized society. The terms Americanism and modernism were therefore used almost synonymously.[10] This connection has long been underestimated in perception research and in writing the history of German-American relations, although since the 1950s sociologists have equated the term modernization with Anglo-Americanization.[11] Detlev Peukert thus drove straight to the core of German images of America in the Weimar Republic when he defined the Americanism of the 1920s as a "cipher for unreserved and unconstrained modernism." According to Peukert, "the public debate over America was about [Germany's] own culture and the challenge of modernity that it faced."[12] The German discussion of America was actually a coming to terms with the social and cultural consequences of the breakthrough to modernism that took place during and after World War I, a connection well recognized at the time by critics of the "America legend."[13] In this way, Americanism developed in the 1920s to a truly European umbrella term[14] that could refer to anything that was "modern" and could even remotely be linked to materialism, efficiency, size, mechanization, standardization, automation, technocracy, uniformity, pragmatism, reform consciousness, naive optimism, spontaneity, generosity, openness, advertising, democracy, or influence exercised upon the masses.[15]

Given this identification of modernization with Americanization at the

---

9 Detlev J. K. Peukert, *Die Weimarer Republik: Krisenjahre der klassischen Moderne* (Frankfurt/Main, 1987).
10 Cf. definitions of the time by Kayser, Zweig, Sieburg, Halfeld, Palitzsch, and Stössinger in the anthology compiled by Anton Kaes, ed., *Weimarer Republik: Manifeste und Dokumente zur deutschen Literatur, 1918–1933* (Stuttgart, 1983), 265–86; Peukert, *Max Webers Diagnose*, 71–3.
11 Cf. Dean C. Tipps, "Modernization Theory and the Comparative Study of Societies," *Comparative Studies in Society and History* 15 (1973): 206; M. Rainer Lepsius, "Soziologische Theoreme über die Sozialstruktur der 'Moderne' und 'Modernisierung,'" in Reinhart Koselleck, ed., *Studien zum Beginn der modernen Welt* (Stuttgart, 1977), 13.
12 Peukert, *Die Weimarer Republik*, 179. In addition to Peukert and Trommler, Nolan showed this particularly well in her excellent book.
13 Cf. Charlotte Lütkens, "Die Amerikalegende," *Sozialistische Monatshefte* 1 (1932): 45–50; Gerhard Desczyk, "Amerika in der Phantasie deutscher Dichter," *Deutsch-amerikanische Geschichtsblätter* 24/25 (1924–5): 98; Hermann Levy, "Amerika als Kulturproblem," *Neuphilologische Monatschrift* 1 (1930): 298.
14 Cf. Frank Costigliola, *Awkward Dominion: American Political, Economic, and Cultural Relations with Europe, 1919–1933* (Ithaca, N.Y., 1984), 140ff, 167ff.
15 See also the presentation in ibid., 167. For attempts at definitions during that period, see Otto Basler, "Amerikanismus: Geschichte des Schlagwortes," *Deutsche Rundschau* 221 (1930): 214–21; Richard Müller-Freienfels, "'Amerikanismus' und europäische Kultur," *Der deutsche Gedanke* 4 (1927): 30–5.

time, the central point of my study of economic America is the question of the relationship between Nazi ideology and the concurrent criticism of modernism. One could also say that, precisely because the Third Reich was the specific National Socialist response to the "crisis of classical modernism" (Peukert), the Nazi image of America reflects, among other things, the central substance of Nazi ideology. Many National Socialists, few of whom expressed themselves coherently regarding the United States prior to 1933, shared the peculiarly inconsistent attitude of an important current in German publicistic literature on America in the 1920s and 1930s. They were enthusiastic supporters of Fordism in the sense of economic Americanization, while just as vehemently rejecting the mass civilization aspects of American culture. Jeffrey Herf has described this paradoxical attitude as reactionary modernism.[16] His remarkable study on the relationship of the Weimar Right to modernism draws attention to a group of writers, engineers, and cultural philosophers who sought to reconcile the romantic, antiliberal, and anti-Western traditions of German nationalism with modern science and technology. On the one hand, they used the "ideas of 1789" to fight the political legacy of the Enlightenment and rebelled against the social and economic reality created by the industrialization and rationalization of all aspects of life. On the other hand, they supported inventions, technological progress, and industrial rationalization measures, although these too were consequences of Enlightenment reason, as long as they conformed to German nationalist ideology.

As Herf has shown, the reactionary modernists were nationalists who, instead of focusing on backward-oriented images of pastoralism, outlined the contours of a new order that would replace the formless capitalistic chaos of the present. The reactionary modernists thus claimed that Germany could be technologically advanced while remaining true to its soul.[17]

Herf's concept is used below to analyze German images of America in the period between the wars. The same authors who valued Ford for his management innovations and his supposed solution of the social question were merciless critics of the culture of the masses that they saw in America. By dissociating Fordism from its historic context and stylizing it into a magic weapon in the battle to eliminate social problems in Germany, the reactionary modernist adherents of Fordism turned it into an ideology that departed drastically from Ford's original intentions. In this

---

16 See Herf, *Reactionary Modernism*, passim; Peukert, *Max Webers Diagnose*, 81ff.
17 Herf, *Reactionary Modernism*, 2–3. Original emphasis.

context, it was decisive for the adherents of economic Americanism, as shown below using the example of Werner Sombart, that America was seen as an exception, an industrial society with no labor movement to speak of, that is, without socialism. The labor question seemed to have been solved brilliantly "without making any kind of concessions to Marxist or Communist thought."[18] Technological progress permitted social harmony and prosperity at home and economic power on the world market, without sacrificing traditional values and hierarchies. Ford was attractive to his reactionary modernist interpreters because his example combined opposition to the political ideals of the Enlightenment with the highest achievement in technological efficiency and control.

Despite the setback of the Great Depression, which this chapter is able to address only tangentially, "America" had not completely lost its value as a symbol after 1933. Since memories of the Weimar debates were still fresh, the Nazis were able to draw some legitimation at first from comparisons with the United States. Their emphasis on parallels reflected the Nazis' conviction that their "German revolution" was part of a worldwide trend. These comparisons referred, above all, to a supposed triumph over Americanism in the United States itself and should by no means be interpreted as signs of an intended Americanization of the Third Reich. As it became apparent that the New Deal was remaining relatively unsuccessful, the old Americanism debate seemed to be turned on its head. America was becoming "Europeanized" in a negative sense, while it was the Nazis who, in their self-perception, were speeding toward a solution to the social question, and this using originally "American" production methods. Of course, the Nazis could no longer call the methods American, particularly as anti-Bolshevist statements were becoming more and more prominent in Nazi reporting on America. No longer was the United States viewed as an exception. America was no longer a land without socialism but rather had become a "breeding ground for Bolshevism" and thus a battleground in the "international civil war of ideologies" (Nolte).

II

The perception of America as an exception is as old as the United States itself and corresponds to a favorite self-image of the Americans.[19] This

---

18 Carl Hollweg, *Columbusfahrt: Politische, wirtschaftliche und soziale Entdeckerbetrachtungen auf einer Amerikareise* (Berlin, 1925), 69.
19 Cf. Eric Foner, "Why Is There No Socialism in the United States?" *History Workshop Journal* 17 (1984): 57–81.

subject of study was first raised in German sociology by Weber and Sombart, who participated in a 1904 study trip to the Congress of Arts and Sciences on the occasion of the World's Fair in St. Louis and who expressed their impressions in a very similar manner.[20] With his treatise on the question, *Why is There No Socialism in the United States?*, Sombart lent the debate a popular slogan that was then often used as the answer in itself. On the one hand, Sombart saw the United States as "the country with the most highly developed capitalism" whose "economic organization [represents Germany's] future."[21] On the other hand, Sombart felt that the open border to the west in the United States created specific conditions that explained the absence of socialism. According to Sombart, the mere theoretical possibility of "being able to choose between capitalism and non-capitalism transforms any embryonic opposition to this economic system from an active to a passive state and dulls the point on any anti-capitalist agitation."[22] Since, according to Sombart, it was impossible for these unique conditions to last, he advanced the prediction that it was only a matter of time until socialism would reach "full bloom" in the United States as well.[23]

By 1923 the "Wild West" had lost its "venting function" and Fordism was available as a new model to explain the economic rise of the United States. This model, too, centered on the relationship between capital and labor and seemed transferable to Germany. The aspects that most interested the reactionary modernists among Ford's followers in Germany were not the internal business management and concrete labor relations in the Ford plants, but rather the question of how Henry Ford had managed to solve the social question without a revolution interfering as it had in Europe. Ford himself gave the send-off to the great Americanism debate with the publication in 1923–4 of his memoirs, *My Life and Work*, in German translation, just as the reichsmark stabilization and Dawes Plan were opening the floodgates for the flow of American capital and American consumer

---

20 On the background of this trip, see Hans Rollmann, "'Meet Me in St. Louis': Troeltsch and Weber in America," in Hartmut Lehmann and Guenther Roth, eds., *Weber's Protestant Ethic: Origins, Evidence, Contexts* (New York, 1993), 357–83; see also Marianne Weber, *Max Weber: Ein Lebensbild*, 2d ed. (Heidelberg, 1950), 329; Wolfgang J. Mommsen, "Die Vereinigten Staaten von Amerika im politischen Denken Max Webers," *Historische Zeitschrift* 213 (1971): 358–81; Friedrich Lenger, *Werner Sombart 1863 bis 1941: Eine Biographie* (Munich, 1994), 316ff; for a comparison of the works of Weber and Sombart on the rise of modern capitalism, see Hartmut Lehmann, "The Rise of Capitalism: Weber versus Sombart," in Lehmann and Roth, eds., *Weber's Protestant Ethic*, 195–208.
21 Werner Sombart, *Warum gibt es in den Vereinigten Staaten keinen Sozialismus?* (Tübingen, 1906), 35.
22 Ibid., 140.
23 Ibid., 142; although it would have been natural, Sombart (at least in the footnotes) did not adopt Turner's frontier thesis.

goods.[24] Two hundred thousand copies of the German edition were printed, making it the best-selling book on America during the period between the wars.[25] His success as the "richest man in the world" lent weight to his arguments, and he used a popular style in offering simple solutions to complex social problems. His business ethics redefined the relationship between capital and labor and promised a solution to the social question in the context of a *Volksgemeinschaft* (national community).[26]

Ford seemed to have satisfied the demand for a harmonious solution to the "labor question" in a manner that was as simple as it was ingenious. Paul Rieppel, whose book the historian Peter Berg considers to be "particularly characteristic of the Ford fervor in Germany,"[27] praised Ford's skill in eliminating the friction in relations between management and labor.[28] More important than the adoption of improvements in the areas of technology and management, according to Rieppel, "is the intellectual content of Ford's methods, which determine the relations between the entrepreneurs, workers and consumers, and accordingly the position of production with respect to capital."[29] In a completely uncritical interpretation of Ford's memoirs, Professor Friedrich von Gottl-Ottlilienfeld of Kiel,[30] who introduced the term *Fordismus* into the German language and popularized it on his lecture tours, considered it to be the differences between Frederick W. Taylor's methods of scientific management and Ford's principles that made the economic attitudes of

---

24 Markham therefore makes that date the starting point of her study. Henry Ford, *Mein Leben und Werk*, German trans. C. and M. Thesing (Leipzig, n.d. [1923]); see also Werner Link, *Die amerikanische Stabilisierungspolitik in Deutschland, 1921–1932* (Düsseldorf, 1970), 356.
25 Information from the publisher to Peter Berg, *Deutschland und Amerika*, 99n. 5. Title of the English original: *My Life and Work* (Garden City, N.J., 1922).
26 Before being abused by the Nazis, the term *Volksgemeinschaft* did not have the negative connotation it has today. It was also used by liberal authors in a positive sense. See, e.g., Moritz J. Bonn, *Geld und Geist: Vom Wesen und Werden der amerikanischen Welt* (Berlin, 1927), 189.
27 Berg, *Deutschland und Amerika*, 101.
28 See Paul Rieppel, *Ford-Betriebe und Ford-Methoden* (Munich, 1925), 26–33.
29 Ibid., 50.
30 Friedrich von Gottl-Ottlilienfeld, born Nov. 13, 1868 in Vienna, died Oct. 19, 1958, in Frankfurt/Main; 1900, private lecturer in Heidelberg; professor in Brünn, Munich, Hamburg; 1924, at Institute for International Economy in Kiel; 1926, in Berlin (see Kürschner's *Deutscher Gelehrten-Kalender*, 1941; *Neue Deutsche Biographie*, vol. 6). Joined the Nazi Party on May 1, 1937, honorary doctorate in Berlin in 1938, Goethe Medal, member of the Academy of German Law (*Akademie für Deutsches Recht*), leading thinker behind a theoretically oriented national economy in the Third Reich, but no longer wrote on issues of Americanization. In a memorandum of the Nazi League of University Teachers (*Dozentenbund*), he was described as "one of the few useful professors of the older generation," because he had become known even before 1933 for his "strong stand against the Jews," but not necessarily as suitable for "establishing a National Socialist economic science." See Gottl-Ottlilienfeld files in the Bundesarchiv, Zehlendorf Branch (formerly Berlin Document Center).

the latter particularly attractive.[31] Whereas the Taylor system was geared toward the "best possible organization for the work to be performed in the company,"[32] Fordism was characterized not only by ensuring every worker his fair wages, shortening the workday, and offering everyone the same chances for advancement, but, above all, by the cultivation of the "spirit of personality," which "blows through the entire enormous company and touches every last worker."[33] Gottl-Ottlilienfeld conceded that workers also profited from higher wages under the Taylor system, but the price they paid was that "the personality of the worker was crushed." If the goal was "animating the company into a true community," the Taylor system was more a parody than a "healthy start." Although Taylorism was theoretically dedicated to the common good, it became obvious in practice that it contributed mostly to the "profit returns" of the entrepreneur while the "general economy took the back seat."[34]

Fordism was therefore more than a revolutionizing of internal business management. It was a redefining of the relationship between capital and labor that affected the entire society. The decisive factor was the manner in which Ford dedicated himself to the common good. Ford's ideology of the "service mentality" was seen as an opportunity to restructure the relationship between individual companies and the economy as a whole. For Rieppel, Ford's business ethics were a virtual reincarnation of old Prussian virtues: "The good old Prussian ideal of service to the people, which has been nearly lost in present-day Germany, has suddenly reemerged in America, this land from which we are used to expecting only the crassest materialism."[35] In his interpretation of Ford, Gottl-Ottlilienfeld depicted a capitalist utopia minus the selfish capitalists. Like Rieppel, he saw in Ford's strategy of price reductions the expression of a "willingness to serve." This was defined positively as "an action based on reason but in the spirit of the community"[36] and was contrasted with the negative "profit mentality" characterized by "propping up prices" in

---

31 Friedrich von Gottl-Ottlilienfeld, *Fordismus? Paraphrasen über das Verhältnis von Wirtschaft und technischer Vernunft bei Henry Ford und Frederick W. Taylor* (Jena, 1924). For evidence of the uncritical handling of Ford, see ibid., 11ff, 30: "From a purely human point of view, I do not doubt his words for a moment. To be sure, we Germans have learned the hard way to be cautious regarding American words, but this is different. Here, words provide simply an interpretation of already accomplished actions."
32 Ibid., 6.
33 Ibid., 12; see also Edmund Keinschmitt, *Durch Werkstätten und Gassen dreier Erdteile: Das soziale Bild von Amerika, Ostasien, und Australien* (Hamburg, 1928), 12, 33ff.
34 Gottl-Ottlilienfeld, *Fordismus?* 8, 11.
35 Rieppel, *Ford-Betriebe*, 29.
36 Gottl-Ottlilienfeld, *Fordismus?* 31.

order to generate dividends. The star witness in Gottl-Ottlilienfeld's reactionary criticism of capitalism was Ford, who he said operated not according to the principle of maximum profits ("buy as cheap as possible, sell as dear as possible," the basic law of the "profit addict") but according to the maxim of "buy at reasonable prices and produce at as low a cost as possible in order to be able to sell for as low a price as possible." Using Ford's methods, the author hoped to provide better for the masses, the end result of which would be not a leveling but "civilization" in the sense of self-actualization of the workers. Gone would be the "competition at the cost of corpses," the profit economy would be defeated, ownership of capital would be merely the expression of a "creative force," of a "leadership of service, . . . called by a self-confident willingness to serve and then chosen by a process of selection along the way."[37] And since "behind every leader in service . . . a following in service [gathers, . . .], the industrial operation is transfigured into a community providing cheerful service to the greater community."

Ford had discovered the "third way." In the words of Theodor Lüddecke, Americanism meant overcoming the old "battle positions" of capitalism and socialism. While in Germany "the best energies of the German people had been used up settling domestic political battles," America pragmatically set about solving the social question. "America does not discuss – America produces."[38] Gottl-Ottlilienfeld discovered with some satisfaction that, under Fordism, the whole development was to take place "free of the changing of forms," maintaining market and price mechanisms as well as the "large-scale technology necessary to life" and the discipline of work, but without the dark sides of modernism, that is, without loss of "creative power," without leveling and without eradicating the differences between cultures. In other words, without revolution, without riots and the "dull push from below," but also without "the uprising of the disinherited in the middle of it all. . . . Pure and simple, no red socialism of demands, that would not have painted the life work of

---

37 All quotations and the following, ibid., 34–7.
38 Theodor Lüddecke, *Das amerikanische Wirtschaftstempo als Bedrohung Europas* (Leipzig, n.d. [1925]), 15. Despite its sensational title, the book was a strong endorsement of Fordism. His most influential contribution to the Americanism debate was the essay "Amerikanismus als Schlagwort und als Tatsache," *Deutsche Rundschau* 221 (1930): 214–21. Born Nov. 17, 1900, doctor of political science, director since 1929 of the Institute for Periodical Science (*Institut für Zeitungskunde*) at the University of Halle, extended visits to the United States in 1923–4 and 1937, joined Nazi Party on Apr. 1, 1930, press secretary for the propaganda departments; see Kürschner's *Deutscher Gelehrten-Kalender*, 1940–1, Lüddecke's files in the Bundesarchiv, Dahlwitz-Hoppegarten Branch, ZB II, 3762/13.

Henry Ford on the wall of our time . . . but rather the white socialism of the pure, enterprising spirit."[39]

The analyses by Lüddecke, Rieppel, and Gottl-Ottlilienfeld, which can be considered representative of a number of Ford interpretations,[40] are characterized by their apparent proximity to the economic thought of the "conservative revolution."[41] Rieppel himself pointed out the similarities between his (that is, Henry Ford's) economic philosophy and that of Oswald Spengler, stating that Ford's business ethics were identical to Spengler's Prussian socialism.[42]

> For Ford's methods signify nothing other than the reawakening of the Prussian-German spirit of service and work. . . . We as a people sensed this instinctively when we attributed to Ford's book a value beyond any we had ever ascribed to any publication on technology or economics. . . . We had a strong feeling that we needed these Ford methods and, above all, we felt that they suited our blood and our soil.[43]

Similar arguments were advanced by retired Admiral Carl Hollweg, who found Ford's principles attractive primarily

> because they express the old Prussian "I serve principle" so often stressed by men like Hugo Stinnes and because they are in contrast to the tired old phrases and false doctrines of German social democrats and Marxist-oriented union bureaucrats [sic] which can be regarded as having now been proven unsuitable for practical development work.[44]

That last clause could indeed have been written by Ford himself, whose ideas Hollweg claimed as part of the Prussian tradition and inter-

---

39 Gottl-Ottlilienfeld, *Fordismus?* 37; see also Waldemar Zimmermann, "Fords Evangelium von der technisch-sozialen Dienstleistung," *Schmollers Jahrbuch* 48 (1924): 491–523.
40 Cf. the assessment in the specialized literature: Beck, *Germany Rediscovers America*, 94–100; Berg, *Deutschland und America*, 99–107; Egbert Klautke, "Die Amerikanismus debatte in der Weimarer Republik," M.A. thesis, University of Heidelberg, 1994, 19–32.
41 Stefan Breuer, *Anatomie der Konservativen Revolution* (Darmstadt, 1993), argues convincingly that the concept of the conservative revolution has become untenable. For practical reasons, I use it within quotation marks, even though Breuer's term "new nationalism" more accurately describes the extremely heterogeneous movement of cultural criticism in the Weimar Republic. For general information on the conservative revolution, see Armin Mohler, *Die Konservative Revolution in Deutschland, 1918–1932: Ein Handbuch*, 3d ed., with a new supplemental volume (Darmstadt, 1989); the term "reactionary modernism," on the other hand, is used not to describe a group of persons but to characterize a certain ideology.
42 Rieppel, *Ford-Betriebe*, 51; Rieppel refers to Oswald Spengler, *Preussentum und Sozialismus* (Munich, 1919).
43 Rieppel, *Ford-Betriebe*, 50.
44 Hollweg, *Columbusfahrt*, 72. The comparison with Stinnes is also made in Lüddecke, *Das amerikanische Wirtschaftstempo*, 26. Hollweg was an engineer and retired Admiral in the Imperial Navy, and traveled to the United States in 1924.

preted as "entirely un-American."⁴⁵ This may be surprising at first, since Ford was the veritable prototype of the American businessman, a classic American success story whose life path had not exactly led him to the top via the obstacle course of a Prussian official's career. Yet Hollweg's claims were not made completely from whole cloth since, almost simultaneously, America was undergoing just as vehement a confrontation with the forces of modernism as was Germany, a difficult process accompanied by vigorous social upheaval and militant protest. Anti-Semitism and hatred of the "plutocratic rulers" of Wall Street were the standard concepts with which "true Americanism" did battle against the "un-American" phenomena of modern times, such as industrialization, urbanization, and mass culture. Aside from the fact that this discussion could hardly take place in the United States under the banner of "anti-Americanism," the two were parallel developments.⁴⁶ Ford's anti-Semitism,⁴⁷ his authoritarian leadership (*Führertum*), and his socioeconomic principles were probably closer ideologically to the "conservative-revolutionary" philosophy of Rieppel and Hollweg than to the ideals of the Enlightenment and liberalism to which the fathers of the American Constitution subscribed and which Hollweg understandably identified as the true American principles.

In addition, proposals of state socialism, such as those presented by Gottl-Ottlilienfeld, were not seen as inconsistent with the freedom of choice of the entrepreneurial class, as an analysis of the economic philosophy of the "conservative revolution" would show.⁴⁸ Spengler, for example, who did not hesitate to speak of American "billionaire socialism," just as he spoke of the English "socialism of money" and of Prussianism as "socialism of the state,"⁴⁹ himself clarified in a reissue of his political writings "that socialism is an 'ethos,' not an economic principle. . . . Idiots are still trying to preach 'national' communism. Socialism, as I understand it, presupposes a private economy with its old Germanic joy in power and its spoils."⁵⁰ For all the political antiliberalism that was Spengler's main thrust, he endorsed a primitive economic liberalism. Through the power

---

45 Lüddecke, *Das amerikanische Wirtschaftstempo*.
46 Cf. Angermann, "Die Auseinandersetzung der Moderne," 58–9; Thomas P. Hughes, *Die Erfindung Amerikas: Der technologische Aufstieg der USA seit 1870* (Munich, 1991), 212–24.
47 Henry Ford, *Der Internationale Jude* (Leipzig, n.d. [1922]); Ford did not espouse a racist-motivated anti-Semitism, but rather supported assimilation because he considered the United States to be a Christian nation in the broadest sense; cf. his contemporary, Arno G. G. Faldix, *Henry Ford als Wirtschaftspolitiker* (Munich, 1925), 40–1.
48 There has been no systematic study; for initial points of departure, see Breuer, *Anatomie der Konservativen Revolution*, 59–70.
49 Oswald Spengler, *Preussentum und Sozialismus* (Munich, 1919), 88.
50 Oswald Spengler, *Politische Schriften* (Munich, 1932), vii–viii.

of politics, he hoped to abolish moneyed capital and unions and weld them together in a Prussian bureaucracy:

> In an organization that fundamentally eliminates the difference between laborers and civil servants by offering every competent person a stable career, from the lowest level of manual labor to the government control boards to the leadership of a business enterprise, the ultimate conservative and proletarian goals will finally coincide under the hand of a born statesman: complete nationalization of economic life not by expropriation but by legislation.[51]

Similar sentiments were heard from Moeller van den Bruck, the authors of *Deutsche Rundschau* and *Deutsches Volkstum*, and the Young Conservatives, all of whom in some way accepted the private economy as the "natural state."[52] The reactionary modernistic Ford boys could fit themselves easily into the scheme presented by Spengler. Gottl-Ottlilienfeld, too, adhered to "market, competition, price," but under the auspices of a *Führersozialismus* (socialism with a strong leader) instead of the conflictual nature of the liberal order.[53]

Compared to these ideological perspectives, many descriptions relegated the purely technical aspects of Fordism more or less to the background. Most descriptions by Ford enthusiasts, particularly the travel reports, included lengthy and lively portrayals of the Ford plants. However, the adoption of specific production methods was seldom taken up as an issue in this literature, whereas technicians and engineers who actually wanted to adopt and implement Ford's methods had a much more skeptical overall assessment of their transferability, even if they shared the basic ideological position of the Fordists.[54] The Ford plants in River Rouge and Highland Park, Michigan, were thus extraordinarily well suited as an heroic stage on which to enact an ideological program. Gottl-Ottlilienfeld acknowledged this expressly in the reissue of his Fordism book in 1926, making a distinction between "Fordism" (the socialism of

---

51 Spengler, *Preussentum und Sozialismus*, 96–7. On Spengler's economic philosophy, see Detlef Felken, *Oswald Spengler: Konservativer Denker zwischen Kaisserreich und Diktatur* (Munich, 1988), 107–14.
52 See Breuer, *Anatomie der Konservativen Revolution*, 62–3; regarding Moeller van den Bruck, see Fritz Stern, *The Politics of Cultural Despair: A Study in the Rise of the Germanic Ideology* (Berkeley, Calif., 1961).
53 Friedrich von Gottl-Ottlilienfeld, *Fordismus: Über Industrie und technische Vernunft*, 3d. exp. ed. (Jena, 1926), 79–81.
54 See Carl Köttgen, *Das wirtschaftliche Amerika* (Berlin, 1925), 46ff. At the time of his trip to America in 1925, Köttgen was director general of the Siemens-Schukert company and executive director of the industry-financed Reich Board of Trustees for Efficiency, the most important institution for the study of rationalization measures; for details on this point, see Nolan, *Visions of Modernity*, 59ff. See also Tilla Siegel and Thomas von Freyberg, *Industrielle Rationalisierung unter dem Nationalsozialismus* (Frankfurt/Main, 1991), 79n. 5.

the service philosophy) and "Fordization" (emulation of specific production methods).[55]

'Fordism,' as the ideology into which it has ultimately developed, has to do with Henry Ford the person, with his actual attitudes and his overall work only inasmuch as a philosophical picture can be distilled from his beliefs or from the intellectual extension thereof: namely, the ideology of community-affirming coexistence known as 'Fordism'![56]

In addition to the hope of reconciling opposing views, Fordism made apparent another leitmotif of reactionary thought – the anticipation of a *Führer*.[57] The fascination with the figure of a *Führer* was transferred to Henry Ford. One author, Fritz Bredow, saw in Ford neither a reactionary nor a revolutionary but a practical man, a "true *Führer*" from whom the Germans could learn how to get back on their feet economically while fulfilling their best character traits.[58] In 1924 Adolf Saager described Ford's career as the rise from unassuming beginnings in a rural area near Dearborn to the ruler of the world automobile market in words and images strongly reminiscent of the later "Hitler myths."

He suggests using the power that a crane wastes when it lowers its arm; he eliminates all useless statistics; he worries about a worker who has stolen; or sends an employee back to the machines if his advancement has gone to his head. He sets prices, inspects the raw materials, proposes studies, drafts new plans. His eyes and ideas are everywhere. This fills him up entirely. His personal needs are minimal – he eats only when he is hungry, doesn't smoke, never drinks a drop of alcohol. His blood circulates throughout the factory, which is his only passion – it even occupies his dreams.[59]

The National Socialists themselves could not escape the phenomenon. Not only did they send an unsuccessful fund-raising delegation to Ford in Dearborn,[60] but the "chief ideologue" himself – Alfred Rosenberg – who belonged to the cultural conservative faction within the Nazi Party, made a big exception for Ford.[61] Peter Schwerber, a Nazi engineer with

---

55 Gottl-Ottlilienfeld, *Fordismus: Über Industrie und technische Vernunft*, 79.
56 In the preface to the second edition (1924) reprinted in Gottl-Ottlilienfeld, *Fordismus: Über Industrie und technische Vernunft*, vi. Faldix also emphasized this point in his criticism of Gottl-Ottlilienfeld.
57 On the rulership concept of the "conservative revolution," see Breuer, *Anatomie der Konservativen Revolution*, 96ff.
58 Fritz Bredow, *Bei Henry Ford: In der Schule eines Weltkindes* (Kallmünz, 1924), 8, 30.
59 Adolf Saager, *Henry Ford: Werden- Wirken* (Stuttgart, 1924).
60 James V. Compton, *Hitler und die USA: Die Amerikapolitik des Dritten Reiches und die Ursprunge des Zweiten Weltkrieges* (Oldenburg, 1968), 13.
61 Alfred Rosenberg, *Der Zukunftsweg einer deutschen Aussenpolitik* (Munich, n.d. [1924]), 99ff, 131ff. Regarding Rosenberg (1893–1946), see Reinhard Bollmus, "Alfred Rosenberg – 'Chefideologe' des Nationalsozialismus?" in Ronald Smelser and Rainer Zitelmann, eds., *Die Braune Elite: 22 biographische Skizzen* (Darmstadt, 1989), 223–35.

philosophical ambitions, published a first official Nazi Party position paper on issues of technology in the *Nationalsozialistische Bibliothek* (National Socialist Library) in 1930.[62] His otherwise very theoretical text cited Henry Ford as one of the few concrete examples from the actual business world.[63] Adolf Hitler, who was not unreceptive to technological innovations, saw in Americanism something like a model for his own new order in Europe,[64] but with the decisive reservation that, with his Malthusian economic ideology, he attributed the strength of the American economy not to technological or management innovations but primarily to the more favorable ratios between geographical expanse, population size, and abundance of mineral resources. Unlike Hitler, most Fordists from the reactionary modernist camp, although they pursued expansive or revisionist foreign policy goals or naively marvelled at the spatial expanses of the United States, still saw in the Americanization of Germany the implicit prerequisite for a revival of Germany's position in world politics. None, however, named territorial expansion as the prerequisite for "German Fordism." Hitler, however, was convinced of the uniqueness of American conditions and his political program of conquering and settling lands to the east can therefore, in this respect, be interpreted as an imitation of the United States. Finally, he used the word "America" as a metaphor in the best tradition of the Weimar debate on Americanism.[65] This had as little to do with the reality of German-American relations[66] as with the actual

---

62 See Herf, *Reactionary Modernism*, 192. One must not assume that such texts (including the party program published in the same series) were binding on Hitler and the National Socialists because the Nazi Party was never a program party bound to decisions made by a party assembly, although there were obviously certain basic ideological patterns that all Nazis more or less shared and that Schwerber reflected in his work.
63 See Peter Schwerber, *Nationalsozialismus und Technik: Die Geistigkeit der nationalsozialistischen Bewegung*, 2d ed. (Munich, 1932), 54.
64 See quotations in Rainer Zitelmann, *Hitler: Selbstverständnis eines Revolutionärs*, 3d ed. (Darmstadt, 1990), 337–8.
65 Hitler's image of America has attracted a great deal of interest among researchers. See, among others, Gerhard L. Weinberg, "Hitler's Image of the United States," *American Historical Review* 69 (1964): 1006–21; Compton, *Hitler und die USA*, 9–40; Axel Kuhn, *Hitlers aussenpolitisches Programm: Entstehung und Entwicklung, 1919–1939* (Stuttgart, 1970), 131–5; Andreas Hillgruber, "Der Faktor Amerika in Hitlers Strategie," *Aus Politik und Zeitgeschichte* 19 (1966): 3–21; Jochen Thiess, *Architekt der Weltherrschaft: Die 'Endziele' Hitlers* (Düsseldorf, 1976); Gordon A. Craig, "Roosevelt and Hitler: The Problem of Perception," in Klaus Hildebrand and Rainer Pommerin, eds., *Deutsche Frage und europäisches Gleichgewicht: Festschrift für Andreas Hillgruber* (Cologne, 1985), 189–94; Zitelmann, *Hitler*, 355–8; Detlef Junker, "Hitler's Perception of Franklin D. Roosevelt and the United States of America," in Cornelis A. van Minnen and John F. Sears, eds., *FDR and His Contemporaries* (New York, 1991), 145–56, 233–6; Enrico Syring, *Hitler: Seine politische Utopie* (Berlin, 1994), 96–104.
66 The Nazis were avowed opponents of Stresemann's concept of peaceful transformation as he related it to the United States. On German-American relations in the era of Stresemann, see Manfred Berg, "Germany and the United States: The Concept of World Economic Interdependence," in Carole Fink, Axel Frohn, and Jürgen Heideking, eds., *Genoa, Rapallo, and European Reconstruction in 1922* (New York, 1991), 77–93.

status of the rationalization movement or even the introduction of assembly line production in Germany, which at that time had barely taken hold in German manufacturing plants.[67]

III

Impressions of the Great Depression complicated the idea of Americanization, not only culturally but also economically, and it gave way to a more sober view. "Amerika abgeschminkt" (America without its makeup) read a 1930 headline in the *Berliner Illustrirte Zeitung (BIZ)*, after Black Friday supposedly exposed the myth of the American economic miracle as "hocus-pocus prosperity." The author of the BIZ self-critically remarked that, in the 1920s, "[we] began to wish in many ways that we were like the happy people over there, and [we] tried to transform ourselves according to their example, to imitate them. But, since we were watching in a spellbound state, we saw a picture blinded by optimism."[68] Even the liberal, America-friendly Moritz J. Bonn found that the Depression was the first major economic crisis in the United States since colonization of the West ended, a process that he said had now lost its venting function.[69] Therefore, he argued, the United States had "to a certain extent, become Europeanized in terms of social issues." The uniqueness of the American social structure, the "classless society," was beginning to evaporate.[70]

This signified an important break with the traditions of German images of the United States. The "conservative revolutionary" critics of liberalism felt vindicated. Hans Wollschläger, one of the most prolific German writers of books on America of all times and the author of one of the key texts of National Socialist anti-American war propaganda, set out to study

---

67 Cf. Jürgen Bönig, *Die Einführung der Fliessbandarbeit in Deutschland bis 1933: Zur Geschichte einer Sozialinnovation* (Münster and Hamburg, 1993), 699.
68 *Berliner Illustrirte Zeitung* 8 (1930): 9, 13, cited in Josef Roidl, "Das Amerikabild der Zwischenkriegszeit in der Berliner Illustrirten Zeitung," M.A. thesis, University of Regensburg, 1987, 79–80.
69 Moritz J. Bonn, born June 28, 1873, in Frankfurt/Main, died Jan. 25, 1965, in London; 1896, received doctorate; 1911, president of the School of Trade (*Handelshochschule*) in Munich; 1914–17 and 1924–26, guest professor in the United States; member of the German delegation to Versailles; expert on issues of reparations in the Reich Chancellory; 1932–3, president of the School of Trade in Berlin; 1933, emigrated to England; lecturer at the London School of Economics; 1939–46, professor in the United States and Canada; see Moritz J. Bonn, *So macht man Geschichte: Bilanz eines Lebens* (Munich, 1953); *International Biographical Dictionary of Central European Emigrés, 1933–1945*, vol. 2, pt. 1: *Arts, Sciences and Literature, A-K* (Munich, 1983), 132.
70 Moritz J. Bonn, *"Prosperity" Wunderglaube und Wirklichkeit im amerikanischen Wirtschaftsleben* (Berlin, 1931), 112, 116; see also Levy, "Amerika als Kulturproblem."

two phenomena, namely, the unemployment picture and the development of American communism, when he traveled to the United States in 1931–32. Two years before it would have been unthinkable to ask such questions. Ferdinand Fried,[71] chief economics editor for the influential journal *Die Tat*,[72] saw national autarky, foreign trade restrictions, large-area economies, and state planning as the worldwide wave of the future.[73] By conjecturing a trend toward state capitalism – in one stroke, he labeled Lenin, Stalin, Snowden, Mussolini, and Hoover the "new men of state"[74] – he paved the way for Nazi publicistic literature that emphasized similarities between the New Deal and National Socialism in the first weeks and months of the Third Reich.[75] The Nazis considered their ideology and policies to be the specific national manifestation of a global trend[76] – even though the National Socialist weltanschauung was primarily tailored to fit the charismatic figure of Hitler as the *Führer* and their politics were primarily geared toward the advancement of the German *Volk*.[77] However, parallels were seen as something natural, a historic necessity.[78] Roosevelt's politics were thus described with the same vocabulary as the domestic "seizure of power" by the Nazis. German reporting on America after March 1933 often spoke of revolution, *Volksgemeinschaft*, allegiance to the nation, *Führertum* and a strong state, subordination of the individual to the common good, public interest over self-interest, dictatorial recovery measures, state socialist programs and revolutionary social programs. However, one should avoid interpreting the drawing of such parallels in Nazi journalism as an indication that the Third Reich was undergoing

---

71 Ferdinand Fried, actually Ferdinand Friedrich Zimmermann, born Aug. 14, 1889, in Freienwalde, died July 9, 1967 in Cuxhaven; professor; economics editor for the *Vossische Zeitung*; 1923–32, with the *Berliner Morgenpost*; beginning in 1929, contributor to *Die Tat*; 1933, contributor to the *Tägliche Rundschau*; 1933–4, contributor to the *Deutsche Zeitung*; 1934, joined the SS and worked in the Office of Race and Resettlement (*Rasse- und Siedlungsamt*); beginning 1949, editor of *Sonntagsblatt*; beginning 1953, editor of *Welt*; see Mohler, *Die Konservative Revolution*, 1:435.
72 Cf. Kurt Sontheimer, "Der Tatkreis," *Vierteljahreshefte für Zeitgeschichte* 7 (1959): 229–60; Mohler, *Die Konservative Revolution*; Breuer, *Anatomie der Konservativen Revolutionen*, 65–6.
73 Ferdinand Fried, *Das Ende des Kapitalismus*, 5th ed. (Jena, 1931).
74 Ibid., 19, 264–5.
75 See the numerous references in Hans-Jürgen Schröder, *Deutschland und die USA 1933–1939: Wirtschaft und Politik in der Entwicklung des deutsch-amerikanischen Gegensatzes* (Wiesbaden, 1970), 93ff.
76 See Friedrich Pohlmann, *Ideologie und Terror im Nationalsozialismus* (Pfaffenweiler, 1992), 199ff, 226ff.
77 See Ian Kershaw, *Hitlers Macht: Das Profil der NS-Herrschaft* (Munich, 1992), 22ff.
78 See, e.g., "Nationalsozialistische Wirtschaftsmethoden im Ausland," *Völkischer Beobachter*, no. 200, July 19, 1933: "The first reports are already coming in from abroad indicating that nearly all civilized nations are undergoing economic transformations which, though they are by no means necessarily an imitation of National Socialism or Fascism, are a natural development and obvious reaction to international liberalism, which is lying in its death throes."

Americanization.[79] The Nazi version of the convergence theory was built clearly on the premise that it was America that was moving toward National Socialism and abandoning Americanism, not vice versa.[80]

Earlier than researchers have assumed,[81] there were tendencies in German reporting that pointed out differences between National Socialism and the New Deal. In addition to the ideological conflict made apparent over the "Jewish question,"[82] press reports emphasized the experimental character of Roosevelt's economic policy.[83] A September 1933 memorandum of the Reich Economics Ministry (*Reichswirtschaftsministeriuml*) stated that "in particular, statements of Roosevelt on various occasions ... [have shown] a striking resemblance to remarks of the Reichskanzler." Upon closer examination, the memo conceded, it is clear "that they are not the same or similar measures, nor could they be," and that the German press was wrong in "calling Roosevelt's program a National Socialist one."[84]

Despite a certain similarity in choice of methods,[85] one could hardly speak of the economic policies as being identical. The National Socialist economic system was an unfree market economy under the dominion of a political system that "formulated ... national power and cyclic stability"

---

79 On the contrary, see Hans Dietrich Schäfer, *Das gespaltene Bewusstsein: Deutsche Kultur und Lebenswirklichkeit, 1933–1945*, 3d ed. (Munich, 1983), 128; for a critique, see Günter Könke, "'Modernisierungsschub' oder relative Stagnation? Einige Anmerkungen zum Verhältnis von Nationalsozialismus und Moderne," *Geschichte und Gesellschaft* 20 (1994): 584–608.

80 This is also the tone of Waldemar Hartmann, "Deutschland und die U.S.A. Wege zum gegenseitigen Verstehen," *National – sozialistische Monatshefte* 4 (1933): 481–94.

81 See Harald Frisch, *Das deutsche Rooseveltbild, 1933–1941*, dissertation (Berlin, 1967); Schröder, *Deutschland und die USA*, 93ff; Schäfer, *Das gespaltene Bewusstsein*, 128–9; see also Junker's contribution to this collection. The image of America held by the Third Reich attracted less attention than that of the Weimar period. In addition to Schröder, *Deutschland und die USA*, 93ff; Ott, *Amerika ist anders*, 243ff; and Diner, *Verkehrte Welten*, 89ff; on the subject of Americanism, see also Hans-Dieter Schäfer, "Amerikanismus im Dritten Reich," in Michael Prinz and Rainer Zitelmann, eds., *Nationalsozialismus und Modernisierung* (Darmstadt, 1991), 199–215; Michael H. Kater, *Different Drummers: Jazz in the Culture of Nazi Germany* (Oxford, 1992); Carsten Laqua, *Wie Micky unter die Nazis fiel: Walt Disney in Deutschland* (Reinbek bei Hamburg, 1992).

82 On the occasion of the boycott of Apr. 1, 1933, e.g., see the files of the Reich Chancellory, Hitler government, I/1, no. 80, Jan. 31, 1933, 277; ibid., no. 78, Mar. 29, 1933, 272, with references to public opinion in the United States, and reports such as "Jüdische Boykottbestrebungen gegen deutsche Waren in Amerika," *Völkischer Beobachter*, nos. 84/85, Mar. 25–6, 1933; "Die jüdischen Propagandisten erweisen ihren Genossen in Deutschland keinen Dienst," ibid., no. 87 (Mar. 28, 1933); "Der jüdische Lügenfeldzug," ibid., no. 88 (Mar. 29, 1933). For detailed information on this subject, see Gassert, *Amerika im Dritten Reich*, chap. 5.

83 See, e.g., "Amerikas Kampf mit der Krise," *Deutsche Wirtschaftszeitung* 30, no. 33, Aug. 17, 1933, 787.

84 Sarnow (Reichswirtschaftsministerium) to the Foreign Office (Auswärtiges Amt), Sept. 8, 1933, Political Archives of the Auswärtiges Amt, R 121331/206.

85 See John A. Garraty, "The New Deal, National Socialism, and the Great Depression," *American Historical Review* 78 (1973): 907–44; Peter Temin, *Lessons from the Great Depression* (Cambridge, 1989), 89ff.

as "top priority objectives,"[86] whereas the New Deal, despite all of its half-hearted and sometimes unsuccessful efforts at regulatory intervention in the economy, never deviated from the principles of a free market economy.[87] As the economic editor of the *Völkischer Beobachter* noted in a remarkable article on "Nationalsozialistische Wirtschaftsmethoden im Ausland" (the practice of National Socialist economics abroad) in July 1933, this fundamental difference from the economic policies of the Third Reich existed despite all the similarities in the choice of methods because Roosevelt was not prepared to give up the "code of healthy competition" and was oriented very strongly toward the interests of "commerce" and the capitalist economic order.[88] The political and institutional limitations of Roosevelt's policies were not concealed in the reporting of the *Völkischer Beobachter*, but instead were cited increasingly as an explanation for the relative failure of the New Deal in comparison to Nazi economic policies:

While the German chancellor can depend on the unreserved allegiance of the German people for all his decisions, Roosevelt must fight in the United States to overcome considerable obstacles created by the behavior of excessively powerful industrialists as well as inflationist farmers.[89]

It was conceded that he "and his braintrust . . . had certainly made monumental efforts," but that "real and lasting success had eluded them."[90]

Newsreels and the press transmitted more and more frequent images and reports of homelessness in New York, "crisis and misery in the farming regions of the U.S.A.," unemployment and social unrest.[91] A general strike in San Francisco made headlines on the front page of the

---

86 See Avraham Barkai, *Das Wirtschaftssystem des Nationalsozialismus: Ideologie, Theorie, Politik, 1933–1945* (Frankfurt/Main, 1988), 230.
87 See, e.g., Herbert Stein, *The Fiscal Revolution in America* (Washington, D.C., 1990); Ellis W. Hawley, *The New Deal and the Problem of Monopoly: A Study in Economic Ambivalence* (Princeton, N.J., 1966).
88 "Nationalsozialistische Wirtschaftsmethoden im Ausland," *Völkischer Beobachter*, no. 200, July 19, 1933.
89 "Roosevelts Absichten," ibid., no. 321, Nov. 17, 1933. Roosevelt's fiscal policy was particularly harshly criticized, e.g., "Inflationsauftrieb in U.S.-Amerika," *Deutsche Wirtschaftszeitung* 30, no. 29, July 20, 1933, 688ff; "Das Hell-Dunkel der U.S.-amerikanischen Währungspolitik," ibid., 31, no. 4, Jan. 25, 1934, 80ff; "Hält Roosevelt seine Goldpolitik durch?," *Völkischer Beobachter*, no. 310, Nov. 6, 1933; "Roosevelts Goldpolitik," ibid., no. 307, Nov. 3, 1933; "Der Kampf gegen Roosevelts Währungspolitik," ibid., no. 330, Nov. 26, 1933; "Neue Inflationsmöglichkeiten in U.S.A.?" ibid., no. 223, Aug. 11, 1934.
90 "Noch immer 10 Millionen Arbeitslose in U.S.A. die Vereinigten Staaten in der Krise-Grundfrage: Die Farmer," *Völkischer Beobachter*, no. 220, Aug. 8, 1934.
91 E.g., "Bilder vom Tage," ibid., no. 338, Dec. 4, 1933 shows "Unemployment Misery in New York: A Woman's Homemade Bed on the Street"; "Not und Elend in den Farmgebieten der USA," ibid., no. 201, July 20, 1934; "Wie Dollarmillionäre wohnen: Amerikas sozialer Kontrast,"

Völkischer Beobachter on July 18, 1934.[92] In the fall of 1934, the Propaganda Ministry firmly expected a defeat for Roosevelt in the Congressional elections. On the day before the election, the Ministry issued instructions to the press aimed at preventing negative reporting in the German press. The press was instructed not to make "any malicious remarks, but to write in an objective, calm and friendly manner about [the elections]. If Roosevelt's party loses a few votes, that need not be particularly emphasized."[93] When Roosevelt achieved a sensational success in the elections, this was presented as further confirmation of the theory that the American people had entrusted themselves "to the leadership of an energetic man" in the face of "the overwhelming problems of the time," a man who had succeeded in "securing for himself the allegiance of the American nation." But even this report did not neglect to point out that the New Deal had yet to achieve a decisive breakthrough in economic policy.[94]

This cautious, somewhat ambiguous reporting stood in stark contrast to the hymns of praise for the accomplishments of the Nazi regime.[95] Comparison with the United States was useful for emphasizing the positive sides of Nazi rule. This is evidenced, for example, by the considerable number of economics publications on the New Deal published between 1933 and World War II.[96] There was hardly an author who did not implicitly include a comparative perspective, although it is impossible to know whether some did this only to legitimize their studies in the eyes of the German authorities or the German readership. And yet, these writings reflect a genuine interest in developments in the United States. The expansion in foreign studies driven by party policy also helped to

ibid., no. 51, Feb. 20, 1935; newsreels: Deulig Tonwoche, no. 149, 1934, censorship date: Nov. 7, 1934; no. 170, 1935, censorship date: Apr. 3, 1935; no. 274, 1937, censorship date: Mar. 31, 1937, copies in Bundesarchiv Koblenz (hereafter cited as BA Koblenz).

92 See "Der Generalstreik in San Franzisko: Eine kommunistische Revolte gegen die amerikanische Regierung," "Tanks auf dem Weg ins Streikgebiet," "Die Streiklage," "Ausschreitungen und Plünderungen," "Der Gegenstoss," *Völkischer Beobachter*, no. 199, July 18, 1934; "Marxistischer Generalangriff: Eine Warnung vor Weltgefahren," "Die USA vor neuen Streiks?" ibid., no. 336, Dec. 2, 1934. Shortly thereafter, reporting was again restricted by the Propaganda Ministry, cf. Brammer collection, July 19, 1934, BA Koblenz, ZSg 101/4/24, no. 610. In the subsequent days, only a few illustrations were published, showing among other things the military being deployed against the strikers, with their weapons raised. See ibid., no. 200, July 19, 1934, and letter from Sallet (German Embassy in Washington) to the Propaganda Ministry, Aug. 3, 1934, ADAP C/III, no. 569, 1087.

93 Sänger collection, Nov. 6, 1934, BA Koblenz, ZSg 102/1/49.

94 "Roosevelts grosser Wahlsieg," *Völkischer Beobachter*, no. 313, Nov. 9, 1934.

95 See, e.g., "Wirtschaftsgesinnung und Wirtschaftserfolg," *Völkischer Beobachter*, 311, Nov. 7, 1934; "Der Erfolg der Arbeitsschlacht 1934: 1,7 Millionen Arbeitslose in Arbeit und Brot," ibid.

96 For a bibliographic overview, see Hans Hainebach, *German Publications on the United States, 1933 to 1945* (New York, 1948).

generate a greater number of publications on America than had appeared since the mid-1920s.[97]

The introductions to a brief study of the economy and Constitution of the United States illustrate this.[98] The publisher pointed out that the book was particularly suitable for publication because it showed "how another large nation attempts to adopt a new economic order" and is related in "a variety of ways to the rebuilding of the German economy."[99] Both author and publisher emphasized, however, how difficult the transformation process was under the democratic conditions of the United States, which, according to another author, was the actual reason for the failure of Roosevelt's "experiment in planned economy." Although Germany and Italy had

> implemented fundamental reform measures in all areas under authoritarian governments, unencumbered by the influences of parliaments and interest groups, [that was] not possible in democratic America, which is why we do not see a straight line there, but rather internal contradictions, concessions first to this side and then to the other, often obstructing the promising paths which had been opened. There was too much experimentation and therefore often too little accomplishment.[100]

In the press reports, the economic image of America was dominated increasingly by constitutional and, ultimately, ideological contrasts. The more unemployment dropped in the Third Reich and the more the contrasts between Germany and America took shape, the more frequent were the references to the low success rate of American economic and social policy.[101] Reports on strikes, unemployment, and social problems now belonged to the standard repertoire of reporting on America[102] and

---

97 For information on the number of publications, see Roidl, *Das Amerikabild der Zwischenkriegszeit*, 182ff; on foreign and American studies, see Sigmund Skard, *American Studies in Europe: Their History and Present Organization*, vol. 1 (Philadelphia, 1958), 277ff.
98 Fritz Ermarth, *Der New Deal: Wirtschaft und Verfassung der USA* (Berlin, 1936), vii; Ermath received his doctorate in Heidelberg, was a fellow at the Brookings Institution, and was a visiting professor at George Washington University in Washington, D.C., in 1936–7. During this time, he wrote a book, *The New Germany*, in which he sought understanding.
99 Foreword by the publisher, attorney Prof. Dr. Karl Geiler, Mannheim-Heidelberg, in *Ermarth, The New Deal*, v.
100 Wilhelm F. Walter, *Das Experiment Roosevelts: Kritische Betrachtungen zur zeitgenössischen Planwirtschaft* (Essen, 1936), 121.
101 See, e.g., "Roosevelts Schwierigkeiten," *Deutsche Wirtschaftszeitung* 32, no. 21, May 23, 1935, 485ff; "Schwankende Konjunktur in USA: Vor einem neuen Rückschlag?" *Völkischer Beobachter*, no. 83, Mar. 24, 1935; "Die amerikanische Krise," ibid., no. 207, July 23, 1935.
102 See, e.g., "USA vor neuen Streiks?" *Völkischer Beobachter*, no. 336, Dec. 2, 1934; "Blutige Kämpfe zwischen Kohlenarbeitern," ibid., no. 33, Feb. 2, 1935; "Aufruhr im Neuyorker Negerviertel," ibid., no. 80, Mar. 21, 1935; "Krach vor einem Neuyorker Wohlfahrtsamt: Beamte von Arbeitslosen bewältigt – Tränengasbomben schaffen Ruhe," ibid., no. 200, July 31, 1935; "Maschinengewehre gegen Streikende," ibid., no. 304, Oct. 31, 1935.

were brought forth especially when it was necessary to counter anti-Nazi protest demonstrations in the United States.[103] This led to an open exchange of ideological blows after Roosevelt addressed pointed words to the autocratically governed nations in his State of the Union address in January 1936. From then on, Roosevelt was charged with having to defend himself against domestic political accusations that he himself had "dictatorial intentions" and governed with "fascist methods." It was, however, more doubtful than ever, Nazi press reports continued, "to what extent this president [stands] on the threshold of really new forms of government." Only time could tell, since FDR had arrived at a turning point in his political career, the reports claimed.[104] The Nazis saw their argumentation confirmed at least by 1937 when, against the backdrop of the escalating Spanish Civil War, an ever stronger anti-Bolshevist element crept into reporting on America and the democracies were accused of failing to address the "communist threat."[105] One report stated that, whereas the United States had long had the illusion of being "immune to social unrest... [it must] today be called the classical land of strikes" and had lost its status as an exception.[106] Another report stated that the "renegade" labor leader and "agent of international communism," John L. Lewis, whose rise was made possible by the New Deal, could claim "to have transplanted the idea of the Marxist class struggle to America at a time in which it was already a thing of the past in the authoritarian-led nations of Europe." Time would tell whether "those who evoked the spirits are also strong enough to rein them in."[107] Yet another report warned that the American public was ill-advised if it did nothing against the "infiltration of Communist ringleaders" who were threatening the "American economy and the entire government order."[108] For behind the sitdown strikers in the U.S., behind the unions of John Lewis, behind the stirred-up crowds in the suburbs of Paris, behind the demonstrating colored

---

103 E.g., "Kommunisten-Überfall auf die Bremen," *Völkischer Beobachter*, no. 210, July 29, 1935 and the subsequent editions: "Sie hätten vor der eigenen Türe zu kehren," ibid., no. 227, Aug. 15, 1935; "Streikausschreitungen in Texas," *Frankfurter Zeitung* 403 (Aug. 9, 1935); see also Brammer collection, BA Koblenz, ZSg 101/6/49, no. 1533, Aug. 8, 1935.
104 "Demokratisches Alibi," *Völkischer Beobachter*, no. 6, Jan. 6, 1936.
105 See "Roosevelt lenkt ab," *Völkischer Beobachter*, no. 263, Sept. 20, 1937. In this connection, see also Ernst Nolte, *Die Krise des liberalen Systems und die faschistischen Bewegungen* (Munich, 1968), 14ff, 33ff; for Nolte, fascism is unthinkable without the "challenge of Bolshevism," which was made possible by the liberal system in the first place. See Thomas Nipperdey, "Der Faschismus in seiner Epoche: Zu den Werken von Ernst Nolte zum Faschismus," *Historische Zeitschrift* 210 (1970): 620–38, here 627ff.
106 "Wem nützen Streiks?" *Völkischer Beobachter*, no. 78, Mar. 19, 1937.
107 "Gewerkschaftskämpfe in USA," ibid., no. 112, Apr. 22, 1937.
108 "Ausbeutung der amerikanischen Arbeiter durch die Komintern," ibid., no. 149, May 29, 1937.

workers of Oran stands Moscow. And its best pacesetter is the weakness and helplessness of a government that does not know how to maintain order in its own house.[109]

Thus, the perspective of Sombart's Nazi propaganda had attained prophetic status. At the same time, the necessary conditions had been fulfilled for integrating America into the historical enemy image of the Nazis. The United States had finally lost its role as a model or, as one scientific study referring explicitly to Sombart found, the possibility could no longer be ruled out "that Bolshevism could prevail in the United States."[110]

In view of this ideological confrontation, it is understandable that there was some concern that phenomena customarily categorized as Americanism since the 1920s no longer be labeled as such. To be sure, Ford still enjoyed preferential treatment in German press and journalism circles,[111] River Rouge remained a major attraction for travelers to America,[112] almost all geography books had pictures and lengthy text passages on the Ford plant in Detroit,[113] and the Film Examiner's Office (*Filmprüfstelle*) in Berlin approved an educational film entitled *Ein Gang durch die Fordwerke Detroit* [A walk through the Ford plant in Detroit] shortly before war broke out.[114] In objective ways, as well, the Nazis attempted to learn from America, for example, by sending the designer of the Volkswagen, Ferdinand Porsche, on two trips to the United States to obtain practical experience at General Motors for building the vertically integrated Volkswagen plant in Fallersleben,[115] or by expending valuable currency to purchase in the United States the Bedeaux evaluation system for in-house

---

109 "Wem nützen Streiks?" ibid., no. 78, Mar. 19, 1937.
110 Christian Wolff, *Amerikanischer Sozialismus? Die geistesgeschichtlichen und gesellschaftlichen Voraussetzungen des revolutionären Sozialismus in den Vereinigten Staaten von Nordamerika* (Munich, 1936), 59. The book is based on a dissertation inspired by Karl Alexander von Müller. See also the long and detailed series of articles by Herrmann Lufft, "Klassenkampf oder konstruktive Lösung der Arbeiterfrage in USA?" *Deutsche Wirtschaftszeitung* 33, no. 14, Mar. 26, 1936, 310ff, and in the subsequent issues.
111 See newsreel from *Deulig Tonwoche*, no. 256, 1936, censor Nov. 25, 1936, copy in BA Koblenz; *Berliner Illustrirte Zeitung*, 47, no. 18, 1938, and 48, no. 30, 1939.
112 See Richard Lies, "Erfahrungen und Eindrücke auf einer Schüleraustauschreise nach USA," *Die Neueren Sprachen* 47 (1939): 72–7, 155–63; *Amerika-Studienfahrt des NS-Rechtswahrerbunds vom 12. Juli bis 2. August 1938 mit den Expressdampfern "Bremen" und "Europa"*, Program of Norddt. Lloyd, Bremen, 1938, 4–6, quoted in Schäfer, "Amerikanismus im Dritten Reich," 204; Helmut Jacobi, *Bericht über eine Studienreise nach den Vereinigten Staaten von Nordamerika und Canada im Frühjahr 1938* (Berlin-Siemensstadt, 1938), BA Koblenz R 58/619/40.
113 See, e.g., Robert Fox and Kurt Griep, eds., *Heimat und Welt: Teubners Erdkundliches Unterrichtswerk für höhere Schulen*, vol. 4: *Nord- und Südamerika*, 5th ed. (Berlin, 1943), 35.
114 See *Lichtbildbühne*, no. 120, May 25, 1939, Filmprüfstelle Berlin, Approvals.
115 Cf. Paul Kluke, "Hitler und das Volkswagenproject," *Vierteljahreshefte für Zeitgeschichte* 8 (1960): 363.

business rationalization measures.[116] Indeed, there is evidence that the rationalization movement did not have its big breakthrough in Germany until after 1934–5,[117] not least of all because the shortage of labor and raw materials caused by the Nazis' politics of autarky and arms buildup required increases in productivity.[118]

It is obvious, however, that this type of Americanization served as a means to an end and took into account only the functional dimension of modernization.[119] After 1933, everyone was talking about "German rationalization measures,"[120] which was strictly differentiated from the egotistic, "liberalistic American" rationalization movement.[121] There was therefore an increasing "de-Americanization" of the word in the Third Reich. For example, in an essay on "true rationalization," the staff of the Ergonomic Institute of the German Workers' Front (*Arbeitswissenschaftliches Institut der Deutschen Arbeitsfront*) criticized the economic leaders of the Weimar Republic, who went on pilgrimages to the United States in the 1920s and blindly adopted American methods without examining what would be good for Germany. Not until "Adolf Hitler's state," the essay continued, were the "conditions for a true rationalization movement" created, putting "people at the center" and

---

116 See Rüdiger Hachtmann, *Industriearbeit im "Dritten Reich": Untersuchungen zu den Lohn- und Arbeitsbedienungen in Deutschland, 1933–1945* (Göttingen, 1989), 208ff; on Charles Eugène Bedeaux (1886–1944), see ibid., 379n. 229.
117 This tentative conclusion was reached by Heidrun Homburg, *Rationalisierung und Industriearbeit: Arbeitsmarkt – Management – Arbeiterschaft im Siemens-Konzern Berlin, 1900–1939* (Berlin, 1991), 527; Wolfgang Zollitsch, *Arbeiter zwischen Weltwirtschaftskrise und Nationalsozialismus: Ein Beitrag zur Sozialgeschichte der Jahre 1928 bis 1936* (Göttingen, 1990), 168; and Hachtmann, *Industriearbeit im "Dritten Reich"*, 76; in addition, the only attempt to date at a synthesis by Siegel and Freyberg, *Industrielle Rationalisierung*, 15–16, who point out, however, that a definitive answer requires additional, detailed studies. For a skeptical view, see Alf Lüdtke, *Eigen-Sinn: Fabrikalltag, Arbeitererfahrungen, und Politik vom Kaiserreich bis in den Faschismus* (Hamburg, 1993), 327.
118 See also Homburg, *Rationalisierung und Industriearbeit*, 527.
119 Unfortunately, the more comprehensive context of the rationalization movement in the Third Reich cannot be addressed here. It should be clear, however, that economic Americanization after 1933 was inseparably connected to preparations for a war of pillage, conquest, and destruction in Eastern Europe and created the conditions necessary for the use of concentration camp slaves and prisoners of war in the Taylorized industries of the Third Reich. See Siegel and Freyberg, *Industrielle Rationalisierung*, 96; Karl-Heinz Roth, "Der Weg zum guten Stern des 'Dritten Reichs': Schlaglichter auf die Geschichte der Daimler-Benz AG und ihrer Vorläufer (1890–1945)," in Hamburger Stiftung für Sozialgeschichte des 20. Jahrhunderts, ed., *Das Daimler-Benz Buch: Ein Rüstungskonzern im "Tausendjährigen Reich"* (Nördlingen, 1988), 27–374; Lutz Budrass and Manfred Grieger, "Die Moral der Effizienz: Die Beschäftigung von KZ-Häftlingen am Beispiel des Volkswagenwerks und der Henschel Flugzeugwerke," *Jahrbuch für Wirtschaftsgeschichte* 2 (1993): 89–136; on the status of research, see Matthias Freese, "Sozial- und Arbeitspolitik im 'Dritten Reich': Ein Literaturbericht," *Neue Politische Literatur* 30 (1993): 403–46.
120 See Fritz Todt, "Die deutsche Rationalisierung," *Der deutsche Baumeister* 1 (1939): 6.
121 "Drei Jahre Rationalisierung," *Völkischer Beobachter*, no. 3, Jan. 3, 1939.

focusing on the "common good."[122] Georg Seebauer, director of the Office of Technology (*Amt für Technik*) in the Reich headquarters of the Nazi Party, director of the Reich Board of Trustees for Efficiency (*Reichskuratorium für Wirtschaftlichkeit*) and deputy director of the Reich Energy Group (*Reichsgruppe Energiewirtschaft*), advocated forced rationalization, which he said had become a "necessity of economic policy" because National Socialism, by eliminating unemployment, had "laid the foundation of rationalization in the first place" and thereby "delivered it from the clutches of a degenerate capitalism."[123] In his address to the Reichstag on January 30, 1939, Hitler himself pointed out the relationship between elimination of unemployment, continued increases in production, the four-year plan (motivated by the armaments industry), and the resulting necessity of "mobilizing a greater and greater work force."[124]

Although the Third Reich portrayed itself as superior to the United States in terms of economic policy, Nazi propaganda was not successful in destroying the myth of an economically strong America. According to reports from a group of exiles, Roosevelt's address of January 1939, to which the Nazis responded with a massive propaganda campaign,[125] had a demoralizing effect on the German population: "It is said that the impression of Roosevelt's speech was very similar to the impression America's declaration of war provoked in 1917."[126] Despite the now intensified anti-Bolshevist and anti-Semitic propaganda regarding America, many Germans were convinced in 1941 that the United States represented a grave threat and that its entry into the war would prolong hostilities for the foreseeable future, if not end all hopes of German victory.[127] In January 1942 a status report from the Security Service of the SS (*Sicherheitsdienst der SS*) reached the conclusion that

---

122 "Die echte Rationalisierung," in Arbeitswissenschaftliches Institut der Deutschen Arbeitsfront, ed., *Jahrbuch 1936* (Berlin, 1936), 189–222. For a detailed analysis of this key document in the Nazi rationalization debate, see Siegel and Freyberg, *Industrielle Rationalisierung*, 77ff; for literature on the Deutsche Arbeitsfront, see Freese, "Sozial- und Arbeitspolitik im 'Dritten Reich,'" 408ff.
123 Georg Seebauer, "Rationalisierung – eine kapitalistische Angelegenheit oder eine volkswirtschaftliche Forderung?" *RKW-Nachrichten* 11 (1937): 161, cited in Siegel and Freyberg, *Industrielle Rationalisierung*, 319; regarding Seebauer, see ibid.
124 Max Domarus, *Hitler: Reden 1932 bis 1945, kommentiert von einem deutschen Zeitgenossen* (Wiesbaden, 1973), 3:1053, Jan. 30, 1939; *Völkischer Beobachter*, no. 32, Feb. 1, 1939.
125 See Brammer collection, Jan. 7, 1939, BA Koblenz, ZSg 101/12/9, no. 24.
126 *Inside Germany Reports*, Apr. 15, 1939, Archiv der Sozialen Demokratie, Bonn, 16; on the United States, see also Klaus Behnken, ed., *Deutschland-Berichte der Sozialdemokratischen Partei Deutschlands (SoPaDe), 1934–1940*, 7 vols. (Frankfurt/Main, 1980), 7:105, Feb. 1940.
127 *Inside Germany Reports*, July 1941, no. 18, Archiv der Sozialen Demokratie, Bonn, 3.

the polemics against Roosevelt's "armaments bluff" . . . [has] not yet succeeded in fully convincing the population. . . . The feeling is frequently expressed that the reports on the American raw materials and supply situation are perceived as favorably "colored." Many *Volksgenossen* [comrades] still believe that England and the United States are far superior to us in production.[128]

The Nazis may have succeeded in temporarily portraying the United States as weakened and nearly incapable of defending against the attack of Bolshevism. However, they were unable to undermine the traditional image of the United States as a *potentially* very strong nation and Germany's most threatening foe.

In the 1920s, reactionary modernizers saw in economic Americanism a third way between the two extremes of unrestricted liberalism and social revolution. Ford was an example that showed that the social needs of the workers could be satisfied without restricting the creative freedom of capital and that it was possible to dissolve social tensions in the context of a *Volksgemeinschaft* by means of rationalization measures. Only under the special conditions of the American economy did this objective appear to have been achieved. The Great Depression began to shake the image of America as an exception, and the situation turned around one hundred and eighty degrees after 1933. The Nazis, who shared the reactionary modernistic philosophy, claimed that they were solving the socioeconomic problems of the modern age while the American society under the New Deal was in danger of sinking "into chaos." While the liberal system in the United States was becoming a "breeding ground for Bolshevism," Fordism was rising to new heights in the Third Reich, albeit with a different name and in the service of a racially defined *Volksgemeinschaft*, a military buildup, the conquest of lebensraum and, ultimately, annihilation of "life unworthy of living."

---

128 See Heinz Boberach, ed., *Meldungen aus dem Reich: Die geheimen Lageberichte des Sicherheitsdienstes der SS, 1938–1945*, 17 vols. (Herrsching, 1984), 9:3154, report no. 250: Jan. 12, 1942.

11

The Continuity of Ambivalence
German Views of America, 1933–1945

DETLEF JUNKER

German views of America have not attracted much attention in the historiography of Adolf Hitler, National Socialism, and the Third Reich. Indeed, no exhaustive analysis of the topic has yet appeared.[1] However, the specialized studies published so far suggest that it is now possible systematically to assess the "views of America" held by Germans between 1933 and 1945; or, to be more specific, to evaluate judgments, prejudices, clichés, stereotypes, and images. The following remarks represent an attempt to provide such a systematic review. It will also incorporate this author's own research on Hitler's perception of Franklin D. Roosevelt and the United States of America.[2]

A chronological summary of the years between 1933 and 1945 leads us to a rather basic and unsurprising observation, namely, that Nazi foreign policy largely determined opinions about the United States and its president. After all, published opinion under the National Socialist regime was the product of a severely controlled press, censorship, and propaganda. During the first few years of the Nazi regime coverage of the New Deal also served to legitimize Nazi rule. The predominant interest that Hitler and the Nazis took in U.S. foreign policy was the crucial factor that finally led to a marked change in the presentation of German views of America. Whereas up to the second half of 1937 Roosevelt and American policies in general received a very warm welcome, or at least met with neutral evaluations, official commentary became increasingly negative in

---

1 For such a study, see Philipp Gassert, *Amerika im Dritten Reich: Die Kritik der amerikanischen Moderne in Ideologie, Volksmeinung und Propaganda, 1933–1945* (forthcoming).
2 Detlef Junker, "Hitler's Perception of Franklin D. Roosevelt and the United States of America," in Cornelis A. van Minnen and John F. Sears, eds., *FDR and His Contemporaries: Foreign Perceptions of an American President* (New York, 1991), 145–56, 233–6.

243

1938–9. After 1938 German propaganda against Roosevelt and the United States assumed a more or less hostile stance, based on what was deemed to be strategically advisable at a particular point in time. However, after the Germans had declared war on the United States, this aversion burst into open hatred. The number of publications on different topics concerning American society and civilization, such as the economy, technology, architecture and cultural matters, everyday life and leisure activities of the American people, Hollywood, and the American "money aristocracy," depended on a variety of factors. For example, the period of relative prosperity in the years between 1936 and 1938 unleashed a tidal wave of publications on America. In these areas, too, the change toward anti-Americanism had become increasingly perceptible by 1939.[3]

America had quickly lost its significance for Germany as a result of the Great Depression, coupled with American isolationism and neutrality legislation. From 1933 to 1939 the United States and Nazi Germany were both metaphorically and literally an ocean apart. On becoming chancellor, Hitler therefore regarded American good will as useful but relatively insignificant. Up to the signing of the Munich Agreement, Hitler had ignored the United States completely; and until the invasion of Poland, he essentially continued to do the same. In no foreign policy decision of those years did Hitler show any consideration for American interests. In key documents, such as the Four-Year Plan or the Hossbach Memorandum, America is not even mentioned.

In the period from 1933 to 1936, Roosevelt, the New Deal, and the United States were in general treated cordially by Hitler and the Nazi press, despite massive and mounting criticism of the terror then beginning

---

3 This general conclusion can be drawn from Hans-Jürgen Schröder, *Deutschland und die Vereinigten Staaten, 1933–1939* (Wiesbaden, 1970); Harald Frisch, "Das Deutsche Rooseveltbild, 1933–1941," Ph.D. diss., Free University of Berlin, 1967; Josef Roidl, "Das Amerikabild der Zwischenkriegszeit in der Berliner Illustrierten Zeitung," M.A. thesis, University of Regensburg, 1987; Günter Moltmann, "Nationalklischees und Demagogie: Die deutsche Amerikapropaganda im Zweiten Weltkrieg," in Ursula Büttner, ed., *Das Unrechtsregime: Internationale Forschung über den Nationalsozialismus*, vol. 1: *Ideologie–Herrschaftssystem–Wirkung in Europa* (Hamburg, 1986), 217–42. See also Hans Hainebach's early postwar publication, *German Publications on the United States 1933 to 1945*, The New York Public Library (New York, 1948), 3: "It will surprise no one to learn that the great majority of the items listed here reflect the ideology of the government then in power, taking a rather negative view of America as compared to Germany. Still, up to 1938, a certain measure of objectivity – attempted or achieved – can be found in many German writings, while hostile attitudes toward the United States are often confined to attacks on the anti-Nazi groups in America. After 1938, anti-Americanism becomes much more outspoken, but is still restrained as long as there seems to be any hope for continued American neutrality. An openly hostile attitude toward everything American is evident in most writings after 1941. Thus, the year of publication can give some indication of the degree of objectivity or aggressiveness to be expected in a specific item."

in Germany that was widely reflected in the American media.[4] Speaking to Louis P. Lochner of the Associated Press on February 24, 1933, Hitler described his government's attitude to the United States as one of "sincere friendship."[5] Hitler's response to Roosevelt's call for disarmament on May 16, 1933, was also couched in friendly if platitudinous terms.[6] On March 14, 1934, Hitler sent a message to Roosevelt through Ambassador William E. Dodd in which he congratulated him on his "heroic efforts on behalf of the American people." The German people, he continued, were watching the president's successful struggle against the economic crisis with interest and admiration.

The following remarks may thus be taken as revealing the official interpretation of Roosevelt and his New Deal in the first years of Nazi rule:

The chancellor is in accord with the president in the view that the virtue of duty, readiness for sacrifice, and discipline should dominate the entire people. These moral demands which the president places before every individual citizen of the United States, are also the quintessence of the German state philosophy which finds its expression in the slogan "The Public Weal Transcends the Interests of the Individual."[7]

According to the German press in those years, Roosevelt was confronted with a revolutionary challenge similar to that facing Hitler and Mussolini; he, too, was a kind of *Führer* or *Duce* using dictatorial measures to intervene in the economy; he, too, had realized that the era of unfettered individualism and parliamentary rule had had its day. Parallels were also drawn between Roosevelt and Hitler as individual personalities. Roosevelt's book, *Looking Forward*, appeared in German translation only a few months after its publication in 1933 and met with a warm reception in National Socialist Germany. The party organ of the NSDAP, the *Völkische Beobachter*, commented, "Many statements could have been written by a National Socialist. In any case, one can assume that Roosevelt has a good deal of understanding for National Socialist thought."[8]

---

4 See Schröder, *Deutschland und die Vereinigten Staaten*, 95–119; Frisch, *Das Deutsche Rooseveltbild*, 31–44.
5 Schröder, *Deutschland und die Vereinigten Staaten*, 98.
6 *Foreign Relations of the United States, 1933*, 1:143–5; *Akten zur Deutschen Auswärtigen Politik*, series C:1933–1937, vol. 1, no. 2:445–50; an English translation of Hitler's speech may be found in John W. Wheeler-Bennett, ed., *Documents on International Affairs, 1933* (London, 1933), 196–208.
7 Hitler's message and Roosevelt's noncommital reply in *Foreign Relations of the United States, 1934*, 2:419.
8 *Völkischer Beobachter*, June 7, 1933. Quoted in Schröder, *Deutschland und die Vereinigten Staaten*, 102. All translations from German primary sources are the author's.

An analysis of the image of Roosevelt and U.S. policies in the biggest European magazine of that time, the *Berliner Illustrierte Zeitung* (*BIZ*), results in the same conclusions for the same years. At Hitler's express wish, that magazine, which belonged to the Ullstein publishing house, was sold at a dumping price to Eher, the NSDAP's publisher, which had produced Hitler's *Mein Kampf*. Once the magazine had been sold, its Jewish editors were dismissed. During the world economic crisis the high-circulation magazine sustained heavy losses in readership, a downward trend that it was only able to reverse when it managed to blend its readers' interest in unpolitical entertainment with subtle forms of propaganda.

In the *BIZ*'s photo and text coverage, President Roosevelt was shown as a strong-willed man with outstanding leadership qualities who had managed to overcome the tribulations of poliomyelitis. Numerous photographs portray an attractive president who liked to spend his leisure time fishing, playing cards, hosting children in the White House, or spending time with his family. Although U.S. foreign policy issues were hardly ever discussed, the alleged similarities between Hitler and Roosevelt, between the New Deal and Nazi economic policies, ranked among the leitmotifs of the *BIZ*. In 1934, for example, the magazine claimed that Roosevelt was trying "to turn the American capitalist economy into a planned economy"; in 1936 it said that the American president was working on "providing a fragmented economic system with a uniform organizational framework."[9]

Evidently, this way of depicting the New Deal served to provide a justification for the economic policy conducted by the Nazis. At the same time photo coverage of labor disputes, strikes, and clashes between the police and protesters became a larger issue after 1937. Although this was not yet explicitly stated, such news implied that the National Socialists had a better record of fighting economic hardships than the Americans. Practically overnight the *BIZ* turned to overtly hostile comments on Roosevelt and American policies. In 1939 undisguised hostilities were the order of the day, following Goebbels's claim in a press statement on February 9, 1939, that "our criticism of Roosevelt cannot be exaggerated."[10]

Roosevelt delivered his famous quarantine speech in Chicago on October 5, 1937. This speech seems to have marked a turning point not

---

9 Roidl, "Amerikabild der Zwischenkriegszeit," 7, 19, 33–4, 53–4, 74, quotation on 75.
10 Frisch, *Das Deutsche Rooseveltbild*, 94; Roidl, "Amerikabild der Zwischenkriegszeit," 76.

only for Hitler but also for Goebbels. Roosevelt's speech met with wide attention even beyond the United States, for it was fiercely critical of the spirit of isolationism as well as the impartial neutrality laws. It seemed to herald an era of active American participation in efforts to suppress the "present reign of terror and international lawlessness."[11] According to Hitler's adjutant Nikolaus von Below, Hitler took this speech "very seriously." Hitler was particularly incensed by Roosevelt's statement that 90 percent of the world's population was being threatened by 10 percent. This, he declared, was clear evidence that Roosevelt did not count the Russians among the aggressors. Hitler believed that Roosevelt's "change of heart" was a reaction to the dramatic downturn of the American economy and the surging figures of unemployment.[12] In Goebbels's diaries, too, the quarantine speech marks a change of opinion that turned completely against Roosevelt. Whereas the few entries in which Roosevelt is mentioned after 1933 reflect a kind of neutral condescension,[13] the entry of October 6, 1937, reads: "Roosevelt gave a mean speech. Hidden attacks against Japan, Italy, and Germany. Stupid and underhanded. Big international sensation. In the German press we better report about it as a minor matter."[14]

Marking a watershed in the perception of America among the National Socialist leadership, the quarantine speech can also help to explain why – with the exception of the highly debatable memoirs by Ernst ("Putzi") Hanfstaengel and Hermann Rauschning – for the period between 1933 and 1936 no anti-American statements by Hitler were publicized. Above all, Rauschning's alleged "talks with Hitler" should no longer be referred to as a source.[15]

---

11 Franklin D. Roosevelt, *Public Papers and Addresses of Franklin D. Roosevelt*, vol. 4: *1937* (New York, 1941), 406–11.
12 Nikolaus von Below, *Als Hitlers Adjutant* (Mainz, 1980), 47.
13 *Die Tagebücher von Josef Goebbels: Sämtliche Fragmente*, ed. Elke Fröhlich for the Institut für Zeitgeschichte in cooperation with the Bundesarchiv (Munich, 1987), vol. 2: *1931–1936*, 716, entry Nov. 5, 1936; vol. 3: *1937–1939*, 11, entry Jan. 15, 1937, 36, entry Feb. 7, 1937, 99, entry Apr. 4, 1937, 211, entry July 24, 1937.
14 Ibid., vol. 3: *1937–1939*, 291, entry Oct. 6, 1937.
15 Ernst Hanfstaengel, *Zwischen Weissem und Braunem Haus: Memoiren eines politischen Aussenseiters* (Munich, 1970); Hermann Rauschning, *Gespräche mit Hitler* (Zurich, 1940). On the problem of reliability of Rauschning's alleged "talks" with Hitler, see Theodor Schieder, *Hermann Rauschnings "Gespräche mit Hitler" als Geschichtsquelle* (Opladen, 1972); Wolfgang Hänel, *Hermann Rauschnings "Gespräche mit Hitler" – eine Geschichtsfälschung* (Ingolstadt, 1984); Martin Broszat, "Enthüllung? Die Rauschning-Kontroverse," in Hermann Graml and Klaus-Dietmar Henke, eds., *Nach Hitler: Der schwierige Umgang mit unserer Geschichte* (Munich, 1986), 249–51. In my opinion Hänel argues convincingly that Rauschning did *not* talk to Hitler "more than a hundred times." Rauschning had an opportunity to talk with Hitler on only four occasions, and during these talks they were never alone.

A systematic chronology of the years 1933 to 1945 leads to a basic conclusion that will probably come as no surprise either: These years saw no change in the traditional ambivalence that characterized the German view of America. On the one hand, judgments and prejudices were revived that had governed German admiration for and criticism of the American nation since the era of Romanticism.[16] On the other hand, attitudes that had developed since the imperial period, World War I, and the Weimar Republic also became crucial factors in determining German views of America. Those attitudes eflected both the rise of the United States to world power status in political, economic, and cultural terms and the debate on "modernism," which the United States embodied.[17]

Apart from continuity there were, as with all historical processes, also unique elements. National Socialist views of America were characterized by one particular critical feature that had been a minor phenomenon since the end of World War I, that is, the anti-Semitic and racist anti-Americanism of the extreme right in Germany. After 1938–9 this element of cultural criticism gradually turned into a determining factor in Nazi attempts to shape public opinion. After Hitler had seized power, the racial factor that marked Nazi-cultivated anti-Americanism was for a while totally neglected, largely for opportunistic reasons coupled with the insig-

16 Ernst Fraenkel, *Amerika im Spiegel des deutschen politischen Denkens: Äusserungen deutscher Staatsmänner und Staatsdenker über Staat und Gesellschaft in den Vereinigten Staaten von Amerika* (Cologne, 1959); Harold Jantz, "Amerika im deutschen Dichten und Denken," in Wolfgang Stammler, ed., *Deutsche Philologie im Aufriss*, 2d ed. (Berlin, 1963), 3:309–72; Manfred Henningsen, *Der Fall Amerika: Zur Sozial- und Bewusstseinsgeschichte einer Verdrängung* (Munich, 1974); Günter Moltmann, "Deutscher Anti-Amerikanismus heute und früher," in Otmar Franz, ed., *Vom Sinn der Geschichte* (Stuttgart, 1976), 85–105; Rob Kroes and Marten van Rossem, eds., *Anti-Americanism in Europe* (Amsterdam, 1986); Hartmut Wasser, "Die Deutschen und Amerika," *Aus Politik und Zeitgeschichte: Beilage zu "Das Parlament,"* B 26/76, 3–15; Walter Kühnel, "Towards the Tricenntial of Happy Misunderstandings: Intercultural Studies of America," in Lothar Bredella and Dietmar Haack, eds., *Perceptions and Misperceptions: The United States and Germany* (Tübingen, 1988), 177–202; Hildegard Meyer, *Nordamerika im Urteil des deutschen Schrifttums bis zur Mitte des 19. Jahrhunderts* (Hamburg, 1929).
17 Peter Berg, *Deutschland und Amerika, 1918–1929* (Lübeck, 1963); Manfred Buchwald, "Das Kulturbild Amerikas im Spiegel deutscher Zeitungen und Zeitschriften, 1919–1932," Ph.D. diss., University of Kiel, 1964; Erich Angermann, "Die Auseinandersetzung mit der Moderne in Deutschland und den USA in den 'Goldenenen zwanziger Jahren,'" *Internationales Jahrbuch für Geschichts- und Geographie-Unterricht* 11 (1967): 76–87; Klaus Schwabe, "Anti-Americanism Within the German Right, 1917–1933," *American Studies/Amerikastudien* 21 (1976): 89–107; Detlef J. K. Peukert, *Die Weimarer Republik: Krisenjahre der klassischen Moderne* (Frankfurt/Main, 1981), 166–90; Frank Costigliola, *Awkward Dominion: American Political, Economic, and Cultural Relations with Europe, 1919–1933* (Ithaca, N.Y., and London, 1984), 167–83; Sara Markham, *Workers, Women, and Afro-Americans: Images of the United States in German Travel Literature, 1923–1933* (New York, 1986); Manfred Berg, *Gustav Stresemann und die Vereinigten Staaten von Amerika: Weltwirtschaftliche Verflechtung und Revisionspolitik, 1907–1929* (Baden-Baden, 1990), 231–73; Mary Nolan, *Visions of Modernity: American Business and the Americanization of Germany* (New York, 1994).

nificance of the United States for Germany as a potential competitor in Europe. Race-oriented arguments only became an integral part of party and of national ideology when Hitler realized that Roosevelt and the so-called "internationalists" had refused to give the National Socialists a "free hand" in creating a racist empire that would extend from the Atlantic to the Urals. An attempt to reconstruct Hitler's image of America in the 1920s reveals that he embodied both traditions, that is, the continuity of ambivalence, on the one hand, and anti-Semitic and racist anti-Americanism, on the other hand.[18]

Thus, we can rightly say that in the 1920s Hitler's attitude toward the United States had been ambivalent. Alternating between admiration and contempt, between *Wunderland* (wonderland) and *Wahnsinn* (madness), Hitler's views never coalesced into a permanent or realistic picture of the United States. Hitler's perception of the United States was circumscribed by his ideological dogmatism, which far surpassed the inevitable ideological bias of other famous German "armchair travelers" to the United States, such as Heinrich Heine, Karl Marx, or Karl May; and it far surpassed the inevitable bias attributed to anybody belonging to the German school of philosophical hermeneutics à la Heidegger and Gadamer. In his role as ideologue and programmatic thinker, Hitler claimed that war and the violent competition of races and peoples for limited space constituted the eternal purpose of world history and set its agenda. In keeping with this theory, the fanatic autodidact Hitler absorbed only those pieces of information about the United States that coincided with his own prejudgments.

Apart from these dogmatic limitations, there existed objective obstacles to Hitler's gaining a realistic understanding of the United States. Hitler did not speak English, he had never been to an Anglo-Saxon country, and

---

18 On Hitler's perception of the United States and Franklin D. Roosevelt, see James V. Compton, *Hitler und die USA: Die Amerikapolitik des Dritten Reiches und die Ursprünge des Zweiten Weltkrieges* (Oldenburg, 1968); Saul Friedländer, *Auftakt zum Untergang: Hitler und die Vereinigten Staaten, 1939–1941* (Stuttgart, 1965); Joachim Remak, "Hitlers Amerikapolitik," *Aussenpolitik* 6 (1955): 706–14; Gerhard L. Weinberg, "Hitler's Image of the United States," in Gerhard L. Weinberg, *World in the Balance: Behind the Scenes of World War II* (Hanover, N.H., 1981), 53–74; Andreas Hillgruber, "Der Faktor Amerika in Hitlers Strategie, 1938–1941," in Andreas Hillgruber, *Deutsche Grossmacht- und Weltpolitik im 19. und 20. Jahrhundert* (Düsseldorf, 1977), 197–222; Andreas Hillgruber, "Hitler und die USA, 1933–1945," in Detlef Junker, ed., *Deutschland und die USA, 1890–1985*, Heidelberg American Studies Background Paper, no. 2 (Heidelberg, 1986), 27–41; Gordon A. Craig, "Roosevelt and Hitler: The Problem of Perception," in Klaus Hildebrand and Rainer Pommerin, eds., *Deutsche Frage und Europäisches Gleichgewicht: Festschrift für A. Hillgruber* (Cologne, 1985), 169–94; Robert Edwin Herzstein, *Roosevelt and Hitler: Prelude to War* (New York, 1989); Detlef Junker, *Hitler's Perception of Franklin D. Roosevelt*; Harald Frisch, *Das deutsche Rooseveltbild*; Enrico Syring, *Hitler: Seine politische Utopie* (Berlin, 1994), 96, 104.

he considered all democratic traditions to be ipso facto Jewish, internationalist, and as such a crime against humanity. His view of the world was Eurocentric, fixed on the European theater and on the power of armies. He never developed anything distantly resembling an adequate notion of the range of Anglo-Saxon seapower. In addition, Hitler personally hated water and the sea. On land, he wrote in 1928, he was a hero, but on the sea a coward.[19]

Hitler was convinced that war was the natural state of history and that it constituted the driving force behind progress. Hence, it is no surprise that his perception of the United States also centered on war. The dominant leitmotif in the very few statements Hitler made on the United States before 1924 is American entry into World War I and the reasons behind it. Between 1924 and the Great Depression his image of the United States was determined by the potential threat to Europe posed by the American nation. As was already mentioned, he took little interest in the weak America that was grappling with the world economic crisis and the neutrality laws. Between 1938 and 1945 his thinking was again governed by the war against the United States. He regarded the United States as a power to be reckoned with when it was actually or potentially involved in European affairs, but as a negligible quantity when it was not.

Hitler blamed the Jews for American entry into World War I. He blamed the Jewish race, the Jewish press, the "international lending capital" held by Jews, and the "capital and trust democracy." Hitler claimed that as their puppet Woodrow Wilson had driven the Americans into the war.[20] This alleged Jewish conspiracy was clearly the leitmotif of Hitler's views in those early years. The European truism about American "materialism" was closely connected with the Jewish issue: "Americans rate business above everything else. Money is money, even when they make it at the cost of human lives. For Jews their purse is the most sacred thing. Americans would have girded up their loins anyway, with or without submarines."[21] In those early years Hitler did not yet use his knowledge of U.S. immigration laws as a basis for an argument asserting Germanic predominance in American society.[22]

Between 1924 and 1928 Hitler wrote *Mein Kampf* and his *Zweites Buch* (or second book). At that time the United States had a strong impact on

---

19 Quoted in Holger H. Herwig, *Politics of Frustration: The United States in German Naval Planning, 1889–1941* (Boston, 1976), 188.
20 Eberhard Jäckel and Axel Kuhn, eds., *Hitler: Sämtliche Aufzeichnungen, 1905–1924* (Stuttgart, 1980), 97, 135, 148, 198, 204, 235, 237, 257, 328, 372–3, 890–1.
21 Ibid., 97.
22 Ibid., 96, 717, 908.

the German economy and civilization. This marked presence was dubbed "Americanism" and unleashed a new discussion about the importance of the United States in which the extreme right also participated. As a result, Hitler had to review his image of the United States and define it more clearly. It is thus no coincidence that longer statements about the United States can only be traced in Hitler's *Zweites Buch*.

If we check *Mein Kampf* for references to the United States, we will notice that the United States plays no role whatsoever in Hitler's program, which is entirely restricted to Europe. Nor is the United States a crucial factor in his thinking about potential allies for Germany. Agitation against the Dawes Plan is notably absent, and the differences between National Socialist ideology and American democracy are either too obvious or too irrelevant to be mentioned. However, in the few cases where the United States does appear in his remarks, the tenor is one of consistent admiration. According to Hitler, the Germanic race dominates the United States in every respect thanks to sound racial and immigration policies, although it is constantly threatened by the Jewish bacillus. For Hitler, the United States was the very model of a state organized according to the principles of race and space. Given its favorable ratio of population numbers and living space – the decisive criterion in Hitler's ideology – the United States was the archetype of a world power, destined to replace the British Empire.[23]

In his *Zweites Buch* these assumptions become even more evident. The United States appears as a prototype of a world power with adequate living space, the right racial policy enforced through immigration laws, a large domestic market, a high standard of living, an extraordinary productivity level, technological innovation, high mobility, and mass production.[24] Indeed, one young Hitler scholar, Rainer Zitelmann, has suggested that Hitler's ultimate goal was not to create an antimodernist utopia based on agriculture and farming, but a highly industrialized economy modelled on that of the United States. While Hitler may have been contemptuous of American society and culture, he was certainly fascinated by the country's economic and technological development, according to Zitelmann.[25]

Jeffrey Herf has effectively captured the essence of this problem by showing how Hitler's fascination with American productivity and tech-

---

23 Adolf Hitler, *Mein Kampf*, 16th ed. (Munich, 1932), 1:313–14, 2:490, 721–3.
24 Adolf Hitler, *Hitlers Zweites Buch: Ein Dokument aus dem Jahre 1928*, intro. Gerhard L. Weinberg (Stuttgart, 1961), 120–32.
25 Rainer Zitelmann, *Hitler: Selbstverständnis eines Revolutionärs* (Hamburg, 1987), 320–4; see Peter Krüger, "Zu Hitlers 'nationalsozialistischen Wirtschaftskenntnissen,'" *Geschichte und Gesellschaft* 6 (1980): 263–82.

nology could be understood in terms of Germany's tradition of "reactionary modernism" – a peculiar reconciliation of the anti-Semitic and *völkisch* traditions of the German right with industrial technology. Herf has demonstrated that the paradoxical combination of irrationalism and technology constituted a fundamental aspect of Hitler's ideology and of National Socialism. Industrial progress was necessary to fulfill the Nazi ideology, and it remained a substantial part of National Socialist thought and practice until the end of the Third Reich.[26]

However, in the *Zweites Buch* the United States appeared not only as the prototype of a world power and the model for a National Socialist organization of living space but also as a simultaneous danger and challenge to Europe and Germany. Hitler criticized what he referred to as the "incredible naiveté of bourgeois nationalists" who thought that such a challenge could be met in the context of an open world economy and free world trade. He also attacked the Pan-European movement of his time for harboring the illusion that American hegemony could be countered adequately by founding a "United States of Europe." An armed conflict with the United States was inevitable, as in Hitler's view of the world there was no such thing as the peaceful coexistence of rival states. Such a war could only be waged successfully by a Europe that was racially regenerated and subjected to German leadership. In Hitler's view only such a united Europe would be able to "stand up to North America in the future." He added that "it is the responsibility of the National Socialist Movement to prepare our Fatherland for this task to its utmost capacity."[27]

This change in Hitler's perception of the United States may be surprising at first sight, but looked at from his racist point of view it represents a quite logical development. This change of heart was a consequence of Hitler's realization that due to its rigorous immigration policy and its resulting high racial quality the United States had become a strong and therefore threatening world power. In that respect, the United States was the exact opposite of Russia, which in terms of living space and population numbers was similar to the United States. However, according to Hitler, Russia was in no position ever to acquire world-power status, because it was a crucible of races and, as he claimed, dominated by Jews.[28] Where, in general, Hitler's opinion was determined by the stereotypes

---

26 Jeffrey Herf, *Reactionary Modernism: Technology, Culture and Politics in Weimar and the Third Reich* (Cambridge, 1984), 222.
27 Hitler, *Hitlers Zweites Buch*, 122, 130.
28 Ibid., 128–32.

created on the extreme German right,[29] in 1928 he came to adopt the view of a group that attributed American imperialism to the victory of the German-Anglo-Saxon elite in the domestic arena[30] rather than to the success story of the Jewish race in the United States.[31] The anti-Semitic leitmotif regained currency for Hitler only at the time when the next war against the United States was imminent.

The decline of America's importance as a result of the Great Depression, its isolationist stance in foreign policy, its neutrality laws, the generally warm welcome given to the New Deal, and the attitude of "reactionary modernism" in Germany had all created a climate in which it was possible for the National Socialists to grant some freedom of expression to the German media. This favorable climate encouraged a continuation from 1933 to 1939 of the ambivalent views of America that had characterized the Weimar Republic. In the Third Reich, the United States was a factor to be reckoned with in many areas of everyday life. Evidently, the Nazis did not believe that it was necessary to counteract this trend, as long as racial dogmas were upheld. Positive and negative assessments of "Americanism" (that is, of America as a symbol of modernism) continued, although less conspicuously than before 1933. Older issues that shaped views of America during the Weimar years – such as technology, rationality, productivity, the media, supply-side America, mass consumption, the leisure industry, sports, and cultivation of the body – also continued to have an impact on public statements about the United States within Germany. Traditional forms and stereotypes of cultural criticism also persisted, such as the tendency to rail publicly against American materialism and lack of culture. The plurality of German images and the ambivalence that characterized the "production" of German views of the United States gave way to a new image only with the outbreak of the war in 1941. From that time on publicly produced opinions about the United States had to be purely negative. Systematic research on "Americanism" in the prewar years of the Third Reich has only just started. Although only a few studies on specific topics are available to date, they might serve as a starting point for the following observations.[32]

29 Schwabe, *Anti-Americanism*, 96ff.
30 See Alexander Graf Brockdorff, *Amerikanische Weltherrschaft?* (Berlin, 1929).
31 See Otto Bonhard, *Jüdische Weltherrschaft?* (Berlin, 1928).
32 See esp. the works of Hans Dieter Schäfer, *Das gespaltene Bewusstsein: Deutsche Kultur und Lebenswirklichkeit, 1933–1945*, 3d ed. (Munich, 1983), 114–46; "Amerikanismus im Dritten Reich," in Michael Prinz and Rainer Zitelmann, eds., *Nationalsozialismus und Modernisierung* (Darmstadt, 1991), 199–215; "Bekenntnisse zur Neuen Welt: USA-Kult vor dem 2. Weltkrieg,"

The ambivalent relationship of the Nazi elite to the United States reflects their equally ambivalent relationship to modernism. The National Socialists were not luddites, but they did claim to provide the one and only acceptable synthesis of technology and the "spirit." Their fascination with technology, production, rationalization, automation, and mass consumption directed not only Hitler's attention to the United States. Their rebellion against the Enlightenment and the "soulless" West was combined with their claim to blend successfully technology and production with the German Aryan spirit, with German "soul" and German blood, with popular aesthetics, and the special relationship of the National Socialists to Providence.[33] Such notions restricted their view of the United States to the themes and patterns of traditional criticism.

The National Socialists were not anti-capitalists or socialists in the Marxist mold. However, capital was to be removed from the hands of "international Jewry" and "plutocrats." The objective was to nationalize but not socialize capital, to use it to help create a war industry and a large self-sufficient economic area, and at the same time to satisfy the need for consumption. On the one hand, the Nazis were full of admiration for the American market's capacity to manufacture products for mass consumption; nor did they reject the idea of competition. On the other hand, however, the German economy's withdrawal from the world market encouraged increasing opposition to American trade and economic policies.[34] Apart from that, for Hitler and his National Socialists war and the military always took priority over the constraints of the marketplace and the requirements of a bourgeois, profit-oriented society. Hitler was a warrior, not a merchant:

The ultimate decision on the outcome of the war for the world market will depend on the use of force rather than on business strategies. . . . Because, after

---

in Deutscher Werkbund e.V. und Württembergischer Kunstverein Stuttgart, eds., *Schock und Schöpfung: Jugendästhetik im 20. Jahrhundert* (Darmstadt, 1986), 383–8. On the special problem of jazz and swing, see Michael H. Kater, "Forbidden Fruit? Jazz and the Third Reich," *American Historical Review* 94 (1989): 11–43; Michael H. Kater, *Different Drummers: Jazz in the Culture of Nazi Germany* (Oxford, 1992); Horst H. Lange, "Jazz: eine Oase der Sehnsucht," in *Schock und Schöpfung*, 320–3; Horst H. Lange, *Jazz in Deutschland: Die deutsche Jazz-Chronik, 1900–1960* (Berlin, 1966); Thorsten Müller, "Furcht vor der SS im Alsterpavillon," in *Schock und Schöpfung*, 324–5. See also Roidl, "Amerikabild der Zwischenkriegszeit," passim; Christian H. Freitag, "Die Entwicklung der Amerikastudien in Berlin bis 1945," Ph.D. diss., Free University of Berlin, 1977, 131–244; and the Marxist interpretation of Wolfgang Röll, "Die USA – das entartete Europa: Zu einigen ideologischen Komponenten des 'Amerikabildes' des deutschen Faschismus, 1933–1945," *Jenaer Beiträge zur Parteigeschichte* 47 (Nov. 1984): 70–88; Carsten Laqua, *Wie Micky unter die Nazis fiel: Walt Disney und Deutschland* (Reinbeck, 1992).
33 Herf, *Reactionary Modernism*, 189–216.
34 See Detlef Junker, *Der unteilbare Weltmarkt: Das ökonomische Interesse in der Aussenpolitik der USA, 1933–1941* (Stuttgart, 1975), 93–116.

all, the economy is a purely secondary matter in the life of peoples and as such it depends on the primary existence of a powerful state. Swords must be given precedence over plowshares, just as the army takes precedence over the economy.[35]

After 1933 the Nazi state indeed gradually took control of the economy. The Four-Year Plan established in 1936 was supposed to prepare the country for war during times of peace. However, the private sector, which was largely free of party domination, managed to survive. It supported a market that continued to cooperate with big American companies and to sell American products and culture to the Germans. Subsidiaries of American companies, for instance, were still represented on the German market. They did not hesitate to participate in the promotion of the German arms industry. In 1935 Opel (General Motors) had a 50 percent market share in the German automobile industry, and by 1939 Opel and Ford were the biggest producers of tanks on the German market.[36] There is no information on the perception of America among Opel and Ford employees. Nor do we know how they reacted when in 1938 Ford pledged to manage production in his company exclusively "with German workers and German material."[37]

We also do not know whether people in Berlin, when they walked past the Berlin Europahaus and looked at the two fifty-meter-long neon billboards of the Ford Company, were actually aware of the fact that Ford was an American company. The same applies to Coca-Cola, which expanded considerably during the Third Reich and which catered great sporting events. It was not only in its advertisements in the Sportpalast, the site of Goebbels's speeches, that the American company invited Germans to drink Coke "eiskalt."[38]

Enthusiasm about cars evolved into a real cult during the 1930s. This too was partly rooted in American culture. The German Automobile Club's magazine, *Motorwelt*, was modeled on American examples. During the 1920s Hitler himself was very much impressed by the degree of motorization achieved in the United States and also by the personal achievements of Henry Ford. After seizing power, he eagerly promoted motorization and highway construction in Germany. When he opened the "International Automobile Fair 1936" he called on car manufacturers

---

35 Hitler, *Hitlers Zweites Buch*, 123–4.
36 Junker, *Der unteilbare Weltmarkt*, 103; Gabriel Kolko, "American Business and Germany, 1930–1941," *Western Political Quarterly* 15 (1962): 713–28; Gerhart Hass, *Von München bis Pearl Harbor: Zur Geschichte der deutsch-amerikanischen Beziehungen, 1938–1941* (Berlin, 1965), 52–63.
37 *Ford-Almanach* (Cologne, 1938), 6; "Ford Works in Germany," *Motor-Kritik* 15 (1935): 711; quoted in Schäfer, *Amerikanismus im Dritten Reich*, 207.
38 Schäfer, *Amerikanismus im Dritten Reich*, 205; Schäfer, *Das gespaltene Bewusstsein*, 118.

to produce cheap cars, declaring that the German people had the same needs as their American counterparts.[39] Even as late as the undeclared war in the Atlantic in September 1941, Hitler claimed, "Modesty is the enemy of progress. In that we resemble the Americans. We are a demanding people."[40] This included the effort to raise living standards for the great majority of *Volksgenossen* (racial comrades) and to produce durable consumer goods modeled on American patterns: electronic ovens, electronic refrigerators, electronic coffee machines, grills, radios, trailers, and tents. Production of such goods started when the arms industry stepped up its activities. When, in 1937, Blaupunkt introduced an overseas receiver for "the discriminating and highly critical audience" it used the Statue of Liberty for its ads and promised that listeners would definitely "enjoy broadcasts from the 'New World.'"[41]

There is ample evidence that before the outbreak of World War II Americans were counted among Germany's "favorite foreigners." Especially between 1936 and 1939 a considerable number of individuals, professional associations, and National Socialist organizations made trips to the United States, many of them promoted by shipping companies. Besides traditional tourist attractions, Germans also visited American automobile companies, department stores, and prisons. They inspected American road construction sites and learned about American methods of law enforcement. German tourism in the United States was given an additional boost by the publication of new guidebooks that painted a new picture of America.[42] (This is another aspect that needs to be investigated more closely.) The Vereinigung Carl Schurz, an association that came under the domination of the German ministry for propaganda in 1933, organized trips to the United States for university professors and students.[43]

The Nazi regime did not want to prohibit the importation of popular American culture, which had reached an initial record high in the mid-1920s. The intention was just to channel it into the right direction, because to a certain extent the Nazi regime tolerated the dynamism displayed by the private sector. Moreover, Hollywood movies as well as jazz and "swing" were very popular, and tolerating them served to improve public acceptance of Nazi rule. Prohibitions and bans usually

---

39 Schäfer, *Das gespaltene Bewusstsein*, 119.
40 Adolf Hitler, *Monologe im Führerhauptquartier, 1941–1944*, ed. Werner Jochmann (Hamburg, 1980).
41 See photo in Schäfer, *Das gespaltene Bewusstsein*, annex.
42 Ibid., 206.
43 Freitag, *Entwicklung der Amerikastudien*, 149–57.

only took effect where the dogma of race was concerned. Attempts to counteract the "Americanism" of popular culture – for example, by dismissing American movies as superficial, trivial, vulgar, and devoid of any sense of culture and art – were unconvincing and probably doomed to failure.

Despite import restrictions and controls on foreign currencies, imported Hollywood movies were smash hits compared to German prewar movies. In the big cities American movies were sometimes shown for up to four months. Until 1940 it was also possible in the cities to see the original or the dubbed version of a new American movie every week. As a matter of course Hollywood stars were part of the celebrity cult that characterized film festivals and magazines during the 1930s.[44] Among them were Clark Gable, Robert Taylor, Joan Crawford, Vivien Leigh, Shirley Temple, Katharine Hepburn, Fred Astaire and Ginger Rogers, and, of course, Greta Garbo and Marlene Dietrich – the latter despite being the victim of a negative press campaign in 1935. The imagination of Germans was much more inspired by the sex appeal of such dangerous "vamps" than by the rather homespun charms of Paula Wessely and Marianne Hoppe.[45]

Jazz and swing, its polished and tamed version, are among the best-researched aspects of popular American culture during the Third Reich.[46] From the National Socialist point of view, jazz and swing had to be dismissed as the "music of Niggers and Jews." They were considered undesirable, but were not generally prohibited during the years before the war. Jazz was banned from radio broadcasting in 1935, but it was only after the outbreak of the war in 1939 that "English music" and then, in 1941, "American music" were outlawed. However, during the years of peace and to some extent also during the war years, the slogan "jazz is where you find it" was a very popular concept. Anybody who wanted to buy jazz records, either imported originals from the United States or German products, could find them in all German cities. Jazz fans had plenty of opportunities to indulge in the music of their jazz icons in "Hot Clubs," "Jazz Clubs," or even at home: Duke Ellington, Fats Waller, Louis Armstrong, Gene Krupa, Wingy Manone, Jimmie Lunceford, Count Basie, Nat Gonella, Harry Roy, Burt Ambrose, but also the first Glenn Miller and Harry James records were all available to the interested listener. Jazz fans, who in general belonged to the well-educated middle

---

44 Roidl, "Amerikabild der Zwischenkriegszeit," 113–18.
45 Schäfer, *Das gespaltene Bewusstsein*, 128–33.
46 See the works of Kater, Lange, Schäfer, and Müller cited in note 32 to this chapter.

class, kept somewhat aloof from the more common-minded "Swing-Heinis" who indulged passionately in jazz and swing dancing (*hotten*), who sometimes saluted each other with "Swing Heil," and who annoyed the National Socialists so much that on October 11, 1938, swing dancing was declared a punishable offense. However, people did not stop dancing and swing music continued to thrive, albeit behind camouflage.

Jazz and swing fans formed loose groups which refused to toe the line, although without going as far as to demonstrate actual political resistance. Their behavior was an indirect protest against intellectual and cultural *Gleichschaltung* (coordination). To a certain extent it represented an opportunity to show disapproval by choosing a certain way of life. After the outbreak of the war the Gestapo closely monitored these groups. Their Anglophile attitude was considered "subversive." In January 1941, Heinrich Himmler decreed that the leaders of young swing fans in Hamburg were to be arrested and sent to concentration camps for two to three years. They were beaten up and sentenced to forced labor.[47]

Although a lot of difficult work remains to be done before we can gain a better understanding of the ambivalence of "Americanism" in the Third Reich, the stereotypical images that Nazi propaganda created of the enemy in World War II are well known.[48] It may be quite difficult, however, to answer definitively the question of how successful National Socialist propaganda actually was in World War II, what Germans really thought, and how they felt about the United States. There is evidence to suggest that Nazi propaganda met with widespread approval only during the Allied terror bombardments, whereas in general its effects were limited.[49] Those who read Hitler's and Goebbels's diatribes, especially their private comments and diary entries, might conclude that as a result of autosuggestion the Nazi leaders fell prey to their own propaganda. During World War II Hitler also dominated everything. Almost all negative images presented in Nazi propaganda to stir hatred against the enemy bore the mark of Hitler's public and private statements about Roosevelt and the United States. They helped to determine the principal

---

[47] Müller, *Furcht vor der SS in Alsterpavillon*, 324.
[48] See esp. the excellent essay of Günter Moltmann, "Nationalklischees und Demagogie"; Detlef Junker, *Kampf um die Weltmacht*, 157–64; Willi A. Boelcke, *Die Macht des Radios: Weltgeschichte und Auslandsfunk, 1924–1976* (Frankfurt/Main, 1977), 379–89; Peter Longerich, *Propagandisten im Krieg: Die Presseabteilung des Auswärtigen Amtes unter Ribbentrop* (Munich, 1987), 81–5; Karl-Dietrich Abel, *Presselenkung im NS-Staat* (Berlin, 1968), 132–3; *Kriegspropaganda, 1939–1941: Geheime Ministerkonferenzen im Reichspropagandaministerium*, ed. and intro. Willi A. Boelcke (Stuttgart, 1966), 693–4, 703–4.
[49] Moltmann, "Nationalklischees und Demagogie," 236–8.

themes that dominated German commentary on the United States from the quarantine speech to the declaration of war on December 11, 1941.[50] Thus, for example, the stereotyped criticism that the United States was completely devoid of culture gained wider currency only after American entry into the war.

The overrriding theme of anti-American propaganda was rooted in Hitler's basic conviction that Roosevelt was not independent in his policies but acted on behalf of international Jewry, Jewish capitalism, and the global Jewish conspiracy which was directed primarily against the United States, the United Kingdom, and the Soviet Union, and which had incited the American people to wage a war against Germany. When Hitler summoned Goebbels on May 3, 1943, and demanded a "powerful anti-Semitic propaganda," he seemed to have been very satisfied with the answer that Goebbels gave him. Goebbels said that anti-Semitic propaganda already accounted for some 70 to 80 percent of German broadcasts aimed abroad.[51] With the advent of World War II Hitler returned to his early perception of the United States, his interpretation of why the United States had entered World War I, and how the policies and behavior of Wilson could be explained.

Anti-Semitism was, of course, the dominant theme of all Hitler's public and private statements between 1937 and his so-called "political testament" in 1945. It is a well-known fact that in Hitler's dogmatic, Manichean teleology of history, the element of total negation, the satanic and evil principle, is embodied in the Jews, because – being a people who for two thousand years had had no living space – they threatened to scuttle the purpose of history.[52] Hitler believed that his mission within the context of world history was to lead the Germanic race and the German people into the final battle against the Jews. As a result, any state that denied his claim to power, any politician who opposed him, became ipso facto an agent of "international Jewry." The fact that America engaged in anti-German policies was apparently enough in itself for Hitler to prove that the Germanic and German elements in the United States had been poisoned and corrupted by the Jews. To support this contention it may be sufficient to just quote a few sentences from his war speech of December 11. According to Hitler it had to be taken into account that "the spirits this man has summoned to his aid, or rather who summoned him, belong to those elements who, as Jews, can have a vested

50 Junker, *Hitler's Perception*, 151–5.
51 Boelcke, *Die Macht des Radios*, 384.
52 See Junker, *Kampf um die Weltmacht*, 39–42.

interest only in destruction, but never in order." It was the Jew in all his satanic malice who gathered around this man (Roosevelt), but of whom this man also wanted to make use. "We know the power behind Roosevelt; it is the eternal Jew who thinks that time is ripe for carrying out on us what we have already seen and experienced with horror in Soviet Russia."[53]

Goebbels's diaries, too, are rife with invective against Roosevelt, who is described as the "servant of Jewry and slave of capitalism" and "the evil genius of American politics."[54] In his war speech Hitler referred to Roosevelt as a "hypocrite," "forger," and "warmonger." He continued:

That he [Roosevelt] calls me a gangster is all the more irrelevant as this term is American and not European in origin, probably due to the lack of such elements here. But quite apart from that I cannot be insulted by Mr. Roosevelt at all, for I consider him – much as I do Wilson – to be mentally ill.[55]

Hitler's negative and hate-filled perception of Roosevelt, in particular his characterization of the latter as a puppet of Jewish capitalism, enabled him to answer a question he had posed himself and which he put before the German people in his war speech: the question why Roosevelt, like Wilson before him, had become a fanatical enemy of Germany. On the very day that Hitler declared war on the United States, he reaffirmed his belief that no real conflict of interests existed between Germany and the United States. According to Hitler, Germany was perhaps the only Great Power never to have possessed colonies either in North or in South America. Furthermore, the United States had drawn nothing but benefit from the immigration of millions of Germans. He continued that the German Reich had never adopted a hostile attitude toward the United States. Regarding the outbreak of World War I, Hitler drew attention to the conclusions of the Nye Committee, according to which capitalist interests in the United States had brought about that country's entry into the war. There were no other territorial or political conflicts likely to affect the interests, let alone the existence, of the United States. The difference in the organization of their respective states being granted, this

---

53 Domarus, *Hitler: Reden und Proklamationen*, 1804, 1807–8; see Hitler's speech of Jan. 30, 1939, in Detlef Junker et al., eds., *Deutsche Parlamentsdebatten*, vol. 2: *1919–1933* (Frankfurt/Main, 1970–1), 288–95. Hitler's reaction to the Lend-Lease Act was similar. See Hildegard von Kotze, ed., *Heeresadjutant bei Hitler, 1938–1943: Aufzeichnungen des Major Engel* (Stuttgart, 1974), 99.
54 Entries of June 22 and Aug. 23, 1940. See entries of Nov. 18, 20, and 24, 1938; Dec. 17, 1938; Jan. 24, 1939; Nov. 12, 1939; June 17, 1940; Sept. 5, 1940; Oct. 8, 1940; Feb. 1, 1941; Mar. 17, 1941; Apr. 27, 1941; June 8, 1941, in *Die Tagebücher von Josef Goebbels*, vols. 3 and 4.
55 Domarus, *Hitler: Reden und Proklamationen*, 1807.

was, according to Hitler, in itself no reason for hostility, as long as one type of state did not try "to step outside its own natural sphere and intervene in others."⁵⁶

When one compares Hitler's statements about Roosevelt and the United States from the period of 1937 to 1941 with the monologues held in the *Führerhauptquartier* (Hitler's main headquarters) from 1941 to 1944 and the surprisingly detailed remarks on the United States in his political testament of 1945, one finds that the latter period witnessed no change or development in his thoughts on the topic. The only apparent change was that his hatred of Roosevelt became more intense. When the president was mentioned it was always as a mentally ill con man, as a pawn of the Jews. Criticism of American culture and the American way of life also became more prominent. A remark Hitler made on January 7, 1942, is most revealing:

Ancient Rome was a colossal, serious state. Great ideas inspired the Romans. This is not true of England today. Yet I prefer an Englishman to an American a thousand times over. With the Japanese we have no inner affinity. Their culture and way of life are too different from ours. However, it is against Americanism that I feel a hatred and abhorrence of the most profound kind. One is closer to any European state. America is in its whole intellectual and spiritual attitude a society dominated by Niggers and Jews.⁵⁷

On February 24, 1945, Hitler once again took up the central idea of his war speech, while at the same time holding fast to his racist world view and anti-Semitic obsessions. The war with America, Hitler dictated for posterity, was a tragic chain of events, as nonsensical as it was against all reason. But an unfortunate historical accident had decreed that his own assumption of power should coincide with the very moment in which "Roosevelt, the chosen representative of world Jewry, took the helm at the White House." In Hitler's eyes this war was senseless, for

Germany does not demand anything of the United States and it has nothing whatsoever to fear from Germany. All conditions for peaceful coexistence are given, and each state will remain in its own sphere. But everything is being fouled up by the Jew who has chosen the United States as his mightiest bulwark. That and only that spoils and poisons everything.⁵⁸

---

56 Ibid., 1801–2.
57 Hitler, *Monologe*, 184. Documentation of Hitler's most important statements about Roosevelt and the United States from 1942 to 1945, in Junker, *Kampf um die Weltmacht*, 157–64.
58 *Hitlers politisches Testament: Die Bormann Diktate vom Februar und April 1945*, with an essay by Hugh R. Trevor-Roper and an epilog by André François-Poncet (Hamburg, 1981), 103ff.

This anti-Semitism was also the centerpiece of three other claims that were crucial for anti-American propaganda in World War II. First, Roosevelt's foreign policy, it was suggested, was practically a flight into war motivated by domestic problems. According to this notion, Roosevelt sought relief in war because he was unable to curb unemployment and get the American economy out of the doldrums. Newsreels and films depicted labor conflicts, police raids against protesters, slums and social hardship in order to illustrate the decline of the American economy. Germans were given no opportunity to learn about the accomplishments of the American war economy. Second, it was asserted that Roosevelt was an arrogant hypocrite who preached about peace but never cared about violating international law. He was a man who insinuated that Germany aspired to rule the world while he himself was subjecting the British Empire to his control and trying to achieve world domination for the United States by force. Third, Goebbels intentionally made use of a stereotypical argument that is probably Germany's and Europe's oldest prejudice against the United States. He claimed that America suffered from a complete lack of culture and was very much inferior to Europe, that it was a country characterized by materialist thinking, false egalitarianism, superficiality, kitsch instead of culture, a fictitious civilization, dominated by gangsters, the old guard, the degenerate, and the morally depraved.[59]

Goebbels's strategy, however, was doomed almost from the beginning. Even if there is some evidence that many Germans were inclined to believe that FDR was a warmonger and the "chief war culprit," or even if they supported Goebbels's and Hitler's notion of a culturally degenerate and inferior America, Nazi propaganda faced the impossible task to balance the deeply ingrained perception of the American economy as potentially strong basis of its war machine.[60] Goebbels himself had to admit in September 1942 that the German armament propaganda had completely been pushed into the defensive vis-à-vis the "American myth."[61] The regime's own public opinion surveys stressed the fact from early 1942 onward that the population considered negative reports on the American supply of raw materials and goods as "rosy" and merely "propagandistic." It consistently refused to believe that England and the United States were not far ahead of Germany in military

---

59 Moltmann, "Nationalklischees und Demagogie," passim.
60 For a thorough analysis of these questions, see Gassert, *Amerika im Dritten Reich*, chap. 6.
61 Cf. Willi A. Boelcke, *Wollt Ihr den totalen Krieg? Die geheimen Goebbels-Konferenzen, 1939–1943* (Munich, 1969), 387, entry for Aug. 24, 1942.

output.[62] In April 1942 the Security Service of the SS reported that many people were convinced that the United States had lots of idle capacities whereas Germany had only very limited room to expand its armament production.[63] The further military developments corroborated these popular views of the United States. The successful campaign in North Africa, the invasion of Sicily and mainland Italy, the strategic bombing of German cities, and, finally, the allied invasion of France convinced more and more Germans that they were facing a strong and determined enemy and not a weak, degenerate America. For young flak helpers who were no longer willing to accept the values of National Socialism, American pilots served as a role model on which they could project their innermost longings and fantasies.[64]

Goebbels, however, attributed the lack of strong opposition in the West to the fact that "the German people considers Anglo-Americans to be more humane than the Russians."[65] However, it was not only the comparison with the Russians that compelled the war-weary population to see the United States as a beacon of hope in the darkness of the final phase of the war, but also the increasingly terrorist nature of the Nazi regime itself, which had started to turn against the general population. Therefore, working-class people expressed their hopes that "if America dictates the peace it will not be so bad. They will only try to conduct their business and, therefore, their capitalist entrepreneurs will be in need of the Germans."[66] Equally, members of the bourgeoisie saw some benefits in the specter of an American occupation because they were hoping that the postwar economy would be more liberal than it had been under the Nazi regime. Pragmatic farmers in the western provinces of the Reich did not hurry with harvesting their crops in the fall of 1944 since they were betting on a timely arrival of American troops, in order to sell their products for U.S. dollars rather than for worthless reichsmarks.[67] As ambivalent as they had been and still were, in 1944–5 Germans were ready to embrace the Americans for a second time this century.

62 Heinz Boberach, ed., *Meldungen aus dem Reich, 1938–1945: Die geheimen Lageberichte des Sicherheitsdienstes der SS*, 17 vols. (Herrsching, 1984), 3:154, report no. 250, Jan. 12, 1942.
63 Ibid., 3639, report no. 277, Apr. 20, 1942.
64 Cf. Rolf Schörken, *Luftwaffenhelfer und Drittes Reich: Die Entstehung eines politischen Bewusstseins* (Stuttgart, 1984), 142–3.
65 Joseph Goebbels, *Tagebücher*, ed. Ralf Georg Reuth, 5 vols. (Munich, 1992), 5:2180–1.
66 Boberach, ed., *Meldungen aus dem Reich*, 6052, report of Nov. 22, 1943.
67 Quoted by Klaus-Dietmar Henke, *Die amerikanische Besetzung Deutschlands* (Munich, 1995), 92.

12

Cultural Migration

Artists and Visual Representation Between Americans and Germans During the 1930s and 1940s

MARION F. DESHMUKH

> On the day I lost my passport I discovered, at the age of fifty-eight, that losing one's native land implies more than parting with a circumscribed area of soil.
>
> —Stephan Zweig, 1943

> Propaganda is something entirely different from art.... you'd better keep in touch with the popular "illustrators." ... they really reach the "beloved" masses.... I'm rather sceptical, we can do very little about [fascism]. Don't overrate the meaning of our "outmoded" profession.
>
> —George Grosz, 1936

The theme of this volume is expansive enough that it can describe a plethora of historical interactions between the old world and the new. America's long relationship with Germany turned problematic once Hitler assumed power in 1933. The severe economic depression, growing militarism, the troubling tales by exiles, all shaped American visions of Germany during the 1930s and 1940s.[1] Recently, the art historian M. Kay Flavell wrote of a

continuing need to trace the continuities and discontinuities between artists ... in exile and the cultural traditions from which they came. We need to

---

[1] For a revealing description of problematic U.S.-German relations in the pre-World War I period, see Frank Trommler's "Inventing the Enemy: German-American Cultural Relations, 1900–1917," in Hans-Jürgen Schröder, ed., *Confrontation and Cooperation: Germany and the United States in the Era of World War I, 1900–1923* (Providence, R.I., 1993), 99–125.

consider how far works produced in a new cultural setting may still be conceived as a contribution to that other tradition, at the same time as they also seek to represent the new environment.[2]

This chapter schematically illuminates three aspects of the German-American encounter. First, it describes the reactions to the events in Europe of two major groups of American artists and art critics. How did American painters respond, both politically and aesthetically, to the totalitarian threats? The decade witnessed heated debates among American painters over the political uses of international modernism versus American regionalism. These debates spilled over into acrimonious ideological discussions between and among artists. Second, it outlines the role German painters played in the United States once they arrived here in the wake of unsettling events in Germany. Those artists can be seen both as symbols of cultural freedom from fascism and as teachers of American art students, instructing those students in often contradictory aesthetic visions. Finally, these remarks address the impact of émigré art dealers upon the American art scene during the 1930s, particularly in relation to publicizing and promoting European modernism. Both the arrival of émigré artists and intellectuals and American aesthetic responses to them provide an interesting angle of vision for understanding German-American relationships during an extremely tumultuous decade.

By the end of World War II, American perceptions of European art had broadened and altered, and New York had replaced Paris and Berlin as the home of Europe's artistic avant-garde. Over seven hundred painters and sculptors migrated to the United States from Europe between 1933 and 1944. These figures do not include museum officials, art dealers, or art historians.[3] The abstract expressionist artist Robert Motherwell once reminisced that, during the war years, one could simply walk down the streets of New York and converse with approximately twenty famous European artists – who included, in addition to German exiles, French, Italian, and Russian artists.[4] As one scholar felicitously phrased it, "one

---

2 M. Kay Flavell, *George Grosz: A Biography* (New Haven, Conn., 1988), 302. Flavell concentrates on George Grosz's years in America. For the artistic exile experience in other countries, see the 1980 exhibition catalogue, *Widerstand statt Anpassung: Deutsche Kunst im Widerstand gegen den Faschismus, 1933–1945*, ed. Badischer Kunstverein, in cooperation with the Elefanten Press (Berlin, 1980). Among the approximately one hundred artists migrating to London were Oskar Kokoschka and John Heartfield. Other artistic centers included Prague and Paris before the Nazi occupation of Czechoslovakia and France (*Widerstand statt Anpassung*, 237).
3 Maurice R. Davie, *Refugees in America: Report of the Committee for the Study of Recent Immigraton from Europe* (New York, 1947), 324.
4 "An Interview with Robert Motherwell," *Artforum* 41 (Sept. 1965): 35.

should not lose sight of another important, unsung educational institution in which German and Austrian émigré art specialists functioned informally, which might best be entitled the Free University of 57th Street and Madison Avenue."[5]

Despite their crucial contributions to the American cultural scene, foreign artists and art dealers faced several disadvantages. Language was among the most critical, but also important were a loss of patronage networks together with social and cultural connections.[6] Compounding the problem of relocation was the fact that the Depression had put approximately one quarter out of an estimated forty thousand American artists out of work. New Deal projects such as the WPA provided limited funding for American artists, but none for foreign refugees.[7] In some cases, American enthusiasm for émigré art instructors was also lukewarm, given the scarcity of Depression-era jobs. For example, even as late as 1944, the American Artists Professional League protested to the New York City Board of Higher Education over the appointment of an émigré as chair of an art department.

[The League] would be remiss in its duty to American artists if it did not protest vigorously, both against the notable discrimination and against this infiltration and teaching of their alien ideologies in an American college which is supported by American taxpayers.[8]

Additionally, as Lewis Coser has noted, U.S. professional and technical requirements, the "rules of the game," could be quite unfamiliar to refugees: "The rules of the games intellectuals play differ between nations, and unfortunately for the referee, it is usually the natives who define how the game is to be played."[9] Finally, the complex issue of influence, whether aesthetic or, more broadly, cultural, is difficult to analyze since, as Colin Eisler (himself a refugee of ten when arriving in the United

---

5 Colin Eisler, "*Kunstgeschichte* American Style," in Donald Fleming and Bernard Bailyn, eds., *The Intellectual Migration* (Cambridge, Mass., 1969), 597. Eisler's very informative essay describes the crucial role scholarly art historians played in transforming the academic enterprise in art history during and after the 1930s and 1940s. He also discusses the importance of artists, curators, and dealers. See also Erwin Panofsky's erudite and often amusing recollections in "Three Decades of Art History in the United States: Impressions of a Transplanted European," in Erwin Panofsky, *Meaning in the Visual Arts* (New York, 1955), 321–46.
6 Davie cites a refugee painter estimating his weekly painting expenses, creating severe financial hardship: "Rent and light for studio and living accommodations: $9.00; [average] expenses for brushes, paint, pastel, canvases: $6.00; model, $6.00" (Stuart Davie, *Refugees in America*, 329).
7 Flavell, *George Grosz*, 82. Cf. Francis V. O'Conner, *The New Deal Art Projects: An Anthology of Memoirs* (Washington, D.C., 1972).
8 Quoted in Davie, *Refugees in America*, 328.
9 Lewis A. Coser, *Refugee Scholars in America: Their Impact and Their Experiences* (New Haven, Conn., 1984), xii.

States from Hamburg in 1941) has suggested, "One is influenced by whatever one wants or is prepared to be influenced by, with as little rocking the boat as possible."[10]

Taken as a group, however, most artists were treated well by their American counterparts; several museums held exhibitions to highlight the émigré artists' oeuvre. A number of painters found work to supplement their often erratic and unpredictable sales opportunities, usually by teaching at art schools or colleges. Several important art dealers continued their occupation in New York and other American cities, founding art galleries and enriching private and public collections with contemporary European art which they or fellow émigrés brought from Germany and which they exhibited and sold to museums.[11]

What sort of artistic milieu awaited émigré artists upon landing in the United States? A broad survey of the American art landscape during the 1930s and early 1940s reveals two major coteries of painters. One included leftist artists grouped around the John Reed Clubs, and, later, the American Artists' Congress, an association founded in 1935 to promote the policies of the Popular Front. It accommodated an aesthetically diverse coalition who fiercely condemned fascism. Included were abstract artists, such as Stuart Davis, as well as social realist painters and illustrators, such as Ben Shahn and William Gropper. The majority of these painters resided in New York. At the time of its founding, the American Artists' Congress's national chairman, Stuart Davis, wrote to a prospective member that "we do not say that you have to join any political party ... in order to fight fascism. All we ask is that artists who realize the real threat of fascism come together."[12] During the 1930s these artists held numerous exhibits and meetings to denounce fascism's pernicious effects on the visual arts. They apprehensively followed current events through the periodical press, newspapers, and contacts with European leftists and communists.

A month after Hitler's appointment as German chancellor, an exhibition of socially committed art opened in New York.

10 Eisler, "*Kunstgeschichte* American Style," 626.
11 For example, the Paul Drey Gallery, on 57th Street in New York City, specialized in both Old Masters and contemporary European art. It opened as a branch of Munich's A. S. Drey in the 1920s and was run by Paul Drey. His wife Elisabeth managed the gallery after his death in 1953. Paul Drey had been a student of the sociologist Alfred Weber and his 1910 social history of German artists, *Die wirtschaftlichen Grundlagen der Malkunst*, is a key monograph on the history of German painting at the turn of the century (letter to author from Emily Fleischmann, secretary, Paul Drey Gallery, July 25, 1983).
12 Stuart Davis to Rockwell Kent, Jan. 29, 1936, Rockwell Kent papers, Archives of American Art, Washington, D.C., quoted in Cecile Whiting, *Anti-Fascism in American Art* (New Haven, Conn., 1989), 39. Whiting's monograph is the fullest account to date of the politics of American art in the 1930s and 1940s.

In a bare loft on lower Sixth Avenue, a significant exhibition of paintings, sculpture, water colors, and prints, provocatively labelled "The Social View Point in Art," was held last month by the John Reed Club of New York. . . . George Grosz, Käthe Kollwitz, Abramovitz, Irwin D. Hoffman and Adolf Dehn contributed sardonic observations, trenchant caricatures, and poignant sketches in black-and-white.[13]

The critic went on to observe that

the club's decision to open its doors to many social viewpoints and varying degrees of class consciousness was responsible for an exhibition, not only interesting as a cross-section of the proletarian ideology that is coloring artistic expression today, but impressive because of its high average of technical facility.[14]

In addition to the social realists (a term deliberately utilized in contrast to the communist artists, ideologically dependent on Soviet models and labeled socialist realists), another type of narrative realism as an aesthetic style could be found among the American scene painters, also called American regionalists. During the Great Depression years, critics aesthetically linked social realism and American regionalism, yet noted their very different political ideologies. The two schools sought a realistic idiom to convey the unique characteristics of urban life on the one hand and rural life, on the other. The socialist realists emphasized and decried the abuses of capitalism in their art and in their politics, looking to the utopian plans in the Soviet Union as positive and possible ameliorative influences. The American regionalists shunned foreign models, both political and artistic, searching instead for native sources to inspire their art. Painters such as Grant Wood, Thomas Hart Benton, or John Steuart Curry represented the regionalist school.

The frightening uncertainties of the Depression, particularly for artists, dealers, and museums, combined with the growing threat of war and fascism, induced a number of American artists to embrace social realism, using it to graphically portray society's ills. Social realism bore traits of Weimar Germany's *Neue Sachlichkeit*, a generally leftist commitment to the little man, the worker, and a distrust, if not dislike, for the capitalist exploiter. The work of several social realists, particularly Gropper and Jack Levine, showed affinities to the art of George Grosz during his Weimar years. As one commentator has noted, "American art was searching for a style at the time Social Realism was urging its

---

13 Gertrude Benson, "Art and Social Theories," *Creative Arts*, 12, no. 3, Mar. 1933, reprinted in David Shapiro, ed., *Social Realism: Art as a Weapon* (New York, 1973), 79–80.
14 Benson, "Art and Social Theories," 80.

claims.... Although the Armory Show (1913) had introduced abstraction to America, it had never overcome the inertia of America's distrust of it as foreign and inimical to native thought."[15] Although the Social Realists looked to the new political and economic experiments in the Soviet Union for ideological reference, their art had Ashcan school elements and reflected the muckraking tones of social criticism common at the turn of the century. The artists used their acid pens and paintbrushes to target the Rockefellers, big business, big finance, and plutocratic capitalists. Similarly, they felt an affinity to the social commentary inherent in the prints of Kollwitz and Grosz in particular.

The second group of American artists, the regionalists, or American scene painters, avoided the New York art world, preferring to remain in the Midwest, where their art was popularly associated with realist depictions of rural life. These artists questioned modernism's value to the general public, seeing in cubism, abstraction, and other forms of the avant-garde idiom an incomprehensibility that distanced art from its natural public.[16] Midwestern painters questioned the ideology of the American Artists' Congress or AAC. Indeed, the AAC promoted the leftist, antifascist policies of the Popular Front. That organization was comprised not only of painters but also of art historians, critics, and journalists. Its membership, for its part, denounced the regionalists as artists who could have safely practiced their profession in Nazi Germany; critics saw little difference between the realist anecdotal genre art favored by Hitler and the indigenous American art espoused by the American scene painters.[17] The regionalists responded by viewing their patriotic art as a national bulwark in the promotion of democracy against fascism. For example, Grant Wood's famous 1939 painting, *Parson Weems' Fable* (Figure 12.1), illustrated, according to the artist,

> that a colorful part of [America's] heritage is being lost as a result of the work of analytical historians and debunking biographers.... I sincerely hope that this painting will help reawaken interest in ... bits of American folklore that are too good to lose. In our present unsettled times, when democracy is threatened on all sides, the preservation of our folklore is more important than is generally realized.[18]

The regionalist artists' own efforts to support American propaganda once the United States entered the war further discredited the group. Its critics

---

15 David Shapiro, "Introduction," in Shapiro, ed., *Social Realism*, 6.
16 Cf. Wanda Corn, *Grant Wood: The Regionalist Vision* (New Haven, Conn., 1983).
17 Whiting, *Anti-Fascism in American Art*, 99.
18 Quoted in ibid., 100.

Figure 12.1. Grant Wood, *Parson Weems' Fable*, 1939. Oil on canvas, 38 3/8" × 50 1/8". Amon Carter Museum, Fort Worth, Texas. Reproduced by permission.

continued to deride the regionalists for being both nationalistic and propagandistic; indeed, the émigré art historian H. W. Janson exclaimed after the war that "almost every one of the ideas constituting the regionalist credo could be matched more or less verbatim with the writings of Nazi experts on art."[19]

During the debates between the American Artists' Congress and the regionalists, some critics saw the arrival of refugee artists as an aesthetic corrective to isolationism. R. H. Turnbull, quoted in the January 1, 1942, *Art Digest*, observed

in the long run American art will probably profit greatly by the presence of stimulating and challenging personalities in our midst. For the blunt fact is that American artists have always tended to be timid and backward in theorizing about their work, and there are even "Regional Schools," self-styled, which

19 H. W. Janson, "Benton and Wood: Champions of Regionalism," *Magazine of Art* 39 (May 1946): 186.

pride themselves on assuming an ostrich-like attitude toward any intellectual development or activity...."[20]

Thus, when German artists arrived in the United States, they faced a series of continuing disputes over international modernism versus regionalist and isolationist impulses. The Germans, mainly working in New York, obviously felt greater affinity to their American social realist and abstractionist colleagues than to the American scene painters.

Included among German artists migrating to the United States were a small number of well-known Weimar painters, such as Grosz, Josef Albers, Herbert Bayer, and Hans Hofmann. Eugen Spiro, president of the Berlin Secession from 1916 to 1933, also left Germany. American artists, particularly those on the political left, quickly recognized the connection between exiles such as Grosz and their own socially connected art. What were these connections? They are not always easily visualized, since, with the exception of Grosz, the political and social commitments of other artists and teachers, such as Hofmann, Albers, or the Bauhaus architects, were in fact more ambiguous.[21] Even Grosz, the most politically radical artist to emigrate in the wake of Nazism's rise, avoided political activism once he arrived in America. When invited to attend a meeting protesting fascism organized by Heinrich Mann, Grosz declined, writing, "I refrain from taking part in such meetings for the simple reason that I do not believe that they will have any really positive results.... This in no way affects my complete opposition to Hitler."[22]

What impact, then, did the exiles have on the American art scene during the 1930s? Over the last several decades, numerous participants have recalled their experiences during those years, and subsequent scholarly treatments have examined the exiles' encounter with America. Similarly, American artists have described their aesthetic and social debts to Germans, especially to the progressive Weimar "culture industry." By examining these narratives, the cultural symbiosis between Germans and Americans – along with missed opportunities and misperceptions – becomes clearer.

20 R. H. Turnbull of the *San Francisco Argonaut*, quoted in *Art Digest*, Jan. 1, 1942, cited in Davie, *Refugees in America*, 332.
21 "Mies [van der Rohe] did not leave Germany until 1938. He has been criticized for his delayed departure; but his apolitical posture, coupled with his loyalty to Germany and a phobia against travel... account at least in part for his reluctance to leave" (William Jordy, "The Aftermath of the Bauhaus in America: Gropius, Mies, and Breuer," in Fleming and Bailyn, eds., *The Intellectual Migration*, 501). On Albers, see the exhibition catalog, *Paintings by Josef Albers: Yale University Art Gallery, New Haven, Conn., Feb. 22-March 26, 1978* (New Haven, Conn., 1978); Neal Benezra, *The Murals and Sculpture of Josef Albers* (New York, 1985).
22 Letter to Kurt Rosenwald, Jan. 27, 1936, quoted in Flavell, *George Grosz*, 152.

At the outset, one can observe several distinctive features of the American-German aesthetic connection during these years: German painters as well as designers and architects, such as the famed Bauhaus founders Walter Gropius and Ludwig Mies van der Rohe, substantially promoted and fostered the development of American abstract art, modernist architecture, and advances in commercial and industrial design during the 1930s and 1940s. The Bauhaus architects, for instance, taught at major universities and attempted to transplant the functionalist idiom into the new American setting. These architects were familiar with the works of Frank Lloyd Wright and Louis Sullivan, and saw in the United States a fertile ground for expanding modernist architecture. According to a contemporary observer, after the arrival of Gropius, every "little school of architecture has had at least to take into account the new teachings."[23]

Because of economic instability, growing threats of war, xenophobia, and anti-Semitism, European artists and intellectuals saw America as a haven, in some cases permanent, in others temporary. For a few, the United States appeared to be a strange paradise indeed. At a 1930s Hollywood party, for example, Thomas Mann was rather startled at being addressed as "Tommy" by a movie producer.[24] Americans' instant informality appeared forced and unseemly to the more formal Central Europeans, some of whom avoided multicolored sports shirts in favor of three-piece suits. Likewise, many Americans viewed the European exiles with a mixture of awe and curiosity, admiring them for their erudition and cultivation, yet not always comprehending the cultural context from whence they came. The more socially engaged American artists of the 1930s were acquainted with the satiric caricatures of Grosz, and several Americans had studied with Hofmann in Munich during the 1920s. For the most part, however, American artists had limited knowledge of German creative efforts.

The exiled artists and intellectuals initially found sustenance among fellow expatriates. Although American newspapers and the periodical press regularly ran stories of Nazi cultural policies, about five years elapsed before Americans realized the extent to which fascism had affected the arts. Emigré dealers and collectors brought with them examples of art rejected by the Nazis. But only after Hitler's notorious "Degenerate Art"

---

23 Anonymous architect quoted in Davie, *Refugees in America*, 368.
24 Cited in Jarrell C. Jackman, "German Emigrés in Southern California," in Jarrell C. Jackman and Carla M. Borden, eds., *The Muses Flee Hitler: Cultural Transfer and Adaptation, 1930–1945* (Washington, D.C., 1983), 109.

Figure 12.2. William Gropper, "One Must Have the Courage to Deliver Europe from the Bolshevik Plague," drawing published in *Liberator*, June 6, 1923. Photography courtesy of the Library of Congress, Washington, D.C.

exhibition in 1937 had showcased Nazi contempt for artistic modernism did Americans in general, in addition to the exiles and the small American intellectual community, begin to take serious notice of the relationship between art and politics.[25] They saw the threats posed by German

---

25 The two leading periodicals that regularly covered cultural events in Germany during the 1930s were the *Art Digest* and *Art News*.

antimodernism and admired the exiled and rejected artists as exemplars of the democratic cause.

This admiration for the Germans already began in a very circumscribed way during the 1920s. In that decade, a small number of American radical artists saw an affinity between the biting graphics of George Grosz and American politics, especially with the Republican "return to normalcy" heralding a break with the Wilsonian call for democratic engagement in world affairs. In the early 1920s, the United States experienced a wave of anti-Bolshevism, epitomized by the Palmer Raids in 1923. Fearful that recent radical immigrants had brought the Bolshevik infection to American shores of the United States, American officials during the 1920s took advantage of intensified antiforeign sentiments to enact new and more restrictive immigration laws. In the year of the Palmer Raids, Gropper, subsequently the best known antifascist illustrator, created a graphic work published in the *Liberator*, which, in style and substance, could have been executed by George Grosz himself. The pen-and-ink drawing, titled "One Must Have the Courage to Deliver Europe from the Bolshevist Plague" (Figure 12.2), shows a military officer cavalierly and ruthlessly shooting what appears to be an innocent victim. Stylistically, the drawing echoes Grosz's graphic techniques to the letter, particularly if one compares it to the German artist's graphics dating back to the beginning of World War I. Grosz's graphics were published in several radical American magazines during the 1920s (Figure 12.3).

By the 1930s, when the growing fascist threat appeared more obvious to Americans, New York galleries held several exhibits of Grosz's and Kollwitz's works on paper. Kollwitz remained in Germany throughout the Nazi period, despite the fact that she was dismissed from the Prussian Academy of Art in 1933 and her art was banned from exhibition. She died in Germany in 1945. Two traveling Kollwitz exhibitions, one arranged by the College Art Association in 1934–5 and the second by the American Federation of Arts, enlarged her American audiences.[26] In 1937 a solo exhibit sponsored by the Hollywood Anti-Nazi League for the Defense of American Democracy took place in Los Angeles; the author Ernst Toller spoke on that occasion, and its patrons included Oscar Hammerstein II.[27] American critics identified Grosz's caricatures with a

---

26 In a 1937 letter describing congratulatory letters for her seventieth birthday, Kollwitz writes, "I am very happy about the deep and wide response my life work has had. . . . outside of Germay also. God knows, I can be happy about that" (letter of July 15, 1937, in Hans Kollwitz, ed., *The Diary and Letters of Käthe Kollwitz* [1955; reprinted: Evanston, Ill., 1988], 174).
27 Hildegard Bachert, "Collecting the Art of Käthe Kollwitz: A Survey of Collections, Collectors, and Public Response in Germany and the United States," in Elizabeth Prelinger, ed., *Käthe Kollwitz*, exhibition catalogue (Washington, D.C., 1992), 126–7.

Figure 12.3. George Grosz, "Prost, Noske! The Young Revolution Is Dead," drawing published in *The New Masses*, April 2, 1927. Courtesy of the Archives of American Art, Washington, D.C.

consistent leftist stance against militarism and clerical conservatism, together with a propensity to lay bare bourgeois hypocrisies. Kollwitz's graphics, while powerful and evocative, represented broader, more generalized universal and humanitarian themes that the Nazis had dismissed as "Bolshevik." Although quite different in their subjects and techniques, Kollwitz's and Grosz's art represented, both to American social realist artists and to a politically sophisticated art public, a visual vehicle with which to denounce Nazi barbarism. That the Nazi government labeled Grosz's art "degenerate," had revoked his citizenship, and had prohibited Kollwitz from exhibiting, forcing her into an inner exile, meant that these artists represented the "other" Germany visually as Thomas Mann represented it verbally and in print. A later observer noted that

> The acid pen of George Grosz had once been the scourge of German profiteers, and his water colors, done with a blurred technique and colors which looked like bloodstains on the paper, had held a distorting mirror, as he said, to the face of hideous reality. Now he found refuge in America and although there was some of that earlier ferocity in his over-dressed Manhattan promenaders, the American Grosz was done with politics; his thoughts turned inward and his vitriol was diluted. He painted his own face brooding among the smoke and ruins of a Europe he could not forget; in his *Wanderer* [Figure 12.4] an old man stumbled through iridescent mud among thickets and brambles, a human spirit in a world of terror, behind him an explosion like a burst of bleeding flesh.[28]

The personal apprehensions Grosz felt for relatives still in Germany and the worsening situation in that country meant that his art had less of a relationship to the American scene than to unfolding events in Europe. His aesthetic gaze toward Europe was noted by several critics, even though Grosz did paint American images. Art exhibitions often paired Grosz and Kollwitz as the preeminent socially engaged graphic artists, the former in exile, the latter in internal exile, both representing an antifascist critique of contemporary society to their more constricted circle of patrons and audiences.

One way this constricted circle widened was through the role of émigré dealers and collectors in advancing Americans' knowledge of formerly rather obscure artists. The émigré dealers had university training, in most cases in Germany, and their connoisseurship was wide-ranging. Among the dealers who long had connections with old master paintings and drawings as well as European modernism were sophisticated individuals such as Tannhauser and Drey of Munich, Paul Rosenberg, and

---

28 Oliver W. Larkin, "Common Cause," in *Art and Life in America* (1949), reprinted in Shapiro, *Social Realism*, 133.

Figure 12.4. George Grosz, "Even Mud Has an End," plate 4, drawing, published in *Interregnum*, 1936. Basis for the oil painting "The Wanderer," 1943. Photograph courtesy of the National Gallery of Art, Washington, D.C. Reproduced by permission of the Estate of George Grosz, Princeton, N.J.

especially Curt Valentin, who astutely promoted American and European sculptors, such as Lipschitz and Alexander Calder.[29] The dealers helped finance and promote the art of émigré painters and graphic artists whose markets had disappeared in Europe. During the Great Depression, American museums faced financial hardships and extremely constrained acquisition budgets, which severely limited the chances for German artists' being bought for their collections. Accordingly, if small sums were available for purchases of contemporary art, American artists had priority over

---

29 On New York dealers generally, see Germain Seligman, *Merchants of Art, 1880–1960: Eighty Years of Professional Collecting* (New York, 1961); Steven W. Naifeh, *Culture Making: Money, Success, and the New York Art World* (Princeton, N.J., 1976); Diana Crane, *The Transformation of the Avant-Garde: The New York Art World, 1940–1985* (Chicago, 1987), esp. chap. 6.

recently-arrived immigrants from Europe. Thus, dealers often served as the financial guardian angels for artists whose public had virtually evaporated. One of the earliest Kollwitz print collectors was the Baltimore dealer Ferdinand Roten. (Obviously, Kollwitz herself could not benefit from Roten's efforts.) Through his gallery, later sold to Brentano's during the 1970s, he disseminated literally hundreds of Kollwitz prints to Americans, beginning in 1933 with an exhibit of her work at the Worcester Art Museum, an event which preceded the more widely circulated exhibitions of the CAA and AFA.[30]

Emigré collectors and dealers, such as Roten, Valentin, and others, brought with them examples of German modernism, making available prints, graphics and paintings which Americans could now appreciate, often for the first time. By sponsoring exhibits at small museums, and by using paintings and prints brought with them, the dealers gave legitimacy to the German artists' oeuvre. They brought with them works of art, particularly contemporary German paintings and graphics, which eventually found their way into private collections and American museums in New York, St. Louis, and Minneapolis. Thus, for example, Carl O. Schniewind of the Chicago Art Institute and Carl Zigrosser of the Philadelphia Museum of Art were early collectors of Kollwitz for their museums.[31] The St. Etienne Gallery in New York City served and continues to serve as a primary exhibition venue for modernist Central European art. Thus exposed to German works, American artists' dependence on exclusively French models lessened. A small but significant number of specialist émigré dealers also promoted graphics, an art form that had not been popular among serious collectors before the 1930s. Emigré patrons helped artists like Grosz survive the uncertainties of life in the new world.[32] Private and public collections of works on paper became an accepted enterprise beginning in the 1930s.

World War I, the uneasy relationship between Germany and the United States during the first part of the 1920s, and, after 1933, the deteriorating political relations between the two countries had obscured German modernism's legacy for Americans. The School of Paris rather than German painting of Berlin or Munich represented the avant-garde and "pure painting" to most Americans. The émigré artists, dealers, and

---

30 Bachert, "Collecting the Art of Käthe Kollwitz," 127. See also Marion Deshmukh, Interview with Ferdinand Roten, Baltimore, Nov. 23, 1974.
31 Bachert, "Collecting the Art of Käthe Kollwitz," 129.
32 Grosz received regular support from I. B. Neumann and Erich Cohn. Cf. Flavell, *George Grosz*, 85, 98.

collectors, however, managed – figuratively and literally – to bridge the cultural divide between America and the European modernist aesthetic legacy.

American artists' understanding of Central European cultural contributions were modified through actual personal contacts within the museum, art school, university, and art galleries of the United States. American artists and key figures in the academic and commercial art scene became acutely involved in the plight of Germans who had fled totalitarianism. German émigré artists arriving in the United States absorbed "American efficiency," while their American students acquired "German methodology."[33] In a 1940 talk at an exhibition of Frank Lloyd Wright's work at the Museum of Modern Art, Mies van der Rohe suggested that "The more we were absorbed in the study of [Wright's] creations, the greater became our admiration for his incomparable talent.... the dynamic impulse emanating from his work invigorated a whole generation."[34] German painters and teachers, such as Albers and Hofmann, linked system and method to the American penchant for "action," anticipating the American abstract expressionists Jackson Pollock and Willem de Kooning during the 1940s. Americans' understanding of the troubling cultural events in the Third Reich was mediated through the influx of cultural refugees.

A number of painters not only had an impact on the major art centers such as New York by their presence but also by teaching at both obscure and famous universities. Albers, a key figure of the Bauhaus, along with Gropius, Mies van der Rohe, Bayer, and Lionel Feininger, had arrived in the United States in the wake of the Nazi takeover. Albers taught at the remote Black Mountain College in the South before joining the staff at Yale University during the 1940s; he remained in New Haven until 1960. Albers's influence was especially tangible, as he taught more or less continuously from the 1930s through the 1950s. The émigré artists struggled to earn a living through teaching, since sales by even very partisan and enthusiastic dealers were uncertain and problematic. Having initially come to New York before Hitler's takeover, Grosz taught at the Art Students' League, where employment as an instructor allowed him to achieve relative material security. He also received a Guggenheim fellowship in the late 1930s, which freed him to paint and not teach for two years. Hofmann, another émigré artist who arrived shortly before Hitler's

---

33 Jordy, "Aftermath of the Bauhaus in America," 491–2.
34 Quoted in ibid., 489.

appointment as Chancellor, taught at his own immensely popular 8th Street School.

Born in Germany in 1880, studying in Munich at the turn of the century and influenced by the Secession exhibits then on view in the Bavarian capital, Hofmann emigrated to the United States in the early 1930s, setting up his school in 1933 after teaching briefly at the Art Students' League. He has subsequently been admired as the "greatest art teacher of the twentieth century, that is, if a teacher's stature is measured by the number of students who achieve national and international renown in their own right."[35] Hofmann influenced two generations of Americans through his instruction: those who studied with him during the 1930s and those who attended the New York School in the 1950s, including some of the major practitioners of abstract expressionism, such as Robert Motherwell, Pollock, Mark Rothko, Clyfford Still, and William Baziotes. Hofmann had an extraordinary impact on American art students. Again, in the rather hyperbolic view of Irving Sandler:

> The earlier generation's need was to join the mainstream of modern art by mastering Cubism and other modern isms. Hofmann could teach them how to make a modern picture – the basics. . . . Stressing the self-sufficiency (indeed, the sanctity) of art while claiming that it could illuminate the working of the universe, his theorizing – conveyed with powerful conviction – was most attractive to the ideology-prone artists of the Great Depression who wanted to justify abstract art in the face of the prevailing Marxist and nationalistic rhetoric that condemned it as either ivory-tower escapism or unAmerican. Almost half of the charter members of the American Abstract Artists, comprising virtually the entire avantgarde of the 1930s, had studied with Hofmann. Although he himself was unsympathetic to geometric abstraction, his former students embraced it in part because of his emphasis on Cubist drawing which was its forerunner.[36]

Hofmann's credo, that "every art expression is rooted fundamentally in the personality and in the temperament of the artist," recalls the late nineteenth-century German and French painterly tradition, particularly the postimpressionists, Fauves, and Secessionists.[37] Young American painters looked to Hofmann as the transmitter of the European tradition, especially School of Paris painting; he was particularly familiar with the latter, having worked and befriended the Parisian artists during the decade before World War I. The critic Clement Greenberg wrote in 1945 that

---

35 Irving Sandler, "Hans Hofmann: The Dialectical Man," in Cynthia Goodman et al., eds., *Hans Hofmann* (New York, 1990), 86. Hofmann's American students included (some of whom studied with him in Munich during the 1920s): Alfred Jensen, Louise Nevelson, and Cameron Booth.
36 Sandler, "Hans Hofmann," 86.
37 Hans Hofmann, "Address," 1941, cited in Sandler, "Hans Hofmann," 165.

"Hans Hofmann is in all probability the most important teacher of our time." He had "grasped the issues at stake better than all the others who tried to 'explicate' the recent revolution in painting."[38] Throughout his career as painter and teacher, the German artist attempted to educate his American students toward an appreciation of the French school while simultaneously stressing the critical importance of pure painting, achieved through direct teaching and through his lectures. As a result of Nazi denunciations of both social satire and modern abstraction, by the late 1930s abstraction had come to be seen in the United States as a nonreferential aesthetic counterpoint to totalitarian realist dogmatism.[39]

In 1991–2, three major American museums cooperated in an exhibition that reconstructed the infamous Munich "Degenerate Art" show of 1937.[40] Prior to the 1937 exhibit in Germany, little publicity had been given to Nazi antimodernist pronouncements. Nor had much attention been paid to Hitler's ferocious xenophobic speeches during the mid-1930s, which extolled the virtues of German art over foreign models. But the "Degenerate Art" show, with its blatant ridicule of contemporary art, appeared to demonstrate to Americans the relationship between antimodernist rhetoric and totalitarianism. Stuart Davis's eloquent denunciation of the Nazi-sponsored exhibition revealed the connection, and further illustrated the idea that simply dismissing the government's art policies as subsidiary to politics was ill-advised. Commenting on Hitler's antimodernist attacks on the visual arts, the artist denounced its implications for society in general:

Because fascism denies democracy in culture just as it denies democracy in science and government, those who would theoretically liquidate art as a reactionary art should give thought to the social implications of their argument. Carried to its logical social conclusion it is an argument against democracy and the peoples' front. It is an argument for totalitarianism.[41]

To Davis, totalitarian art and politics were intimately linked. The "Degenerate Art" exhibition displayed and pilloried five Grosz paintings, two of his watercolors, and thirteen graphics. In letters denouncing the exhi-

---

38 Sandler, "Hans Hofmann," 93.
39 A number of art historians have questioned the apparently apolitical nature of American abstract expressionism, viewing it as integral to post-1945 Cold War ideology. Cf. Serge Guilbaut, *How New York Stole the Idea of Modern Art: Abstract Expressionism, Freedom, and the Cold War* (Chicago, 1983).
40 Cf. Stephanie Barron et al., *"Degenerate Art": The Fate of the Avant-Garde in Nazi Germany*, Los Angeles County Musuem of Art (Los Angeles, 1991). The exhibit was shown at Chicago's Art Institute and the Smithsonian Institution, Washington, D.C., before it traveled to Berlin.
41 Stuart Davis papers, Aug. 27, 1937, quoted in Whiting, *Anti-Fascism in American Art*, 76.

bition, Grosz lamented the fact that "in Germany I am now regarded as one of the madmen, 'Art Bolshevists.' or whatever their term is."[42]

After 1945, a number of émigré artists, including Grosz and the French painters Marc Chagall and Fernand Léger, returned to a physically desolate and culturally shattered Europe. Other artists remained in America, including the architects Gropius and Mies van der Rohe and the painters Hofmann and Albers. Their impact on American culture was critical, both during the interwar years and after 1945. Architects such as Gropius and Mies van der Rohe played an obvious and tangible role through their building projects and their teaching. Gropius was fifty-four when he arrived in the United States, Mies in his late forties. As one American admirer noted: "America could not have nurtured Mies, Europe could have not fulfilled his promises. He has perhaps gained more, and given more, to the US than any other émigré outside the realm of atomic physics."[43] Likewise, Hofmann and Albers mentored several generations of art students in the vocabulary of modernism. There can be no doubt that the interaction between German and American artists, art historians, museum officials, and dealers during the tumultuous 1930s and 1940s demonstrates the critical importance of German contributions to American aesthetic developments. The American cultural scene was unquestionably enriched and enlarged through the elements of encounter summarized previously: The German artists both taught and exhibited, thereby transplanting the legacy of modernism to American shores. The art dealers exposed Americans to art discredited by the Nazis. At the same time, however, one can also suggest that the Germany legacy was ambiguous, and tempered by the fact that, for example, Grosz's defining work had been substantially created in Weimar Germany rather than Depression-era and wartime America. For all its brilliance, the Bauhaus did not always manage to enlarge or refine its earlier modernist message after its move to the United States.[44] In short, there were cultural losses and gains from the émigré communities that continue to be calculated in the histories and memories of both Germans and Americans.

---

42 Quoted in Flavell, *George Grosz*, 180. See also Beth Irwin Lewis, *George Grosz: Art and Politics in the Weimar Republic* (Princeton, N.J., 1971; rev. ed.: 1991), 228; Barron et al., *"Degenerate Art"*, 245.
43 Quoted in Laura Fermi, *Illustrious Immigrants* (Chicago, 1968), 236.
44 Leslie Humm Cornier, "Walter Gropius: Emigré Architect, Works and Refuge, England and America in the 30s," Ph.D. diss., Brown University, 1986, 68.

13

Representations of Germans and What Germans Represent

American Film Images and Public Perceptions in the Postwar Era

BEVERLY CRAWFORD AND JAMES MARTEL

INTRODUCTION

The movie "Schindler's List" was a Hollywood sensation. Holocaust survivors, in particular, claimed that the film evoked the reality of their experience. What critics and audiences did not say, however, was that this film was one of a handful in American media history that presented a positive portrayal of a German. Oskar Schindler is, to be sure, a self-centered, smug swindler, vaguely affiliated with the Nazi Party. But unlike the portrayal of most Germans in American film, his character did not carry the baggage of an entire package of stereotypes that accompanies German characters. In him we see a multidimensional character, and by the film's end, Schindler appears to us to be not just a German but a decent individual who struggles to do the right thing in the face of tremendous adversity.

Although this may appear to be an unremarkable achievement, it is a rarity in Hollywood cinematographic history. Prior to this film, no portrayal of Germany was complete without recourse to a series of stereotypes and damning stereotypes at that. We find that virtually all American images of Germans in popular postwar Hollywood films are negative; when a positive image appears, it is often coupled with a negative one. Germans are portrayed as bumbling Prussians with Teutonic rolls of fat and sprouting moustaches; they are monomaniacal mad scientists who engage in unscrupulous experimentation; they are Nazi monsters, sadistic dentists, terrorists, and seductive (but wicked) or blond (but ugly) vamps. The "good" German is shown together with the "evil" one; communal camaraderie and gemütlichkeit are portrayed as the cultural glue that binds Germans together in a frightening and barbaric mission.

Despite these negative images, however, American public opinion surveys suggest Germany's increasing popularity with the public and widespread American identification with Germans. What then, explains Hollywood's particular images of Germans? What is Germany and who are Germans in the minds of Hollywood filmmakers? How are Hollywood images linked with popular perceptions? Have Hollywood images of Germans changed over time? And what larger social, cultural and political issues are represented in these images?

These are important questions because cultural representations and national stereotypes produced in the American media are profoundly political and deeply affect relations between America and Germany. The media portrayal of Germany has wider implications as well; a powerful Hollywood film industry presents an image of Germany and Germans to the world, affecting Germany's relationship with every country on earth. An examination of film images and popular perceptions is especially important in the new and unstable post-Cold War era: The American political elite has been deprived of an enemy that long served to define the self-image of the United States (that is, the Soviet Union); the institutions that provided a set of stable expectations for relations seem no longer relevant; and unification suddenly gives Germany a new role in international relations. In periods of flux and uncertainty, one nation's image of another becomes an important definer of new international relationships.

This chapter explores these national images of Germans and Germany as produced by directors of American films and reflected in public attitudes in the postwar period. We are particularly interested in films and television programs that are part of popular culture and reach a wide audience, although we consider several more "serious" films as well. The discussion is divided into four parts. The first suggests that representations of Germans in American postwar film are dominated by three often overlapping images: Prussian bumblers, mad scientists, and cruel Nazis often juxtaposed against the weaker image of the "good" German. The second section examines how the images have changed throughout the postwar period – how some images come to dominate and others recede. We argue that the dominant image, emerging fully in the 1970s, is that of the stylized Nazi, and that the first two images have merged into the Nazi image. The third and fourth sections of the chapter are devoted to the task of explanation and interpretation; we offer a solution to the puzzle of the discrepancy between negative mass media images and positive public perceptions, and we explore deeper meanings of the stereotypes and what they tell us about American cultural dilemmas.

REPRESENTATIONS OF GERMANS IN
POSTWAR AMERICAN FILMS

It is commonplace to note that stereotypes dominate the images of one culture produced in another. American literary portrayals of Germans are no exception: Throughout American literature we see multifaceted but still stereotypical images of Germans as evil militarists, deranged scientists, bovine women, industrious, honest, economical, obsessively clean, and hardworking people. They are portrayed as gluttons, Huns, and the geniuses of Western civilization.[1] The stereotypes presented in film, however, are less differentiated and contrast sharply with the more complex images of Germans in German films widely distributed in America, that is, "Baghdad Cafe" or "An American Friend." In these films, stereotypical German characteristics, that is, cleanliness, orderliness, and camaraderie can be portrayed in a "normal" or even positive way. This is not the case in American film.

When Germans appear on the American screen, three images dominate. The first is the World War I pig-faced Prussian who was once portrayed as a barbaric bayonetter of babies – but is now transformed into the bumbling and harmless comic figure of "Hogan's Heroes." He still huffs and puffs with an air of official indignation, and growls in guttural officious tones. But the monstrous image of the Teutonic Prussian Hun, dominant in literature and film of the interwar years, has become a parody of himself in the post-World War II period. The epitome of this image is Sergeant Schultz of "Hogan's Heroes," a popular comedy serial produced for American television in the 1960s. Set in a World War II prisoner of war camp, Stalag 13, Schultz – waddling in his quaint Prussian overcoat and perpetually wearing his World War I helmet – is a stupid and comical stereotype. Schultz grovels in fright before his superior, the hapless monocle-clad Colonel Klink. Meanwhile, the American prisoners continually outwit them both, heightening the image of Germans as stupid, officious, and absurd, but ultimately harmless.

---

1 For excellent examples, see the essays in Peter Freese, ed., *Germany and German Thought in American Literature and Cultural Criticism* (Essen, 1990). For more on the visual representations of Germany in America, see Marion Deshmukh's chapter in this book.

Like the laughable cabbage-head Prussian, the second image – that of the mad scientist – is not purely evil but does invoke the picture of a character in single-minded pursuit of knowledge at the expense of all else, often unwittingly unleashing untold catastrophe with his bold scientific experiments. This figure has been an important stereotype in American literature from the nineteenth-century tales of Nathaniel Hawthorne to Thomas Pynchon's 1973 novel *Gravity's Rainbow*.[2] It is the absent-minded but brilliant professor with wild hair and wide eyes behind thick glasses whose curiosity overtakes both reason and emotion. In the 1984 comedy "Splash," for example, the hero, played by Tom Hanks, falls in love with a mermaid. He is thwarted by Walter Kornbluth, a monomaniacal, arrogant, and paranoid mad scientist whose single-minded goal is to capture the mermaid in order to conduct medical experiments on her. Kornbluth's efforts to thwart the budding love affair between the mermaid (Daryl Hannah) and the hero (Tom Hanks) prove fruitless; nonetheless he will stop at nothing to capture her. He continues his pursuit despite suffering a number of accidents along the way, chasing her even after suffering broken arms and legs.

Finally, the image of the Nazi dominates the other two in post-World War II film, often combining elements of each in the portrayal of Germans as cruel, unscrupulous, murderous, crazed and single-minded, but ultimately stupid and self-destructive. Not surprisingly, this is the central and most enduring image of Germans in postwar American popular film. In the 1950s and 1960s, we see this image coupled with the image of the "good" German soldier; in the 1960s permutations of this character represent the communist adversary; in the 1970s and 1980s, this image is both contrasted to the "good" German or the heroic American and is even sometimes portrayed as being indistinguishable from "us" as Americans.

Nazis themselves were experts at style and logoization, using the swastika, the stylized eagle, the SS uniform, the jack boots, and the Hitler mustache as their own symbols. For Hollywood, these symbols came as prepackaged images of evil, and Nazi propaganda films like "Triumph of the Will" provided American filmmakers with a model for the Nazi embodiment of horror and cruelty. High cheekbones, blue eyes, and hard strong bodies become an indication of hidden menace, even as for the Nazis themselves they signified ultimate beauty. The thicker the German

---

2 For a discussion of this image in nineteenth- and twentieth-century American literature, see Peter Freese, "Exercises in Boundary-Making: The German as the 'Other' in American Literature," in Freese, ed., *Germany and German Thought*.

accent, the more evil the character. Even in a film like "Little Drummer Girl" (1984) the cold, manipulative character who heads the Israeli intelligence unit that is tracking down Palestinian terrorists is played by Klaus Kinsky as a German Jew, with a thick guttural accent, on a calculating monomaniacal mission. The Aryan-looking German who works for the Israelis turns out to be a homosexual and a murderer; the female German terrorist working for the Palestinians, a vicious and aggressive lesbian. Homosexuality and evil are inextricably linked in these images.

In "Raiders of the Lost Ark" (1981), pure evil is represented by a character who combines the symbols of Nazism with the physical characteristics of the bumbling Prussian. The villain is bald and fat; his beady eyes peer from behind thick glasses; sweat beads his face and drips from his chin. He merges the meticulous efficiency of the Nazi with the bumbling of the fat Prussian; he is both a cunning perpetrator of nasty tricks to trap and kill our American hero, Indiana Jones, and the stupid victim of Indy's own traps.

In film representations, the image of the German as Nazi is often contrasted with the benign portrait of the lowly Wehrmacht soldier. The characterization of the Wehrmacht, always shown in contrast to the SS, is often used to represent soldiers everywhere and to demonstrate the virtues of loyalty and good soldiering. In "The Odessa File" (1974), for example, the plot revolves around Peter Mueller's search for the Nazi war criminal, Edward Roschmann, who killed Peter's father, a Wehrmacht soldier, during the war. In the final scene between Peter (the new generation "good" German) and Roschmann (the old generation "bad" German), Roschmann says, "someone has been filling your head with sentimental claptrap about war crimes. A soldier obeys his orders; he doesn't ask whether they are right or wrong." Peter, defending his father – and ultimately defending his own heritage and the roots of the "new" Germany – replies angrily, "you are an executioner, a butcher – don't compare yourself with a soldier."

The image of the Nazi is combined with that of the mad scientist to add a new element of horror to the Nazi image. Here, Germans are portrayed as doctors and dentists or pure scientists – who under Hitler had ideological license to engage in atrocious experimentation and torture of their human subjects, as well as to build instruments of mass destruction. In this recurring character we see the very real Nazi doctor who performed ruthless experiments on his supposedly inferior victims and who perfected the executioner's technology of the concentration camps. These characters are intended to portray the dark side of German efficiency, brilliance, and hard work.

Whereas the mad scientist is a tragic figure, with wild eyes and glasses askew, the Nazi doctor is a figure of consummate evil who knows what he is doing and does it with disciplined and monomaniacal obsession. An important aspect of the particular sense of horror in films like "Frankenstein" is that the mad scientist is well intentioned but unwittingly creates evil. The Nazi scientist, however, has no such confusion; he knows he is committing evil and does so cold-bloodedly and brutally. Dr. Josef Mengele, the chief doctor at Auschwitz, and the villain in "The Boys from Brazil" (1978), is an apt example. Having experimented extensively with twins and injected blue dye into the eyes of children to make them acceptable Aryans, he now has cloned tissue from Hitler's body to create ninety-four young Hitlers in order to "fulfill the destiny of the Aryan race." Boasting arrogantly of his project to create new Hitlers and place them everywhere, he proclaims, "The whole world is my laboratory. . . . Hitler was thrilled when he learned that I could tailor make the right Hitler for the right time, for the eighties, the nineties, and beyond." In the final scene, Bobby (one of Mengele's clones of Hitler) displays similar characteristics. In an act of cold calculation he orders his dogs to attack Mengele and watches placidly while the dogs kill him. "Holy Shit," he says, fascinated but unmoved by the murder.

One of the most riveting films to portray this image is "Marathon Man" (1976). Dustin Hoffman plays Babe Levy, a red diaper American Jew, writing a Ph.D. dissertation on authoritarianism in order to understand his father's suicide after having been fired from his position as a professor during the McCarthy era. Levy is captured by a Nazi group headed by Klaus Szell, a Nazi war criminal living in South America, otherwise known as "Der weisse Engel" of Auschwitz who took out the gold teeth of Jews before they were exterminated. In an excruciating scene, Szell tortures Babe with the dentist's drill, alluding to the experiments he conducted at Auschwitz.

In typical self-referential fashion, Hollywood repeats this image of the Nazi dentist/doctor in other films. In "Splash," for example, when the mad scientist Kornbluth sees the error of his ways, a sadistic dentist replaces him as the evil character. As he is about ready to work on Kornbluth's tooth, broken in one of his attempts to capture the mermaid, Kornbluth says, "I don't want painkiller." Oh, says the dentist in a thick and guttural German accent, "you vant pain. vell, I aim to please." He picks up his instruments of torture and – now comically – repeats the torture scene from "Marathon Man."

Nazi horror is intensified in American film when the characters are highly cultured and refined, rendering them at once seductive and repulsive. Mengele, for example, is played by the upstanding, grave, and even Lincolnesque Gregory Peck;[3] impeccably dressed, he dances gracefully to Strauss waltzes. In "Swing Kids" (1993), the Nazi sent to recruit the rebellious Peter for the Hitler Youth is cosmopolitan and well-bred; he seduces Peter's mother with his genteel behavior, fine wine, and Swiss chocolate. We almost believe that he is a humane and sympathetic man, until we see him turn on Peter in the final scene; having failed to recruit him he instantly betrays his calculating cold-blooded nature, sending him to the work camps and most likely to his death.

Similarly, communal carousing in the affable German spirit of gemütlichkeit is portrayed as a thin veneer covering the barbaric Nazi heart of the German people, and it is intended to arouse dread in the audience and signal the terror to follow. In the "The Odessa File," Mueller attends the reunion of soldiers who fought in the World War II Siegfried Division. Bavarian music, laughing distinguished old men, and beer mugs open the scene, only to dissolve when their general stands up rigidly, clicks his heels to proclaim that "Germany believes that she doesn't need us now, but one day she will see that she does." The throbbing crowd can barely resist raising their arms in a "Sieg Heil!"

Or in "Cabaret" (1972), the only musical sequence not performed in the cabaret takes place in a pleasant beer garden, where families sit and chat at picnic tables under beautiful green shade trees. An angelic blond boy begins to sing "Tomorrow belongs to me" in an angelic voice; only after we are captivated by the music does the camera reveal his swastika armband. Gradually the crowd stands to join in song; the voices grow louder and join in harmony, and the scene culminates in a crescendo of emotional German voices committed to the fascist mission.

These scenes represent a further theme pursued in the unfolding of the image of German as Nazi; Nazis are among us and they are everywhere. To maintain the diabolic Nazi image in films set in the current period, the old "evil" Germans lurk among the new "good" Germans. Normal looking people might be Nazis at heart; one doesn't know. As the head

---

3 See Anna Insdorf's critique in her *Indelible Shadows: Film and the Holocaust* (Cambridge, 1989), 10–12.

of British intelligence tells Quiller in Harold Pinter's "The Quiller Memorandum"(1966),

nobody wears a brown shirt now, you see. No banners. Consequently, they're difficult to recognize – they look like everybody else. They move in various walks of life all over the country but they're very careful and quite clever and they look like everybody else.

This motif is repeated in American films throughout the 1970s and 1980s. In "The Odessa File" the secret organization, The Odessa, has infiltrated all government organizations in Germany and is manufacturing biological weapons to use against Israel. In his search for the war criminal Roschmann, Peter, too, finds that "they are everywhere," particularly in police forces throughout Germany. In "Raiders of the Lost Ark" Indy discovers that his old archaeological competitor is secretly working for the Nazis. The theme is symbolically represented in "The Boys from Brazil" in a scene where Nazi hunter Ezra Lieberman (modeled after Simon Wiesenthal) visits the home of the first man murdered by Mengele's "Comrades Organization." As the boy (Hitler's clone) opens the door, we see his image reflected and multiplied in the hall mirror. The Nazi can be endlessly replicated and appear everywhere. In "The Little Drummer Girl" Nazis have become terrorists, and we don't know who they are. They are everywhere.[4] We see the theme emerge as recently as 1991 in the "made for T.V. movie," "Hitler's Daughter." According to the plot, Hitler's mistress bore a child in the United States, a daughter, who is masterminding the rise of the Fourth Reich. She is running a vast secret American operation to discredit and kill her opponents and become president of the United States; members of that organization have infiltrated the highest circles of government.

This motif has also been transformed into the idea that we are *all* culprits. "Judgment at Nuremberg" (1961) opened this theme with its implicit argument that if the Germans are guilty of the Nazi atrocities, then we are all guilty. Here, the judge reminds the court that "if these murderers were monsters, this event would have no more moral significance than an earthquake." Instead, he warns, it can happen easily and

---

4 This theme of terrorists as metamorphosed Nazis is explored in Jillian Becker's *Hitler's Children: The Story of the Baader-Meinhof Gang* (New York, 1978). As Anton Kaes writes in *From Hitler to Heimat: The Return of History as Film* (Cambridge, Mass.: Harvard University Press, 1989), the English translation of the title is a misnomer. In fact, most young German members of terrorist gangs that emerged in the 1970s and 1980s were fiercely antifascist and believed that the FRG was simply a continuation of the fascist regime. Nonetheless, older Germans linked the terrorism of the young Germans in the 1970s with the terrorism of the Nazi regime (pp. 24–5). This linkage was obvious in American film images as well.

anywhere. Later American films explore this theme by examining explicit American complicity with Nazis, Nazi war criminals, and ex-Nazis. "Marathon Man" shows how American government agents protected Nazi war criminals in exchange for information. In "The Music Box" (1981) we see refined American attorneys downplaying the acts of Nazi war criminals by arguing that the United States was forced to put Nazis on the payroll because there was no one else to do the job of fighting communism. In the scene from "Cabaret" described previously, the viewers are drawn into the collective emotion expressed in the music; the clear message is that we could just as well be "them."

Finally, the Nazi image is often coupled with the image of the "good German." In films that juxtapose these two images, one is able to separate the new Germany from the old. "Voyage of the Dammed" (1976) provides an excellent example. Based on a wartime incident, the film shows the predicament of a group of Jews permitted to leave Germany in 1939 who head for Havana but are refused permission to land by the Cuban authorities. Max Von Sydow plays the noble German captain of the ship who protects the Jews until they are safe. His character is contrasted with the cruel (Nazi) purser of the ship who is cold, calculating, and blind to their plight.

In "The Odessa File" the "good" German, Mueller, played by John Voight, has a very slight German accent; in the final scene he confronts the "bad" German, played by Maximillian Schell, and asks him what it was like in the Nazi period. "It was like ruling the world," replies Schell in deep guttural tones.

For years they looked down on us, but we showed them, because we did rule the world, we Germans. We beat every army they threw at us. They looked down on us, but we showed them what we were working for. And we succeeded. You shouldn't be critical of us. You should be grateful. You can point that gun at me, but we are really on the same side. Same destiny. Same people. Why should it matter what happened to a few miserable Jews? Germany was crushed to pieces in 1945, but now we are rising again, slowly and surely. And what brings all this about? Discipline. Discipline and management. Harsh discipline and harsh management. The harder the better. You see my estate, my electric company. My factory and hundreds of others like it. We did this.

Peter replies, "Whatever prosperity there is in Germany is because of millions who work hard and never murdered anyone in their lives." The stereotypical "German" quality of hard work and discipline is finally separated from the characteristics of the obsessed and monomaniacal Nazi.

In "Swing Kids," the Nazi is contrasted with ordinary teenagers, rebellious and apolitical. Set in 1939, the "Swing Kids" defy the Nazis by dancing to the American jazz music of blacks and Jews. Their heroes are Americans, their identity and therefore their reason to resist is formed by cultural icons outside of Germany and *in* the United States. The message of this film stands in contrast to that of the German film, "The White Rose"(1983), whose plot revolves around the actual resistance rather than rebellion of young people to the Nazi regime. In this film, the urge to resist has its origins in German culture. These students have been trained in a humanist German tradition; naively they believe that if other Germans similarly trained simply knew about the atrocities, they would no longer support Hitler. Such messages about the role of German culture in creating the "good" German are rarely seen in American film.

As we mentioned at the outset of this chapter, "Schindler's List" (1993) is rather unique in its depiction of its hero, Schindler. Unlike other treatments of the "good German," the film does not Americanize its hero, setting the American ideal in clear contradiction to the evil German archetype. Schindler is portrayed as being very much a German; he profits from the war and at least initially does not seem all that bothered by the specter of the approaching holocaust. Schindler's opposition to the holocaust comes, not from an external, Western source, such as rock and roll or identification with America, but rather organically, from within the context of Nazi Germany. Schindler is affiliated with the Nazi Party, is himself an Aryan and fully acculturated into German society. The remarkable feature of this movie is that this "good German" is a fully developed character, not purely good or purely evil. This achievement is especially noteworthy since the temptations to indulge in Nazi stereotyping are abundant. The holocaust sets the context for the entire movie and there are clear and uncompromising portrayals of evil Nazis, including the sadistic camp leader, Amon Goeth. But even in this case, "Schindler's List" refuses to make the division between "good" and "evil" Germans all that apparent or easy for the viewer. The relationship between Schindler and Goeth is for most of the movie at least cordial and at times downright friendly. This movie does not allow us to make a facile "us" versus "them" distinction about Germans during the holocaust. It points to the complexities of German society at the time and shows that simple dichotomies fail to capture the experience of Germany during World War II. We are forced to accept Schindler as he was; a German citizen of the Nazi regime, with all of the complexities that this implies. Even Goeth is not a completely one-dimensional character. Although a thoroughly evil figure, who is shown, for example, shooting hapless Jews from his balcony when they slack off their labors, Goeth does allow Schindler to export the Jews under his employment despite clear orders to the contrary. In short, Schindler's list is an American movie about Germany and what happened there, not a movie that is set in Germany but one that serves to reinforce American images and stereotypes about Germany.

THE EVOLUTION OF IMAGES AND POPULAR PERCEPTIONS

During the 1950s and 1960s, the image of the Nazi as the pure representation of evil was rarely visible in American film. In the 1970s and 1980s, however, the Nazi image flourished in all its complexity, and subsumed the others. The images themselves were not created in a vacuum; they were formed in a particular cultural and historical context. In this section, we turn to that context to show how they functioned, what kinds of images were suppressed and how the images worked in the context of the films. Our description of this context is crucial to an understanding of how these images were produced and received by the wider public.

Loath to touch controversial themes, Hollywood did not make one anti-German or anti-Nazi film during the first seven years of the Nazi regime. The major exception to this silence was Charlie Chaplin's "The Great Dictator," made against the advice of virtually every Hollywood mogul. Chaplin's own power as a film star gave him the clout and resources to buck the trend and produce a major picture with a controversial theme.[5] During the war itself, Hollywood churned out anti-Nazi movies. Many of the films were propaganda movies. Take, for example, the Walt Disney cartoon, "Reason and Emotion." Two protagonists, Reason and Emotion, are given human form. Emotion is essentially good until he becomes a Nazi represented by his spiked helmet and bayonet. As such he becomes evil, capturing Reason and imprisoning him in a concentration camp. Here Nazism represents irrationality. The use of the Nazi icon creates an illusion of critical distance between the viewer and the message, allowing the viewer to discern the message for himself, thus internalizing it more completely. We read this cartoon as a warning to Americans not to lose control of their own emotions lest it captivate their own sense of reason. We see for the first time the message in film that it could happen here and they could be us.[6]

---
5 Ilan Avisar, *Screening the Holocaust: Cinema's Images of the Unimaginable* (Bloomington, Ind., 1988), 93, 134.
6 Richard Shale, *Donald Duck Joins Up* (Ann Arbor, Mich., 1982), plate 14.

The images of Germans and Germany changed dramatically during the early Cold War period. Prominent individuals and influential groups, as well as members of the political elite and the public at large, still distrusted Germany intensely.[7] Polling data during this period showed that 66 percent of the people polled had grave misgivings about Germany; and 39 percent felt that ex-Nazis were coming back into positions of influence in German politics and business. But for the American policy elite, communism had replaced Nazism as the world's threat, and the task was to undemonize Germany. After years of opposing Germany and encouraging negative images of Germans in the American media, the government of the United States found itself in the position of promoting in American society a difficult transition from representations of Germans as archenemy to the image of Germany as a stable ally and trading partner. This was necessary because the Marshall Plan was a five billion dollar a year cash transaction aimed largely at rebuilding Germany from the pockets of American taxpayers. How did Hollywood handle this transition?

A series of films was produced in the early 1950s and even later that sought to portray various German episodes in World War II in a more positive light. The 1951 film "The Desert Fox" provides an example. James Mason stars as Rommel, portraying him as a great general and a loyal citizen of Germany. Rommel is not represented as simply the lowly soldier just "following orders"; when it becomes clear that Hitler will destroy Germany, Rommel takes part in an assassination attempt and dies for his efforts. According to Ilan Avisar, Rommel in fact never betrayed Hitler and was a great supporter of fascism.[8] Although Rommel was indeed forced by Hitler to commit suicide in 1944, and the evidence in this case is not complete, what is essential to note here is that the film portrays Germans for the first time after the war in a more complex and differentiated way.

Subsequent films focused on the ordinary and upright German soldiers who were portrayed as the hapless victims of Hitler and their military officers. Judith Crist writes of the films of this era: "[In World War II

---

7 See, e.g., Drew Middleton, *Renazification of Germany*, distributed by Community Relations Service (New York, 1950); Franklin D. Roosevelt Jr., resolution requesting the president to appoint a bipartisan commission relating to American policy in Germany, House Resolution 585, 81st Congress, second session, May 2, 1950; and Anti-Defamation League of B'nai B'rith, *Why We Are Losing in Germany* (New York, 1950).

8 Avisar, *Screening the Holocaust*, 110–11. Our own research parts company somewhat from Avisar's conclusions. According to some sources, Rommel did plot to overthrow Hitler although unlike most of the conspirators he did not plot Hilter's assassination. Avisar is apparently right that Rommel had been an enthusiastic supporter of Nazism and Hitler up until the latter part of the war.

movies you are sure to find] a Nazi who, just before his capture, and especially thereafter, makes it clear to us that he was against Hitler all along and then proceeds to save the day for Americans by Nazi know-how or, at the very least, returns to his homeland a confirmed democrat."[9] As examples Crist lists films such as "The Bedford Incident" (in which a postwar Nazi helps against the Russians) and "Battle of the Bulge" (in which Robert Shaw is a tank commander who does not trust Hitler).[10]

Beginning in the early to mid-1960s, the image of Nazism was expanded to incorporate a new enemy: communism. Two films produced in 1964 exemplify the phenomenon of conflating communism and Nazism: "The Spy Who Came in from the Cold" and "Dr. Strangelove." In "The Spy Who Came in From the Cold," the film adaptation of John Le Carré's novel, we see the dreary world of Cold War espionage through Le Carré's eyes. Human character is distorted and fragmented in the world of spies; because the job of waging the Cold War requires doing evil in the name of good, the ability to exercise moral judgment is warped and even destroyed on both sides. If this process of eroding all that is human does not lead to alcoholism, depression, and self-destruction (as it does in the case of the British spy played by Richard Burton) it leads to the single-minded pursuit of power and the destruction of others, as we see in the character Mundt, the East German communist agent. Le Carré chose East Germany rather than the Soviet Union as the site for the drama of these two characters to unfold; his images portray communism as a facade for the perpetuation of Nazism and anti-Semitism. In "Dr. Strangelove" we see the horrific but comic representation of the mad scientist-turned-Nazi-now-working-for-the-Americans who is ready to destroy the world because of the Cold War rivalry. The usual German stereotypes are all present: Dr. Strangelove has a thick German accent; he is curt and pompous. In addition, Stanley Kubrick has added an element of farce. A former Nazi in hiding, Dr. Strangelove must constantly control his arm from raising in the Nazi salute.

The popular T.V. cartoon of the 1960s "Rocky and Bullwinkle" provides an excellent example of the representation of communists as Nazis. Here, the two Soviet spies, Boris and Natasha, take their orders

---

9 Judith Crist, *The Private Eye ... The Cowboy ... And the Very Naked Girl* (New York, 1967), 159.
10 There was a similar evolution in German films of this period as well, and these American films were also popular in Germany. The theme emerges again in the film "Das Boot" (1982), a German film that was extremely popular in both Germany and the United States. See Kaes's *From Hitler to Heimat*, 16–17.

from the "Fearless Leader," the bumbling Prussian-Hun-Nazi. The "Fearless Leader" is wicked looking and ugly, with a monocle, an SS uniform, and deep scars gouging his face. On his bulging chest is an iron cross medallion, warped slightly to resemble a swastika. In this cartoon, then, the Hun/Nazi general image reemerges to direct communist spies from behind the scenes, throwing tantrums and cursing at his own impotence. In another television series, "Get Smart," we see Max Smart, an American spy working for "Control," a parody of the CIA. His archenemy is "Kaos," purportedly a parody of the KGB but represented as a parody of the SS. Its leader speaks with a guttural German accent, wears a monocle, and continually clicks his heels together while he stands at rigid attention.

During the period of détente and after – the 1970s and 1980s – a series of films were produced that addressed the phenomenon of Nazism in ways that had only been treated sporadically in film. It is in this period that Nazism became a mass-produced and often stylized Hollywood image that we see most vividly portrayed in "Raiders of the Lost Ark" and in the 1983 television miniseries "The Winds of War," where heroic and affable Americans battle obsessed and evil German Nazis.[11] During this recent period as well, a number of films were produced that criticized America's relationship with ex-Nazis and Nazi war criminals in the 1950s, and chided both Americans and Germans for not pursuing the war criminals more vigorously. Films such as "The Odessa File," "The Boys from Brazil," and "The Music Box," discussed previously, provide examples. In the T.V. miniseries, "The Great Escape II" (1988), Major Dodge and two of his comrades return to Germany shortly after the war to prosecute the murderers of their fifty comrades killed by the Gestapo after having escaped from a prisoner of war camp. But Dodge and his friends learn that the Allied forces have no interest in prosecuting war criminals because the Nazis are needed for the fight against the Russians.[12] It is in this period that we see the continued differentiation of the "good" German from the "bad" German and the new Germany from the old. We thus see an attempt to stylize the Nazi image and separate it from an

---

[11] Kaes discusses the iconography of the Nazi era that has evolved from this period and had its origins in the international art films of the early 1970s – Lucchino Visconti's "The Damned," Louis Malle's "Lacombe Lucien," François Truffaut's "The Last Metro," and Liliana Cavani's "The Night Porter." He argues that these films "presented the fascist past through imagery so powerful that most subsequent films about the Third Reich were invariably influenced by [them]" (Kaes, From *Hitler to Heimat*, 22).

[12] Lothar Bredella, "How to Cope with Evil? References to the Holocaust in American Films of the 1970s and 1980s," in Freese, ed., *Germany and German Thought*, 70.

image of Germans as a whole, an image only vaguely alluded to but still present in these films.

Even in the two films already discussed ("Cabaret" and "The Odessa File") that show German gemütlichkeit associated with evil in the culture, the context in which these images appear forces the viewer to either differentiate or universalize the experience and ultimately separate the image from a picture of the German people as a whole. Recall that in "The Odessa File" the scene previously described portrays only the "old" Germans. Mueller (pronounced like the American "Miller" throughout the film) looks awkward and out of place. He looks and talks more like an American than a German. This portrayal allows us to differentiate the good from the evil German and relegate the old customs of camaraderie to the Nazi past. In "Cabaret," the impact of the scene portraying collective gemütlicheit is actually to *universalize* the Nazi horror by drawing the viewer into the emotional experience. In films of this period, then, not all and not only Germans are associated with the evil Nazi.

We saw only one film, "Hitler's Daughter," that treated the issue of German unification. The film's second scene opens with the American vice-presidential debates in a fictive 1990 election campaign. The opposition party's vice-presidential candidate is a woman, Leona Gorden, who is secretly Hitler's daughter. She is shown accusing the incumbent vice president of opposing German unification, spoofing his views that a united Germany might be a security threat to the United States and to Europe as a whole. She herself clearly supports the unification, and we see it as the basis on which Gorden's Fourth Reich will be built. Clearly the message of this horror film is that Germany threatens once again to become a menace to the West.

In short we see an evolution of the images of Germans in American popular film throughout the postwar period. The anti-German propaganda films receded as the Cold War began, and the ordinary German was portrayed as the good soldier, always in contrast, of course, to the evil Nazi. Later, Americans could laugh at the wartime enmity between America and Germany in "Hogan's Heroes," as the barbaric Hun was transformed in the bumbling, overweight, and stupid Prussian. At the height of the Cold War, the prepackaged Nazi image provided a shorthand way to portray the new enemy, communism. Here, there was no need to couple the Nazi with his "good German" counterpart. It was widely believed throughout the Cold War that Nazism and communism had similar roots in totalitarianism, and therefore the connection seemed obvious. Furthermore, the Soviet hammer and sickle could not quite match the emotional value of the swastika in striking terror in the hearts of Americans; Nazi symbols were simply better in their connotations of evil. Finally, it was only in the 1970s and 1980s that American films began to stylize the Nazi image for its own sake as a symbol of pure evil and began to deal with the Nazi phenomenon and its lingering postwar issues.[13] For the most part, these later films separated the good German from the bad, often universalizing the Nazi guilt. Nonetheless, the "good" German was always portrayed *alongside* the bad German and was never represented alone as a normal human being.

Did perceptions of the wider American public also change with this shift in images? The answer is not readily available. The public opinion polls we examined are superficial and blunt instruments in their capability to measure American perceptions of Germans; we can only offer a few clues here. We did not have empirical studies at our disposal that could assess the impact of the films we discuss on the American public. Instead, we analyze images and public perceptions separately, and we suggest that both have their origins in wider political phenomena.

Not surprisingly, American approval ratings of Germany as a country increased as memories of World War II receded, as Germany became a military ally, and as the Cold War progressed. In 1954 Germany had an approval rating in the United states of 52 percent, in 1966, it was 73 percent, in 1967, 75 percent, in 1974, 74 percent, and in 1976, 77 percent.[14] Measuring not only approval but similarity and interest, the poll suggests that the American public will strive to achieve a measure of congruity between its level of approval for a foreign nation and the extent to which the foreign nation is perceived as similar to the United States in terms of certain salient attributes, as well as the extent to which the nation contributes to the perceived American national interest. For the most part the study showed that beginning in the mid-1960s, Americans felt as similar to Germans as they did to Danes, Australians, and Canadians

---

13 This is not to say, of course, that all of these images did not emerge throughout the postwar period. We only suggest here that certain themes dominate certain periods and that a pattern of representations seems to have evolved.

14 Miroslav Nincic and Bruce Russett, "The Effect of Similarity and Interest on Attitudes Toward Foreign Countries," *Public Opinion Quarterly* 43, no. 1 (Spring 1979): 68–78. The percentages were arrived at by taking the Gallup Opinion Index for twenty-five foreign nations in which respondents were asked to rate each nation on a scale ranging from +5 to −5, weighing the percentage of the public that rated a particular nation at each point on the scale by the value of each scale point, and summing the weighted total for each nation. The rating in 1976 was the same as the rating for Sweden, lower than Australia with 85 percent, Canada with 91 percent, England with 87 percent, but higher than Italy and Japan.

and also felt that Germany contributed to their own national interest. Thus, feelings of similarity are highly correlated with the feelings of approval.

More disaggregated data, however, might suggest more nuanced perceptions. We found only three polls of this type. First, the German *Emnid-Informationen* both tabulated others' opinion polls and conducted their own, attempting to survey dominant stereotypes of Germans among the population of the United States between 1942 and 1961. In 1942 the adjectives that over 50 percent of those surveyed felt most accurately described Germans were "warlike," "industrious," and "cruel." In 1961 the dominant adjectives were "intelligent" and "industrious." Only 13 percent said "cruel," and 20 percent said "warlike." Forty percent used the term "progressive" to describe the Germans. Only 12 percent thought Germans were "normal."[15]

In a survey conducted in July 1961, after Adolf Eichmann had been captured by Israelis in Argentina and brought to Jerusalem to stand trial, 31 percent of a national sample thought Eichmann should be executed, while another 43 percent said he should be imprisoned for life. Nevertheless, only a minority reported a decreased sympathy for Germans. Whereas a preponderant majority of Americans were convinced of Eichmann's guilt and felt that he should be severely punished, only one in six reported that they had become less sympathetic toward Germany and Germans as a result of the trial. Shock at the Nazi atrocities publicized during the trial did not result in a generalized change in attitude toward Germany and Germans.[16] What this survey suggests is that Americans separated their views of the individual Eichmann – or their judgment of a group of war criminals – from their image of Germans as a whole. Another disaggregated survey, however, captured a negative collective stereotype of Germany. In 1982 Germany was ranked fifth highest in approval by Americans in a Gallup Poll, but in the same year, when another Gallup poll posed the question "How much freedom is there in West Germany?" a low 32 percent of Americans felt that there was a high degree of freedom in that country.[17] Twenty-one percent of Americans (compared to 4 percent in the population polled in West Germany) felt that there was "little or no freedom" in West Germany.

---

15 *Emnid-Informationen* 13, no. 17 (Apr. 29, 1961), 9.
16 Irving Crespi, "Public Reaction to the Eichmann Trial," *Public Opinion Quarterly* 28, no. 1 (Spring 1964): 91–103.
17 John D. Treadway, "Germany in the American Media," in Lore Amlinger, ed., *Germany and The United States: Changing Perceptions/Danger and Hope* (Stuttgart, 1987), 80.

What was the American public's reaction to German reunification? In February 1990 the *Gallup Monthly Report* published poll results showing that 72 percent of Americans thought that German reunification was a good thing, and 59 percent were not concerned – or at least not very concerned – that a united Germany would become an aggressor nation as it was in World War II.[18] "Hitler's Daughter" notwithstanding, public opinion clearly followed American policy toward reunification, and provided a good indicator of the public's view that Germany's society, political culture, and political system had been fully transformed in the postwar period.

EXPLAINING REPRESENTATIONS AND PERCEPTIONS

How do we explain these phenomena? How do Hollywood images originate, and what explains their congruence or incongruence with public perceptions? The question of how cultural images are produced has long been an issue of theoretical contention. The debate has focused on the relationship between elites and the mass public in the promulgation of these images. Pareto held that culture, and the cultural images produced by the media, originated with elites and conformed wholly to elite interests as an instrument to manipulate the public at large. In a more complex view, Horkheimer and Adorno argued that the culture industry represented complex issues in ready-made images and thus limited the world of associations possible for those who partook of those images. Mosca qualified Pareto's contention in his claim that elite manipulation of culture will be powerful only if it resonates with the subjective experience of the audience; only if elites shape their message to reflect and manipulate popularly held images, will they be the ultimate arbiters of cultural images. In a more nuanced view, Geertz argued that the production of culture drew its power from the producers' ability to make sense of social realities and render them meaningful to individuals.

In the popular production of images, Hollywood has acted as an elite and semiautonomous commercial institution that offers shorthand, predigested images to represent complex phenomena; it packages ideas and viewpoints in such a way as to please an audience. The images it produces are not only products of cultural stereotypes; they are products of talented

---

18 Graham Heuber, "Most Americans Do Not Seem Worried About a Reunified Germany," *Gallup Monthly Report*, no. 293, Feb. 1990.

artists and Hollywood's own organizational and historical particularities. Recall, for example, our brief discussion of the making of Chaplin's "The Great Dictator" against the wishes of Hollywood moguls. Hollywood elites do not always produce images according to the wishes of political elites. Indeed, many of the images of Germans in American film can be traced to émigré German filmmakers. The image of the German as mad scientist, for example, is particularly influenced by German film and emigrant directors. Fritz Lang's "Metropolis" (1926) brought to the American public a vision of a (German) negative utopia run by science gone crazy. The "German style" of film in the 1930s was a Hollywood interpretation of the dark silent German movies of a decade earlier.[19]

Another major influential émigré was Billy Wilder, who was born in the Austro-Hungarian Empire. Wilder began his career-making movies in Austria and Berlin but fled to America to escape the Nazis. Despite his wholehearted adoption of American film culture (something which he had admired greatly from Austria and Germany), Wilder maintained many elements of his Central European training and had many linkages to the German émigré film community.[20]

Nonetheless, as our discussion of the evolution of images suggests, the Hollywood film industry has had a long and sometimes incestuous relationship with the American government, particularly when its films touched on issues of concern to the American national security establishment. In the 1940s and 1950s, Hollywood exercised self-censorship through the Hays Office; every foot of film passed through its censorious hands; in these years, films that dealt with political issues clearly reflected American policy while protecting the commercial interests of the industry.[21]

If we accept the argument that the film industry's interests often correspond to the political establishment's preferences, particularly when it portrays sensitive political issues, we can more clearly understand the dramatic change in the film images of Germans and Germany produced during the early Cold War period. As communism replaced fascism as the official national security threat, Germans as a whole were undemonized in American film. Images of heroic and moral Germans –

---

19 Andrew Tudor, *Monsters and Mad Scientists: A Cultural History of the Horror Movie* (Oxford, 1989), 27–30.
20 For information on Billy Wilder, including links with German directors and German émigrés, see Maurice Zolotow, *Billy Wilder in America* (New York, 1977).
21 John Izod, *Hollywood and the Box Office, 1895–1986* (New York, 1988), 69–71.

ironically, images of those Germans with moral values – particularly those Germans who fought against the allies in World War II, such as Rommel in "The Desert Fox" – replace the image of the German people as the enemy.

It is important to note that this was not the only form of representation possible in the pursuit of representing Germany. An alternative path would have been to construct an image of those antifascist Germans who fought against the Nazis during the Third Reich. These groups were, in fact, excluded from public service in postwar West Germany, and the occupation governments even banned organized activities on the part of former leftist partisans.[22] We can only speculate that because many of the antifascist Germans were also socialists and committed communists, this representation of the "good" German was also suppressed in American films. Instead, Hollywood chose to humanize or joke about German soldiers who fought in both wars, always, of course contrasting them with their militaristic Nazi and heroic American counterparts. In doing so, American films portrayed Germans as representing the more universal and positive values associated with the military, that is, loyalty, discipline, obedience, and commitment to duty. The range of possible representations was narrowed to this one image in the context of the emerging ideological battle with communism.

Indeed, the Nuremberg trials had cast doubt on these military values. In the new climate of the Cold War, these doubts could not be tolerated. The task, then, was to confine the criticism of blind obedience and unquestioning respect for authority to the Nazi period alone and to *universalize* military virtues associated with soldiering everywhere by embodying those virtues in the "good" soldier whether German or American. This explains the emergence of the image of the "good" or even the comic Wehrmacht recruit. Films like "Judgment at Nuremberg" and "Dr. Strangelove" kept alive the Nuremberg critique, but in the 1950s and 1960s, these films were few and far between. Indeed, during this period, "good" Germans were represented as universal soldiers, and "bad" Germans were the Nazis transformed into communists. Recall the line from "The Odessa File" in which the "good" Peter calls the "evil" Roschmann an executioner and a butcher and aggressively decouples those characteristics from the characteristics of a real soldier who is simply "doing his duty."

22 See William Graf, *The German Left Since 1945: Socialism and Social Democracy in German Federal Republic* (Cambridge, 1967). As Kurt Schumacher once bitterly said of the German socialists, "we were sitting in the concentration camps while other peoples were still forming alliances with the Hitler government" (quoted in Graf, *German Left Since 1945*, 68).

After détente in the early 1970s relaxed the image of the communist enemy, American filmmakers could explore Nazism and the Holocaust for their own sake. That exploration continued to separate "good" Germans from "bad" Germans, but now the portrayals were more nuanced and less associated with military images. In official policy, on Hollywood sets, and in the minds of Americans, it was the "old" Germany that was the enemy, not the new democratic Germany. The task of rehabilitating Germany in the minds of Americans for political purposes was now complete. Without implicating present-day Germany, the phenomenon of Nazism could be resurrected as an important historical episode and as a symbol for unmitigated evil. As the scene in "Cabaret" discussed previously suggests, Nazism could now represent a universal, not a particular German phenomenon; we are all culpable.

The Vietnam War and its aftermath created a cultural space for the exploration of the complicity of American government officials with Nazi war criminals in the fight against communism, and the general indifference to Nazi war criminals still at large. Films such as "Marathon Man" and "The Music Box" portrayed that relationship in a highly critical manner and join with "The Spy Who Came in from the Cold" and "The Little Drummer Girl" to go so far as to criticize the state (represented by its intelligence agencies) – including the American state – as an immoral institution.

In short, our discussion has suggested that media images of Germans throughout the postwar period have their roots in both literary and officially produced stereotypes, and they are produced in the minds of Hollywood directors and producers, most often in congruence with official United States policy toward Germany. Perceptions of Germans in the wider public are formed by a confluence of forces, including experience, official policy, and media images. These perceptions are congruent with traditional stereotypes, official policy, the public's self-image, and cultural values that place the individual above the collectivity in the making of more complex judgments and assessments. Therefore, although the image of Germans that we see on film are, for the most part, negative stereotypes, they are framed in such a way as to separate the image portrayed from a collective image of Germans as a whole. If we accept the Gramscian notion of cultural hegemony, this explains, in part, the apparent incongruence between negative film images of Germans and the positive popular perceptions of Germany. In other words, since the advent of the Cold War, images of Germans in American popular film and television represent something other than the

German people themselves. It is to this final issue that the discussion now turns.

WHAT DO IMAGES OF GERMANS REPRESENT?

Our conclusions can only be speculative. On the portrayal of America in German films, Eric Rentschler has written that "German directors have made films set in America not so much 'in order to understand another culture'; rather they have used the signs of another country to establish an enriched relationship to their own." Citing Walter Abisch, he writes that such a procedure reduces everything to a set of signs and images that require interpretation.[23] It is our hunch that we must approach the meaning of German images in American films in a similar way. Images of Germans in American films reveal more about how Americans see themselves than about how Americans see Germans. But there are important differences between the treatment of Americans in German film (as Rentschler interprets it) and the treatment of Germans in American films. The images discussed here project negative characteristics onto Germans, often in ways that permit Americans to avoid confronting their own cultural conflicts. In American films that address these conflicts, that is, between good and evil, between the "old" and the "new" generation, between principle and pragmatism, Americans and American values of heroism and individualism are pitted against collective and negative "German" characteristics; in this battle, the Americans usually win. Under these conditions, it is difficult for Americans to examine their own anxieties and dilemmas.

As the opinion poll data suggests, the American audience has a deep identification with Germany. Indeed, German immigrants have been a dominant group in American society. Therefore, the Nazi episode posed an agonizing challenge to American middle-class identity: the Nazi regime grew out of Europe, the cradle of "civilization." Firm believers in the idea of progress and enlightenment, Americans watched Europe regress into unparalleled savagery. Nazism was at once brutal and clearly a product of modern culture. The premises of Nazi ideology were couched in the language of social science; religion and magic were scorned and a secular atheistic creed preferred. Their war machine was efficient and modern, their soldiers disciplined and loyal. In short, they

---

23 Eric Rentschler, "How American Is It: The U.S. as Image and Imaginary in German Film," *The German Quarterly* 56 (Fall 1984): 607.

were like "us." Subjugation, genocide, and enslavement were hardly foreign to the American experience. Nazi images serve as a mirror to the American past and present; more extreme, exaggerated, but still recognizable. The evils represented by Nazism could be everywhere; they are not only potentially among us, but they are us. Although a few films explore that theme and universalize that guilt, most have solved the dilemma by continuing to separate "them" and "us." In contrast, "Schindler's List" has taken yet another option, namely, looking at Germany and German citizens in all of its and their complexity.

Similarly, the mad Nazi scientist often represents America's ambiguous relationship with technology. Technological development is both the foundation of American ideology and a source of deep anxiety; it destroys traditional life and institutions. Just as the Nazis represented the possible dark side of Western culture and rationality, so does the mad scientist represent the dangers of technology. The German is at once seen as familiar and threatening. As Peter Freese suggests, the mad-scientist/Nazi connection represents "the close connection between genius and madness, scientific accomplishment and ruthless immorality – perhaps our attempt to consider the enigma of a people steeped in a rich cultural heritage and perpetuating atrocious evils."[24] In the image of the Nazi scientist, Americans projected onto Germans their own confusion and anxiety over the enigma of the Third Reich and the enigma of Western civilization. But it was the United States, after all, who first developed and then actually *used* the atomic weapon. Unable to disassociate their own culture from those dangers, Americans use images of Germans as a screen onto which they project their own anxieties and doubts.[25]

This argument is reinforced when one examines American film portrayals of the Japanese, as compared with American images of Germans. Japan inflicted much greater damage on American troops and soil than did the Germans; nonetheless the enduring image of the enemy is that of the Nazi and not the Japanese militant fascist. Because of America's complex identification with Germans and Germany, the postwar film industry has been obsessed with German, not Japanese images as representations of evil.

Americans are not alone in projecting their own cultural conflicts onto another culture in its media images. In Chinese and Hong Kong "Kung

24 Freese, "Exercises in Boundary-Making," 130.
25 Other psychoanalytic themes appeared in the films we viewed as well: the struggle with the father, patricide as a prerequisite for Nazi control, and generational struggles. Although they may be significant, we do not have the space to explore these representations here.

Fu" films, the Japanese frequently (if not always) represent evil; although they are portrayed as excellent fighters, they are always depicted as cheaters. Often, in these films, a Chinese "fifth column" betrays its own side, allowing the Japanese a short-term victory. The drama of World War II is played out through imagery and allegory again and again, both in Asian and in American cinema. Just as the Germans are represented as the "other" to the American population even as a close identity is established, so the Japanese represent the "other" to their Asian neighbors and thus occupy a similar position cinematically.

And what of the future? Like World War I and World War II, the Cold War and the Soviet enemy are now history. In the Gulf War of 1991, Saddam Hussein was repeatedly compared to Hitler by both policy elites and the media. The image of American technology in Saddam's hands was transformed in the media to instruments of calculating and immoral destruction. The use of Nazi images and the image of our technology in the hands of madmen to rouse hatred of new enemies is too convenient, too evocative, and too entrenched to disappear. The fascination with the Nazi phenomenon is likely to continue in media imagery if the dilemmas discussed in this chapter are real. What is all too likely is that the future will repeat the past for some time to come; negative collective representations will continue to be represented in the American media by "the other," and positive individual images will continue to be represented by Americans. On the one hand, this phenomenon allows Americans to separate out the individuals in a foreign culture from the negative stereotypes; on the other hand, it prevents Americans from engaging in serious cultural self-examination. We are encouraged, therefore, by the appearance of a film such as "Schindler's List," which suggests that as far as American media portrayals of Germany are concerned, it may be possible to produce future works that neither ignore the past nor forget that German citizens are as varied and complex as anyone anywhere else.

14

Chancellor of the Allies?
The Significance of the United States in Adenauer's Foreign Policy

HANS-JÜRGEN SCHRÖDER

Foreign policy has played an exceptionally prominent role in the history of the Federal Republic of Germany since its founding. A central task of the young republic, in addition to forming a new government and rebuilding the economy, was to reestablish ties with other nations. The government of Chancellor Konrad Adenauer worked gradually and persistently to win back Germany's right to engage in foreign policy and its equal status in the international community of nations. On May 5, 1955, nearly ten years to the day after the total defeat of the Third Reich, the western part of Germany formally received its sovereignty. This victory was made possible for the most part by three interrelated elements of West German foreign policy: concentration on economic issues, even in the realm of foreign relations; a close association with the United States; and, as the central element of Germany's desired Western orientation, conciliation with its Western European neighbors, especially France. "Our stance is firm in the area of foreign policy," stated Adenauer in a personal letter in August 1949. "It is oriented primarily toward establishing a close relationship with our neighbors in the Western world, particularly the United States. With all our energy, we will work toward the goal of having Germany admitted as soon as possible as a full member of the European federation, with all the rights and responsibilities thereof."[1]

Just five days after he was elected chancellor, Adenauer sketched out

---

This chapter was translated from German by Sally E. Robertson of Arlington, Va. This chapter was previously published in German in Josef Foschepth, ed., *Adenauer und die Deutsche Frage* (Göttingen, 1988).

1 Adenauer to Helene Wessel, Aug. 27, 1949, in Hans Peter Mensing, comp., *Adenauer: Briefe, 1949–1951* (Berlin, 1985), 97; see also Hans-Peter Schwarz, *Adenauer: Der Aufstieg: 1876–1952* (Stuttgart, 1986), 671.

these basic foreign policy guidelines for the public as well in the governmental declaration of September 20, 1949.[2] As for the area of economics, Adenauer considered it an important initial task of domestic policy to increase the integration of the German economy into the world economy. It was necessary, he said, "to eliminate systematically the structural defects in the German economy caused by fifteen years of a state-controlled and wartime economy" and to lay the foundation for social and economic life by ensuring the competitiveness of the German economy. Adenauer emphasized the foreign policy dimension of Germany's world market orientation by noting the significance of scientific research "to benefit economic production." Only if Germany succeeded, he argued,

in distinguishing itself with its performance on the world market will it be possible for us to survive there. For a weak nation, a politically weak nation, is always in danger of being disregarded in the economic competition with other nations if it does not accomplish something exceptional.

As regards the geographic focus of his foreign policy, there was for Adenauer

no doubt that we belong to the Western European world by virtue of our origins and our attitudes. We want to maintain good relations, including personal contacts, with all countries, but particularly with our neighbors, the Benelux countries, France, Italy, England, and the Scandinavian nations. The Franco-German conflict which has dominated European politics for hundreds of years and given rise to so much war, destruction, and bloodshed, must be wiped from the face of the earth once and for all.

The climax of the declaration was the wish, expressed by Adenauer, to acknowledge the United States:

at this hour with special gratitude. . . . I do not believe that there has ever in history been a victorious nation that has tried to help the defeated nation and contribute to its rebuilding and recovery in such a way as the United States has done and continues to do with respect to Germany.

History, he said, would record this behavior on the part of the United States "as a greater deed" than its "struggles in war." The chancellor referred to "innumerable Americans" who

showed true personal involvement and charity by the moving way in which they helped Germany in our time of greatest need, when hunger and poverty ruled the land here. The German people must not and will not ever forget these actions by the American people.

2 *Verhandlungen des Deutschen Bundestages: Stenographische Berichte* 1 (1949): 22–30.

Addressing the concrete form of West German foreign policy, Adenauer referred to the difficulties arising from the fact that foreign policy was reserved to the Allied High Commission. This, he said, was the reason that he had not established a ministry for international relations as he had been asked to do. This did not mean, however, that the Federal Republic was going to "avoid any activity in this area." Adenauer saw it as a "paradox" of the German situation that "Germany's foreign affairs are being handled by the Allied High Commission" but that, at the same time, "any action by the federal government or federal parliament, even in German domestic affairs, involves some kind of foreign component." He argued that Germany was "more closely entwined with foreign nations than ever before as a result of the occupation, the Ruhr Statute, the Marshall Plan, and so on."[3]

I

The Marshall Plan was not only an illustration of the intricate connection between domestic and foreign policy, but was also significant inasmuch as the inclusion of West Germany in the European Recovery Program was a signal from Washington of its determination to achieve the economic and political stabilization of West Germany. These stabilization measures were executed on the basis of important decisions regarding the foreign policy orientation of the young republic which were made even before it was established.

As in the 1920s, Germany after World War II was the centerpiece of American policy in Europe.[4] When laying down the details of the Marshall Plan, its architects quickly realized that it could be successful only if it included Germany.[5] A summary analysis by the State Department in the summer of 1948 stated that, at least potentially, Germany was one of the most important suppliers of such urgently needed goods as coal, mining machinery, and industrial equipment. At the same time,

---

3 See also Adenauer's remarks before the CDU/CSU Bundestag faction on Sept. 14, 1949: "We now have the paradox that, although Germany has no foreign minister, its entire politics are viewed as foreign policy, even the things we do domestically. Everything will be seen from the point of view of foreign policy" (Udo Wengst, comp., *Auftakt zur Ära Adenauer: Koalitionsverhandlungen und Regierungsbildung 1949* [Düsseldorf, 1985], 365).
4 An essay of critical importance in this regard is Werner Link, "Zum Problem der Kontinuität amerikanischer Deutschlandpolitik im 20. Jahrhundert," in Manfred Knapp, ed., *Die deutschamerikanischen Beziehungen nach 1945* (Frankfurt/Main, 1975).
5 See Hans-Jürgen Schröder, "Marshallplan, amerikanische Deutschlandpolitik und europäische Integration, 1947–1950," *Aus Politik und Zeitgeschichte*, supplement to the weekly newspaper, *Das Parlament* B 18 (1987): 3–17, listing additional references and sources.

Germany was a potentially significant market for European products. For this reason, the analysis continued, the economic recovery of Germany was vitally necessary to overall European economic recovery. Conversely, the economic recovery of Germany depended to a great extent on the economic recovery of the other European nations, because they were the main markets for German exports. The policy of the United States, as put forth in this analysis, was to address as much attention as possible to this interdependence in order to make the overall European Recovery Program as effective as possible.[6]

The integration of West Germany into the Marshall Plan strategy had far-reaching consequences for the orientation of West Germany's domestic policy, as well as its foreign policy, which is the subject of this chapter. Political and economic leaders in the Western zones clearly recognized the integrative momentum of the Marshall Plan and exploited it for the gradual development of West German foreign policy. The chairman of the Administrative Council of the Bizone, Hermann Pünder, repeatedly pointed out that the Marshall Plan had great significance, reaching far beyond its economic significance, for West Germany and for Europe as a whole. For example, he said, the work of the Organization for European Economic Cooperation in Paris (OEEC) already showed "a very agreeable start in the direction of truly pan-European thinking by all participating nations." From a German point of view, he continued, this organization "must be given special credit for [showing] an ever-greater understanding for our situation and for West Germany's capability of contributing to the economic recovery of Europe" and for beginning, from these realizations, "to draw conclusions [affecting] not only economics but their entire attitude toward Germany.... Particularly important for us" were precisely these "conclusions going beyond the economic realm in an attempt to smooth the way for a new, democratic Germany to rebuild itself in the European family of nations." Pünder stated that Germany was proceeding from the conviction that the European cooperation brought to life by the Marshall Plan would not be limited to the duration of the European aid program, but would last beyond it.[7]

The "declarations of intent delivered [by Pünder and other Bizone representatives] on the future form of foreign relations... fit perfectly into the international economic and security plans of the United States."

---

6 Department of State Policy Statement, Germany, Aug. 16, 1948, *Foreign Relations of the United States* (hereafter cited as *FRUS*) 2 (1948): 1310.
7 Institut für Zeitgeschichte and German Bundestag, eds., *Wörtliche Berichte und Drucksachen des Wirtschaftsrates des Vereinigten Wirtschaftsgebietes, 1946–1949*, vol. 2 (Munich, 1977), 1525.

This was stressed with reference to the Marshall Plan and to the foundation of the Bizone and currency reform. The "structural framework of economic and political integration into the West began to emerge even in the Bizonal phase preceding the establishment of the Federal Republic."[8] The Western orientation of the Western zones inaugurated in the initial phase of the Marshall Plan was not limited to economics. The economic integration of West Germany had a political and security dimension analogous to the dual economic and political functions of the Marshall Plan. Only in the context of European integration did it seem possible to guide not only the economic but also the "political and spiritual forces of Germany onto a healthy and peaceful track."[9]

In addition to the extensive foreign policy implications of the Marshall Plan's economic and foreign trade mechanisms, Adenauer was also cognizant of the component that involved power politics in a narrower sense, as embodied by the Occupation Statute of April 1949 in which the Western allies reserved for themselves elementary control rights. The general idea was that the government of the Federal Republic could gradually expand its scope of action, moving not in opposition to, but in cooperation with, the Western Allies. Adenauer acknowledged that the Occupation Statute was anything but an "ideal." However, he said, it was "progress compared to the lawless state in which we lived before the Occupation Statute took effect." For the German people, he said, there was no other way "to regain our freedom and equal status" than to ensure that Germany walks "the path upward together with the Allies after the complete collapse bequeathed to us by National Socialism." The only path to freedom, he explained, "is to seek to expand our freedoms and responsibilities bit by bit in agreement with the Allied High Commission."[10]

The United States necessarily played a key role in this regard, according to Adenauer's calculations. Not the least of his reasons for perceiving the United States in this role was the shift in power within the international system that had taken place during the course of World War II. Pointing out the loss in power experienced by France and Great Britain,

---

8 Manfred Knapp, "Die Anfänge westdeutscher Aussenwirtschafts- und Aussenpolitik im bizonalen Vereinigten Wirtschaftsgebiet (1947–1949)," in Knapp, ed., *Von der Bizonengründung zur ökonomisch-politischen Westintegration: Studien zum Verhältnis zwischen Aussenpolitik und Aussenwirtschaftsbeziehungen in der Entstehungsphase der Bundesrepublik Deutschland (1947–1952)* (Frankfurt/Main, 1984), 73.
9 Speech delivered by American High Commissioner John McCloy in Great Britain on Apr. 4, 1950; German text in *ERP Information* 5 (1950), Deutsche Bundesbank, Historical Archives, 3365 (Vock reference files: Marshall Plan).
10 *Verhandlungen des Deutschen Bundestages: Stenographische Berichte* 1 (1949): 29.

Adenauer repeatedly stressed the position of control that Washington occupied in world politics:

Since 1914, the United States of America has developed into a first-class world power. Without exaggeration, one can say that never since the time of the Roman Empire of Emperor Augustus has a nation had such power in its hands as the United States now possesses. It is the strongest military power, the strongest economic power on earth.

The chancellor described it as "very lucky for humanity that the American people are freedom-loving, progressive, and resolute." They "have grasped surprisingly quickly the role that has now fallen to them in history"; they "clearly recognize the responsibility to humanity as a whole that has been placed on them by their power and wealth."[11] In the following years, Adenauer repeatedly addressed this powerful position of the United States, but mostly treated it as an "unspoken assumption" forming the consistent basis of his analysis of domestic and foreign policy situations. "Let us always be clear," Adenauer cautioned the CDU/CSU faction in the Bundestag in mid-September 1949, "that the Americans may at any time hang our breadbasket so high as to put us in a very serious situation."[12]

Adenauer's fanatic opposition to the Soviet Union and his clear diagnosis of the power of the United States led him almost inevitably to the conclusion that the freedom of action of the Federal Republic could be expanded only in cooperation with the Western Allies and not in opposition to them. Moreover, a confrontation with the Western powers would have increased solidarity among the three Western Allies, thereby significantly complicating, if not preventing, Germany's attempts to exploit to Bonn's advantage the differing priorities in the German policies of France, Great Britain, and the United States. Cooperation with the Western powers opened up the prospect of developing special relations with Washington that would subtly force the Parisian hand. Immediately after establishment of the Federal Republic, this vision of Adenauer found expression in the Petersberg Agreement.

---

11 Hans-Peter Schwarz, ed., *Konrad Adenauer: Reden, 1917–1967: Eine Auswahl* (Stuttgart, 1975), 184. (Speech of Oct. 20, 1950, on the subject of "Germany's Position and Mission in the World" at the first national convention of the CDU.)
12 Before the CDU/CSU faction of the Bundestag on Sept. 14, 1949, cited in Wengst, *Auftakt zur Ära Adenauer*, 365.

II

It was entirely in line with this policy that the preamble to the Petersberg Agreement signed on November 22, 1949,[13] expressed the determination of the parties "to develop progressively their relations on the basis of mutual trust." One urgent objective was to "integrate [the Federal Republic] as a peace-loving member of the European community." The government of the Federal Republic had succeeded in obtaining important concessions, above all, permission to establish trade and consular relationships, which was important from a foreign policy perspective. In addition, the Federal Republic was promised admission into those international organizations in which German "expertise and cooperation could contribute to the common good," analogous to its already-granted participation in the Organization for European Economic Cooperation. In return, the government of the Federal Republic promised above all its "firm determination" to "maintain the demilitarization of the territory of the Federal Republic" and "prevent the renewed establishment of any kind of armed forces," and its willingness to cooperate with the Office of Military Security (*Militärisches Sicherheitsamt*).[14] The close connection between safety from Germany and concessions to Germany was expressed in the linkage that the Allies established between an essential halt to the dismantling program and the entry of Bonn into the International Authority for the Ruhr (IAR). It was far and away this point that ignited domestic political conflict in the Federal Republic, the clearly audible climax of which came in the Bundestag debate of November 24–5, 1949. The SPD criticized this "mentality of linkage and trading in which they will forego a bit of dismantling if we will swallow a bit of Ruhr statute."[15]

In response, Adenauer first defended the "method of our foreign policy" by noting the security needs of the Allies. The Germans, on the one hand, and the Allies, on the other, "will naturally see the same state of affairs from two different points of view." However, "we Germans should not forget what happened from 1933 to 1945; we must also not forget what agony the National Socialist regime caused for the entire

---

13 See the excellent edition by Horst Lademacher and Walter Mühlhausen, eds., *Sicherheit – Kontrolle – Souveränität: Das Petersberger Abkommen vom 22. November 1949: Eine Dokumentation* (Melsungen, 1985).
14 Ibid., 87ff.
15 *Verhandlungen des Deutschen Bundestages: Stenographische Berichte* 1 (1949): 487.

world." Furthermore, one must also "not forget that nearly all the people of the world are still suffering badly from the consequences of this war." Finally, he said, Germany must be clear "in everything we do . . . that we are powerless as a result of our total collapse." Therefore, the "psychological factor plays a very important role" in negotiations with the Allies, which are being conducted with the objective of "progressively taking greater and greater possession of our sovereign power." One cannot "immediately expect and demand full trust." Just as "it would be unworthy and wrong to pursue a policy of servile submissiveness, a policy of boastfulness would be just as stupid, unintelligent, and futile." Therefore, the "method of German foreign policy" must be one of "moving slowly and incrementally forward." This method had proven successful in the Petersberg negotiations, Adenauer continued, as evidenced by the purely external fact that the German text was accorded the same validity as the French and English ones. In paying tribute to the result of the negotiations, the chancellor mainly pointed out that German wishes had been 90 percent accommodated in the area of dismantling. During the Petersberg negotiations, Adenauer had pointed out that the dismantling issue had implications reaching far beyond the economic ones:

For us Germans, [it is] an issue of great economic significance, but also an issue of great psychological significance, and I expressed more than once the fear that the word "dismantling" would one day occupy the same place in domestic political agitation that the word "Versailles" occupied in the 1920s.

Precisely since he was so conscious of the emotional charge of the dismantling issue, Adenauer should have realized that it would be interpreted as unbridled provocation when he alleged that the SPD would rather "let the dismantling program continue to the end." This was what caused SPD Chairman Kurt Schumacher to originate the much-quoted appellation of Adenauer as the "chancellor of the Allies."[16]

In a political tribute, Adenauer classified the agreement as "a great success. . . . For the first time, we will return to the international sphere," the chancellor commented appropriately in the aforementioned Bundestag debate. However, his claim that "our equal status has been officially recognized for the first time since the collapse,"[17] which he also made in his memoirs, does not hold up to historic appraisal but documents instead the chancellor's negotiating strategy of going "the way of the equal partner, rather than that of a mere taker of orders, from the very

---

16 Ibid., 397, 472, 524–5.
17 Ibid., 476.

beginning."[18] There is no question about this in the documentation of negotiations with the Allies. Notwithstanding the criticism of this overestimation of the Petersberg Agreement with regard to Germany's equal status, which was certainly motivated by domestic politics, it is certain that the Petersberg Agreement

> ended once and for all the era in which the three Western Allies made far-reaching decisions regarding the future of Germany without prior negotiations with German representatives.... The government of the Federal Republic began, though within narrow bounds at first, to conduct German foreign policy, even though this was officially still one of the rights reserved to the Allies.[19]

In this context, one must not overlook the indirect foreign policy effects of the negotiated economic relief. The near stoppage of the dismantling program improved the economic and social situation in West Germany and, therewith, the general "start-up conditions" for the young republic.[20]

In the domestic political controversy over the Petersberg Agreement, Adenauer cautioned "against speculation ... that we can somehow prosper from the lack of unanimity among the other major powers."[21] In a very subtle form, however, this is exactly what the government of the Federal Republic practiced, notably in forging special relations with the United States. This was demonstrated shortly after the government was established when Bonn had to react to the devaluation of the British pound. Although the final decision regarding establishment of a new parity for the German mark was the responsibility of the High Commissioners, discussions within the cabinet revealed the determination of the German federal government that their U.S. orientation be expressed in the reestablishment of the external value of the German mark. For example, Minister of Economics Ludwig Erhard warned of a 30 percent devaluation following the British example. Such a measure, he said, would give the impression "that we were tied by a total dictate to the English pound."[22] The president of the *Bank deutscher Länder* (Central bank of the German federal states), Wilhelm Vocke, wanted to avoid "under any circumstances" going along with "the English automatically

---

18 Lademacher and Mühlhausen, eds., "Introduction," *Sicherheit*, 59.
19 Hans-Peter Schwarz, *Die Ära Adenauer: Gründerjahre der Republik, 1949–1957* (Stuttgart, 1981), 67–8.
20 See Lademacher and Mühlhausen, eds., "Introduction," *Sicherheit*, 61.
21 *Verhandlungen des Deutschen Bundestages: Stenographische Berichte* 1 (1949): 472.
22 Transcript of the cabinet meeting of Sept. 21, 1949, in Ulrich Enders and Konrad Reiser, comps., *Die Kabinettsprotokolle der Bundesregierung*, vol. 1 (1949) (Boppard/Rhein, 1982), 286.

and pari passu." This would entail the risk, he explained, that the Federal Republic would be considered part of the Sterling bloc in the future, which would have several negative consequences: "We would no longer be directly that which we are today, namely, an advocate of American policy," for Bonn would be "controlled and directed" from London.[23] This would threaten the free market economy and the standard of living. These assessments were largely shared by the federal chancellor. In his own contributions to the discussion, however, he concentrated on the issue of moderating the upward trend in prices in Germany caused by the devaluation. Effective September 19, 1949, the exchange rate for the German mark compared to the dollar was set at 23.8 cents per mark ($1 = DM 4.20). This meant a return to the exchange rate of the Weimar period and was evidence of the high value placed on America by Germany.

This close link to the United States, which had become evident on the currency issue, doubtless played a role in the decisions made by the German federal government in connection with the Petersberg negotiations. An initial indication of the special significance of the United States is seen where the Petersberg Agreement mentions the "intention of signing a bilateral agreement with the government of the United States of America regarding aid under the Marshall Plan."[24] In discussions held in the Foreign Affairs Committee of the Bundestag regarding the advantages and disadvantages of Germany joining the International Authority for the Ruhr, committee chairman Professor Carlo Schmid (SPD) assumed a close German-American relationship as if it were a given. German membership and the accompanying voting rights could acquire "decisive importance" in the event that the IAR instituted "a policy of export restrictions." With "the votes of the United States, adverse consequences for Germany could perhaps be prevented."[25] In the next few weeks, numerous cabinet members also argued in favor of the strategy of joining the IAR in order to open up new avenues of influence. It was therefore doubtless a skillful move on Adenauer's part to appoint Franz Blücher, federal minister for matters related to the Marshall Plan, as the German delegate to the IAR. Significantly, both London and Paris tried to torpedo Blücher's appointment. Adenauer explained to union representatives that the German delegate to the IAR should "represent not only the

---

23 Ibid., 296.
24 Lademacher and Mühlhausen, eds., *Sicherheit*, 87.
25 Ibid., 306, notice of Oct. 28, 1949 regarding the debate over the Ruhr Statute in a meeting of the Committee on the Occupation Statute and Foreign Affairs on Oct. 26, 1949.

interests of industry in the Ruhr" but "his name should also guarantee that the general viewpoint of economic cooperation with the Western European nations and the United States will be taken into account."[26] Thus, German entry into the IAR was cleverly put in the context of America's European Recovery Program. In an interview with *Die Zeit*, Adenauer said that he did not regard the Ruhr control authority as a yoke to be borne, but as the "first step toward control of all European heavy industry."[27]

III

The foregoing American policy toward Germany completely justified this optimism. It had been evident since 1947 that the Truman administration was determined not to let its stabilization policy in West Germany be impeded by either British concepts of order, such as the planned socialization of Ruhr industry, or by French desires for security. In particular, the security concerns raised repeatedly by the French government were either downplayed or completely ignored by Washington. American diplomats often used terms such as "obstructionism" and "intransigence" to describe French criticism of Washington's policy toward Germany.[28] Understanding was expressed in principle for French fears of a rebuilding of German military potential. At the same time, however, there was no doubt regarding the American government's determination to make no cutbacks of any kind in its policy of stabilization in West Germany.

Correctly assessing the priorities of American policy toward Europe, which allotted a special role to both Great Britain and the Federal Republic and ruled out long-term control of German industrial potential by France, French diplomatic efforts seized the initiative in May 1950 with the Schuman Plan. The danger of economic dominance by the Federal Republic was to be at least partly averted by the French offer of cooperation in the coal and steel industry. This motive for the Schuman Plan was clearly recognized, even by observers at the time.[29]

26 Ibid., 518; notation regarding the discussion between Adenauer and union representatives, Dec. 22, 1949. See also Adenauer's letter to Johannes Albers of Cologne on Dec. 22, 1949: "The ERP minister would seem to be the most suitable delegate, precisely because we must work toward expanding the principles of the Ruhr Statute to all of Western European heavy industry" (cited in Mensing, comp., *Adenauer: Briefe, 1949–1951*, 148).
27 Adenauer's *Zeit* interview of Nov. 3, 1949, in Lademacher and Mühlhausen, eds., *Sicherheit*, 341.
28 E.g., Murphy to State Department, Dec. 13, 1948, in *FRUS* 2 (1948): 1340.
29 E.g., in a cabinet document of June 26, 1951, "[T]he Schuman Plan appears as the last attempt by the French to retain some control over German heavy industry. Their aim is now to replace

American reaction to the Schuman Plan was fundamentally positive. From a historical perspective, this is not surprising, since certain American diplomats had worked quietly to bring it about. In Washington, there was particular relief at this sign of possible Franco-German conciliation. In a press conference on May 18, 1950, President Truman described the Schuman Plan as a "constructive, statesmanlike act" capable of placing Franco-German relations on a "completely new foundation." Schuman's initiative, Truman continued, was among the most encouraging European developments since the end of the war. Implementation of this plan could contribute to ending the Franco-German rivalry and could help build a peaceful, productive Europe.[30] For tactical reasons, the Truman administration had tried to avoid anything that would have been viewed as Washington intervention into negotiations on the Schuman Plan. This was done primarily to avoid possible negative repercussions among the French public and the fundamental opposition of the British government. Numerous American diplomats including the American high commissioner in the Federal Republic, John McCloy, worked behind the scenes at the direction of their government to constructively guide the contacts between the French and Germans. McCloy then provided "assistance in drafting the relevant articles of the Treaty Establishing the European Coal and Steel Community."[31]

The Marshall Plan delegate Paul Hoffman emphasized in this context the functional importance of the Federal Republic in American policy, namely, the possibility of "restoring Western European competitiveness via Germany."[32] The general prospect that was opening up for American diplomacy, therefore, was that of pushing the development of European industrial capitalism "in a direction ... consistent with the conditions of the Pax Americana."[33] Franco-German conciliation was to form the germ cell for Western integration to be made available to other nations as well. As regards Adenauer's foreign policy approach, the Schuman Plan and its overall positive assessment by American diplomats are the visible evidence of the success of the chancellor's strategy of cooperation. Adenauer's ambition, on the signing of the Petersberg Agreement, that control of the

some of their evaporating powers by obtaining influence indirectly in a manner politically acceptable to the Germans." Public Record Office, London, CAB 134/230.
30 *Public Papers of the Presidents of the United States: Harry S. Truman*, vol. 1950 (Washington, D.C., 1965), 418, 476.
31 Volker R. Berghahn, "Montanunion und Wettbewerb," in Helmut Berding, ed., *Wirtschaftliche und politische Integration in Europa im 19. und 20. Jahrhundert* (Göttingen, 1984), 267.
32 Cited in Berghahn, ibid., 270.
33 Ibid.

German economy by the Western Allies be converted as soon as possible into an all-European cooperation, had become reality with amazing speed in the coal and steel industry. The eagerness for Franco-German conciliation and the consistent consideration of American interests probably contributed very decisively to this success.

A further step toward emancipation was the decision regarding Germany's contribution to Western defense. At first, Adenauer rushed unquestioningly ahead of his time in late 1949 by presenting nearly unrestricted offers of German defense contributions. The outbreak of the Korean War in June 1950 brought this problem to a relevant stage of discussion sooner than expected. By December 1950, the foreign ministers of the United States, France, and Great Britain had agreed in principle on a German contribution to Western defense. It was to be accomplished not on a national, but on a supranational level. The foreign ministers had essentially adopted the ideas of French Prime Minister René Pleven, whose concept went down in history as the European Defense Community (EDC). With his offer of German troop contingents, Adenauer was essentially pursuing three objectives, which he summarized as follows in his memoirs: "1. achieving sovereignty as a result of rearmament; 2. security against rearmament of the Soviet zone by the Soviet Union; and 3. creation of a European federation."[34]

It was understandable that the arrangements for German rearmament could not be carried out at high speed so soon after the end of the war. Not least of the reasons for the delay in negotiations between the Western Allies and the Federal Republic was that Bonn had linked its defense contribution to a demand that the Occupation Statute be amended. "The dilemma in which we find ourselves with our policy," read a February 1951 State Department memorandum on American policy toward Germany, "is particularly clear on the question of German involvement in the defense of Europe. Since Soviet pressure makes early use of German aid inevitable, we believe that Germany must be integrated as soon as possible into the Western European system of defense. In the consultations regarding rearmament, however, the Germans have demanded equal status in the military cooperation."[35] In addition, "the Germans, with an eye toward regaining full sovereignty, are linking rearmament to demands for extensive political concessions from the Western powers." One solution, the memorandum continued, would be

---

34 Konrad Adenauer, *Erinnerungen, 1945–1953* (Stuttgart, 1973), 345.
35 Cited in Rolf Steininger, *Deutsche Geschichte, 1945–1961: Darstellung und Dokumente in zwei Bänden* (Frankfurt/Main, 1983), 2:402–3.

to involve the Federal Republic in the Western European integration process. Consequently, it could

turn out to be necessary to draw up a treaty governing relations with the Federal Republic, with the result that the Federal Republic will want to have equal rights in significant areas and actively assume the obligations of a member in the community of Western nations.[36]

The State Department herewith pointed out the path that was subsequently taken, leading to signing of the corresponding treaties in the spring of 1952.

It was doubtless a visible sign of success for the German federal government when, after long debate over a suitable location for the signing of the treaties, the Convention on Relations Between the Three Powers and the Federal Republic of Germany, which Adenauer called the Germany Treaty, was signed in Bonn on May 26, 1952. The EDC treaty was signed the following day in Paris. In a tribute to the treaties before the *Bundesparteiausschuss* (National Committee) of the CDU, Adenauer mainly emphasized the gain in sovereignty for the Federal Republic:

With these treaties, we again become a subject of policy and strategy, after having been only an object. With these treaties, we again have a voice in the political questions that decide the destiny of the German people. And with the treaty establishing the EDC, we also have a voice in the strategic vision for Germany and Europe. Before this, we did not have this option or this right.

Adenauer also pointed out that not only member nations of the European Defense Community were present at the signing of the EDC treaty in Paris but also representatives from England and the United States, as well as all the NATO countries. This made it clear, he said, that "the isolation of Germany will come to an end, if this is ratified, and that we will then be integrated into the great alliance of Western nations, which have set themselves one goal only – to preserve peace and order in Europe and in the world."[37]

However, the EDC and with it the Germany Treaty (as with the Petersberg Agreement, a linkage had been established) got stuck in the turmoil of French domestic politics. The longer the ratification process dragged on in France, the more clearly the European integration process entered a state of crisis, even before the defeat of the EDC in the French

---

36 Ibid.
37 Political status report at the meeting of the CDU's *Bundesparteiabschuss* in Bonn on June 14, 1952, in Schwarz, ed., *Adenauer: Reden*, 252–3. See also Adenauer's remarks before the national committee of the CDU on June 13, 1952, in Günter Buchstab, comp., *Adenauer: "Es musste alles neu gemacht werden": Die Protokolle des CDU-Bundesvorstandes, 1950–1953* (Stuttgart, 1986), 111ff.

national assembly on August 30, 1954. This affected the very core of both German and American policy on Europe. It is not surprising in this situation that both Washington and Bonn sought to intensify their bilateral relationship.

IV

Given the premise of Adenauer's policies, it is natural that the German federal government aspired to expand bilateral German-American relations. This was all the more necessary in view of the stagnation in policy regarding Western Europe. Some of the most important points of departure for an intensified policy toward America were unquestionably in the area of economics. This was true, in general, as a result of the significance of economic matters in both German and American foreign policy. On the German side, there was the additional factor that Bonn had gained sovereignty in trade policy with the Petersberg Agreement and therefore had greater freedom in this area, at least on paper. For Washington, too, bilateral economic negotiations with Bonn were of additional importance because there were no formal requirements in this area to take the other two Western Allies into consideration. Three important agreements on economic cooperation between Bonn and Washington should be mentioned: the Agreement on Economic Cooperation between the Federal Republic of Germany and the United States of America on December 15, 1949, the temporary reinstatement of the German-American trade agreement of 1923, and the Friendship, Trade, and Shipping Treaty of October 29, 1954. In these agreements, among other things, the Federal Republic accepted the liberal international economic order promoted by Washington. This economic cooperation with the United States also had a strong political component. This was evident in the conscious references to the Weimar era. In the cabinet briefings on the trade treaty of 1954, the Foreign Ministry emphasized the political significance that went far beyond the economic sphere. For the United States, the Foreign Ministry claimed, it was "the most important treaty of its kind." For the Federal Republic, it was:

the first and most important classical trade treaty after the war.... Even the old treaty of 1923, in its time, had political significance by virtue of its mere existence. The new treaty with the leading nation of the Western world will have no less an effect.[38]

---

38 Cabinet document of Oct. 1954 from the Foreign Ministry, Political Archives of the Foreign Ministry, Bonn, Länder Department III, *Vorbereitung und Abschluss von Handelsverträgen: Allgemeines*, vol. 1.

The first visible high point of Adenauer's systematic development of bilateral relations with the United States was his trip to the United States in April 1953.[39] In its handling of the nearly two-week visit, Washington signaled the improved status of the Federal Republic in American foreign policy. The chancellor received ample opportunity to explain his political ideas to the press, to the Senate Committee on Foreign Relations, and, especially, to President Eisenhower and Secretary of State John Foster Dulles. At the airport upon Adenauer's arrival in Washington, Vice President Richard Nixon declared that Washington wanted to go back to the "old relationship," in other words the German-American cooperation of the 1920s.[40] The restoration and deepening of this relationship was also the goal of the Federal Republic, confirmed the chancellor in his first meeting with the American president.

After his return, Adenauer told the executive board of the CDU (*Bundesvorstand*) of his gratification over his reception in the United States. It was "so surprisingly good . . . that one could hardly have imagined it being any better." The "reception by President Eisenhower himself" was really "such that . . . German-Americans, older people, came to me afterward in Chicago and New York, with tears in their eyes, and said 'Thank you for coming. Now we Americans of German origin have had the last shadow removed that was placed on us by the last war.'" Adenauer's visit to Arlington National Cemetery made a particular impression on him, which he described on many occasions. In accordance with American protocol, it was staged very effectively with gun salutes, national anthems, and presentation of the German flag. "The whole thing," according to Adenauer, "was a demonstrative welcome for the Federal Republic of Germany, which one could not conceive of having been done better or more effectively." This occasion reinforced the chancellor's view of the importance of good relations with the United States: "It is natural that we shall try now, as before, to maintain very close and good contact with Washington." However, the chancellor also warned against overestimating German options in the realm of international politics. "We Germans should be clear that we are still not very significant in world history at this time." When one sees the "power of America," Adenauer continued, and considers "what extensive connec-

---

39 See in particular *FRUS* 7 (1952–4): 424ff; Hans-Jürgen Grabbe, *Unionsparteien, Sozialdemokratie und Vereinigte Staaten von Amerika, 1945–1966* (Düsseldorf, 1983), 192ff.

40 "United States Delegation Minutes of the First Meeting of Chancellor Adenauer and President Eisenhower, The White House, Apr. 7, 1953," dated Apr. 17, 1953, *FRUS* 7 (1952–4): 426.

tions Great Britain [still has] in the world, . . . then we Germans are really not in the same class."[41] Precisely in light of this situation, it must be asserted that the chancellor's first trip to America was a successful stage on the way to equal status for the Federal Republic.

The chancellor's visit to the United States in April 1953 also had an important domestic political function. In the days preceding the second Bundestag election, it was invaluable to the CDU/CSU that the chancellor was received so grandly in the United States. The campaign strategists could present Adenauer as a guarantee of good German-American relations and increased German standing in the world. This was done, for example, in a film produced for the campaign entitled *Adenauers Amerikareise* (Adenauer's trip to America), which was classified as extremely effective advertising by the national headquarters of the CDU.[42] Opinion polls confirmed that the trip to the United States was a hit in the elections. Whereas only 30 percent of those polled in late 1952 said they agreed with the chancellor's policies, this percentage increased to 41 percent after his trip to America.[43]

During his visit to Washington, Adenauer also asked the American government in thinly veiled form for support in the upcoming elections, and his request was granted. American diplomats discussed this internally without embarrassment.[44] Washington took particularly spectacular steps in the form of statements by the president and secretary of state. On June 17, 1953, Eisenhower took the opportunity to praise Adenauer's stability and his policy on Germany.[45] The president affirmed that the shared the opinion that reunification of Germany could be achieved only through continued Western European integration. At a press conference, Secretary of State Dulles was even more direct. With respect to the German question, he expressed his conviction that it would be devastating for Germany if Adenauer were unable to continue his work as federal chancellor after the elections.[46]

The chancellor's foreign policy and, notably, his support by the American government certainly contributed to the positive outcome in the Bundestag elections of 1953. With 45.2 percent of the votes on the

---
41 Minutes of the meeting of May 22, 1953, in Buchstab, *Adenauer*, 516–82, quotations on 519ff.
42 See Grabbe, *Unionsparteien*, 193.
43 Ibid.
44 In late July 1953, however, the State Department warned against making support of Adenauer's campaign too public, for fear this could expose the chancellor to increased criticism from the opposition that he was a "puppet of the Americans" (State Department communication to the High Commissioner for Germany [HICOG], July 30, 1953, *FRUS* 7 [1952–4]: 499).
45 Ibid., Eisenhower to Adenauer, July 23, 1953: 491ff.
46 See ibid., editorial note, 532.

second ballot, the CDU/CSU gained the absolute majority of the seats. In contrast to the "Erhard election" of 1949, the Bundestag election of 1953 could therefore be characterized as the "Adenauer election."[47] The outcome of the Bundestag election illustrates the entanglement of domestic and foreign policy where the American factor is concerned. Adenauer's successful American policy contributed to success at the ballot box and, conversely, the impressive performance of the CDU and CSU had repercussions for the chancellor's status with respect to the United States. The Eisenhower administration was confirmed in its view that it had bet on the "right horse" in its policy toward Germany, and that it was in interests of the United States to have continued confidence in Adenauer. Internal American status reports confirm this.

The American High Commission, for example, used the end of the first session of the German Bundestag after the elections of 1953 as an occasion to produce a detailed evaluation of the most important political events in the Federal Republic since it was established.[48] This report yields important insights into the evaluation of Adenauer's policies by the American diplomatic corps. The very introduction refers to the "skilled and powerful leadership" by Federal Chancellor Adenauer, which placed the legislative branch "on the shadow side of political events." The German federal government had been able to implement its most important programs without notable amendment by the parliament, the report continued. In view of this dominance of the executive branch, the report concluded, any analysis of the West German political system would first of all have to address the function of the chancellor and his governing apparatus.

The strong position of the chancellor, the report went on, resulted partially from the fact that the constructive vote of no confidence anchored in the Basic Law provided him with more independence from the parliament than was the case in other European parliamentary democracies. Thus, Adenauer had a position comparable in strength to that of the president of the United States, despite the narrow majority with which he was elected chancellor in September 1949. This constitutional status of the chancellor was reinforced by German tradition and mentality, which also tended to favor a stronger executive branch. The position of the

---

47 See Grabbe, *Unionsparteien*, 193.
48 U.S. HICOG, Bonn, to State Department, July 12, 1954: "Some Observations on West German Political Developments," National Archives, Washington, D.C., RG 59, 762A.00/7-1254. See also Williams memorandum, ibid.: "I think it will be valuable to keep the despatch in mind as a desirable base for briefing papers that may be required of us and for quick instruction of officers who come to see us for a day or two before proceeding to Germany on assignment."

federal chancellor had been further bolstered by the CDU/CSU victory in the Bundestag elections of 1953. Under these conditions, Adenauer had and used the opportunity to leave a decisive mark on the development of the Federal Republic.

The report also found the strong position of the executive branch evidenced by Adenauer's "kitchen cabinet" and suggested comparisons to Roosevelt's New Deal. In the weight of the office of chancellor, the report also spotted a weakness of the young democracy, because the small, influential group surrounding Adenauer had made no moves so far to increase the number of people involved in the political decision-making process. This potential weakness in the government was exacerbated by the chancellor's tendency to often leave even party colleagues and coalition partners in the dark regarding his true intentions, particularly in the area of foreign policy. Nor did Adenauer involve the opposition in the foreign policy planning and decision-making process. The events of 1949–54 therefore confirmed the assessment of the first German chancellor made by the American High Commission at the inception of the Federal Republic: Under the given circumstances, Adenauer may have been the best solution for the young republic.

This positive assessment of Adenauer was corroborated by reference to the chancellor's status report that progress toward his most important political objectives was possible only by moderating his policies on the development of Germany. Both his private and official statements clearly showed his recognition of the fact that Germany could play a major role in a unified Europe only by not undertaking too much too soon.

One important factor in the chancellor's strength, the U.S. report continued, was his success, especially the economic prosperity and partial restoration of Germany's international standing. The big foreign policy successes promised by the chancellor, however, had yet to be attained, namely, the regaining of sovereignty and the right to defensive rearmament, plus progress on Western integration in a manner that opened up new development prospects for Germany. The promises linked to signing of the treaties with the West had yet to be fulfilled. If Adenauer's policy of "enlightened realism" gradually proved impractical, his attractiveness would abate and his leadership powers disappear, for the chancellor's program, which was so successful in the Bundestag campaign of 1953, essentially rested on three pillars: prosperity, reunification, and Western integration.

Whereas the first pillar, prosperity, was proving stable, the report found that the second, the reunification policy, was precariously propped. Particularly in view of the chancellor's repeated reminders that integration with the West was the only path to reunification, Western integration gained central importance in this respect as well. For if this element of Adenauer's vision should also prove unsuccessful, then the ground would be pulled out from under the entire policy to which Adenauer's prestige was linked. Stagnation in policy toward the West would therefore have domestic and foreign policy consequences for the Federal Republic. There were already signs of growing impatience, disillusionment and budding anti-Americanism. This was true not only of the SPD opposition but also for groups that had previously been among the most reliable supporters of America's policy toward Germany. Moreover, there was the danger that continual stagnation in European policy would lead to a drastic reorientation in German political thought. Germany might succumb to the temptation to make a virtue of necessity and use the forced demilitarization as an argument for obtaining national unity through neutrality, pursuing a seesaw policy between East and West or even striving for direct German-Soviet cooperation. Under these circumstances, the report concluded, the chancellor would be able to exert effective control over developments in Germany only if he produced concrete foreign policy results. After the defeat of the EDC, this line of thought led Washington to arrange for Germany to contribute to Western defense through NATO, thus establishing one of the prerequisites for the granting of formal sovereignty to the Federal Republic. The events of May 5, 1955, were therefore the result of close German-American cooperation.

V

The close cooperation between Germany and the United States should not mask the fact that there was at least considerable latent potential for conflict between the two, as summarized by the terms "neutrality fear" and "Rapallo trauma." Adenauer was repeatedly gripped by a sort of neutrality panic, by the idea that Washington might reach an agreement with Moscow on German neutrality. In gloomy tones, the chancellor depicted the consequences of such a policy:

The Soviet threat is a reality and there is no point in closing our eyes and denying its existence. This danger exists not only for Germany; it threatens all the countries of Western Europe. It would be a fateful error for certain European countries to believe that Soviet Russia will content itself with maintaining its current power status or drawing only the Federal Republic into its sphere of influence. The political goal of Soviet Russia, in my opinion, is very clear, very logical and very consistent. Soviet Russia wants to ensure the demilitarization of Germany at all costs. It then wants to achieve the withdrawal of Western Allied troops from a demilitarized Germany *neutralized* by paper treaties, and it wants this because it knows that . . . the Federal Republic would then fall very quickly into the Soviet sphere of influence. However, if Soviet Russia achieves this goal, then European integration would be impossible. . . . If European integration becomes impossible, if the Soviet influence in Western Europe continued to grow in this way, then the United States would certainly one day lose interest in Europe. Then Soviet Russia would have achieved its goal: it would rule all of Europe. If Soviet Russia were successful in becoming the ruler of Europe, then it would also be a very serious opponent for the United States. Division of the world into a Soviet and an American sphere of influence would then be a distinct possibility, and we, we Europeans and England as well, would belong to the Russian sphere of influence. That would truly be the end of the Christian West.[49]

In retrospect, however, Adenauer's fear of neutrality was unjustified, since neutrality as an alternative to Western integration was not a subject for serious debate in American diplomatic circles. Even the plans and discussion papers of the American government dealing with formal neutrality always proceeded on the assumption that Germany would retain at least its economic ties to the West and that, in this way, at least a factual dominance of American influence would be maintained. There is no evidence in American policy toward Germany and Europe of the danger, repeatedly invoked by Adenauer, that Germany would be surrendered to the Soviets.

Analogous to Adenauer's fear of neutrality, internal American analyses, in an exaggeration of the Rapallo trauma, repeatedly articulated the fear that the Federal Republic would align itself with the East. According to a memorandum from the German desk of the State Department in March 1950,[50] there was a danger that Soviet references to Russo-German friendship under Bismarck or to Stresemann's idea of Germany serving a bridging function between East and West would find fertile ground in the Federal Republic. Moreover, the Treaty of Rapallo showed that communism was no obstacle to Russo-German cooperation since both the economic and political implications of a Russo-German arrangement would give Germany a chance to ascend again to the status of a superpower. Finally, reference was made to the unsolved problem of German reunification. Precisely this German wish for reunification carried with it

---

49 Speech on Sept. 14, 1951, in Bad Ems, in Schwarz, ed., *Adenauer: Reden*, 230–1 (original emphasis).
50 Cox memorandum, Mar. 13, 1950, *FRUS* 4 (1950): 608ff.

the risk of German alignment with the East and had to be taken into consideration in formulating U.S. policy toward Germany. The Rapallo fear expressed repeatedly by American politicians and diplomats is just as unjustified with respect to Adenauer's foreign policy. A seesaw policy between East and West was not an option for Adenauer.

Even a sober historical analysis cannot change the fact that, for those involved in the decision-making process in West Germany and the United States, the German neutrality fear and the American Rapallo trauma were potentially disruptive elements for German-American relations, which started to become apparent in the late 1950s in the course of American efforts toward détente in the East–West conflict. At the high point of East–West confrontation, the neutrality fear and Rapallo trauma had a stabilizing effect instead, because they further increased the value of the Federal Republic in the eyes of American leaders and the central significance of the United States in Bonn's domestic and foreign policy. This was another reason for the rapid resurgence of West Germany.

In retrospect, Adenauer emphasized the significance of the United States for the West German emancipation process in a pointed manner. "What have we accomplished in foreign policy?" he asked in a statement on fundamental foreign and domestic policy issues in March 1966 before the fourteenth convention of the CDU in Bonn. He answered the question as follows:

Hitler wantonly started the war without provocation. Hitler and his people committed the most shameful crimes against humanity. For this reason, the German name was disgraced around the world and, in the first years after the war, other nations thought only of what the Germans had done under the Hitler regime. We therefore had to win back the trust of the other nations – this is one of the most fundamental principles of any foreign policy – especially trust in our constancy.

From the very beginning, he said, the United States was particularly important in this trust-building process.

The United States was actually the first to trust us again. I am deeply moved as I remember sometimes that day at Arlington National Cemetery near Washington when I laid a wreath on the Tomb of the Unknown Soldier.... The first foreign minister to visit us here in Bonn was Dean Acheson, the American secretary of state under Truman. Truman showed great understanding of us and our situation. In the main, however, it was Eisenhower and John Foster Dulles... who gained such a degree of trust in us and our policies that we could discuss with them everything that was in our hearts. We could be assured that they were listening with benevolence and would keep what we said in confidence.

The "main guiding principle of our whole foreign policy" was "joining the free nations of the West.... In this process, we had to fight the massive resistance of the opposition." Consistent implementation of this policy, however, despite all the resistance, brought about a "closer and closer connection between the Federal Republic and the free nations of the West." And the former Federal chancellor correctly surmised "that, if someone had predicted in 1945 what path the Federal Republic would take, no one – probably not even I – would have believed this prediction."⁵¹

From the perspective of a permanent solution for the western part of Germany, Adenauer's strategy of incrementally regaining sovereignty in cooperation with the Western Allies was an unquestionable success. The Petersberg Agreement manifested the first gain in economic, political, and psychological terrain, which was won in a hardy struggle with the Allies. This early emergence of Adenauer's self-confident and demanding negotiating style clearly refutes the charge made by his domestic political opponents that he was "chancellor of the Allies" or a "puppet" or a mere "taker of orders." At the same time, it cannot be denied that Adenauer was the ideal partner for the Western Allies, especially the two Anglo-Saxon powers, by virtue of his foreign policy program and the domestic political stability he achieved.⁵² This was particularly true for Washington, as impressively documented by the American High Commission's analysis in the summer of 1954, as cited previously. Washington was able to advance significantly its goals of economic, political, military, and cultural integration of the West through close cooperation with the Adenauer government and through opportunities for informal or even direct influence. Adenauer was the "dream partner" for Washington, and the chancellor began "his rise in Germany and Europe as a man of the Americans."⁵³ The Federal Republic enjoyed economic and political stability as a result of Western integration and support from the United States. Of course, it must not be overlooked that, in the course of these developments, Adenauer's vision of reunification dried into a mere rhetorical formula.

51 Speech before the fourteenth convention of the CDU in Bonn, Mar. 21, 1966, in Schwarz, ed., *Adenauer: Reden*, 477–8.
52 See also Steininger, *Deutsche Geschichte*, 2:360–1.
53 Schwarz, ed., *Adenauer: Reden*, 687.

15

American Policy Toward German Unification

Images and Interests

KONRAD H. JARAUSCH

The peaceful revolutions of 1989–90 toppled regimes and transformed international relations. After four decades in which time itself seemed to have become frozen, events rushed forward at a dizzying pace. In a nutshell, the collapse of Communism in Central and Eastern Europe overthrew the Soviet empire, destroyed the Warsaw Pact, and dissolved the Council for Mutual Economic Assistance (COMECON). The unexpected rising of suppressed peoples shattered the relative stability of the Cold War and ushered in a period of rapid and unpredictable change.[1] By ending the East–West confrontation, this rupture opened up undreamt-of vistas of action which also tested the established relationship between the United States and the Federal Republic of Germany. It was in effect a redefining movement in transatlantic relations that was fraught with exciting possibilities for crises and new beginnings.

Not surprisingly, American opinion responded to the new situation much like an individual reacts to an unforeseen event, namely, in terms of its prior experiences with the Germans. The Central and East European rising stirred up layers of public images in the United States that had accumulated through personal contact and media projection over two centuries. In the case of Germany negative stereotypes, created by the enmity of the world wars and the shock of the Holocaust, predictably raised old fears of aggression and domination. But earlier historical memories of immigration as well as education, and recent impressions based on private contacts and the stability of the Federal Republic, also engendered

---

1 Timothy Garton Ash, *The Magic Lantern* (New York 1990); Ralf Dahrendorf, *Reflections on the Revolution in Europe* (New York, 1990).

more positive views that spurred new hopes.[2] These mixed feelings sparked a lively debate in the American press and academic community which, although ostensibly about the future, was largely couched in terms of the past.

Because the public remained divided, the decisions taken by the president and his advisers were shaped less by such images than by sober calculations of American national interest. Although welcoming the unexpected upheaval, the Bush administration had to scramble to develop a policy that it wanted to pursue toward the crumbling of communism. In its initial "strategic review," inherited Cold War reflexes of competition with the Soviet Union and ideological distrust clashed with bolder analyses that emphasized the potential for cooperation with those leaders and called for a fresh willingness to take political risks. As public opinion and expert advice often conflicted, the government had to reconcile different personality traits, agency proclivities, and group agendas. Efforts of Bonn and Washington experts who had built up an intricate network during decades of contested cooperation to exert some influence on decisions further complicated the task of policy formation. What some saw as a threat to established patterns, others could view as an opportunity for new or previously ignored departures.[3]

Analysts have rarely studied the American role in German unification, since they are more concerned about its future implications. Those transatlantic accounts that do discuss the question are in remarkable agreement that Washington acted wisely in championing German unity.[4] In contrast to media criticism of the passivity of the Bush-Baker team, insiders praise their exceptional self-restraint, which sought not to spook President Gorbachev. Owing to the happy ending, the remaining disputes between the Bonn and East Berlin embassies, staffers in the State Department and the National Security Council, or NSC, as well as members of the German and American governments revolve around who deserves most of the credit.[5] This unanimity raises the unusual interpretative

---

2 Konrad H. Jarausch, "Huns, Krauts or Good Germans? The German Image in America, 1800–1980," in James F. Harris, ed., *German-American Interrelations: Heritage and Challenge* (Tübingen, 1985), 145–59; and Willi Paul Adams and Knud Krakau, eds., *Deutschland und Amerika: Perzeption und historische Realität* (Berlin, 1985).
3 Michael Beschloss and Strobe Talbott, *At the Highest Levels: The Inside Story of the End of the Cold War* (Boston, 1993), and James A. Baker, *The Politics of Diplomacy: Revolution, War and Peace, 1989–1992* (New York, 1995).
4 Stephen F. Szabo, *The Diplomacy of German Unification* (New York, 1992), and Heinrich Bortfeldt, *Washington, Bonn, Berlin: Die USA und die deutsche Einheit* (Bonn, 1993).
5 Philip Zelikow and Condoleezza Rice, *Germany Unified and Europe Transformed: A Study in Statecraft* (Cambridge, Mass., 1995), and Richard Kiessler and Frank Elbe, *Ein runder Tisch mit scharfen Ecken: Der diplomatische Weg zur deutschen Einheit* (Baden-Baden, 1993).

problem of having to explain the surprising consensus in U.S. policy. In doing so, it is necessary to go beyond the public debate on Germany and to analyze those factors that actually determined the final decisions.

I

Views of other countries tend to derive both from old recollections as well as from new information. Such attitudes are the product of decades of reporting and reflection that fill entire libraries and create something called national stereotypes. Popular images are the result of discursive contests over imaginary space that often have more to do with the problems of the country in which they take place than with the traits of the country they purport to describe. Intellectual criticism of their inaccuracy, although inevitably correct, is therefore largely beside the point: what matters is, rather, the relative saliency and distribution of such views of others. Because they mostly draw on past experience, their vocabulary generally tends to be historical.[6] In the case of German unification, which of the competing images governed the American popular response?

In this first television revolution, the role of the media was crucial in generating public feelings. Although Tom Brokaw of NBC news scored a coup with his report from the opening of the Wall, news coverage of this lead-issue was rather spotty on the whole. T.V. excelled in conveying dramatic moments like embassy occupations, mass demonstrations, or police repression, but it had difficulty in communicating the complex implications of those events. Increasingly caught up in the excitement, newspaper correspondents provided more depth in their reporting, but they had to mediate between rapid changes on the spot and incomprehension at home. Magazines took more time to reflect on developments in special issues or to proclaim a prominent politician like Helmut Kohl to be "man of the year." But in their commentaries, editorial writers, remote from the feeling of the action, tended to articulate domestic fears.[7]

As a result of such uneven reporting, powerful pictures all too often overwhelmed critical reflection. Events moved with such speed that

---

[6] Kurt H. Stapf, Wolfgang Stroebe, and Klaus Jonas, *Amerikaner über Deutschland und die Deutschen: Urteile und Vorurteile* (Opladen, 1986); Gordon A. Craig, "Die Bundesrepublik Deutschland aus der Sicht der USA," in Werner Weidenfeld and Hartmut Zimmermann, eds., *Deutschland-Handbuch: Eine doppelte Bilanz, 1949–1989* (Bonn, 1989), 669–78.
[7] Michael E. Geisler, "Mehrfach gebrochene Mauerschau: 1989–1990 in den US Medien," in Rainer Bohn, Knuth Hickethier, and Eggo Müller, eds., *Mauer-Show: Das Ende der DDR, die deutsche Einheit und die Medien* (Berlin, 1992), 257–75.

academic analysis was almost always out of date the moment it appeared in print. Instead, television pictures of children penned in embassy gardens, singing demonstrators carrying candles, or club-wielding policemen evoked powerful emotions in an audience half a world apart. Television conveyed the drama of refugees fleeing, protesters asking for basic human rights, and opportunist communists promising reforms. But political reflection on the causes and consequences of these images never quite managed to catch up with the changes, and failed to construct a rational barrier against human compassion. Bypassing the concerns of informed commentators, graphic newsclips created so much public sympathy for East German aspirations for freedom that they were difficult to oppose.[8]

In contrast, old fears of the German problem tended to dominate the more extended commentary. A classic representation of this attitude was *The New York Times* editorial of November 17, summing up the aversion of Germany's neighbors to its unification.[9] Some intellectuals like Arthur Miller went all the way back to Kaiser Bill to warn against authoritarianism; columnists like William Safire polemicized against German aggression in the world wars; other editorialists like Abraham Rosenthal invoked Hitler's racial genocide in the Holocaust; and former policy makers like Henry Kissinger recalled the danger of national neutralism and cautioned against a new Rapallo deal between Bonn and Moscow. The Anglo-Irish publicist Conor Cruise O'Brien summed up the general anxiety when he flatly predicted the rise of a "Fourth Reich."[10] These warnings sought to activate negative stereotypes according to which 79 percent of Americans considered Germans "aggressive" and 55 percent called them "arrogant."

Other voices, however, expressed new hopes for a united Germany, based on more recent postwar experiences. Although these counterarguments looked less dramatic, they could cite a wide array of positive factors. To begin with, regular people recalled favorable impressions of German immigrants as hardworking and decent citizens; political observers stressed Bonn's behavior as a star pupil of democracy after World War II; clergymen emphasized Germany's virtually complete break with militarism and its rejection of nuclear arms after 1945; business circles applauded the

---

8 Wolfgang G. Gibowski and Holli A. Semetko, "Amerikanische öffentliche Meinung und deutsche Einheit," in Wolfgang-Uwe Friedrich, ed., *Die USA und die deutsche Frage* (Frankfurt/Main, 1991), 391–406.
9 "One Germany: Not Likely Now," *New York Times*, Nov. 19, 1989.
10 Diverse commentaries reprinted in Harold James and Marla Stone, eds., *When the Wall Came Down: Reactions to German Unification* (London, 1992), 167–217.

performance of the economy and its firm integration into the European Community; and military analysts noted the dependability of the Bundeswehr within the Western Alliance.[11] These optimistic assessments played on favorable stereotypes, according to which 89 percent of Americans called Germans "disciplined," 81 percent "efficient," 70 percent "caring," 65 percent "friendly," and 55 percent "trustworthy."

In many ways, these contradictory images represented a clash between different perceptions of the German past. American skeptics drew on the negative experiences from World Wars I and II and the horrible memories of the Holocaust; the optimists cited the more positive record of the postwar era and the stability of West Germany. On the one hand, there were deep suspicions of a German otherness that had provided the dark counterfoil to liberal democracy in the twentieth century; on the other hand, there was also much pride in American remaking of the Germans as trustworthy democrats after 1945. No wonder that potential solutions were phrased in historical terms such as an Austrian version of continued GDR independence or confederation schemes, such as the nineteenth-century German *Bund*. Eventually the more recent positive experiences won out: Between November 1989 and February 1990, the *Washington Post* gradually began to support unification, while *The New York Times* took until May 20, 1990, to accept its inevitability.[12]

As a result of such coverage, public attitude toward the possibility of German unification turned surprisingly favorable. Opinion surveys still displayed some earlier ambivalences, but approval both gained in breadth and increased in strength during the spring of 1990. Moreover, the replies were consistent among different polling organizations, suggesting that the responses were robust enough to be independent of the questions asked. Already in January 1990 61 percent of those surveyed by the *Los Angeles Times* favored German unity; by March a German poll found 67 percent positive respondents, while 77 percent of a *Wall Street Journal* sample agreed; in April even 76 percent of the more skeptical *New York Times* readers supported unification; and in May ABC pollsters discerned an impressive 84 percent approval rating.[13] Considering American memories

---

11 Contrasting arguments in Gary L. Geipel, ed., *The Future of Germany* (Indianapolis, Ind., 1990), a Hudson Institute Report.
12 Editorials in the *Washington Post*, Nov. 1989 to Feb. 8, 1990, as well as in the *New York Times*, Nov. 1989 to May 20, 1990. Cf. also Frank Trommler, ed., *Amerika und die Deutschen: Bestandsaufnahme einer 300jährigen Geschichte* (Opladen, 1986).
13 Arthur M. Hanhardt, "Die deutsche Vereinigung im Spiegelbild der amerikanischen veröffentlichten Meinung," in Friedrich, ed., *Die USA und die deutsche Frage*, 407–17; and Bortfeldt, *Washington, Bonn, Berlin*, 71–4.

of World War II, these responses represented a greater amount of unanimity than in most other foreign policy questions.

Such global ratings, nonetheless, hid an undercurrent of unease that surfaced only in more precise analyses. Already the aggregate data revealed a substantial amount of respondents, ranging from one-quarter to one-seventh, who were skeptical of unification, with less than 10 percent bitterly opposed. In response to a different question, 37 percent considered reunified Germany a danger because of its potential expansionism (21 percent), current economic power (26 percent), the possible return of fascism (27 percent), and for other reasons (26 percent).[14] In other words, even some of those who were willing to grant the German wish to be reunited harbored considerable doubts about the future course of such a larger Germany. These reservations were neither strong nor widespread enough to compel the Bush administration to oppose unification, but they were sufficient to persuade policy makers to be circumspect.

The social distribution of opinion also favored a cautiously supportive course. Proponents of unification were strongest among Americans with German relatives, friends on the continent, or personal experience in the old country. Most members of the business community, military who had served there, and academic specialists with professional expertise tended to be sanguine as well. But owing to the memory of the suffering, many American Jews were opposed (42 percent against but still 56 percent for), world war veterans or older people had doubts, and citizens with ethnic ties to Poland or other victimized countries also remained skeptical. Interestingly enough, intellectuals were more fearful than the normal folk (only 57 percent of the college-educated in favor versus 72 percent of the general population).[15] Although a considerable segment of the elite continued to worry, even among critical groups a majority was willing to overcome its doubts, whereas the regular people were more optimistic yet.

Because American policy makers had to respond to a host of competing issues, the contextual framing of the events proved important as well. Washington debates did not focus on Germany alone, but were preoccupied with the bilateral confrontation with the Soviet Union and the fate of its domestic reforms. For the White House, the German issue was embedded in a wider question of how the Western Alliance should deal

---

14 Gibowski and Semetko, "Amerikanische öffentliche Meinung," in Friedrich, ed., *Die USA und die deutsche* Frage, 397–8.
15 Ibid., 400–3; Hanhardt, "Deutsche Vereinigung," 409.

with the "End of the Cold War" in general. If the military threat were really decreasing, progress might be possible in disarmament and even the long-dormant trade with Russia might revive. From this broader perspective the East German awakening appealed as a potential solvent of the Eastern Bloc that would weaken the Red Empire, if not destroy it altogether.[16] Such rhetoric provided a wider world-political perspective that created the conceptual space within which to attempt a German settlement.

In the larger "Collapse of Communism," the German question was only a subsidiary issue to Americans. Compared with the intractable difficulties of reforming the Soviet Union, overcoming the division of Central Europe seemed an eminently solvable task. If Germany were no longer preoccupied with its own reunification, might it not serve as an anchor of political stability and help manage the transition of the post-Communist states to democracy? If the leading economy on the continent were enlarged by one of the most productive of the East, might it not speed the transformation of the bankrupt planning system to capitalism with aid and investment? By acting as an American partner, a grateful Germany might make up for economic or military limitations of U.S. power, engaged elsewhere in the world and hamstrung by domestic discontent. This wider framing helped to change perceptions of Germany from a past problem to a potential solution, thereby paving the way for American approval of unity.[17]

It also helped that both domestic camps in the United States had readymade interpretations for German unification. The Reaganesque Right could view the disappearance of the GDR as part of the triumph of capitalism and proof of an elemental human urge for freedom. Military circles might congratulate themselves on the diminution of the Soviet threat and the crumbling of the cornerstone of Russian empire that was likely to prevent its future reemergence. At the same time, the liberal Left could applaud the democratic awakening in East Germany as a stirring example of grassroots democracy and people power. Whereas some intellectuals might mourn the collapse of "real existing socialism," others could hope for a "Third Way" between both systems or for the liberation of social reform from the shackles of post-Stalinism.[18] Although contradic-

16 Michael Haltzel, "Amerikanische Einstellungen zur deutschen Wiedervereinigung," *Europa-Archiv*, no. 4 (1990): 127–32.
17 Bernard Gwertzman and Michael T. Kaufmann, eds., *The Collapse of Communism* (New York, 1990); and Timothy Garton Ash, *In Europe's Name: Germany and the Divided Continent* (New York, 1993).
18 Burkhard Koch, lecture on the U.S. reaction to German unification, Stanford University, Spring

tory, these readings overlapped enough to keep German unity from becoming the focus of a major ideological debate among Americans.

II

On the whole, American policy toward German unification proved remarkably supportive. In spite of elite reservations or intellectual anxieties, there was little struggle over its basic direction, with arguments largely limited to its implementation. Earlier disagreements between Washington and Bonn like the clash on modernizing short-range nuclear forces seemed forgotten and had hardly any impact on decisions. Of course, diverse treaty clauses and a long list of public statements had publicly committed the American government to the cause of German unity. But because other Western powers seemed less bound by prior assurances, the speed with which the United States converted the rhetoric of German unity into policy remains astounding in retrospect. Because the majority of the public agreed with the aim of keeping Germany away from French or Russian influence, Washington decisionmakers could dedicate themselves to the grand game of bringing unity off rather than having to build support for their policies.[19] What was so different about the actual American contribution to German unification?

To begin with, fewer actors than usual were involved in the shaping of the decisions. In Washington the key player was President George Bush, a World War II veteran and former CIA director as well as Ambassador to China. Although he harbored no strong feelings about Germany, he had much foreign policy experience, felt an ideological kinship to the conservative Kohl government, and understood the rising importance of the FRG in Europe. His right hand was Secretary of State James A. Baker, a successful lawyer and domestic advisor who had been a tough negotiator as secretary of treasury but was a novice in international affairs which made him receptive to fresh ideas. In the State Department the most influential advisors were Counsellor Robert Zoellick and Policy Planning Staff Director Dennis Ross, while in the NSC Brent Scowcroft was an able coordinator and the head of the European desk, Robert

---

1992; and Michael Minkenberg, "Das neue Deutschland amerikanische Reaktionen auf die deutsche Vereinigung," MS, Cornell University, 1993.
19 Essays by Wolfgang Krieger, Klaus Schwabe, Hans-Jürgen Schröder, Ernst-Otto Czempiel, Clay Clemens, Wolfram Hanrieder, and Gerald R. Kleinfeld in Friedrich, ed., *Die USA und die deutsche Frage*, 79–390.

Blackwill, an experienced professional. In Bonn the businessman ambassador, Vernon Walters, loudly advocated unification without much impact at home, while in East Berlin the career diplomat Richard Barkley promoted the reform of the GDR and had Baker's ear.[20]

This was an extraordinarily narrow circle of decisionmakers for an issue of such momentous importance. Policy was determined by the president and secretary of state, supported by the relevant specialists in the NSC and at State, about a dozen people in all. Leaving the vast intelligence, military, and diplomatic bureaucracies to spin their wheels meant that important decisions could be shielded from the influence of lobbyists and journalists, ordinarily so potent in protracted policy struggles. Because hardly any of the key players had personal ties to Germany, their views were only affected by a general professional rapport, built up during decades between the Bonn and Washington establishments. Hence those responsible could act on the basis of a hardheaded assessment of what they considered to be in the best interest of the United States. The narrowness of this inside group made bold decisions possible and helped to override any lingering fears about German unity.[21]

As a result, the negotiating process resembled "a classic tale of 'great power' diplomacy." Talks proceeded between heads of state and their foreign ministers, with preparations limited to a few NSC staffers, such as the political scientist Condoleezza Rice for the Soviet Union and the lawyer Philip Zelikow for Germany. There were countless personal chats between decisionmakers of various countries as well as several important instances in which they conferred as a group. The heads of state exchanged many phone calls, letters, and messages, keeping closely in touch and seeking to influence one another. This confidential, not to say secret, procedure allowed complicated discussions to proceed outside of the glare of publicity. The intensity and frequency of the meetings gradually created an atmosphere of trust between the key players that permitted the resolution of conflicts of opinion by compromise. Only to announce the results in press conferences was not particularly democratic, but it seems to have worked effectively.[22]

---

20 Other important figures were Robert Gates, the deputy national security advisor, and Raymond Seitz, head of the European Bureau of the State Department. Baker, *Politics of Diplomacy*, 17–36; Zelikow and Rice, *Germany Unified*, 20–4.
21 Robert D. Blackwill, "German Unification and American Diplomacy," *American Council on Germany, Occasional Paper 1994*, no. 3. Cf. Manfred Knapp, "Die Aussenpolitik der USA unter George Bush," *Aus Politik und Zeitgeschichte*, B 44 (1992): 43–54.
22 Numerous entries in Horst Teltschik, *329 Tage: Innenansichten der Einigung* (Berlin, 1991) and Bortfeldt, *Washington, Bonn, Berlin*, 188–92.

The consultations took place in several configurations, superimposed upon each other. This complex diplomacy consisted essentially of a "double synchronous bilateralism" between Washington and Moscow, Bonn and Moscow, Washington and Bonn, and to a lesser degree, Bonn and Paris. Contacts between the United States and the Federal Republic were particularly close, reaching down to the working level and facilitating the exploration of ideas as well as the drafting of proposals. Less frequent were multilateral exchanges, involving the United States and its Western Allies, Britain and France, as well as Germany; in contrast, the Soviet Union hardly brought its own Warsaw Pact partners into the deliberations. Smaller states were merely consulted on single issues, like the Polish border question.[23] Formal organizations like the Conference on Security and Cooperation in Europe (CSCE) were only used to ratify the results of previous decisions taken in the inner circle. This limitation of participants created some resentment by those countries that were left out like Poland, Israel, or Italy, but it brought positive results.

Already in May 1989, U.S. policy makers had began to reassess the relationship with Germany and to debate the implications of the upheaval in the East. Instead of insisting on the modernization of short-range nuclear missiles which were largely targeted on East Germany, Washington compromised with Bonn by proposing conventional force reductions that delayed the decision. Not bound by historical images or "personal animosity," the White House decided to shift toward Bonn as "partner in leadership," because its increased economic weight made it dominant in the European Community. Viewing a potential collapse of the GDR as opportunity rather than as threat, the president was receptive to Chancellor Kohl's argument that "you and I are witnessing events beyond our wildest dreams, the ideological breakdown of a political and economic system." In order to demonstrate presidential leadership, Bush seized the initiative by announcing as a new vision "let Europe be whole and free."[24]

Although it played little part in the refugee crisis, Washington sent unmistakable signals that encouraged the reopening of the German question. In spite of wanting to maintain progress in detente with Moscow, the State Department tried to help the mass exodus by mediating with Hungary and Czechoslovakia and worried increasingly about the immo-

---

23 Bernd W. Kubbig, ed., *Transatlantische Unsicherheit: Die amerikanisch-europäischen Beziehungen im Umbruch* (Frankfurt/Main, 1991); and Kiessler and Elbe, *Runder Tisch*, passim.
24 Baker, *Politics of Diplomacy*, 92–6, 159; Zelikow and Rice, *Germany Unified*, 24–32; and Hans-Dietrich Genscher, *Erinnerungen* (Berlin, 1995), 623–5.

bility of the Socialist Unity Pary (*Sozialistische Einheitspartei Deutschlands,* or SED). In an early October interview, Baker professed "no concern about a unified Germany which is integrated into the democratic community of European nations" and in a later speech he "supported the reconciliation of the German people" in peace and freedom. After Erich Honecker's fall on October 18, the president similarly commented in *The New York Times*: "I don't share the concern that some European countries have about a reunified Germany," since he believed in Bonn's loyalty to NATO. Still groping toward a clear policy, these initial reactions gave a tentative green light, provided things did not move too fast.[25]

The fall of the Wall, nonetheless, caught the U.S. leaders somewhat by surprise. While feeling "overwhelming euphoria" at the toppling of this Cold War symbol, the secretary of state was at the same time concerned that a potential incident might escalate out of control. In order not to make the Soviets feel "that we are sticking our thumb in their eye," the White House decided to welcome the change so unemotionally that the uncomprehending media accused the president of showing insufficient enthusiasm. By telephone Foreign Minister Hans-Dietrich Genscher thanked "the American people for what you've done for Germany since World War II" and during a subsequent visit assured President Bush that Germany wanted self-determination but would continue to stay in NATO. Despite Soviet warnings against the consequences of "political extremism," the White House remained committed to supporting the democratization of East Germany and rejected the convocation of Four Power talks.[26]

To promote "prudent evolution," Washington subsequently tried to define its own prerequisites for unification. The White House was miffed at not having been consulted before the announcement of Helmut Kohl's Ten Point Plan for a confederation between the two Germanies, but acquiesced, since the proposal was consonant with its own views: "The real question was how to bring along Moscow and, to a lesser degree, London and Paris." To this end, the State Department defined four cardinal principles: (1) "self-determination . . . without prejudice to its outcome"; (2) "continued commitment to NATO" by West Germany; (3) "a peaceful, gradual . . . step by step process"; and (4) a guarantee of existing borders according to the Helsinki Agreement of 1975. At the

---

25 Baker, *Politics of Diplomacy,* 161–3; Zelikow and Rice, *Germany Unified,* 80–1; and Genscher, *Erinnerungen,* 641–2, 645–7, 650–1.
26 Baker, *Politics of Diplomacy,* 163–5; Zelikow and Rice, *Germany Unified,* 105–9; Genscher, *Erinnerungen,* 664–8.

Malta summit, the Bush–Baker team reassured President Gorbachev in early December that the United States supported his domestic reforms and would not seek to take unilateral advantage of the collapse of communism. And at the subsequent NATO meeting in Brussels the president made the four conditions public, thereby providing clear policy targets for the West.[27]

By mid-December growing criticism of the speed of German unification began to dampen the enthusiasm of the Bush administration. For domestic reasons this was a sensitive issue to the Soviets, while neither the French nor the British could muster much enthusiasm and some influential American commentators also opposed the prospect. To reassure the many critics, Secretary Baker sketched before the Berlin press association a broader security architecture that would include the Conference on Security and Cooperation in Europe and inaugurate a "new Atlanticism." In order to establish an independent channel to GDR leaders, he also visited the East and discussed the need for "reform and peaceful change" with Prime Minister Hans Modrow as well as with Lutheran Church leaders. The firsthand impressions, gathered in this visit, confirmed the view that East Germany was crumbling faster than expected and that the population would allow no turning back from the path toward some form of economic unity with the West.[28]

When the GDR actually imploded in January 1990, the State Department proposed a diplomatic framework for negotiating unity. To keep the process from spinning out of control, Dennis Ross and Robert Zoellick developed the "Two Plus Four" concept as a compromise between Four Power talks and German-German negotiations. Since Genscher demanded that the Germans be included on equal terms and rejected a general peace conference (such as the thirty-five member CSCE) as too unwieldy, bringing together the German states with the World War II victors seemed a suitable alternative. Bonn and East Berlin could work out the domestic side of unification among themselves and settle the international aspects with the Four Powers, while the CSCE could ratify the final product. Baker had to work hard to sell this approach to a skeptical NSC and the reluctant French and British as well as to convince the initially suspicious Soviets. Announced at the Open Skies Conference in Ottawa in mid-February, this negotiating framework

---

27 Baker, *Politics of Diplomacy*, 166–71; Zelikow and Rice, *Germany Unified*, 113–34; Beschloss and Talbott, *Highest Levels*, 153–71; Genscher, *Erinnerungen*, 681; and Karl Kaiser, *Deutschlands Vereinigung: Die internationalen Aspekte* (Bergisch Gladbach, 1991), 50–8.
28 Baker, *Politics of Diplomacy*, 171–6; Zelikow and Rice, *Germany Unified*, 142–8.

proved effective in giving the Russians a voice without letting them slow the process down.[29]

In preparing for the negotiations, Washington sought to create a unified Western position through close consultations with its allies. The French were worried that they would lose their leadership within the European Community, while Britain bridled at the prospect of giving up the last remnants of its World War II victor status. In Bonn, the Foreign Office under Genscher was willing to make larger concessions to Soviet security fears by upgrading the CSCE, while in East Berlin the new Foreign Minister Markus Meckel, a pacifist pastor, still harbored neutralist dreams. In repeated bilateral talks with President François Mitterrand and Prime Minister Margaret Thatcher, the White House succeeded in getting support for continued German NATO membership through reinterpreting the defense doctrine of the Western Alliance in order to make it less threatening. By depriving the Soviets of the possibility of playing off one ally against another, the common Western stance made a major contribution to the diplomatic settlement.[30]

Acting as a disinterested mediator, American policy also helped defuse the Polish border quarrel. Because he needed refugee votes in the upcoming general election in the fall of 1990, Kohl had refused to issue a binding guarantee of Germany's new Eastern border before unification. By recalling the diplomatic double standard of the interwar period, his obstinacy created a furor abroad, because it seemed to confirm all the worst fears about Germany's future intent. In February 1990 Washington feared that this issue might derail the diplomatic process, since it made the East Central European states ambivalent about the departure of Soviet soldiers. Gentle but unmistakable pressure from Bush at a Camp David summit coupled with Senate preparations for a hostile resolution, amplified by Genscher's threat of breaking the Bonn governing coalition, finally forced Kohl in early March 1990 to approve joint parliamentary resolutions that restored international confidence.[31]

During the actual negotiations, American diplomats time and again kept the talks from bogging down. In bilateral briefings such as the

---

29 Baker, *Politics of Diplomacy*, 195–216; Blackwill, "German Unification," 35; Genscher, *Erinnerungen*, 695–7, 709–11, 716–18, 724–31; Szabo, *Diplomacy of German Unification*, 53–9; and Zelikow, *Study in Statecraft*, 165–97.
30 Kiessler and Elbe, *Runder Tisch*, 77–105 and Ulrich Albrecht, *Die Abwicklung der DDR: "Die 2 + 4 Verhandlungen"* (Opladen, 1992).
31 Baker, *Politics of Diplomacy*, 232–4; Genscher, *Erinnerungen*, 720, 743–4; Zelikow and Rice, *Germany Unified*, 217–22; Konrad H. Jarausch, *Die Unverhoffte Einheit, 1989–1990* (Frankfurt/Main, 1995), 193.

Windhoek meeting, they reassured the Russian leaders that keeping Germany in NATO would actually help control the Bundeswehr rather than strengthen the West. When the Soviets demanded illogically to decouple the internal from the external negotiations or to have a unified Germany remain a member of both opposing alliances, U.S. representatives listened politely, but refused to let Germany be "singularized" by discriminatory conditions. Instead they kept the Western allies in line and searched with the Germans for common ground on which to build enticing offers. In this process Washington developed a remarkably selective hearing, always responding to liberal Soviet hints and ignoring threatening Russian grumbling. By keeping tempers from flaring, this tactic worked in the end, since it helped liberal Moscow leaders overcome the resistance of their domestic hardliners and kept the process moving forward.[32]

To wear down Soviet opposition to German NATO membership, Washington, in consultation with Bonn, proposed a series of compromises. In mid-May Baker presented a nine-point package of incentives to Gorbachev that included: (1) follow-on conventional force reductions in Europe; (2) new disarmament efforts in short-range nuclear forces; (3) German repudiation of atomic, biological, and chemical (ABC) weapons; (4) no NATO forces in East Germany for a transition period; (5) a respectable time-frame for Soviet troop withdrawal; (6) a general revision of NATO strategy; (7) German border guarantees; (8) an enhancement of the CSCE role; and (9) stronger economic ties between Germany and Russia. During the Soviet-American summit in Washington in late May, Bush's assurances suddenly persuaded Gorbachev to jump over his shadow and concede "that nations can chose their own alliances." Prepared at Turnberry, the subsequent London declaration transformed NATO into a less frightening political alliance, while the Houston world economic conference opened the door for financial assistance.[33]

By mid-July the ground had been so well prepared that Americans did not even need to be present at the final breakthrough. Facilitated by parallel Soviet-German talks about economic aid, the settlement of the outstanding diplomatic questions during Kohl's visit to the Caucasus mountains took place largely within the parameters of the earlier U.S.

---

32 Edvard Shevardnadse, *Die Zukunft gehört der Freiheit* (Hamburg, 1991); Beschloss and Talbott, *Highest Levels*, 197–8, 207–9; Baker, *Politics of Diplomacy*, 234–9; and Genscher, *Erinnerungen*, 750, 755–6, 768–80, 824.

33 Julij Kvitsinskij, *Vor dem Sturm: Erinnerungen eines Diplomaten* (Berlin, 1993); Kiessler and Elbe, *Runder Tisch*, 144–59; Zelikow and Rice, *Germany Unified*, 260–7, 275–85; Baker, *Politics of Diplomacy*, 252–9; and Genscher, *Erinnerungen*, 787–8, 802–4.

proposals. Because Western concessions had helped him weather a crucial meeting of the Party Congress, Gorbachev felt free to accept German NATO membership and to end Four Power rights more quickly. In return the Soviets received a bilateral treaty of cooperation, generous economic aid, and political support in rejoining the rest of Europe.[34] Initially Washington was stunned by the bilateral bargain, but at closer inspection it could feel pleased, since the deal realized its own most important aims. Although some sticky details remained to be worked out in the final Two-Plus-Four session, the Caucasus agreement was also an indirect credit to American diplomacy.[35]

Because of its absence at the final deal, the U.S. government has not gotten much credit for this major foreign policy success. Chancellor Kohl's and Foreign Minister Genscher's effusive expressions of gratitude to President Bush have largely been dismissed as political rhetoric. In Germany, public opinion has remained focused on Mikhail Gorbachev's role and on the surprising extent of Soviet concessions. In the United States, Bush's low-key response to the fall of the Wall and his refusal to gloat over Soviet setbacks created a pervasive image of White House passivity. Only insiders appreciate the extent to which U.S. reticence was a deliberate strategy, designed to make it easier for the Russian leadership to make the necessary concessions without inflaming its own domestic enemies.[36] Because of this confusion, it is important to clarify Washington's precise role in German unity.

The most obvious U.S. contribution was the ending of the Cold War. Because German division was largely a result of confrontation with the Soviet Union, unification could only proceed through a reduction of superpower tensions. Washington's slow endorsement of the Russian reform process made possible a series of bilateral signals to Moscow that, taken as indication of a larger reversal, transformed the relationship from confrontation toward cooperation. Most visibly, the improved personal climate between Bush and Gorbachev as well as Baker and Foreign Minister Eduard Shevardnadze facilitated a series of disarmament breakthroughs that produced a Soviet-American rapprochement. As a result the White House could promote the unification negotiations by explaining

---

34 Teltschik, *329 Tage*, 319–42; Kiessler and Elbe, *Runder Tisch*, 168–79; Hans Klein, *Es begann im Kaukasus: Der entscheidende Schritt in die Einheit Deutschlands* (Frankfurt/Main, 1991); and Theo Waigel and Manfred Schell, eds., *Tage, die Deutschland und die Welt veränderten* (Munich, 1994).
35 Beschloss and Talbott, *Highest Levels*, 238ff; Zelikow and Rice, *Germany Unified*, 328–45.
36 "USA: Den Kalten Krieg am Ende doch gewonnen," *Weserkurier*, Oct. 3, 1990; and discussion in U.S. Senate, Executive Session, Oct. 10, 1990, in Friedrich, ed., *Die USA und die deutsche Frage*, 423–42.

German wishes, testing the limits of Soviet flexibility and proposing a series of potential compromises. Because of its reluctance to exploit Russian weakness, Washington acted effectively as honest broker between Bonn and Moscow.[37]

Almost as important was the American role in creating a united front among the Western Allies. Because of greater public fear in Paris and London, the French and British governments were less enthusiastic about unification. Left to their own devices, they might have joined a refusal front with the Soviet Union or tried to stretch the negotiating process out for years. After all, Mitterrand briefly sought to reenact the Franco-Soviet alliance in a meeting with Gorbachev in Kiev, while Margaret Thatcher played with reviving the Anglo-French entente. Only persistent American lobbying convinced the Western capitals that they might be able to influence the shape of German unity if they accepted the substance, however reluctantly. By stressing its continued commitment to Europe, the White House placated most anxieties and managed to pull the Allies along.[38] In the end, the British could console themselves by having saved NATO, while the French could assuage their consciences through closer integration within the European Community.

At the same time, Washington played a crucial role in shielding the negotiations from the interference of smaller states. All German neighbors were justifiably concerned; some countries like Italy wanted to participate to bolster their prestige; and other states, like Israel, felt they had a moral claim to be involved. For practical and psychological reasons, the United States accepted the German argument that a general peace conference would be too unwieldy, smacked of another Versailles, and could lead to large reparation demands. On American insistence, only Poland was included in the negotiations concerning the sole topic of its own borders, while all other countries had to be content with ratifying the result in a concluding CSCE meeting. Keeping the bargaining confined to a half-dozen governments kept the complications down and made a speedy conclusion of the talks possible.[39]

The final contribution was U.S. support for the conservative version of unification within Germany. Against leftist preferences for a loose confed-

---

37 Beschloss and Talbott, *Highest Levels*, 238–43; Zelikow and Rice, *Germany Unified*, 364–70.
38 Renata Fritsch-Bournazel, *Europa und die deutsche Einheit* (Stuttgart, 1990); Margaret Thatcher, *The Downing Street Years* (New York, 1993), and the just published memoirs of Jacques Attali.
39 Peter Merkl, *German Unification in a European Context* (University Park, Pa., 1993), 303–51; and Adam D. Rotfeld and Walther Stützle, eds., *Germany and Europe in Transition* (New York, 1991).

eration, a gradual merger of the economies, and military neutrality, Washington endorsed the Kohl-Genscher fast track approach to unity. By seeking to exploit the window of diplomatic opportunity, the White House accepted the Federal Republic's decision to manage unification via Article 23 of the Basic Law that permitted the immediate accession of East German states rather than Article 146 that would have required a constitutional convention first. By separating the domestic from the foreign dimensions of unity, the Bush-Baker team also allowed the currency union of July 1, 1990, to be worked out between both Germanies alone. Finally, through consistent opposition to neutralization, Washington managed to keep united Germany safely within the Western Alliance.[40] This evidence clearly suggests that important aspects of the German unification process bear the imprint of American policies.

III

Without a doubt, American support contributed considerably to the success of German unification. In spite of some anxieties over strengthening the CSCE, Washington viewed unity more favorably than any other capital besides Bonn and East Berlin (after the democratic elections of March 1990). Ambassador Walters's enthusiasm even indicates that some U.S. officials were more committed to unity than many young, leftist or Western Germans themselves. A simple counterfactual consideration supports this conclusion: What would have happened if the leader of the Western Alliance had been opposed or lukewarm to the accession of East Germany to the Federal Republic? Because of French doubts, British resentment, Russian fears, Polish concerns, and the skepticism of smaller neighbors, it is highly unlikely that German unity could have come about. Even if Moscow held the key to German unity, Washington's persistent pressure was essential to making it turn and unlock the door.[41]

In the contest for public opinion, new hopes won out over old fears of a greater Germany. In contrast to the stirring images that played on T.V., the print media – especially longer commentaries – were dominated by concerns about the shadows of the past. But in debates such as the Chequers meeting in Britain, where distinguished academics advised Margaret Thatcher on German policy, the recent positive history of the

---

40 This dimension is often overlooked in the purely diplomatic analyses. Cf. Bortfeldt, *Washington, Bonn, Berlin*, 188–92.
41 Konrad H. Jarausch, "Die Amerikaner und die deutsche Vereinigung," *Leipziger Volkszeitung*, July 5, 1991.

Federal Republic as ally, trading partner, and democracy prevailed over darker memories of the Second or the Third Reich.[42] Unlike intellectuals who were preoccupied with reliving the past, the chief actors in the White House and the State Department were largely free of such historical ballast. Instead, they remembered countless constructive meetings with their German counterparts in the diplomatic corps, the military service or the business community which had created a more reliable image. It is the length and closeness of the many-tiered working relationship between Washington and Bonn that facilitated communication and produced sympathy for the German point of view.[43]

In its deliberations the White House defined national interest in a manner surprisingly consonant with the aspirations of the Federal Republic. The basic direction was determined by Bush's decision that, since unification seemed inevitable, the United States could best influence the process and reach its own aims by supporting it. In a political sense Washington saw the reunion of the Germanies as an opportunity for creating a strong, democratic core in Europe that could help stabilize the newly independent states of eastern Europe. In military terms, the NSC was interested in preserving the cohesion of the NATO alliance that guaranteed American influence in transatlantic defense and kept German arms under multilateral control. In the economic realm, the U.S. government wanted a continental partner that would keep the European Community trading door open enough to allow access for its own goods.[44] Ignoring earlier transatlantic frictions, this analysis produced a remarkable combination of altruism and enlightened self-interest that guided White House policy.

In contrast to other issues, Washington hardly wavered in its support of German unification. In the initial debates about the fall of the Wall, the advice of East Berlin Ambassador Barkley to support the reform of an independent GDR outweighed Bonn Ambassador Walters's outright advocacy of unity. Moreover, after the surprise of Chancellor Kohl's Ten Point Plan, Secretary of State Baker's December visit to East Berlin suggested that Washington wanted to slow down the destabilization of Central Europe.[45] But once it had taken the plunge in January 1990, the White House pressed ahead, and did not allow occasional differences

---

42 Charles Powell, "What the PM Learnt About the Germans," reprinted in James and Stone, eds., *When the Wall Came Down*, 233–9.
43 Hans Gatzke, *Germany and the United States: A "Special Relationship?"* (Cambridge, 1980).
44 Elizabeth Pond, *Beyond the Wall: Germany's Road to Unification* (Washington, D.C., 1993), 249–69. Walther Mahnke, ed., *Amerikaner in Deutschland: Grundlagen und Bedingungen der transatlantischen Sicherheit* (Bonn, 1991).
45 Vernon A. Walters, *Die Vereinigung war voraussehbar: Hinter den Kulissen eines entscheidenden Jahres* (Berlin, 1994), versus G. Jonathan Greenwald, *Berlin Witness: An American Diplomat's Chronicle of East Germany's Revolution* (University Park, Pa., 1993).

between a cautious NSC and a more optimistic State Department to obstruct the process. When congressional leaders attempted to force Kohl into a public commitment to the sanctity of Poland's western border, the Bush-Baker team sought to defuse the issue and helped overcome other last-minute obstacles to the process. In retrospect, American policy therefore looks remarkably steady and consistent.[46]

During the improbable trajectory from East German awakening to German unity, the involvement of the United States became increasingly important. To the initial breakthrough of October–November 1989, which overthrew Honecker's post-Stalinist regime, America contributed only by encouraging a general lessening of East–West tensions. The refugee exodus from East Germany, the mass demonstrations and the revolt of SED pragmatists were fueled by the internal dynamics of communist collapse. During the second acceleration of January–February 1990, which doomed the attempt to renew the GDR, Washington intervened more actively. Although economic stagnation, Round Table dreams, and Premier Modrow's mistakes had domestic roots, Gorbachev's decision to write off his East German ally was facilitated by American insistence. In the final rush that determined the internal and external shape of unity, the United States played an even greater role. Whereas Germans themselves negotiated the currency union and the unification treaty, international acceptance of unification on Western terms owed much to Washington's guidance.[47]

Only the future can tell whether support of German unity was the right decision. No doubt, the relationship between Washington and Bonn has become less asymmetrical, since the latter has become fully sovereign, larger, and more powerful. In the short run, the greater Federal Republic has been somewhat overwhelmed by the new demands on its leadership, because it has had to redefine its international stance and sense of identity. That rethinking is painful, as German scruples about participating in the Gulf War or the Yugoslav Crisis attest. But in the long run, unification has laid the foundation for more normal relations between the two allies, because the Germans will be able to articulate their own interests and the desires of their neighbors more forcefully. With the newly won freedom of action, they ought to be able to shoulder more of the burden of responsibility for European stability.[48]

---

46 Baker, *Politics of Diplomacy*, 156–8, 213–16; Genscher *Erinnerungen*, 871–3.
47 Zelikow and Rice, *Germany Unified*, 367–70; and Jarausch, *Unverhoffte Einheit*, 307–27.
48 Baker, *Politics of Diplomacy*, 298–9, 639; Kubbig, *Transatlantische Unsicherheit*; and Charles Weston, *Transatlantische Neuorientierung: Amerikanisch-europäische Bündnispolitik nach der Ära des Kalten Krieges* (Munich, 1993).

Although gratitude in international affairs is an unreliable currency, American support for German unity has created a large capital of good will. In his memoirs former foreign minister Genscher praises the Americans for making a contribution of "inestimable value" to gathering international approval for the solution of the German question: "They took up German unification as well as the freedom to decide about alliance membership as their own cause so to speak." During virtually the entire process Washington and Bonn acted with so much consonance that potentially troubling issues like differing attitudes toward the CSCE could be resolved before they could become divisive. "Without [U.S. support], what happened in 1990 would not have been possible, at least not in that fashion." In the inevitable future disagreements between the "old" and the "new" continents, one can only hope that neither partner will squander this asset willfully.[49]

49 Genscher, *Erinnerungen*, 788, 877; "Perspectives on German Unity: Recollections and Views of the Political Participants," *Deutschland*, Aug. 1995, 49. Cf. also Konrad H. Jarausch, ed., *After Unity: Reconfiguring German Identities* (Providence, R.I., 1996).

16

Unification Policies and the German Image
Comments on the American Reaction

FRANK TROMMLER

For many Americans who watched on television in November 1989 as thousands of young people celebrated the opening of the Berlin Wall, the surprise was twofold. They were stunned, of course, by the sudden decision to open the grim symbol of the Cold War between communism and the Free World. Yet they also discovered that they were surprisingly sympathetic with the Germans who mounted and then tore down that ugly monument against the idea of freedom. In radio interviews or letters to the editor, many Americans confessed that they had not seen, for such an extended period, so many ordinary Germans. Unexpectedly, they found them to be rather similar to themselves, concerned with family, work, and pleasure, suspicious of politicians, fond of freedom and worn-out jeans.

Opening such a revealing window onto ordinary Germans might count as one of the less often mentioned byproducts of the fall of the Berlin Wall. It stands out as one of those rare occasions when the power of stereotyping between nations was momentarily revealed and challenged. What commentators preferred to call history in the making was consumed as an encounter with "real people" of another nation. The encounter lasted until the surprise effect had vanished from the faces of those people. For some time, TV journalists tried to prolong or resurrect it, until other similarly gripping events that accompanied the fall of communism in Czechoslovakia and Rumania turned American attention away from the Germans.

What exactly was the challenge to the established stereotypes about Germany? One could argue that the surprise on the part of the Americans reflected the customary portrayal of Germany as an economically successful country that produces both shiny BMWs and ugly memories of Nazi crimes. If this was the case, the next question would be whether the images associated with the fall of the Wall created different assumptions about Germany. Was the concurrent invocation of Nazi images a routine reply to reassure American viewers about German continuities, while ordinary Germans themselves were simultaneously shown in the unusual role of allies in the celebration of freedom? Or was the extended coverage simply one part of the visual takeover of the process in which a system that had suppressed the freedom of communication was being destroyed, thus returning the fate of the two Germanies to the people in the streets?

A thorough analysis would have to go into many aspects both of the political processes and the media-based public participation in them. It would have to start, however, with a reflection of the assumption that spread exponentially in the past decades and thus came to dominate many facts and factors that led to the unification of Germany: that an event of such historical proportion is inevitably shaped by television. Did not the world learn of the plight of the East Germans through TV coverage of the beleaguered West German embassies in Prague and Budapest? And later through the images of the demonstrations in Leipzig, Dresden, and Berlin? Was not the opening of the Wall in the presence of the NBC anchorman Tom Brokaw a TV production, "eine Fernsehinszenierung"?[1] Were not the subsequent reactions of Mikhail Gorbachev, George Bush, Margaret Thatcher, François Mitterrand, and Helmut Kohl strongly influenced by the effects of these pictures, geared to respond to TV coverage?

The TV dimension of Germany's unification was obviously less unforeseen than the event itself. The assumption is almost automatic that an event does not happen unless it happens on television. By now the supposed inevitability of the televised transformation of reality matches the notion of inevitability that Max Weber, at the beginning of the century, attributed to the ever-increasing rationalization of all human endeavors in the modern bureaucratized world. Weber's "iron cage" of rationalization which we cannot escape has given way to the notion of television as an "iron box" which we also cannot escape. Declaring this phenomenon to be a stereotype probably underplays its enormous power both in the political world and in the world of academic analysis. Yet it

---

1 Michael E. Geisler, "Mehrfach gebrochene Mauerschau: 1989–1990 in den US-Medien," in Rainer Bohn, Knut Hickethier, and Eggo Müller, eds., *Mauer-Show: Das Ende der DDR, die deutsche Einheit und die Medien* (Berlin, 1992), 260.

might be quite suitable for a brief exploration of the interplay of unification politics and public images.

Konrad H. Jarausch's chapter in this book, "American Policy toward German Unification: Images and Interests," can be read as a comment on the effect of television on the politics of unification. Simply put, Jarausch's analysis of American policy, in particular the recourse of President Bush and Secretary of State James Baker to traditional low-profile diplomacy, dispels the notion that the media had particular influence either on the process or the outcome of the intense political activities that led to the unification of the two German states. To be sure, there is a powerful public dimension of unification politics, especially in Germany and the United States, which Jarausch does not explicitly integrate into his analysis. Further studies are necessary in order to assess its changing importance for the political process; it seems, though, that television's worldwide appeal contributed substantially to the success of the peaceful revolutions of 1989–90. Nevertheless, the crucial maneuvers of the four powers plus the two Germanies toward the historical compromise of 1990 displayed all the signs of traditional diplomacy, mostly behind closed doors. Jarausch soberly and thoroughly dissects the tactics of the Bush administration, explaining the success of American diplomacy as closely linked to the conscious avoidance of the glare of publicity, in turn motivated mainly by the fear of alerting Soviet suspicions. While he comments that "the U.S. government has not gotten much credit for this major foreign policy success," others, focusing on the unfavorable media coverage, interpret Bush's policy as reactive rather than active, a testimony to the weakness of his administration.[2]

There is much room for disagreement about the broader implications of this policy. What seems less contested is the close relationship between Bush's *Realpolitik* and its scant attention to long-standing stereotypes about the Germans, their bloody past and arrogant ambitions. As properly highlighted by Jarausch, Bush, Baker, and the American foreign-policy establishment hardly concerned themselves with the intensive debate about Germany's devastating past in the twentieth century, which dominated the discussions of the issue in major newspapers, magazines, universities, and intellectual circles. Although critical voices were occasionally heard within the administration, an affair similar to the Chequers seminar, at which the British prime minister, Margaret Thatcher, tried to develop arguments based on Germany's behavior in recent historical times, was

2 Geisler, "Mauerschau," 257–75.

not in the cards.³ A crucial ingredient of Bush's *Realpolitik* was his reliance on the close cooperation with the West Germans which had emerged in the preceding forty years of the Cold War, encompassing not only diplomatic and military affairs but extending to the whole realm of Western economic integration. Although a conscious decision to disengage from the anglophile position of the Reagan administration may have predetermined a more favorable stance toward the Germans ("partners in leadership"), the "length and closeness of the many-tiered working relationships between Washington and Bonn" (Jarausch) gave Bush's and Baker's policy its momentum.

In its disregard for the dramatic invocations of history which so often tend to coagulate into ritualistic exercises, Washington reacted with its own version of pragmatic presentism. The ambiguities, however, remained visible even if scant attention was paid to the interplay of public actions and the immediate impact of television imagery. Not every objection against German unification was based on stereotypes and, in turn, not every stereotype about the Germans was negative or critical. Objections based on the memory of the Holocaust and the immense costs of twelve years of National Socialism are not to be equated with beliefs in the flaws of the German character which have lingered since World War I, and even less with the usual fare of nationalist pettiness of which Americans are as culpable as any other nation.

Scholars have not been particularly astute in keeping up with the sophisticated use of stereotypes on the part of politicians and journalists in the age of television. The function of stereotypes as a quick information unit within communication – and not necessarily as ontological matter – is now becoming better understood.⁴ There is more awareness of the communicative structure of a particular encoding of information, even when it distorts reality. At the same time, the limits of public and private usage of these information units become more noticeable; they can be used or not used, but seldom transformed or rationalized. They "contain collective experiences which carry a kind of truth that can never be reached or touched by the empirical facts of science." They "operate on a different level of discourse."⁵

---

3 Günther Heydemann, "Partner oder Konkurrent? Das britische Deutschlandbild während des Wiedervereinigungsprozesses 1989–1991," in Franz Bosbach, ed., *Feindbilder: Die Darstellung des Gegners in der politischen Publizistik des Mittelalters und der Neuzeit* (Cologne, 1992), 201–34.
4 See Penelope J. Oakes, S. Alexander Haslam, and John C. Turner, eds., *Stereotyping and Social Reality* (Oxford, 1994).
5 Anton C. Zijderveld, "On the Nature and Functions of Cliches," in Günther Blaicher, ed., *Erstarrtes Denken: Studien zu Klischee, Stereotyp und Vorurteil in englischsprachiger Literatur* (Tübingen, 1987), 26–7.

This leads back to the question as to what extent stereotypes regarding Germany and the Germans were challenged by the events of 1989–90. If they operate on a different level of discourse, they may not have been affected by these upheavals – an observation that also might account for the fact that negative stereotyping did not seriously affect the construction of a pragmatic policy toward German unification. However, too many Americans asserted that the fall of the Berlin Wall was catalytic for their sense of American responsibilities in the world, and that it had an impact on how they understand their country's relationship with Germany. Was there a change in the overall perception of Germany aside from the fact that opinion polls routinely report a rather steady distribution of (more) positive and (less) negative views concerning that country?[6]

Instead of reiterating the long historical agenda of mutual images between Americans and Germans which scholars have assembled, especially in recent years, I will turn to a comparison with the images of Japan that developed after 1945 in seemingly similar ways.[7] Akira Iriye, the foremost scholar in the field, has pointed to the fact that individuals relate themselves to the world in a number of different contexts and from a combination of various motives and preconceived notions. Consequently, their "images and subimages of another country are likely to consist of several symbols that contain various connotations in different contexts. At the very least, it seems possible to identify five types of symbols: globalism, cosmopolitanism, nationalism, particularism, and provincialism."[8] Iriye's application of these symbols to the mutual perceptions of Americans and Japanese also provides insights into the case of the Germans. The ambiguities of cooperation and competition were similarly subsumed under America's postwar patronage.[9]

---

6 See Andrei S. Markovits, "Die Deutschen: Ansichten aus Amerika," in Günter Trautmann, ed., *Die hässlichen Deutschen? Deutschland im Spiegel der westlichen und östlichen Nachbarn* (Darmstadt, 1991), 291–302; Michael Minkenberg, "Das neue Deutschland – amerikanische Reaktionen auf die deutsche Vereinigung 1989–90," in *Amerikastudien/American Studies* 38 (1993): 273–88.

7 Among the recent publications about this topic are Lothar Bredella and Dietmar Haack, eds., *Perceptions and Misperceptions: The United States and Germany* (Tübingen, 1988); Peter Funke, ed., *Understanding the USA: A Cross-Cultural Perspective* (Tübingen, 1989); Peter Freese, *"America": Dream or Nightmare? Reflections on a Composite Image* (Essen, 1990); Peter Freese, ed., *Germany and German Thought in American Literature and Cultural Criticism: Proceedings of the German-American Conference in Paderborn, May 16–19, 1990* (Essen, 1990); Frank Krampikowski, ed., *Amerikanisches Deutschlandbild und deutsches Amerikabild in Medien und Erziehung* (Baltmannsweiler, 1990); Lothar Bredella, ed., *Mediating a Foreign Culture: The United States and Germany* (Tübingen, 1991).

8 Akira Iriye, "Introduction," in Akira Iriye, ed., *Mutual Images: Essays in American-Japanese Relations* (Cambridge, 1975), 17. See also the more recent book by Paul Gordon Lauren and Raymond F. Wylie, eds., *Destinies Shared: U.S.-Japanese Relations* (Boulder, Colo., 1989).

9 For an extensive exploration of similarities and differences in the postwar cultural developments of Japan and Germany, see Ernestine Schlant and J. Thomas Rimer, eds., *Legacies and Ambiguities: Postwar Fiction and Culture in West Germany and Japan* (Baltimore, 1991), and Ian Buruma, *The Wages of Guilt: Memories of War in Germany and Japan* (New York, 1995).

In the volume *Mutual Images*, Priscilla Clapp and Morton Halprin specify the classification of images which Americans have held toward Japan since the victory of 1945. They distinguish three themes: inevitable harmony, partnership, and inevitable conflict. The first, inevitable harmony, "is the notion that the interests of the United States and Japan are identical and that Japan can be counted upon to act as an agent of the United States in Asia."[10] This theme can be transferred to the Federal Republic after its founding in 1949, and in terms of America's orientation toward Europe rather than Asia. Under the auspices of the Cold War, Bonn often acted as an agent of the United States, receiving the appropriate respect or, for that matter, disrespect on the part of the Americans. The second theme, creating a partnership, points to the "diligent efforts on both sides to overcome the differences inherent in the two cultures, as well as divergent national interests."[11] This theme can also be transferred to the German-American relationship in its reflections both in the sphere of political decision-making and in terms of public opinion. The third theme, the inevitable conflicts of interests, "includes a multitude of pessimistic feelings about the future of the relationship." It is a less coherent philosophy about the relationship and serves more as a catch-all category for a variety of tactical and ad-hoc approaches to the relationship.[12] When it comes to negative images, there is, of course, always more than meets the eye, but Clapp and Halprin's basic description also applies to the case of Germany, the other defeated nation that rose from defeat to new prosperity.

Clapp and Halprin follow up with a historicization of these factors, placing them in a rough sequence since the 1940s, though with a strong emphasis on the fact that the seemingly contradictory images of the other country also occur simultaneously, depending on the constituency and the political and economic climate. These images can be entertained by the same individual on different occasions: "It is conceivable, for instance, that a businessman may feel threatened by Japanese competition (inevitable conflict) but at the same time have an aesthetic appreciation of Japanese culture (harmony) and believe in the wisdom of continuing the Japanese alliance (partnership). These would all be genuine images and emotions, and it would be difficult to say that only one of them in particular represented his view of Japan."[13]

10 Priscilla A. Clapp and Morton H. Halprin, "U.S. Elite Images of Japan: The Postwar Period," in Iriye, ed., *Mutual Images*, 210.
11 Ibid.
12 Ibid.
13 Iriye, "Introduction," 17.

A similar configuration, embracing contradictory views toward the former enemy country in Europe, can be elucidated in regard to the multitiered American relationship with Germany. One can locate the different views within the sequence of postwar developments in the order of "proprietary harmony" in the 1950s, "creating a partnership" in the 1960s and 1970s, and thereafter a stronger intermingling of the theme "containing a competitor" with earlier images. One can also, of course, locate these dispositions in one individual at a given time, building a case for the simultaneous use of ten contradictory images and stereotypes. Defining stereotype without contextualization is hardly worth the effort.

Iriye's model of coalescing synchronic and diachronic manifestations of mutual images helps us understand the postwar dynamics of occupation and partnership, dependency and competition, patronage and antagonism. Although it is sobering to discern the ubiquity of stereotypical patterns on the part of Americans, one can also compose a clearer picture of the determining forces on the part of the other two nations. There seems to be little doubt that, in terms of adversarial imagery in the United States, Japan has moved far ahead of Germany since the 1970s. In turn, Germany, having been freed from the Wall and the remnants of the postwar occupation, has lost the claim for a special status within the American orbit.

Given the fact that foreign countries generally attract only limited interest in American everyday life, the term "special status" might already stretch the case. And yet, Germany's reemergence after its total defeat by the allies in 1945 had become a special segment in the story of America's leadership as the Western superpower, not least because the common cultural tradition had been so strong and Germany's downfall as a bastion of Western civilization under Nazism so devastating. In a similar vein, the confrontation with the communist adversary during the Cold War was nowhere as emotionally charged as in Berlin, where American troops were completely encircled by the Soviets. The crucial images of the onetime enemy, nazism, and the current enemy, communism, were connected with Germany. Any version of the American tale of the twentieth century or, for that matter, any employment of the narrative of the superpower referred, in one form or another, to the involvement of the Germans. Millions had been stationed as soldiers in West Germany or Berlin, or knew of relatives who had spent time there. A sizable part of the military establishment had lived there in comfort. Businessmen had found the Germans to be particularly suited for expanding business practices. It was hardly surprising that many Americans who had lived through World War II, the subsequent economic take-off, and the confrontation with the communist bloc, observed Germany's rise as a democratic Western power with a kind of proprietary interest.

For most of them, America's story in the twentieth century as a story of democratization and a triumph over despotism found its last spectacular expression in the fall of the Wall. Many were deeply moved by the November events. One more time Germans could be considered proxies for the Americans: this time in the celebration of freedom. This had little to do with the everyday use of stereotypes about Germans and their national characteristics. It resulted from the reflection of the interconnectedness of national identity with post-World War II history, destined to fade out with the younger generations that have grown up after the erection of the Wall in 1961.

In contrast to the proprietary interest in a democratic Germany, but similarly far-reaching, was the spurning of Germans as the perpetrators of the Holocaust. Again, different from the distancing perceptions concerning the Japanese, Americans constituted a substantial part of their mission as the leader of the West in a painful engagement with the German affliction with anti-Semitism and racism, an engagement that provided not only a moral agenda but also the moral high ground for keeping the emerging democratic Germany in check. While there are many contradictory and compensatory concerns at work, the free access to images of evil through the invocation of the Nazi crimes has long been domesticated – and successfully exported with the American mass entertainment culture that always uses clear distinctions between good and evil. Studies on film and television confirm the instrumentalization of the Nazi period, deeply ingrained in the arguments of American public debate, as the dramatic contrast for the visual representation of the morally just cause. Whether the Nazi period has been detached from Germany and become a "free-floating signifier" is, however, questionable.[14] Memory, as the Jewish community has proven time and again, holds on to historical reality and is a kind of reality, not a free-floating signifier. With the establishment of the United States Holocaust Memorial Museum in 1993, the struggle between the needs for generalizing and those for historicizing the Holocaust has taken on a new public dimension. It will continue to define an engagement with the historical

---

14 Lothar Bredella, Wolfgang Gast, and Siegfried Quandt, *Deutschlandbilder im amerikanischen Fernsehen: Inhalte, Formen, Funktionen* (Tübingen, 1994), 243.

Germany, as opposed to the mere use of critical stereotypes which is going on between all nations.

As Europe always remained an integrating part of American self-definition,[15] it played a crucial role in the projection of the triumph of the American empire after World War II. The importance of Germany in the process, dating back to World War I, was enhanced by the fact that Hitler's reign of terror provided a handle on this relationship that helped extinguish the remnants of a cultural inferiority complex. Germany's failure as a modern power even helped overcome America's moral uncertainty as the only power that had used the atomic bomb. Unlike Japan at the end of the twentieth century, Germany has little to offer for the narrative of the decline of America's position in the world. It should try to stay out of it. The emotional bridges between the two nations that balanced the use of critical stereotyping have disappeared since the fall of the Berlin Wall. As Europe and the United States are moving further apart, a new wave of stereotyping may not be the worst factor that needs to be addressed. More ominous is the general loss of interest in the other continent among broad segments of the population despite official statements to the contrary.

15 Daniel J. Boorstin, *America and the Image of Europe: Reflection on American Thought* (New York, 1960).

Index

AAC; see American Artists' Congress (AAC)
abolitionists, 102
Abramovitz, Max, 269
academics, 152–4; see also elite opinion; intellectuals
Acheson, Dean, 330
Adams, Brooks, 137
Adams, H. C., 165
Adams, Henry, 137
Adams, Herbert Baxter, 138, 143
Adams, John, 26
Adams, John Quincy, 41, 42, 50
Adams, Willi Paul, 5
Adenauer, Konrad, foreign policy of, 15, 309–31
Adorno, Theodor, 302
AEA; see American Economic Association (AEA)
Albers, Josef, 272, 280, 283
alienation, 187
Althoff, Friedrich, 138
Altschul, Charles, 140
American Artists' Congress (AAC), 268, 270–1
American Artists Professional League, 267
American Economic Association (AEA), 164, 165
American freedom, 12, 19–40; see also religion and religious liberty
"American Friend, An" (film), 287
American identity, 51–2, 62–3; regional, 50

American studies, see Amerikakunde
Americanism, 10, 220–2, 228, 239, 253
Americanization: deplored by German writers, 85–6, 115–16; and modernization, 11
Amerikabild, 35
Amerikakunde, 65–7
Amerikanisches Magazin, 65
Amory, Martha Babcock, 50n30, 51
Angermann, Erich, 9
Anglo-Americanization, modernism as, 220
anti-Semitism: of Ford, 228; of Hitler, 246, 248–50, 253, 259–62
Appel, Karl-Otto, 167
Archenholtz, Johann Wilhelm von, 30; *Minerva*, 35
architecture, modernist, 273
Armory Show (1913), 270
art, 265–83; American critics' views, 266–9; artistic representation, 265–83; Central European, 279–80; degenerate, 273–4, 277, 282; émigré art dealers, 266, 277–9; émigré artists, 266–8, 272–83; regionalist, 269–71; socially committed exhibition, 268–9; see also film
Art Institute of Chicago, 279
assimilation, as alienating, 149
Auerbach, Berthold: *Luzifer*, 76
authoritarianism, German, 80, 142
autocracy, versus democracy, 140
autostereotypes, 135, 146

BABS; see Bochumer Auswandererbriefsammlung (BABS)
"Baghdad Cafe" (film), 287
Bahrdt, Carl Friedrich, 27–8
Baird, Robert, 50n31, 50n33, 54, 55, 59
Baker, George, 179
Baker, James A., and German unification, 340–1, 344, 347, 349, 350, 355
Bancroft, George, 41, 42n11, 45–6, 47, 50n30, 50n34, 52, 59, 60; *History of the United States*, 65
Barkley, Richard, 341
Barrer, Stephan, 25
Bauer, John, 101, 106
Bauhaus architects, 272, 273, 283
Baumgarten, Siegmund Jakob, 20, 21n1
Bayer, Herbert, 272, 280
Baylor, Charles Goethe, 131, 134, 154
Baziotes, William, 281
"Bedford Incident, The" (film), 297
Benton, Thomas Hart, 269
Berg, Peter, 224
Bergstraesser, Arnold, 71
Berlin Secession, 272
Berlin Wall, 353–4, 357, 359–61
Bernstorff, Johann Heinrich Count von, 153
Betz, Friedrich, family letters, 24–5
bilateralism, 323–8, 342, 347
"Birth of a Nation" (film), 118
Blackwill, Robert, 340–1
Blucher, Franz, 318
Blume, Mathias, 25
Blümner, August, 90
Blümner, Carl, 90
Bochumer Auswandererbriefsammlung (BABS), 89, 92, 126–7
Bollmann, Justus Erich, 36–7
Bolshevism, in America, 222, 239, 242; in art, 277, 283
Bonn, Moritz, J., 232
Boxer Rebellion, in China, 147
"Boys from Brazil, The" (film), 298
Brauns, Ernst Ludwig, 72, 82
Breckinridge, Robert, 50n31
Bredow, Fritz, 230
Breen, Timothy H., 44n12
Bronson, Charlotte B., 51
Brooks, Sidney: *America and Germany, 1918–1925*, 179
Brooks, Van Wyck: *America's Coming of Age*, 148

Bruck, Moeller van der, 229
Bruen, Mathias, 50n33
Bruns, Bernhard, 95–7
Bryant, William Cullen, 47–8, 50n31, 50n35
Buchanan, James, 79
Buckminster, Joseph Stevens, 50n30, 50n33
Bülow, Adam Dietrich Freiherr von, 35–6, 66–7
bureaucratization, 161
Burgess, George, 50n30, 50n34
Burgess, John W., 137, 138, 139
Burke, Edmund: *Reflections on the Revolution in France*, 38
Burr, Aaron, 50, 54
Bush, George, foreign policy of, 340, 355–6
Butler, Nicholas Murray, 145, 152
Buttner, J. G., 54n49

"Cabaret" (film), 291, 293, 299, 305
Calder, Alexander, 278
Calvert, George H., 50n32, 50n34, 55
capitalism, 175, 187, 188
Carl, Johann Jacob, 27
Carlsbad Decrees, 74
Castle, William R. Jr., 15, 196; on American World War I involvement, 198; on German foreign policy, 198–205; head of Western European Affairs Division, 193, 196–7; on Polish security, 204
Catholicism, 23, 95–9, 102, 104, 106, 107
Chaplin, Charlie, 295, 303
Chicago Art Institute; see Art Institute of Chicago
Christianity, 37, 39; attacks on, 29; European, tolerance for, 20; and state, 33–4
Ciechanowski, John, 204
cinema; see film
Civil War, American, 10, 13, 87–107
Clapp, Priscilla: *Mutual Images*, 358
Clark, John Bates, 165
Cleveland, Richard Jeffry, 48–51; *Narrative*, 49
Coggeshall, George, 50–1
Cogswell, Joseph Green, 43n11, 46, 47, 50n30, 50n34

Cold War: and Berlin Wall, 353–4, 359–61; ending of, 339, 347–8; film images during, 296, 303–4
collectivism, versus individuality, 61, 80
Collier, Price, 141
communism: collapse of, 333, 334, 339; development of American, 233
comparisons, 51–61, 189–90
Conference on Security and Cooperation in Europe (CSCE), 342, 344–5, 348–9
conservatism, 66–7, 80; versus popular sovereignty, 68; and religion, 28, 32, 37; *see also* liberalism
constitutionalism, 178, 184; and American freedom, 19, 21, 29–40; and liberalism, 79–80
constructionists, 9
Coolidge administration, on reparations plan, 193
Cooper, James Fenimore, 47, 50n31, 50n35, 51, 54–5, 59–60, 62–3
Coser, Lewis, 267
Council for Mutual Economic Assistance (COMECON), 333
Creel, George, 147
Crist, Judith, 296–7
critics; *see* art
Crowninshield, Clara, 47, 48–9, 50n30, 54, 55–8, 60n79
CSCE; *see* Conference on Security and Cooperation in Europe (CSCE)
Cubism, 281
cultural chauvinism, 149–50
cultural images, 2, 155–70, 265–83; of Imperial Germany, 131–54; information channels for, 136–44; *see also* art; film; popular images
cultural migration, 15, 265–83
cultural values: and free associations, 7; and image formation, 3; low/high culture, 148, 152
Curry, John Steuart, 269

Dahlmann, Friedrich Christoph, 76
Davis, Stuart, 268, 282
Dawes Plan (1924), 191–2, 196, 200, 203–14, 223, 251; *see also* reparations question
Degenerate Art exhibition, 273–4, 282
Dehn, Adolf, 269
deism, 22, 29

Delbrück, Hans, 140
demagogues, patriotic intellectuals as, 74
democracy: versus autocracy, 140; and liberalism, 68, 72, 80; mass, 174–5; organic, 186–7; pluralist, 157–8; representative, 80; *see also* republicanism
Depkat, Volker, 34–5
Depression; *see* Great Depression
"Desert Fox, The" (film), 296, 304
Deutsche Rundschau, 229
Deutsches Volkstum, 229
Deutschtum, in America, 73–4
Dewey, John, 167–70, 178–9
Dewey, Orville, 50n30, 50n33
Dieden, John, 97, 106
Diehendt, Johann Daniel, 21n1
Dilthey, Wilhelm, 168
diplomatic service, modernization of, 194
Dippel, Horst, 30, 34
Disney, Walt, 295
"Dr. Strangelove" (film), 297, 304
Droppers, Garrett, 164
Du Bois, W. E. B., 166
Duden, Gottfried, 74, 81
Dulheuer, Heinrich, 22
Dulles, John Foster, 324, 325, 330
Dünnebacke, Joseph, 94–5
Dwight, Henry E., 44, 45, 47, 50n30, 50n34, 51–2
Dwight, Timothy, 44, 45n15

Ebeling, Christoph Daniel, 36, 65–7
Ebert, Friedrich, 199
EDC; *see* European Defense Community (EDC)
egalitarianism, republican, 104
Eichmann, Adolf, 301
Eisenhower, Dwight D., 324, 325, 330
Eisler, Colin, 267–8
Eliot, Charles W., 152
elite opinion, 14–16, 78–9, 90–106, 137–8, 150–2; *see also* academics; intellectuals
Ely, Richard T., 165, 169
emancipation, 95, 101, 103
emigration; *see* immigration
empiricism, and religion, 20
Enderis, Guido de, 211
Endress, Christian, 37
Engels, Friedrich, 80–1
Engelsing, Rolf, 85

Enlightenment, political ideals of, 217
equality, 120; republican, 62, 63; social, 128
Erhard, Ludwig, 317
ethnic images, 2
Eucken, Rudolf, 152
Eulenberg, Johann Heinrich, family letters, 24–5
European Defense Community (EDC), 321–2, 328
Everett, Edward, 47, 50n30, 50n34, 68–9, 83
expansionism, 150
Eyre, Lincoln, 211

Fay, Theodore S., 79
federalism, 183–4, 189
Federalist Papers, 30
Feininger, Lionel, 280
feudalism, 160
Feuerbach, Ludwig, 78
Fichte, Johann Gottlieb, 168
Fillmore, Millard, 82
film: importation of American, 257; representation of Germans, 15, 285–308
Fisk, Wilbur, 50n30
Flavell, M. Kay, 265–6
Follen, Karl, 74–5
Follenius, Paul, 75
Fontane, Theodor, 113
Ford, Guy Stanton, 139, 140
Ford, Henry: anti-Semitism of, 228; as Führer, 230; *My Life and Work*, 223–4
Fordism: Ford plants, 229, 239, 255; in Germany, 15, 217–42, 255–6
foreign policy: of Adenauer, 309–31; American in 1920s, 197–8; of Bush, 355–6; effect of stereotypes on, 194; Nazi, 243; of Roosevelt, 246; of Weimar Germany, 191–2, 197–8
Forster, Georg, 28
Forty-Eighters (48ers), 78, 87–9, 93–5, 97–8, 103, 107
Four-Year Plan, 244, 255
Francke, Hugo, 140, 145, 147–9
Franckesche Stiftungen, 21n1
Franco-Prussian War, 174
"Frankenstein" (film), 290
Franklin, Benjamin, 21, 26, 45

free trade, 118
freedom, American; *see* American freedom
Freud, Sigmund, 156, 157; *Totem and Taboo*, 3
Freytag, Gustav, 113
Fried, Ferdinand, 233
frontier, 188
Frühkonstitutionalismus; *see* constitutionalism
Fuerts, E. A., 142
Führer: and Fordism, 230; Hitler as, 233; Roosevelt as, 245

Gagern, Heinrich von, 61
Gall, Ludwig, 68–9
Gatzke, Hans W., 146
Gay, Peter, 6, 8
Geertz, Clifford, 302
Geiger, Heinrich, 24
Geiger, Jacob, 24
Geisberg, Franz, 95
Genscher, Hans-Dietrich, 343, 345, 349, 352
Gentz, Friedrich von, 68; *Historisches Journal*, 37–8
Gerard, James W., 151
German unification; *see* unification, German
Gerstäcker, Friedrich, 73, 81
Gerstein, Dietrich, 93–4
Gestalt psychology, 4
"Get Smart" (television show), 298
Gilbert, Seymour Parker, 15; reparations agent, 193, 195, 205, 208–14; versus Schurman, 205–10
Gleichschaltung, 258
Goebbels, Joseph, 246–7, 259–65
Goering, Jacob, 29
Goethe, Johann Wolfgang von, 9, 38, 43, 48, 60, 74, 136, 151
Goldberger, Ludwig Max, 116–18
Gorbachev, Mikhail, 347, 348
Gottl-Ottlilienfeld, Friedrich von, on Fordism, 224–30
Gottlieb, Alexander, 21n1
Great Depression: and art, 267, 278; German view of, 232, 242, 244, 253
"Great Dictator, The" (film), 295, 303
"Great Escape II, The" (television mini-series), 298
Greenberg, Clement, 281

Greene, George Washington, 47
Grellet, Stephen, 50n31, 50n33
Greverus, Ina-Maria, 84
Grimm, Herman, 113
Gropius, Walter, 273, 283
Gropper, William, 268, 269; "One Must Have the Courage," 274, 275
Grosz, George, 265, 269, 272, 275–7, 280, 283; "Even Mud Has an End," 278; "Prost, Noske," 276
Gutberlet, C., 166

Habermas, Jürgen, 167
Haddock, Samuel, Jr., 60
Hadlock, Samuel, 50n30, 51
Haeckel, Ernst, 152
hagiography, 65–6
Hall, Fanny W., 51
Halprin, Morton: *Mutual Images*, 358
Hamilton, Alexander, 80
Hammerstein, Oscar, 275
Hanfstaengel, Ernst ("Putzi"), 247
Hanks, Tom, 288
Hannah, Daryl, 288
Hansen, Marcus Lee, 85
Harginet, Jacob, 25
Hauptmann, Gerhart, 113
Hawthorne, Nathaniel, 288
Haymarket Riot (1886), 148, 165
Hazen, Charles D., 139, 140
hedonism, 70
Heeren, Arnold Hermann Ludwig, 68
Hegel, Georg Wilhelm Friedrich, 168
Hegewisch, Dietrich Hermann, 36, 65
Heidegger, Martin, 167
Heine, Heinrich, 72, 112
Helbich, Wolfgang, 13, 83, 155–6
Helmuth, Justus Heinrich Christian, 20–1, 27–9, 36–7, 39
Herbst, Jurgen, 142–3
Herder, Johann Gottfried von, 38
Herf, Jeffrey, 221, 251–2
Hermann, Friedrich Wilhelm, 30
Herrmann, Richard K., 4
heterostereotypes, 135, 146, 153
Hexamer, Charles J., 149
Hiestand, Henry, 50n32, 50n33, 57, 58–9
Hilferding, Rudolf, 188
Himmler, Heinrich, 258
Hindenburg, Paul von, 213, 214
Hitler, Adolf: anti-Semitism of, 246, 248–50, 253, 259–62; appeal to working class, 215; Degenerate Art exhibition, 273–4, 282; on Fordism, 231; foreign policy following, 330; as Führer, 233; Hitler myths, 230; *Mein Kampf*, 246, 250–1; on Roosevelt, 243–9, 260–2; on unemployment, 241; and World War I, 178; *Zweites Buch*, 250–2; *see also* National Socialism
"Hitler's Daughter" (television movie), 292, 299
Hoffman, David, 33–4
Hoffman, Dustin, 290
Hofmann, Hans, 272, 273, 280–3
Hoffman, Irwin D., 269
Hoffman, Paul, 320
"Hogan's Heroes" (television show), 287, 299
Holleben, Theodor von, 153
Hollweg, Carl, 227–8
Holst, Hermann von, 141–3
Honecker, Erich, 343, 351
Horkheimer, Max, 302
Hossbach Memorandum, 244
Houghton, Alanson B., 198, 210
Howe, Samuel Gridley, 50
Hugenberg, Alfred, 214
Hülsemann, Johann Georg Ritter von, 67–8
humanitarianism, of immigrants, 104
Humboldt, Wilhelm von, 43
Hussein, Saddam, 308
hyperinflation; *see* inflation

idealism, 99–100; American, 186; and Civil War, 101; German, 116, 129, 135, 151; racial, 89, 100; republican, 98, 106–7; versus self-interest, 105; versus utilitarianism, 129
identity; *see* American identity; cultural identity; nationality
imagery, 111
images: definition and usage of term, 2, 43–4, 110–11; and information, 129; as interdisciplinary study, 5, 110; and memory, 16; versus perceptions, 111; and projection, 129; as realistic concept, 110; versus stereotypes, 111; *see also* perceptions; stereotypes

immigration: books written for, 114–16; and German images of United States, 65–86, 87–107, 109–29, 148–50; letters of German-Americans, 87–107; and perceptions of United States in 19th-century Germany, 65–86; 109–29
Imperial Germany (1870–1914): American perceptions of, 131–54; popular images of, 131–54
imperialism, 129, 135, 150, 177
individualism: versus collectivism, 61, 80; loss of, 179; versus state regulation, 177
industrialization, 71, 80–1, 134, 177, 179
inflation, in Weimar Germany, 191, 197
intellectuals, 14, 155–70; as demagogues, 74; German, 71, 85–6, 138, 153; travelers, 47–8; *see also* academics; elite opinion
intransigence, 319
Iriye, Akira, 359
Irving, Washington, 41–2, 43n11, 50n31, 50n35, 51n39, 53–4, 56

J. P. Morgan and Co., 196, 205, 209, 216
Jacoby, Günther, 167
Jaeckh, Ernst, 181
James, Edwin, 211–12, 214
James, William, 162–3, 166–9; *Pragmatism*, 166
Janson, H. W., 271
Japanese, film portrayals of, 307–8
Jarausch, Konrad H., 16, 355
jazz, importation of, 257–8
Jefferson, Thomas, 39; as deist, 29; and freedom of choice, 35
Jewett, Isaac A., 50n35
Joas, Hans: *Pragmatism and Social Theory*, 167
John Reed Clubs, 268, 269
Jones, Ernest, 156
journalism, 11; images reflected by, 120–2
"Judgment at Nuremberg" (film), 292, 304
Judson, Harry P., 141
Junker, Detlef, 15, 219

Kamphoefner, Walter D., 12, 13, 82–3
Kant, Immanuel, 161, 167–70, 195
Kapp, Friedrich, 78
Keener, Lewis; *see* Kuhner, Ludwig
Keller, Gottfried, 113
Kelley, Florence, 163
Kellogg, Frank B., 206
Kent, James, 33–4
Kernberg, Otto F., 3
Kinkel, Gottfried, 78, 82, 91
Kinsky, Klaus, 289
Klineberg, Otto, 5, 6, 8
Kloppenberg, Ignatz, 155–7
Kloppenberg, James T., 14
Knapp, Johann Georg, 19
Kohut, Heinz, 4
Kollwitz, Käthe, 269, 275–7, 279
Kooning, Willem de, 280
Kossuth, Lajos, 91–2
Kotzebue, August von, 74
Krakau, Knud, 5
Krause, Albert, 99–100, 105
Krieger, Leonard, 169
Krüger, Peter, 14, 218–19
Kühner, Ludwig, 99–100
Kürnberger, Ferdinand: *Amerika-Müde*, 69–70, 112

labor, organization of, 177
Lafayette, Marquis de, 21, 26, 36
laissez-faire, 163, 166
Lamont, Thomas, 212, 216
Lang, Fritz, 303
Lassalle, Ferdinand, 80
Le Carré, John, 297
Legaré, Hugh Swinton, 50n32, 50n34, 54
Léger, Fernand, 283
Lenau, Nikolaus, 70–2, 75, 78, 112
Lenz, Christian, 101–2
Levine, Bruce, 88, 102
Levine, Jack, 269
Lewis, John L., 238–9
liberal nationalism; *see* nationalism
liberalism: American, 77, 188; and constitutional movement, 79–80; and democratization, 68, 72, 80; European, 79; and freedom, 31; German, 67, 68, 77; and modernization, 68; and religion, 28, 32, 37; *see also* conservatism; laissez-faire

libertinage, 65
liberty; *see* American freedom; religious liberty
Lieber, Francis, 76-7, 79
Liliencron, Detlev von, 113
Lincoln, Abraham, 88, 97, 102, 107
Lippmann, Walter, 45, 110
Lipschitz, Rudolf, 278
List, Friedrich, 75, 76, 84
literati, 48
literature, German image of United States in, 111-14
"Little Drummer Girl" (film), 289, 292, 305
Locarno Conference, 213
Löher, Franz von, 72
Longfellow, Henry Wadsworth, 41, 43n11, 47, 49, 50n30, 58
Lüddecke, Theodor, 226-7
Luebke, Frederick C., 148, 152
Luhmann, Niklas, 190
Lutkens, Charlotte, 188

McClellan, George, 94
McCloy, John J., 320
McGrath, Gates, 205-6
McLellan, Henry Blake, 50n31, 50n34
Maltzan, Ago von, 199, 203-4
Mann, Herman, 272
Mann, Thomas, 273; *Königliche Hoheit*, 113
maps and mapmaking, 2-3
"Marathon Man" (film), 290-1, 293, 305
Marbury versus *Madison*, 33
Marschalck, Peter, 87
Marshall Plan, 296, 311-14, 318, 320
Martens, Frederick, 100n32
Martin versus *Hunter's Lessee*, 33
Marx, Karl, 80-1
Marx, Wilhelm, 201
Marxism, 160
Mason, James, 296
mass democracy; *see* democracy
mass media, 120-2
mass opinion: American, 16; and image formation, 3, 81-2
materialism: American, 61, 71, 113, 128, 135; German, 178; versus service, 225
May, Henry F., 136
Meckel, Markus, 345

media; *see* mass media
Mellon, Andrew, 196
memory, and images, 16
Mencken, H. L., 137; "American Credo", 186
Mengele, Josef, 290
Mennonites, 22
Methodism, 27
"Metropolis" (film), 303
Meyer, Eduard, 152
Mies van der Rohe, Ludwig, 273, 280, 283
militarism, 138-40, 146, 147
Milius, August Johann, 21n1
Miller, Arthur, 336
Mills, C. Wright, 169
misperceptions: about America, 10; versus misinterpretations, 172; versus misunderstandings, 9, 171-2, 190; roots of, 4; and stereotypes, 4, 5-6
missionaries, 23, 39, 43
Mitterrand, François, 345, 348
modernism: American, 11, 113, 220-1, 240; German, 187; and liberalism, 68; reactionary, 219-21, 231, 242, 252; *see also* industrialization
Modrow, Hans, 344, 351
Mohl, Robert von, 79
Möllhausen, Heinrich Balduin, 113
Mommsen, Wolfgang J., 183n23
monarchy, versus republican government, 51-2
Monroe, James, 68
moralism, 135
Morgan (J. P.) and Co.; *see* J. P. Morgan and Co.
Morrow, Dwight, 196
Moser, Johann Jacob, 30
Motherwell, Robert, 266, 281
Motley, John Lothrop, 43n11, 46, 47, 50n30, 50n34
Motorwelt, 255
Mott, Valentine, 50n31, 50n35, 52
movies; *see* film
Mühlenberg, Heinrich Melchior, 27, 36
Munch, Friedrich, 74-5
Munro, Dana C., 140
Münsterberg, Hugo, 116-19, 145
"Music Box, The" (film), 298, 305
mysticism, and religion, 35

Nagler, Jörg, 13–14, 87
National Liberal Party, 78
National Socialism, 4, 189; on America, 218–42; and Americanization, 233–4; critique of modernism, 221, 254; economic policy, 234–5, 241, 255; and Ford, 230; and New Deal, 233–8, 242, 244–6, 253; on popular American culture, 256–8; propaganda of, 243, 258–9; and seizure of power, 233; and unemployment, 237, 241
national unity, 131, 178
nationalism: American, 143; and cultural superiority, 149; German, 72, 80, 104–5, 173, 175; liberal 73–4, 76, 78; and patriotism, 72
nationality, American, 51–2
Nationalsozialistische Bibliothek, 231
nativism, of Republicans, 88
Nazism; *see* National Socialism
Neudeutschland, in America, 72
Neuhaus, Helmut, 31
neurobiology, and image formation, 6–7
neutrality fear, 328–30
New Deal: projects for artists, 267; and National Socialism, 233–6, 242, 244–6, 253
New York Evening Post, 212
New York Times, The, editorial coverage of Weimar Germany, 193, 211–13, 215–16
Niebuhr, Barthold Georg, 76
Nietzsche, Friedrich Wilhelm, 167
Nixon, Richard M., 324
Nolan, Mary, 11
Notestein, Wallace, 141
Noyes, Alexander, 212, 216
Nueces Massacre, 103

object relations, 3
objective reality, and subjective perception, 5, 6
O'Brien, Conor Cruise, 336
obstructionism, 319
Ochs, Adolph S., 211, 216
"Odessa File, The" (film), 289, 291, 292, 298, 299, 304
Ogden, Rollo, 212, 216
Olin, Stephen, 50n32, 50n33, 56
opinion: generational, 144–8; social distribution of, 338; surveys, 337–8; *see also* elite opinion; mass opinion; public opinion
organic democracy; *see* democracy
other/otherness, and perception, 1, 42, 44

Pack, Nicholas, 94–5
Paine, Thomas: *Age of Reason*, 29
painters; *see* art
Palmer Raids, 275
Pareto, Vilfredo, 302
parliamentary government, 177–8, 183, 184
particularism, 70, 78
patriotism: German, 72; and nationalism, 72
Pax Americana, 320
Paz, Octavio, 171
Peabody, Francis, 145
Peck, Gregory, 291
perceptions: definition and usage of term, 2, 43–4, 111; versus images, 111; mutual, 190; and personal experience, 8; versus reality, 189; and social reality, 4, 14; subjective, 5, 6; *see also* images; misperceptions; self-perception; stereotypes
Perkins, Thomas H., 50n30, 50n33
Petersberg Agreement, 315–19, 322–3
Peukert, Detlev, 220
Philadelphia Museum of Art, 279
pietism, 19–20, 28, 31, 35, 36
Pintor, Harold: "Quiller Memorandum," 292
Pleven, Rene, 321
Poincaré, Raymond, 200
Poland, and Weimar German foreign policy, 204
political psychology, 6
political science, 4
political systems, 14, 78–9, 171–90; *see also* constitutionalism
Pollock, Jackson, 280, 281
popular images, 15, 16; of Germany, 13, 131–54; importation of, 256–8; of unification, 335–40; *see also* art; cultural images; film
Porsche, Ferdinand, 239
positivism, 167
Postl, Karl; *see* Sealsfield, Charles
Potter, Mary Storer, 49
pragmatism, 166–7

press; *see* journalism
Preuss, Hugo, 183–4
Priestly, Joseph, 29
propaganda: versus art, 265; of National Socialists, 243, 258–9; *see also* war propaganda
Protestantism, 22, 39
psychoanalysis, 3–4, 7
public opinion, 28, 172, 185–6
Putnam, George Palmer, 50
Pynchon, Thomas: *Gravity's Rainbow*, 288

Quakers, 27, 59

Raabe, Wilhelm, 113
racism, 119
radicalism, plebeian, 88
"Raiders of the Lost Ark" (film), 289, 292, 298
Rapallo trauma, 328–30, 336
rapprochement, 347
rationalism, 71, 161, 170, 219, 220, 240–1; radical principles of, 20; and reason, 187; and religion, 20
Raumer, Friedrich von, 79
Rauschning, Hermann, 247
reactionary modernizers, 15
"Reason and Emotion" (cartoon), 295
reciprocal visions, 14
reform movement; *see* social change
regionalist art; *see under* art
Reichel, Johann Friedrich, 22
Reichsgericht, 32
Reisebeschreibungen, 34
religion and religious liberty, 19–29, 31–40; American versus German, 59; feminization of, 58n68; and social reform, 59
reparations question, 191–3, 198, 200, 210, 213; *see also* Dawes Plan (1924)
representative democracy; *see* democracy
Republican Party: Democratic, 35; idealism of, 98; and ideology of progress, 107; nativism of, 88; reform elements of, 97–8
republicanism: American, 61–3, 104; and decadence, 61; European, 104; German, 91; liberal, 105; and lifestyle, 62–3; versus monarchy, 51–2
reunification; *see* unification, German

Reuss, Johann August von, 31
revivalism, and religious liberty, 22
Rice, Condoleezza, 341
Rieppel, Paul, 224, 225, 227
Rights of Man, 38
Robinson, Edward, 50n30, 50n35
Robinson, James Harvey, 138
"Rocky and Bullwinkle" (cartoon), 297–8
Rodgers, Daniel, 164, 165
Romanticism, 38, 69–71, 79–80
Rommel, Erwin, 296, 304
Roosevelt, Franklin D.: economic policy, 234–8; expected defeat of, 236; as Führer, 245; Hitler on, 243–9, 260–2; *Looking Forward*, 245; and seizure of power, 233; *see also* New Deal
Roosevelt, Theodore, 145
Roschen, Pastor, 23
Rosenberg, Alfred, 230
Rosenberg, Paul, 277
Rosenthal, Abraham, 336
Ross, Anna, 155–6
Ross, Dennis, 340, 344
Rossi, Robert, 101
Roten, Ferdinand, 279
Rothko, Mark, 281
Rotteck, Karl von, 79
Ruhr Crisis, 191
Russell, James E.: *German Higher Schools*, 154
Russell, Jonathan, 50

Saager, Adolf, 230
Safire, William, 336
Sage, Henry W., 195
St. Etienne Gallery (New York), 279
Sand, Karl Ludwig, 74
Sandler, Irving, 281
Sands, David, 50n31, 50n33
Sauer, Christopher: *Almanac*, 57
Schäfer, Johann Edward, 19, 40
Schäfer, Johann Georg, 19, 20, 22, 40
Scheler, Max, 167
Schell, Maximillian, 293
"Schindler's List" (film), 15, 285, 294–5, 307
Schlözer, August Ludwig: *Staatsanzeigen*, 30, 35
Schmid, Carlo, 318
Schmidt, Johann Joseph, 26

Schmoller, Gustav, 164
Schneider, Christian Wilhelm, 20
Schniewind, Carl O., 279
Schoepf, Johann David, 34
Schönmann, Friedrich, 186
School of Paris, 279, 281
school textbooks, images reflected by, 122–5
Schubert, Carl von, 199, 209
Schumacher, Kurt, 316
Schuman Plan, 319–23
Schurman, Jacob Gould, 15, 180; American ambassador to Germany, 193, 194–6, 201–3, 205–10; Gilbert versus, 205–10
Schurz, Carl, 77–8, 82, 88, 119, 145
Schweber, Peter, 230–1
Sealsfield, Charles, 72–3
secular reports, by travelers, 43
security, individual and family, 20
Sedgwick, Catherine M., 50n30, 50n35, 53, 54, 61
self-determination, 79, 104, 343
self-perception, and images of other, 16
Seligman, H. L. A., 165
service, as Prussian ideal, 225
Shahn, Ben, 268
Shaplen, Joseph, 215
Shelley, Percy Bysshe: *Prometheus Unbound*, 1, 13
Shepard, Walter, 177–8
Shevardnadze, Eduard, 347
Simmel, Georg, 167
skepticism, 51
slavery, 57, 94, 102–3; versus freedom, 100; versus republic, 98, 106; *see also* abolitionists; emancipation
Small, Melvin, 150
Smidt, Johann, 76
social change, 187; and religion, 59
Social Democracy, 80, 121, 152, 164, 180, 182
social equality, 128
social inferiority, 120
social psychology, 3; and stereotypes, 5, 6
social realism, 44, 269–70
social science research, 3, 4
socialism, 159, 177, 228–9; Prussian, 227
Socialist Unity Party, 342–3
sociology, 5
Sombart, Werner, 116, 118, 188, 222, 223

Sparks, Jared, 50n30, 50n35, 57
Spengler, Oswald, 227–9
spiritual autobiographies, 43n9
Spiro, Eugen, 272
"Splash" (film), 288, 290
Sprague, William B., 50n31, 50n33, 58
"Spy Who Came in from the Cold, The" (film), 297, 305
stabilization policy, 319
stereotypes: of America, 69, 82, 175; definition and usage of term, 43–5; and emigration, 69; and experiential factor, 6; forming, 137; function of, 16; historical foundations of, 6; versus images, 111; and misperceptions, 4, 5–6; and reality, 5; transcending, 15; by travelers, 45, 47; truth in, 194; *see also* images; perceptions
Sternburg, Herman Speck, 153
Stetson, John, 204
Stiles, Ezra, 36
Still, Clifford, 281
Stoll, Elmer E., 140, 141
Stow, Baron, 50n30, 50n33
Stowe, Calvin Ellis, 50n32, 50n35
Stresemann, Gustav, 197, 201–4, 214–15
Sturm und Drang literary movement, 68
subjective perception, and objective reality, 5
Sullivan, Louis, 273
Sumner, Charles, 47, 50n30, 50n35
"Swing Kids" (film), 291, 294
Sydow, Max von, 293

Tannhauser and Drey, 277
Taylor, Frederick, W., 224–5
television, 16, 335–6, 354, 356
temperance movement, 59
territorial behavior, and emigration, 84–5
Texas, German émigrés in, 103–4
textbooks; *see* school textbooks
Thatcher, Margaret, 345, 348, 349, 355
Third Reich; *see* National Socialism
threat, perceptions of, 4
Ticknor, Anna Eliot (Mrs.), 56, 57
Ticknor, George, 45, 47, 50n30, 50n34, 52
Tieck, Ludwig, 71
time, perceptions on concept of, 53–5
Tocqueville, Alexis de, 8, 61
Topliff, Samuel, 50n30

trade agreements, 323
travel and travelers: perceptions of, 11, 13, 41–63, 116–20; regional identity, 50; types of, 47–51
Treaty of Berlin (1921), 191
Treaty of Rapallo (1922), 199
Treaty of Versailles; see Versailles Treaty
Treitschke, Heinrich von, 140
Treutlein, Edward, 96, 106
"Triumph of the Will" (film), 288
Truman, Harry S., 319, 330
Turnbull, R. H., 271–2
Turner, Frederick Jackson, 143
Turpin versus *Locket*, 33

Unbehagen (uneasiness), in modern culture, 3
unemployment: during Depression, 233, 237; in Third Reich, 237, 241
unification, German, 10, 16, 106, 178; American policy toward, 333–52; American reaction to, 353–61; Gallup poll on, 302; television during, 335–6, 354, 356; Ten Point Plan, 343, 350
unionism, 87–8, 103; see also Civil War
utilitarianism, 161; American, 129; versus idealism, 129
utopia, United States as, 67

Valentin, Curt, 278–9
Van Wart, Sarah, 41
Veblen, Thorstein, 169, 178–9
Velthusen, J. C., 23
Versailles Treaty, 191, 197, 202
visual representation; see art; film
Vocke, Wilhelm, 317
Voight, John, 293
Volkan, Vamik, 6
Vormärz, 32, 68, 74
Voss, Dirk, 46, 50n35
Vossler, Otto, 8
"Voyage of the Damned" (film), 293

Wagner, Adolph, 164
Wagner, Richard, 148
Walters, Vernon, 341, 349
war propaganda, 133, 153, 174
Warburg, Max, 182
Ware versus *Hilton*, 33
Washington, George, death of, 29
Weber, Max, 156–63, 170, 182–3, 219,

223, 354
Weimar Republic, 173, 177, 179–88; American views on, 191–216; constitution, 184; rationalization during, 11; see also Third Reich
Welcker, Karl Theodor, 79
Wellek, René, 112, 114
Weltpolitik, 144
White, Andrew Dickson, 138, 142, 145, 195
"White Rose, The" (film), 294
Wiebe, Robert H., 133, 134
Wilder, Billy, 303
Williams, John Sharp, 138
Willis, Nathaniel P., 50n30, 50n35
Willkomm, Ernst: *Europamüde*, 69, 73, 112
"Winds of War, The" (television miniseries), 298
Wissenschaftspolitik, 138
Wittenberg, Albrecht, 30, 35
Wittke, Carl, 87, 88, 91
Wolff, Christian, 21n1
Wollschläger, Hans, 232–3
women: American, and German writers, 119; and domesticity, 58; émigrés to America, 85; German, 56–7, 63; New England, 58
Wood, Grant, 269; *Parson Weems' Fable*, 270, *271*
Woolman, John, 59
world-philosophy, 144
World War I, 14, 131–6, 173–9, 182
World's Fair (St. Louis, 1904), 223
Wright, Frank Lloyd, 273, 280
Wright, Hezekiah Hartley, 50n33

Yankees, 48n25, 91, 117, 147
Ybarra, A. S., 211
Young Conservatives, 229
Young Germany movement, 76
Young, Owen D., 196
Young Plan, 210, 214, 215

Zelikow, Philip, 341
Zigrosser, Carl, 279
Zimmermann, Ferdinand Friedrich; see Fried, Ferdinand
Zitelmann, Rainer, 251
Zoellick, Robert, 340, 344
Zucker, Adolf, 87
Zweig, Stephan, 265

For EU product safety concerns, contact us at Calle de José Abascal, 56–1°, 28003 Madrid, Spain or eugpsr@cambridge.org.

www.ingramcontent.com/pod-product-compliance
Lightning Source LLC
LaVergne TN
LVHW091528060526
838200LV00036B/521